VIOLENT SCREEN

A critic's 13 years on the front lines of movie mayhem

by
Stephen Hunter

Delta
Trade Paperbacks

A Delta Book
Published by
Dell Publishing
a division of
Bantam Doubleday Dell Publishing Group, Inc.
1540 Broadway
New York, New York 10036

ISBN: 0-385-31652-6

Reprinted by arrangement with The Bancroft Press

Manufactured in the United States of America
Published simultaneously in Canada

January 1997

10 9 8 7 6 5 4 3 2 1

BVG

To the Baltimore Sun, *which has allowed me to indulge myself as its film critic since 1982.*

Acknowledgments

Grateful acknowledgment is made to the Baltimore Sun *for permission to reprint the following pieces, in whose pages they originally appeared.*

Thanks go too to my wife Lucy, who manned the home fires while I was spending too many nights in too many Multiplexes, and who maintained the family archives from which most of these pieces were picked.

The author would also like to thank his editors and supervisors over the past thirteen years for their belief in his career and for their willingness to grant him the widest possible latitude in interpreting the concept of "film critic." Kathy Lally, largely responsible for getting me the job, should be mentioned first of all; then, in no particular order, thanks go to Steve Parks, Rob Howe, Karol Menzies, Mary Curtis, Eric Siegel, Dennis Moore, Steve Proctor, Jan Warrington, Gil Watson, Karen Hunter, Kim Marcum and Tom Clifford. Apologies to anyone whose name has been pushed out of my brain by too many bad movies.

The author would also like to thank Dee Lyon, of the Baltimore Sun's *library staff, for helping him dig two dozen or so pieces out of the newspaper archives. They couldn't have appeared here otherwise.*

Finally, the author would like to thank his publisher, Bruce Bortz, and his editor, Ann Sjoerdsma. Bruce thought this was a fine idea, and came up with the money and the production expertise to make it happen; it was Ann who delivered the idea of focusing on violent films, giving the collection an organizational spine as well as a meaning. She then pored over hundreds of reviews and essays, grouped them by category, wrote the title notes, and performed the line editing and the proofreading. Again, my gratitude to them both.

Contents

VIOLENT SCREEN

INTRODUCTION
June 6, 1995

I write at a curious moment in the history of the republic. A little more than a month ago, some very bad boys blew up a federal building and killed 168 of their fellow citizens. One would think that such a thing would dampen America's thirst for violence considerably. Yet, the No. 1 film in the country is "Die Hard With a Vengeance," in which some very bad boys plant bombs in various precincts of New York City and detonate them. The smoke and debris and the body parts fly; it takes a keen eye to detect the difference between the special effects of Hollywood and the grotesque effects of hatred.

What a perfect microcosm for our complex responses to violence: We abhor the authentic stuff, and turn in national revulsion from it. Then we go pay seven bucks to watch it in Technicolor in the mall. In our heart of hearts, in our secret places, we crowd into dark, anonymous spaces and lose ourselves and our souls in its celebration.

In that way, movie violence divides us almost into halves: the half that tsk-tsks and tut-tuts its vulgarity, cravenness, rudeness, noise and gore, and the half that "gets with" the exact same values. Reconciling the two may be the movie critic's most difficult dilemma, particularly a movie critic who doubles as a suspense novelist and in the private world of his fiction has killed hundreds. In fact, I would venture to suggest that I have more blood on my hands than any movie critic or movie killer in history.

I have even sold books to Hollywood, and if any ever get made into movies (doubtful, as I write, but who knows?), the screen will crackle with machine-gun fire, bullet strikes and blood puddles, and all across America people who look and think a lot like I do will write learned pieces on What It All Means.

It's even more difficult for a movie critic who writes violent novels whose own father was murdered; thus, in the most melancholy of ways, I have learned something of the squalor, devastation and immense sense of violation that a violent crime leaves in its wake and I know that it's something the movies never, ever get right.

So when I examine what I have written on the subject of violent movies over close to a decade and a half on duty in America's bijoux and look for a grand pattern, I come up empty-handed: no grand patterns, no deep and penetrating observations on the esthetics of violence in the American cinema, no meaningful conjectures on the influence of movie violence on real violence. It's too big and messy a subject for generalities; let's leave that to politicians seeking a goose in the polls.

But I have always felt it a point of honor as a movie critic not to pretend that, as an advanced thinker, I am somehow above the lure of violence in a film. Indeed, my best pieces here seem to be about movies where I've made some emotional contact with violence and have let it sweep me away, fire off all my synapses, liberate my imagination. In fact, I think one of the reasons that we go to movies is FOR the violence: It enables us to project ourselves and our hostilities into some form of righteous rage and take charge of and triumph in a world of the imagination where a world of reality obdurately refuses to be taken charge of or to allow triumph.

I'm not sure this is necessarily the bad thing that so many assume it to be. Critics of American movies love to zero in on the relatively few copycat killings that the odd picture will inspire, but nobody's able to chronicle the times that angry men have seethed toward violence but been released from its mandates when a story so gripped their imaginations that they lost hold of themselves and their anger in witnessing it. That's one reason why stories — novels as much as films — will never die: In offering us a chance to enter another, more grandly imagined life, they also offer us a chance to forget the bitterness of our own smaller existences. It's escapism in the best possible sense.

Some of this has to do with the sheer dynamism of the medium. That's why they call them "movies," after all: The eye is drawn to action, and if it's skillfully mounted, clearly photographed, gracefully choreographed and vividly edited, it viscerally draws you in. You are responding to the most basic of cues — movement and sound, and at some primitive level, your excitement centers are stimulated and you cannot, no matter who you are, deny the urgings of your limbic system.

And yet violence as spectacle is never quite enough. The great films that happen also to be violent are great not because of the violence or in spite of it; rather, they are great because the violence amplifies the character and the conflict in the drama. Peckinpah's great "The Wild Bunch" is the ultimate case in point, as I argue in one of the pieces here. No one would or even could deny that it's one of the most violent movies ever made, with its fetishist's concentration on bullets blowing into and usually through bodies, and that its rhythms draw you in even more and more. But the violence, however gross, is never arbitrary: It's reflective of the corrosive nihilism that infects each of the cast members and compels him to celebrate his own extinction as he rides to the ultimate end of the road.

In far too many other films, however, violence is unrelated to character and story or, in some cases, takes the place of character and story; it feels arbitrary, injected entirely for its prurient effect. When I began in this business, the common fodder of low-end cinema was the slasher pic: for week after week I'd head out on Friday afternoon to see some el cheapo atrocity flick that specialized not merely in depicting violence itself but in celebrating it from the point of view of the killer, of encouraging us to feel his pleasure as he drew near to the kill and to exult in his strength as he delivered the blow on the cowering, quivering and almost always female victim.

Such headaches you cannot imagine. Happily, the market adjusted; the slasher movies are basically dead in a way that their hero Jason never was. Now we're in an era of ironic violence, in which young film school or video market geniuses offer us hip, knowing takes on mayhem, with ample nods to other movies and a wink that communicates the information that it's only a movie. Alas, far too few people are hip or ironic enough themselves to get the joke: They insist on seeing blood as blood, torture as torture and death as death. That is their right, though possibly movie critics might be of some help to them. (Try explaining your enthusiasm for "Pulp Fiction" to a lecture hall full of Republican women. It isn't pretty.)

Does this mean we are at the saturation point? How much more violent can a film get than "True Romance" or "Reservoir Dogs"? It's hard to know, but I suspect that the man knew what he was saying when he proclaimed, "Folks, you ain't seen nothing yet."

Stephen Hunter
Baltimore, Md.

FILM NOIR

"All hail sleaze and evil"

RESERVOIR DOGS
December 25, 1992

The boys are back in town — and how. "Reservoir Dogs," Quentin Tarantino's astonishing debut feature, appears to be set in a theme park called Testosteroneland, where nature isn't only red in tooth and claw, it's black as the heart of man and dank as any rag-and-bone show of the human spirit.

Yet its first astonishment is that in contrast to the relentless violence of the material, the movie itself is flashy, slick, giddy, audacious. It's a movie made by a man who has seen too many movies and can regurgitate technical credits from forgotten '50s B gangster melodramas with the best film nerds in America. The overarching sensibility is the showoff's: Everything is studiously placed for maximum sensation. It's the "Citizen Kane" of the gag reflex.

Of course, it's hopelessly immature. Tarantino is 29 but seems much younger: The film is one of those pulpy endorsements of nihilism that ends up with just about everybody in the movie, and several poor souls in the first rows of the theater, on slabs. It has to be made by a man who has never seen anybody die except in movies. Yet at the same time it's inconveniently dazzling — driven, beautifully made and completely wacko at once. It's pure outlaw art.

Tarantino's subject — that is, besides B movies and his own damned precociousness — is the honor among thieves and the lack of it among policemen. It basically takes place in a single setting, with flashbacks, as the surviving members of a robbery gang gather in a warehouse and try to hash out what happened in a bungled job in a wholesale diamond exchange that left half of them and dozens of square johns and cops dead in downtown Los Angeles.

The movie is radically structured, after the fashion of Kubrick's first film, "The Killing," another famous heist movie but one in which the heist was actually shown. Tarantino's glitziest stroke is never to show the main event: He backtracks in time and point of view half a dozen times, showing what led up to it and what happened after it, but the actual raid itself goes undramatized.

The robbers are a hyper-masculine crew of tattooed tough guys who dress like Blues Brothers and carry — what else? — .45s. Each is given a color code name by "Joe," the leathery old mastermind (Lawrence Tierney, who looks as if he could chew his way out of Alcatraz). Yet as hypercharged and kinetic as "Reservoir Dogs" is, it keeps stopping for riffs and it's only halfway through when one realizes that, under the torture scenes, the gunfights, the screams of a wounded, bloody man who slowly dies on screen for about 97 minutes, the movie is really a comedy.

Tarantino writes pointed, vivid comic solos that literally halt the movie in its tracks and take on a life of their own, like performance pieces. The weaselly Steve Buscemi, as Mr. Pink, is the author of many of these (Buscemi is a performance artist, so possibly he's incorporating some of his own material). At one point, he breaks up a tense planning meeting with a five-minute kvetch on the agonies of being code-named "Mr. Pink"; in another, he contributes a cracked, inane disquisition on the absurdity of tipping.

But the competing centers of authority in the film are Mr. White (Harvey Keitel), who is a "responsible thief," and Mr. Blonde (Michael Madsen), who is a psycho killer. The two seem to struggle for control of the aftermath, as they attempt to figure out whether one of their own is an undercover cop. Meanwhile, Mr. Orange (the British actor Tim Roth, who, amazingly, played a Cockney contract killer in Stephen Frears's "The Hit," yet here seems as American as tacos) lies bleeding to death on the floor.

It is Madsen who shuffles through the film's most controversial moment, cutting the ear off a captured policeman while doing a hipster's jig to the tune of a piece of '70s fluff called

"Stuck in the Middle with You." The scene is horrible to watch, contrasting psychotic power with utter helplessness in a dance of pure sadism, but in fact it's so outrageous, like an Ice-T song, that what it elicits is hilarity, not outrage.

ROMEO IS BLEEDING
April 22, 1994

Some months ago, I received a letter from a man who shall go nameless, telling me that he was sure I was right about a particularly loathsome movie called "The Real McCoy" (Kim Basinger as a bank robber), but that he would see it anyway.

"You see," Mr. —— confided, with what must have been a nervous little giggle, "I simply adore Strong Women films!"

Well, Mr. ——, have I got a movie for you!

Mr. ——, meet Mona Demarkov. Mona, don't you think Mr. —— could use some discipline? Possibly it would do to tie him up, knock out his teeth and shoot off his toes? Or possibly, Mona dear, you would enjoy cutting an ear off? Mr. ——, stop that squirming now! You *adore* strong women, remember?

Mona, played at full toot boogie by the heretofore sedately seductive Swedish actress Lena Olin, is the significant icon in "Romeo Is Bleeding." In fact, she's the only reason for seeing the movie, which is only alive when she's going nuts with a Ruger or kicking the stuffing out of whatever poor guy gets in the way.

Femme fatale? This woman's a femme Armageddon!

"Romeo Is Bleeding" revels in its own trashiness. It aspires to join that small circle of near-outlaw works set on the grimy edges of film noir, along with "Reservoir Dogs" and "True Romance" — defiant champions of ultra-violence, campy outrageousness and dime-novel nihilism. Alas, it's nowhere near as good as those two, but it has a certain zany charm.

The "hero" — hero being a relative term here — is a New York detective named Jack Grimaldi, who makes Harvey Keitel's "Bad Lieutenant" look like Mr. Rogers. It does nobody any good, however, that Jack is played by one of the most talented and yet least interesting actors around, Gary Oldman. Oldman has extraordinary technical skills, yet whatever it is that the camera loves to record in an actor's presence, he hasn't got it.

Anyway, when the movie opens (it's actually a flashback in form, as a chastened but ruined Jack recalls his fall), Jack is playing both sides — the NYPD and the Mob — against the middle, and he's got a potful of money in the backyard to prove it. His personal life is equally an issue of equipoise, with a wife (Annabella Sciorra) in one corner and a mistress (Juliette Lewis, in yet another trampy role) in the other.

It all comes apart when he's asked to bodyguard the recently captured Mona. Mona quickly seduces him into setting her free and then declares war on the Mafia boss (Roy Scheider) who set her up, at the same time involving poor Jack in the game in ways he's not quite clever enough to figure out.

This is one of those cases where the villain — Mona — is so overpowering that she seems to drain the power from all around her. She's so titanic that the movie, the characters, the whole plot go away; nobody can stand up to her, not in the story and not in the film. Even director Peter Medak, who once shepherded wild boy Peter O'Toole through "The Ruling Class," seems a little afraid of her and backs off.

In the end, only Mona remains. For Mr. ——, that surely is enough; as for the rest of us, I have my doubts, though I'd appreciate it if you didn't tell Mona.

THE LAST SEDUCTION
January 20, 1995

"The Last Seduction" certainly bears out the biblical injunction that the last shall be first: It's the first good movie of the year. It may be the first good movie of last year. It's an archly ironic film noir that whirls along like a dervish on shore leave, teasing its own conventions exactly as it fulfills them.

It's of the noir subset No. 7A — the femme fatale — built around a beautiful, predatory woman who has no moral compass, deploys her body as a lethal weapon, and uses the weaker sex as one might use tissue: to soak up fluids and to dispose of. Linda Fiorentino, briefly big years ago after "Vision Quest," is big all over again as sultry, leggy Bridget Gregory, a New Yorker married to a weak-willed physician (Bill Pullman) whom she's bullied into selling pharmaceutical cocaine to street hoods. Profit: $750,000.

But Bridget is too large to remain married to a nervous piker like Pullman's Clay, particularly when he briefly rebels and smacks her in the mouth. One of Fiorentino's great accomplishments here is that she really makes you feel her relish for the damage she's doing, and the pleasure she takes in the power of her own charisma. There's not a quiver of ambivalence anywhere in her: "I am bitch," she says in this performance, "hear me roar." For smacking her, she punishes her husband by walking out with the $750,000. What's he going to do, call the cops?

Actually, he calls a private detective, as the situation is somewhat urgent. Each week he can't pay back a loan shark, he gets a finger broken, and when he runs out of fingers, the goons will probably break something bigger, like a neck. She knows this. It's part of the joke.

Bridget sets up in western New York, a rural town called Beston for which the "Big City" is Buffalo, while she figures out her next move. Sitting in a bar on her first night, her next move walks in: dewy-eyed, blond hunk Mike Swale (Peter Berg), a self-hating small-towner who is attracted to her exactly as he is frightened of her. It's not much of a match — the spider woman and the boy fly. When Bridget rivets him with her dark eyes and gropes him under the table, he melts like a chocolate soldier in a microwave. "You're the designated ——," she tells him, her idea of a romantic line.

In fact, at heart the mechanism of the film is its inversion of romantic ideals. The men — Mike and even mildly forgiving Clay — are true romantics, the clingy, nurture-needing, valentine-sending, battered-husband types. They look on Bridget and her beauty and cogitate sweet feelings of yearning and togetherness. She looks on them and sees . . . smack, smack, chomp, chomp . . . free lunch. Her great weapon is that love is a complete con to her. She feels nothing for anybody but herself and can therefore manipulate like a chess master, laughing to herself as she does it.

This same contempt relates to geography, too. Isolated in Beston, she's like Attila in a day-care center. Everywhere she sees nothing but marks and fools who weren't tough enough to make it to New York. "There's a place for losers and quitters," she tells Mike. "It's called Beston."

John Dahl, who directed this film and is a specialist in noir (he also did "Red Rock West"), has a true feel for sexual tension at the heart of the melodrama. So overwhelming is Bridget, so cunning and darkly charismatic, that she truly becomes the movie. One can feel the snares being lovingly draped around poor, dim Mike, though the suspense mechanism is somewhat peculiar: Though Bridget is the point-of-view character, we never know her true agenda.

Eventually, the movie seems to lead into another area, as Bridget uses Mike's computer knowledge (he's a claims adjuster) to isolate a set of wealthy women whose husbands' credit records suggest they are keeping mistresses on the side. Bridget, who clearly has an entrepreneurial gift, sees a service she can offer to such people. But Dahl brings this offshoot back into the original story line in a convincing way.

The movie will remind many of "Body Heat," Laurence Kasdan's great film from 1981. It's not as good as "Body Heat," and the big secret that Bridget learns to give her total control over Mike turns out to be pretty ridiculous. The ending could have been stronger; one feels a mousetrap snapping closed at the end, not a chrome steel trap on ball bearings. But "The Last Seduction" seduces us, early.

BLOOD SIMPLE
March 8, 1985

All hail sleaze and evil, hot blood, cold beer, murder, sex, Texas and Volkswagens.

These are the prime components of "Blood Simple," a stunning debut film from Joel and Ethan Coen (Joel directed, Ethan produced, both wrote). Made for $1.5 million by two guys who'd never even been on the set of a real movie before, the film shows how much can be done with brains instead of money, and talent instead of connections.

"Blood Simple" is, generically, a noir pastiche. It's a black, biting murder thriller that plays on — without ever really imitating — the conventions of the movie past. Those conventions — their high-water mark was late in the '40s — took the form of convoluted, beautifully filmed plots of guilt and violence, betrayal, anxiety in an ever-present vapor of fear. They were fatalistic, gloomy, weirdly kicky: Alienated men in scary cities of the night, trying to play the angles and getting creamed for their efforts.

"Blood Simple's" distance to these old noirs is one of the shrewdest things about it: It's neither an exercise in bogus nostalgia nor a crude recycling of old gimmicks. It never stoops to "quote" old sequences, except one forgivable lapse when Joel Coen slams a zoom in on Frances McDormand in shaky homage to his pal Sam Raimi, from whose "The Evil Dead" the shot was taken. That mistake aside, the movie uses atmosphere, a brooding sense of evil, imagery and ideas, not cliches. It feels old and new at once.

You might liken it to "Body Heat," another excellent noir pastiche, except that it's a good deal less sensual: The Coens like violence, not sex, and their movie derives its energy from its sudden bursts of physical damage, not its sexuality.

At the same time, it's extremely funny, cut to an exquisite, jokey rhythm (a horror-movie rhythm, actually) that prevents its ugliness and violence from acquiring the weight that would destroy it. It starts giddy and stays giddy.

But more important, it returns something to movies that has

long been absent: cleverness. As young directors have taken over the business and mastered the technical aspects of movie-making, they seem to have forgotten the narrative. The Coens are a refreshing return to the days when plots had to make a kind of sense.

It's not that the movie is realistic; it's that, within the confines of its world and from the premise of its plot, everything that happens happens for a purpose. It's a tidy movie; the Coens set out the ingredients in the beginning and by the end, they've used everything and used it well. And yet it's also got the system of visual logic so beloved of other young directors that supplies an additional sinew of organization.

The situation is classic James M. Cain, calling up the wonderful sordidness of roadhouse squalor of the 1930s pulp-writer who, 30 years after he peaked, was finally recognized for the brilliant stylist he was.

Like Cain's "The Postman Always Rings Twice," we begin with a crummy but wealthy husband, Julian Marty (Dan Hedaya, familiar from a lot of TV roles), who owns a prosperous bar called "The Neon Boot" on some unspecified, seedy Texas highway. Marty's wife Abby (Frances McDormand) has left him, run off with Ray (John Getz), one of Marty's bartenders.

Marty — one of the movie's cleverest, subtlest strokes is that everybody, even his own wife, calls him by his last name — hires a sleazo private eye to follow the couple, then having confirmed their union, to kill them. But the private eye (M. Emmet Walsh) sees another possibility: Instead of killing the two, he kills — or seems to kill — Marty. And this is just in the first few minutes.

From this permutation of the fatal triangle gambit there unfolds a problem in devious human geometry of inordinate complexity, angles yielding to fresh angles and perspectives that are crazed to the point of surrealism yet austerely consequential to the prime stroke.

The central dynamic in the film is misunderstood information: Each of the characters misreads a crucial situation, and it is this misreading that sends them into such a collapsing gyre of destruction. Yet at the same time, the audience always knows more than they do, and can keep the story sorted out in ways they can't.

What impresses is the power of Joel Coen's eye. The movie is built around a series of riveting images. But more to the point, the pretty pictures have meaning in terms of the narrative: They're informed with ideas, they hold the movie together.

Here's an example. There comes a moment when Ray and Abby, standing in the front door of Ray's seedy little house, attempt to penetrate the confusions that have ensnared them. Suddenly — the image is extraordinary — a thrown newspaper hurtles through the air with the stunning shock of a darting bat; we see it approach before they do and we flinch; we see it hit the storm door window with a bang and we duck — a second before they do.

Brilliant, brilliant, brilliant. In that one shot, Coen has summed up the principle of the movie and foreshadowed its ending. The newspaper — what else could it be? — is reality, banging against the transparent, fragile but still tenable glass of their illusions and confusions. It scares them, but not us, because we see it coming and they don't. (They never see it coming, as they never see *anything* coming.) And finally, it sets up a moment later in the film when they will stand before another window, locked behind their illusions again, and this time reality will hurl against the window in the form of a heavy caliber bullet.

M. Emmet Walsh, a longtime character actor, really takes command of the film as the sleazy private eye, Visser. In a grungy leisure suit, he's raunchy, sardonic evil. Walsh makes you love his ugly mind and his avuncular willingness to do terrible things for relatively small amounts of money. He's got a high nasal laugh that sounds like a tin cup going through a meat grinder, and a low cunning that's almost lovable in its purity. There's no gutter too slimy for this smiling insect to crawl through. Another Coen joke: He drives an old VW; he's a "bug."

Hedaya is also fine, mean enough to die but not quite evil enough to die that way. The two romantic leads, McDormand and Getz, are perhaps the weakest elements in the picture, but fail to harm it excessively. Getz is earnest, not terribly bright, a born chump; McDormand isn't quite clear enough. Is she meant to be a tramp or an innocent? This is the one answer the Coens don't quite have.

But, no, there is another answer lacking: That is, what is the movie saying? Well, it's saying, "Give us your money and we'll give you some fun," which by current standards is a great bargain. It's pure entertainment. But the old noirs, the real noirs, they were really about something. They used their gloomy looks, their seedy characters, their small-scale betrayals as paradigms for a neurotic age. The Coens, in their rush to give everybody a nice day, don't let the film ever really be about anything except $4.50's worth of fun.

But if this mischievous, cunning, stylish exercise in showing off isn't the deepest film ever made, it is surely one of the most enjoyable. With more curlicues than a wrought-iron balcony and more visual jokes than a stand-up routine by Federico Fellini, it's the rare film for both literates and post-literates. It's for people who like to listen to movies and it's for people who like to look at them.

PULP FICTION
October 14, 1994

Quentin Tarantino's "Pulp Fiction" is a Saturday Night Fever dream: a hot, dense, wicked disco of tough-guy posturings, vivid dips of violence and literally unbelievable plot moves.

Set on a single deconstructed weekend in a hyperbolically exaggerated Los Angeles criminal netherworld, it blithely slides through three main, marginally interconnected narratives, throwing away dazzling chunks of screwball dialogue, doing effortless deadpan comic riffs with the ease of a con man, while re-arranging time sequences for better thump. It is a prime post-modernist work: part wicked parody, part high-tech atrocity, part megalomaniacal solo spin by its brazen young director

— all cut to the snappy rhythm of a music video, somehow both artificial and moving at the same time.

If "Pulp Fiction" lacks anything, it's the shattering intensity of Tarantino's mind-blowing first film, "Reservoir Dogs." In that movie, he stunned you with the discordant notes: a torture sequence set to sleepy '70s rock, as a droopy-eyed psycho did a shuffle-off-to-Buffalo while slicing off a policeman's ear. It was horrifying and hilarious at once, and hypnotic.

Rather, "Pulp Fiction" stuns with the glib twists of its plot. It is absolutely unfigurable. Just when you think you've got it nailed, it finds a whole new direction to go, and then when you adjust to that, again it permutes. I think of it as a stress fracture shooting across a pane of glass, jagging this way and that, moving with utter unpredictability and utter confidence.

In story one, two hit men — Jules (Samuel L. Jackson) and Vincent (a heavier, duller John Travolta) — fulfill a professional obligation by popping an apartmentful of yuppie crooks who have absconded with a crime lord's suitcase full of, well, we never learn. But they don't just kill; rather, they turn the execution into an eloquent examination of fate. Think Rosencrantz and Guildenstern with .45 automatics and you get the picture — although to be fair, it's Jules, the smart one, who turns pensive in the face of his mission. Poor Vincent, played in a humorously moronic stupor by Travolta, is a man moping through in the lazy, hazy days of a drug high; he never quite gets with the rap.

That job done, the two report to the bar where the crime lord — Ving Rhames — is holding court with a lumpy boxer (Bruce Willis). Soon we're off on another adventure: Travolta's "date" with Rhames's wife (Uma Thurman), who is very sexy. But Travolta knows if he gets romantic, he gets dead. So he commits himself to being a good boy. They go to a loony '50s bar, dance a twist contest (Tarantino sends up Travolta's dance contest sequence from "Saturday Night Fever"). All this is very droll: She's much smarter than he is, plays adroitly with him, but somehow we feel his personality imprinting himself on the situation. They return to her place and just when you think,

"OK, now I know what this is all about," it turns out to be about something entirely different.

Then we turn to the boxer (Willis) whom we've seen earlier. He becomes the center of the film after a brief, comically strange soliloquy by Christopher Walken. Set to throw a fight, Willis's Butch Coolidge instead bets on himself, kills his opponent, and escapes, knowing that if he can collect on his bets he's a millionaire. If he gets caught, he'll get killed. So the movie covers his attempts to flee town while being hunted by killers — among them, Travolta; this would be the day after his date with the boss's wife. It's this story that veers into the strangest territory.

Suddenly lurching into a cross between "Deliverance" and "The Collected Works of the Marquis de Sade," it puts Willis and Rhames at the merciless mercy of rednecks with really nasty ideas on their minds. Favorite, weird, unexplained touch: the little guy in the leather hood who comes out of the box.

But we're not done with the day before.

After the boxer story plays out, we slide back in time to the previous day, when we learn why the hit men showed up in strange college-guy clothes. It's because after the first hit, they took one of their spies home with them. While gesturing dramatically with a gun, Travolta learns why the first rule of gun safety is never point a gun at something you are not willing to destroy. The gun, as guns do, goes bang; the young man, as young men do when hit by bullets, goes ker-blooie. Thus ensues a bizarre adventure in post-shooting hygiene, in which the two hit men, a suburban buddy (played by Tarantino himself) and an elegantly mysterious fixer (Harvey Keitel) deal with the problem of scrambled brains all over the upholstery.

That, in part, is what "Pulp Fiction" is about. But only sort of. More to the point, it's about attitude and voice. Tarantino has much of both: He's hypercool, a kind of third-generation hipster who loots his routines from pop culture with the aplomb of Willy Sutton, presumably because that's where the laughs are.

His world is astringently amoral: Killing isn't a sin; being uncool is. Drugs are life, guns are death, bright patter and cunning are everything in between. (Curiously, Tarantino doesn't really identify with the powers-that-be in such a world, but with the scufflers, the good soldiers trying to get through the day.) It has almost nothing to do with the real world and almost everything to do with the pretend one.

THE GRIFTERS
January 25, 1991

Grifters are the coyotes on the great plains of crime. They hover at the edges, afraid to go after the really big kills, afraid of the implicit violence in big-money stings, but nibbling, scuffling and pawing for the unattended few bucks left over.

Jim Thompson is the poet laureate of this low-rent moral twilight and Stephen Frears's version of Thompson's "The Grifters" chronicles the vicious games that members of this demimonde play upon each other. It comes to the conclusion, depressing enough as it is, that the grift is thicker than blood.

It should be a great movie, given that Frears, in his last film, "Dangerous Liaisons," showed an extraordinary relish for the cruel gamesmanship between sexual predators, and that his dark view of the world seems perfectly matched to Thompson's. But, despite arousing considerable activity in the pleasure centers, the movie finally more or less implodes on Thompson's ramshackle plotting, his deep affection for coincidence and his simple ignorance of the way the world works.

The movie is set in a Freudian jungle, as two women compete for the affections of a young man, although neither of them seems to really love him. For his part, he mistrusts both, especially the one who happens to be his mother.

John Cusack plays Roy, with the tiny mouth and innocent face of a child, but he's always looking for a way to trade a nickel for a dime on the theory that dimes more quickly add up to dollars. His grifts are somehow childish — "I'll give you a dime for every quarter you can balance on end," he tells a sucker, thereby trading 10 dimes for $2.50 in loose change.

So why does a sensational dish like Myra go for him? Frears can't really make us see it, until he finally reveals that Myra, played by Annette Bening, is a grifter herself, and sees in the yet-unformed Roy a chance to work her way up to the big time where she'd once labored as a "sweeper" — using her beauty as a sucker-magnet for a legendary con man. But, in her quest for dominion over Roy's heart and glands, she is opposed by Lily (Anjelica Huston), who's not only a mere 14 years older than Roy but also his mommy.

Lily's in the grift, too; she's some kind of traveling odds-twiddler for a Baltimore bookie named Bobo Justus (Pat Hingle, Jr.), and it's not to the movie's credit that it can never quite explain how Lily makes a living by thumping money against long shots in order to lower the odds and create a window of opportunity for the hotshot Mafia guy back in Baltimore (a misconception, actually; Baltimore is not a big organized crime city).

The races bring Lily to L.A., where she re-establishes contact with long-lost Roy and takes umbrage at Myra's cheap dominion over him; the two women are like sharks circling a bleeding goat treading water, each trying to lead him in a different direction as he tries to make up his mind between the kinds of lust he feels for each and wonders why he feels dimly that neither has his own best interests in mind.

All right, why John Cusack? I can't answer; he seems to lack the charisma or the energy that would make him attractive to either woman, including Mom. Cusack's curious dimness does a lot to leach the center from the movie. Bening and Huston, however, are both excellent: Bening's character has a kind of merry self-awareness and mercenary gusto that's very attractive, and Huston seems stronger than cast iron or ancient oak.

When it plays on the theme of sexual competition in this kinky neighborhood, "The Grifters" is terrific, particularly as Frears dwells on the incisive nastiness of the characters and the predatory instincts of their calling. But the movie keeps lurching through false starts and down blind alleys, wasting time on characters (like Hingle) who appear vividly, then completely disappear. It's not a plot that grows organically from a single premise, it's not of a piece; rather, it's as if Thompson simply started anew each day, unsure where he'd end up at sunset.

Finally, when it turns violent, it turns absurd. One of the primary "gimmicks" just doesn't work, not in this world: It turns a bullet wound to the face so grievous that the police can't identify the body — possibly true when Thompson was writing in 1963, but a doubtful proposition in today's era of sophisticated forensics. And it ends with an accidental killing in a hotel room that is simply ludicrous and cheapens the long movie that comes before it by its arbitrariness.

In the end, you feel the "The Grifters" has conned you.

Article:
OLD FILM NOIR FLICKERS IRONICALLY THROUGH NEW NOIR
January 22, 1995

In 1972, then-film critic Paul Schrader wrote a seminal essay on the dark and mesmerizing post-war American cinema of deceit, murder and betrayal known as film noir. He broke it down into three phases, the last of which, the "manic," had just ended — or so he thought. He didn't know, of course, that he himself would write the last great film noir of the "manic" phase, "Taxi Driver," in 1976.

He also didn't know that there was a fourth stage yet to come, one that has blossomed of late into full, gnarled bloom. It might be called the "ironic" stage, or as some have christened it, "nouveau noir." It took root in 1981 and has now reached maturity in the works of John Dahl, the latest of whose films, "The Last Seduction," has just opened.

Ironic noir is the antithesis of manic noir. Manic noir, whose two highest accomplishments were "Taxi Driver" and, before that, "Kiss Me Deadly," Robert Aldrich's jazzy spin on the Mickey Spillane novel, celebrated the last pure product of America: craziness. They were by definition over the top and took as their protagonists men who lost control. In "Taxi

Driver," Robert De Niro's Travis Bickle shot his way into the American subconscious as a twisted version of Arthur Bremer, who would inspire an equally twisted John Hinckley. The movie ended in an excess of massacre as Bickle, under a Mohawk haircut and spattered with blood, blew away everything that moved in a New York brothel, convinced it was his messianic role to cleanse the world.

Nothing so impolite would happen in ironic noir. It's not about screwballs, psychos, gun people or anything. It doesn't celebrate craziness, but rather another pure product of America: movies. In fact, it has the cool, detached humor of a good movie review, which in a sense it is. It's sublimely self-aware — as opposed to the genuine spontaneity of the original noir works — as directed by young men who are completely conscious of everything they do. Their primary goal is to do a film that both celebrates and parodies the genre. They lack the reflexively pyrotechnic drive of such noir greats as Billy Wilder ("Double Indemnity," 1944), Joseph Lewis ("Gun Crazy," 1950) or Rudolph Mate ("D.O.A.," 1950), and, of course, they've seen too much film noir.

If you asked Wilder, Lewis or Mate or any of the others about film noir, they'd say, "Huh?" Then they'd have the unit publicist kick you off the set. Ask John Dahl about film noir (I did), and he says, "Well, the three greatest influences on my work were . . ." and then proceeds to discuss with clinical detail three films — "Double Indemnity" and "Sunset Boulevard" by Wilder, and "A Place in the Sun" by George Stevens (not exactly a film noir but, courtesy of Theodore Dreiser, about a murder) — and how he set about to recreate their impulses.

That's not necessarily bad; it is necessarily inescapable. One of the real changes in film culture over the past, say, 30 years, is the sense in which it's turned in upon itself. The first few generations of sound movies were made by men who were pioneers as much as they were artists. They were flying by the seat of their pants. Most came from stage or newspaper backgrounds, most worked under intense studio pressure (the studios being literal factories that turned out 200 "units" a year), and most just did what worked without thinking about larger meanings until later. They were eminently practical men, and in their interviews they tended to make fun of the earnest young intellectuals who asked Big Questions.

Why did you shoot the concluding sequence from "Hell on Four Wheels" through the reflection of the broken mirror? Was it to indicate Bill's advanced state of psychosis?

Er, no. I saved about 8,000 bucks that way. We had a whale of a cast party with that money.

That sort of thing.

Yet given the helter-skelter nature of its inventors, film noir nevertheless has such a coherence to it you wonder if it was engineered by a single brilliant mind, or at the very least a learned committee.

There are many explanations for its emergence as the dominant film mode at the end of World War II. The most common is that it somehow reflected post-war exhaustion and pessimism. We had just won a giant victory and what did we win? Yet another war with yet another ominous super enemy, this time made all the more potentially lethal by the possibility of nuclear extinction.

Add to this the infusion of refugee technicians (cinematographers, lighting technicians, makeup artists) who had no homeland to return to — the emergence of a proto-counter-culture in the rigidly conformist '50s — and you get a cinema with a dark streak, satiny, existential, full of doomed suckers and smart ladies.

I favor a more literary explanation: that film noir was a decade-late cinematic extension of the literary movement called "hard-boiled." That genre had reached its full flower in the '30s with the diamond-hard prose of such geniuses as Dashiell Hammett, James M. Cain (both of whom hailed from Maryland) and the great Raymond Chandler. They all but reinvented American prose before the war by somehow desentimentalizing it. They refused to see the city as a world of glittery possibility, but instead as a neon-lighted sewer where death was hiding in an alley. When that sensibility eventually reached the movies, it took the form of film noir, with its concentration on squalid little tales of death without redemption.

Why did noir die, or at least go into eclipse, sometime in the late '50s? One reason may have been utterly stylistic, reflecting the ancient question scholars of the genre argue: Is noir a philosophy or a look, a content or a style?

If it's a style, then the death of black-and-white filmmaking in the late '50s pretty much explains things. Somehow, noir didn't work in color. It lost its meanings. Just look, say, at Robert Siodmak's brilliant "The Killers" of 1946. The vivid cascade of blue-gray shadings, the exquisite placement of shadow on faces, the use of lighting (as in the gun flashes that illuminate the dark as Swede's hand slips off the bedpost, signifying his surrender to death) — all give the movie a visual distinction that exactly communicates its view of a fate-haunted, doomed universe.

In 1964, Don Siegel, a great director, remade (and reinvented) the movie with an especially hip cast that included Lee Marvin and Clu Gulager as the killers, John Cassavetes as the betrayed quarry (played by the young Burt Lancaster in the original), and as ace bad guy, in his last film, Ronald Reagan. Subtract the weirdness that attends any movie with Ronald Reagan as a bad guy, and the movie still doesn't work. It's shot in almost pastel colors against generic studio backgrounds, and it feels feather-light and silly. It needed a much darker palette to give its weighty themes density.

Another reason for the demise of film noir was television. The ubiquitous made-for-TV movie came along halfway through the '60s to take over the economic stratum — that is, the B-movie niche — that had been the exclusive province of film noir. By the mid-'70s, there were no B-movies anymore; they had moved entirely to television, and the studio product tended to be big-budget and demographically driven. A film like "Taxi Driver" (1976) was something of a fluke, ramrodded home by a tough producer (Julia Phillips), a brilliant young director and star (Martin Scorsese and De Niro), and Paul Schrader's exceptional script. That "Taxi Driver" exists at all says more about the unique momentum that talent develops (in this case Scorsese's) than anything about the systemic acceptance of the genre.

So noir was dead, or at least exiled to television. Then, in 1981, Lawrence Kasdan all but reinvented it with "Body Heat," making stars out of William Hurt and Kathleen Turner in the process. "Body Heat" was the first ironic noir, and it established the pattern to come. It was both a film noir and a parody of a film noir. Immensely assured, it took place in two zones: the literal, where it was really happening, and the ironic, where it was echoing in our minds with associations to other films.

Of classic noir themes, it was a reiteration of the "black widow" or "femme fatale" variant — the frightened male fantasy about the sexually voracious and predatory female who uses men to advance her ends, then spits them out and moves on. Turner, tawny as a leopard and just as fierce, wrapped Hurt around a Popsicle stick and seemed to enjoy every second of it. But the lines were so campy with double entendre and cynicism they could never have been uttered in a literal noir. "You're stupid," she purrs to him. "I like that in a man."

The noirs that have followed are almost all in that film-savvy tradition.

Quentin Tarantino, in particular, is a movie-maker so arch you can see each of the 5,000 movies he's seen spinning behind his eyes as he works. "Reservoir Dogs" is a treasure trove of noir tough-guy conventions, but for true devotion to the cult, consider the even denser "Pulp Fiction" in terms of the movies that invented it and the classic noir themes it plays with: There's the couple on the run (Tim Roth and Amanda Plummer) from "Gun Crazy" and "They Live by Night"; there's the hit-man couple (John Travolta and Samuel L. Jackson) from "The Killers" I and II; there's Bruce Willis as the boxer getting even with the fixer (John Garfield in "Body and Soul"); there's Uma Thurman as the femme fatale ("Double Indemnity," "The Postman Always Rings Twice") almost luring poor Travolta into Big Trouble; there's Ving Rhames as the Big Boss (Richard Conte in "The Big Combo," Louis Calhern in "Asphalt Jungle"). Is this a movie or a film-school class?

Of course, Tarantino dumps all this into the Cuisinart of his own sick imagination, pushes the No. 10 button, and the whole thing comes out sliced, diced, mulched and crushed into something that's entirely old but feels entirely new.

Of the '80s and '90s noirs, only one feels utterly isolated from the ironic mode: Carl Franklin's brilliant "One False Move," which could be called "country noir." This film feels so fresh and powerful it seems to have been made by a director who's seen no other movies, though it too cleaves to classic themes (couple on the run, plus one; small-town sheriff against big-time criminals).

The Dahl films fall somewhere between Tarantino and Franklin. They're not so playful and allusive that they become catalogs. They do, however, pay genuine homage to what's come before and in some way comment ironically on that work. They're also not nearly so violent as either Franklin or Tarantino. Dahl is attracted to the menace and the plot twists of noir, but not to the gut-wrenching, modern violence of either Tarantino or Franklin.

"Kill Me Again" was a private-eye caper, somewhat undone by the fact that the private eye who should have been played by a Bogart clone was played by a 22-year-old kid (Val Kilmer). "Red Rock West" was a classic innocent-man-in-the-wrong-place tale, in which a drifter (Nicolas Cage) is taken to be a hit man, and people keep giving him money to kill other people, until the real hit man shows up. Complications ensue.

"The Last Seduction" is by far Dahl's most accomplished film, and it, too, is built around a classic theme, the femme fatale. In fact, the movie feels in some sense like a remake of "Body Heat," though moved to a cold-weather clime (a small western New York town). Linda Fiorentino plays a wife who's stolen $750,000 from her mildly abusive husband (Bill Pullman), money that the couple had earned by selling stolen hospital cocaine to street dealers.

What kind of a woman is she? Let's put it this way: She'd give Medea the willies. She takes off for Chicago, but instead lays up in Beston, N.Y., and begins a casual affair with a somewhat defenseless claims adjuster (Peter Berg). Berg is the sucker, the Hurt analog. She jerks him this way and that until she finally sees a use for him and sends him on his way, even as she's being stalked by her husband who, mildly and surprisingly, only wants half the money back.

The great kick in the movie isn't the plotting or the surprises (not as well done as in "Body Heat") but the guilty pleasure of sharing Fiorentino's manipulations. She's the point-of-view character (in "Body Heat," it was Hurt). The true seduction in the film isn't hers of him, but its of us — it makes us feel the subversive joy of using and destroying another human being. And it mandates that we smile while we do it.

That would have been impossible in the old noirs, where evil was eventually punished. In the fourth-stage world of irony and metaphor, there's no room for such outdated concepts as good and evil.

THE OUTLAW LIFE
"Sex and death entwined in style"

ONE FALSE MOVE
August 20, 1992

The temptation is to go too far and proclaim "One False Move" a masterpiece, the best movie of the year, blah, blah, blah. Of course it isn't. But it's a hell of a movie.

The picture almost slipped into oblivion, and much praise goes to Gene Siskel and Roger Ebert, who championed the movie on their nationally syndicated television show, and pretty much invented its life ever since.

This is exactly the sort of film Hollywood has forgotten how to make: the small-scale, extremely tense, character-driven thriller, so bitingly authentic that in its last few moments, when its antagonists come together, guns drawn, and you know that someone's going to die, it's heartbreaking. You believe in the characters good and bad, and you will grieve their loss, good and bad.

It's of a small sub-genre that might be called "country noir," which takes the nihilism and violence of the city and deposits them in some bucolic pasture with devastating results. "Bad Day at Black Rock" is perhaps the sine qua non of such works; but now "One False Move" threatens to replace it.

The setting is Star City, Ark., where local Sheriff Dale "Hurricane" Dixon would spend the rest of his days jawing with the boys down at the cafe over hot coffee and doughnuts, and locking up the odd miscreant, the loud drunk or the wife beater, on weekends. But, no, on their way to Dale City are three losers with guns and the will to use them: a white trash tattoo museum called Ray (Billy Bob Thornton, who co-wrote the script); Pluto (Michael Beach), a chillingly remote stud with a knife; and Fantasia (Cynda Williams), who is beautiful and confused. Their specialty is ripping off drug dealers; and in the movie's horrifying opening moments we watch as they wipe out a birth-day party.

They are the scariest of the scary. Far from master criminals, they're sloppy, impulsive, mean and stupid, like the Dick and Perry of Truman Capote's "In Cold Blood"; they have no place on the moral compass, except for Fantasia. She's the film's best character; one feels her regret and her helplessness. A drug addict, she despises what she's become; yet she's powerless to stop it, and when she has to, she'll kill, too. Williams manages to capture this ambivalence and sense of fragile denial exquisitely.

Hurricane is played by Bill Paxton, an agreeable smaller presence in many bigger films (most famously, he was the cowardly corporal in "Aliens 2"). In the early going, he's like a big sloppy dog, and when two shrewd L.A. detectives come to town, he slobbers and throws himself at them like an eager pup. (The two are played with flawless world-weariness by Jim Metzler and Earl Billings.) But ultimately, he manages to bring it together when he realizes it's not like it is on TV.

Director Carl Franklin manipulates these strands with vivid brio, aided immeasurably by the cleverly plotted script from Thornton and Tom Epperson. I love the way every little bit of information is used, and how what seems so obvious and straightforward in the beginning is ultimately revealed to be part of a more complex order, particularly with regard to Dale and Fantasia.

"One False Move" doesn't make a single false move. It's as tough and gripping as they come. It's the first movie I've seen in months about which I thought to myself, as I was walking out, "Damn! I wanna see that one again!"

WILD AT HEART
August 17, 1990

Imagine a version of "The Wizard of Oz" in which, at the end, the dim Dorothy still doesn't quite "get" the lesson that

"There's no place like home." So the munchkins beat the crap out of her.

That's pretty much "Wild at Heart," the new David Lynch film that, like his legendary TV triumph "Twin Peaks" and his much loved and hated "Blue Velvet," is full of murder, violence, perversion, bizarreness, cruelty, madness, violence, bad teeth, violence, trashy Southern accents, gratuitous gore, violence and pure romantic love. In other words, it's a comedy.

Lynch could never be accused of restraint, and if he pushed the envelope as far as it could go on television, he's straining at the bounds of the feature film here (as it is, the movie just missed an X by a whisker, based on a scene in which a shotgun and a head mix it up in a most frightening manner). It's definitely for graduate level movie-goers.

The film is indeed a gloss on "The Wizard of Oz," following a romantic voyager through a wondrous though peril-filled new land, yielding, in the end, to the wisdom that there is no place like home. The new land, however, isn't Oz, and I have a feeling we're not in Kansas anymore, either; It's the land of Scuz, and Lynch is its Wizard.

Working from a novel by Barry Gifford, Lynch follows the Gothic-baroque path of Sailor Ripley and Lula Fortune, two American kids doing the best that they can, considering the fact that Lula's mother is trying to kill Sailor, because she thinks he saw her lover pour kerosene on her husband and turn him into a gandy-dancer flambe. Sailor (Nicolas Cage) is a killer, having, in the movie's first few merry moments, literally beaten the brains out of an attacker hired by Mama. When he gets out of jail, who sails up in a black T-Bird ragtop but Lula (Laura Dern), Mama's scrawny-trashy daughter. The two check into a motel for a night of love, but he won't go the final step — crooning "Love Me Tender" — because they aren't married yet. See, they have morals. The next morning, they begin their journey.

They drive two-lane blacktops across the deep South, and get as far as the town of Big Tuna, Texas. Meanwhile, Mama — Dern's real mother, Diane Ladd, in a Wagnerian performance as a white-trash Valkyrie — sets a private detective after them (the hapless Harry Dean Stanton) and then throws in with a criminal boss to dispatch hit men.

The movie, to put it mildly, is a hoot from hell. Lynch has something almost completely missing from other American movies, a vanishing integrity, and that's what people respond to. This is his movie, like it or not, and he probably doesn't care whether you like it or not. It is unabashedly its own self.

It follows the conspiratorial design Lynch pioneered on "Twin Peaks": The movie seems to ever widen in its plot, bringing in still new levels of grotesque connivance, and then it finishes in an abrupt blast of violence, when Sailor and one of his tormentors run into a straight-shooting Texas lawman. As the density increases, you are continually disoriented.

To bring this off, the performances can't be "ironic," or intellectualized. The actors have to open up and give. Consider, for example, the performance of Willem Dafoe as Bobby Peru, one of the hit men Mama sends after Sailor and Lula. This is truly one of the strangest turns in an American film. Bobby is a piece of work: His teeth are as black as his soul and his polyester, country music-star wardrobe; his eyes are weirdly lit by fires within, and he sports one of those used-car salesman lizard mustaches — he's a combination of John Waters, Randy Travis and Warren Oates. But what's so astonishing about him is the way that Dafoe just surrenders to the concept: He wades in so far you can't imagine he could find his way out.

The same is true of Cage and Dern. Cage's Sailor is wild at heart, an Elvis-manque in a snakeskin jacket — "the symbol of my individuality," as he explains with labored earnestness — and a penchant for other people's trouble. His hair is slicked back, his droopy eyes radiate sexual heat, his brain is just about empty of everydamnthing except bad country music: He's white knight as white trash. Dern is also wonderful: She's had too much Dr Pepper and too many Stuckey's nut rolls in her time, and all the carbonation and nougat have gotten to her brain, if ever she had one.

Yet even as these two aren't exactly Romeo and Juliet or even Archie and Veronica, and still less Dorothy and the Scarecrow in any but the jokey sense, their love feels genuine amid all the perversity; and their lovemaking certainly looks genuine, so much so that Lynch comes back to it time after time.

When you leave "Wild at Heart," you're not really sure what you've seen; but you know you've seen something, *that* I guarandamntee you. It's like being slugged over the head with a bag full of pulp novels by a madman who may be onto something. It's scary and exhilarating. It feels alive.

THELMA & LOUISE
May 24, 1991

"Thelma & Louise," from Ridley Scott and starring Susan Sarandon and Geena Davis, is being hailed as a breakthrough film, the first female buddy picture that works. But it's nothing new at all. In fact, it's still the same old story, a fight with guns for glory, until time goes by.

So sad. It begins as a well-observed tale of bonding in which two Arkansas women, who've been shunted aside by the men in their lives, set out for a mildly irresponsible weekend of fun.

What they find is the lure of the gun, the sense of power and freedom it confers, and the sense of contempt for its victims. In the end, so seduced by it, they abandon everything for the bold new life they've discovered.

If this movie didn't have the camouflage of political correctness — it's about women, see, and therefore sports the fashionable feminist subtext — it either wouldn't have been made or would be denounced savagely.

Louise (Sarandon), a waitress, and Thelma (Davis), a housewife, are best friends, taken for granted by their men. Out for a weekend, they decide to take a revolver along. They stop for a drink, Thelma has a few too many and she gets into a fix with a clearly dangerous guy. He rapes her in the parking lot; Louise breaks it up with the gun, but in a fit of rage pulls the trigger, shooting the guy stone dead.

The movie doesn't pay a lot of attention to details. The shooting was ambiguous enough to qualify as self-defense. But the two women panic and take off on an odyssey across the Southwest, pursued by a kindhearted Arkansas state policeman (Harvey Keitel).

The two become involved with a variety of losers as they flee, including a hot young cowboy stud who gives Thelma her first orgasm (liberating), teaches her the ins and outs of robbery (enlightening) and steals all their money (terrifying). This last stroke compels them toward a life of crime.

What's so terrifying about the movie is the degree to which violence is seen as liberation. As they progress into empowerment by handgun, they lose their dumpiness. Finally, when they pull their pieces to humiliate a tank-truck driver who's been dogging them, they're *Vogue* models: Lean and tan, slick and cool, they brandish their pistols like fashion accessories. They love the power the guns give them to drive this scumsucker to earth and light off his 10,000 gallons of fuel in the desert.

Arthur Penn's "Bonnie and Clyde" advanced this same line back in 1967, demonstrating how two outcasts in the clinch of the Depression found their identities in the violence that they wreaked. But in that year, about 75 people were murdered in — to pick a city — Washington, D.C.; the times were somehow more innocent. This year, in that same city, 500 are likely to perish. The message that seemed so revolutionary then now seems utterly irresponsible.

And besides, "Bonnie and Clyde" played fair: It demonstrated, without romanticism, the inevitable ending of such adventures, as its protagonists were blown apart.

By contrast, "Thelma & Louise" is at its most dishonest in chronicling its heroines' end. (Read no further if you don't want to know.) Faced with the prospect of a return to society — as represented by a phalanx of troopers — they turn instead to the edge, and hurl their pink T-Bird over it. The camera freezes on that last image of them, locked in the air.

But if the camera had rolled for another few seconds, think what the last image would be: two beautiful women, smashed to pulp on the rocks, reduced to meat and blood, a lunch for flies. For what? For nothing.

And that's liberation?

KALIFORNIA
September 3, 1993

The French, who have a wondrous phrase for nearly everything, have a particularly vivid one for an all-too-common banality among the educated: nostalgie de la boue, or "nostalgia for the mud." This describes the morbid preoccupation of some intellectuals with matters of squalor and violence, with which they have no acquaintance.

"Kalifornia" is nostalgie de la boue distilled and purified into an essence so dedicated it all but knocks you out of your socks. It's more boue than nostalgie, as a matter of fact. It follows a dreamy young writer named Brian Kessler who is fascinated with serial killers — he romanticizes them into "children" in need of "treatment," not punishment. Of course, he and his girlfriend end up sharing a violent cross-country odyssey with the real McCoy, in the shape of a creep named Early Grayce. The killer is far from the specially touched wild child of the writer's delicate imagination: He is, instead, greasy, grubby scum with the IQ of a fish and the moral imagination of the fly who feeds on the road kill smeared along Route 66.

It's a promising concept, albeit melodramatic, but what keeps the movie from halfway working is its infernal preciousness. Consider that oh-so-ironic name of the killer: "Early Grayce," so literary and archly amusing. That pretty much establishes the artistic agenda of the film. Every detail has been polished and honed for maximum irony and abstract beauty. The self-consciousness extends into the film's visual presence. It's one of those extremely galling pieces that is so in love with the fact of its own "movieness" that every frame has the look of a window in a trendy SoHo boutique. It should have been directed by Helmut Newton; instead, it was Dominic Sena, who perfected his style in music vids and commercials. Big surprise, huh?

But the big news in the film is its casting, with Brad Pitt, who's played more than a few pretty boys (as in "A River Runs Through It"), as Early, under a matting of grease, fading tattoos, lank, sullen hair and the surly attitude of a much-cuffed junkyard dog. His girlfriend Adele (pronounced, of course, A-dell) is played by Juliette Lewis, and even in the casting one senses insincerity. These two are currently flavors-of-the-month in Hollywood. There's something deeply irritating about their need to subsume their beauty and good fortune in portraying the wretched of the earth. It has the haughty stench of young lords slumming among fishmongers.

The intellectual couple, Brian and Carrie, are played by Richard Gere look-alike David Duchovny and Michelle Forbes, who comes up with the movie's best performance. Duchovny and Forbes are offered up-front as conventional liberal sophisticates, full of the usual prejudices and fascinations of that breed, but Forbes's Carrie at least has an instinct for the practical. When, by plot machinations too facile to be believed, Brian signs up Early Grayce and Adele as ride-sharers on a Pittsburgh-to-L.A. run, with stopovers at the sites of notorious multiple murders (so that the writer can "feel the pain"), Carrie takes one look at this stunted, slovenly mutant from the planet of the scum and his waif-like Poor Pitiful Pearl of a girlfriend and realizes that he's bad news. Later, director Sena comes up with an even more graphic image: When Early takes off his boot at a rest stop, she catches a sniff of his foot — it's like a slap in the face and the odor of decay represents his spiritual decay. But only she smells it, while Brian persists in the usual excuses about how "it's not his fault, it was his upbringing, he's a victim," etc, etc.

Like oh so many intellectuals, Duchovny's Brian is fascinated by his brush with the actual, rather than the theoretical. Of course, he's unequipped to process the data correctly, so flattered is he by Early's seemingly earnest attentions. Soon they're shooting guns and hanging out in biker bars, where Early's masculine power and remorseless recourse to violence are liberating to the uptight, sensitive Brian. But . . . Duchovny's character is conceived as so utterly stupid and oblivious, it's difficult to care for him. His idiocy is the key factor in his upcoming victimization.

What pleasure there is in "Kalifornia" is of the dark comic variety, much of it class-based. Everybody in the film feels superior to Adele, including Lewis; thus the character is denied even the smallest shred of dignity and her ignorance is treated as a source of much merriment. There's an air of sanctimony in the film that grows increasingly irritating.

"Kalifornia" really loses steam and interest as it travels down those hot dusty highways. Once the tension between the two couples is spent and it becomes clear who Early is, the movie becomes a less than routine and never more than predictable violent thriller, and the violence isn't filmed with enough originality to make it interesting. The climax is more convoluted than a blueprint of a computer.

And the movie even walks away from its themes. Seeming to begin as an account of an idealistic liberal's education in the dark reality of the world, it's so overwrought by the end that it doesn't have a moment to consider its moment of highest irony: when Early, leaking blood and venom, comes careening toward Brian, the liberal, anti–capital punishment zealot squeezes the trigger on that most hated of all liberal icons, the semiautomatic pistol.

NATURAL BORN KILLERS
August 26, 1994

"Natural Born Killers" is about as "natural" as Natural Lite Beer or naturally mentholated cigarettes.

In your face like a drunk with a bad attitude problem, the movie hammers, yammers, blurts and blasts. There's not a single moment of repose or reflection; it grabs you by the lapels and sprays saliva in your face for two and a half hours.

Oliver Stone thinks he's making a satire, but he has no idea what a satire actually is. The point being made, under the coarse bombast, would seem to have something to do with that modern bugbear that has replaced "the system" as the generic target of opportunity for blowhards, "the media." Leaving aside the hypocritical irony that no man in this century has benefited more from media adoration than Oliver Stone, it's clear that

Stone hasn't thought rigorously about the media, isn't quite sure who or what "the media" are, nor is he offering suggestions as to how to improve them. He's just brazenly throwing the whole kitchen sink at the audience under a mantra of hip, and daring the squares to call him on it.

Under the craziness, there's a worm of a story. Originally based on a screenplay by a real *enfant terrible* of the movies, the twisted genius punk Quentin Tarantino, who wrote and directed "Reservoir Dogs" and whose "Pulp Fiction" won the Palme D'Or at the Cannes Film Festival, the movie tells the story of Mickey and Mallory Knox (Woody Harrelson and Juliette Lewis), two American kids from the heartland, trying to do the best that they can. But the only thing they're any good at is killing people, which they do as reflexively as breathing.

One presumes (one can never know) that Tarantino's original thrust was acidly ironic: sleazy white trash with the IQs of turnips but the feral instincts of rabid weasels, wandering the landscape, blowing people away, covered by media that apotheosized them for their beauty and daring without regard to the moral compass. Possibly that could have been a great movie, and someday I'd like to see it; but Stone and cohorts David Veloz and Richard Rutowski (Tarantino now receives only a story credit) have so front-loaded the meager narrative materials with sheer technique that nothing in it is felt, and the plot line all but disappears. It reminds me of Pauline Kael's great line about "One From the Heart": It's one from the lab.

Building on techniques he pioneered brilliantly in "JFK," Stone shifts radically back and forth between film modes, not sequence by sequence but actually shot by shot within the sequences. The images rattle back and forth between high stylizations, almost recapitulating the history of film in every scene; black-and-white film noir, over-exposed color, slow-motion, odd angles, raw videotape, even animation.

When Stone did this in "JFK," it had a thematic justification: He was chronicling an authentic event from dozens of sources, some legitimate, some not, many contradictory. What emerged was a kind of nightmare metaphor for the difficulty of ever truly knowing the truth. We had an impression of a reality lost under the dizzying profusion of possibilities. But the story of Mickey and Mallory doesn't have the mythic weight or the sheer historical meaning of the assassination of JFK. It's too slight to sustain the technique, so the technique becomes an end in itself; it comes to feel wholly arbitrary and unrelated. The result is to aestheticize the characters and the violence. They have no meaning under all the razzle-dazzle. The considerable mayhem — mostly point-blank executions of helpless clerks — has no power to disturb.

Occasionally, the movie is quite clever. In an early sequence, it re-imagines Mallory's squalid childhood as a bad '50s TV sitcom, with the vulgar Rodney Dangerfield as her sexually abusive father. Occasionally, it's quite powerful. The first sequence, a roadhouse robbery that's really just an excuse for massive bloodletting (and is probably closest in spirit to the original Tarantino script) is a terrifying yet weirdly hilarious account of the lethal whimsy of some very bad young people who play eenie-meenie-miney-mo to determine who will survive (it has something of the subversive power of the torture sequence in "Reservoir Dogs").

But as a story, "Natural Born Killers" is a mess, as if it's been cut and re-cut so many times no one can remember what it was originally about, and no copy of the script can be found. Characters come in late, make no impact and depart. Tom Sizemore, as some kind of Wambaugh-like writer-cop who's pursuing Mickey and Mallory for his own ends, is one example, but he's just there; his influence on events is meaningless. Tommy Lee Jones, in a performance that's mostly about his hair, appears at the movie's end as the warden of a prison that Mickey and Mallory stir toward apocalypse.

"Natural Born Killers" is full of death, but it's not particularly worried about it. There's no real engagement with the troubling problem of random American violence and our own fascination with it. Stone is far more obsessed with the attempts of a feckless Australian journalist, Wayne Gale (Robert Downey Jr.), to get Mal and Mickey on tape for his tabloid TV show. Gale stands for all the slick purveyors of media violence, making a buck off real crime.

But Downey all but subverts the film by becoming its one recognizable character and the only one about whom we care. His fate, meant to be a case of just desserts, instead provides the movie with its only stab of real pain. As for Harrelson and Lewis, they struggle to play the unplayable and manage not to play it. Harrelson doesn't have the feral depth, the instinctual cunning, to make Mickey anything but a lewd joke; Lewis has better luck, but it's virtually the same performance she gave last year in "Kalifornia."

As for Stone, self-decreed king of the issue pictures, his hectoring and bleating grow wearisome after a bit. It turns out that not only does the emperor not wear any new clothes, but he's not even an emperor. He's just a guy with a $50-million budget but without a clue.

TRUE ROMANCE
September 10, 1993

Whatever "True Romance" lacks in artistic refinement or high intellectual and moral purpose, it has this one undeniable virtue: never a dull moment.

A blazingly violent bad-boy story from the hyperfervid id of the same Quentin Tarantino who wrote and directed "Reservoir Dogs," "True Romance" is "It's a Wonderful Life" for the '90s, except that the wonders of life include guns, drugs, gaudy convertibles, great sex, and this time the hero is named Clarence, not the angel. The angel is named Elvis. Are we talking sentimental or what?

The true romance in it is screenwriter Tarantino's for movie violence and style. It's a melody in the key of BLAM! that represents an adolescent's yearning fascination with the power of the gun and the power of having a blonde on your arm. Sex and death are its entwined strands of DNA and, like "Reservoir Dogs," it wears this tin-pot nihilism like the badge of honor. And somehow, it's red, white and true-blue American: red blood, white trash and blue dialogue.

But it's not as good as "Reservoir Dogs," which had the core strength of being about professionals in a hard and violent trade and was as unsentimental as a spent cartridge case. This one — which, admittedly, Tarantino wrote before "Reservoir Dogs" — has the far less rewarding theme of the lucky amateur, as a dreamer finds himself in the middle of the hardball drug-dealing culture. His magic talisman: not a Kevlar Threat II ballistic vest, but . . . true love.

Our hero is Christian Slater, as Clarence Worley, a dreamy, movie-mad clerk in a comic book store who, one dreary Detroit evening, sits in an all-night theater watching three Sonny Chiba flicks (if you don't know who Sonny Chiba is, the movie's probably not for you). Who should sit next to him and start yapping cheerfully about nothing at all but that fabled creature: the girl of his dreams (Patricia Arquette).

She's blonde, pert, sexy, funny, wild and . . . she really likes him. What has to happen does happen and only the next morning does he learn she's named Alabama Whitman and is by trade a prostitute, paid for by his kindhearted employer as a birthday present. But — here's the fairy-tale part — she falls in love with him and wants to leave her pimp.

Clarence has seen all the great John Woo films, just as has Tarantino, so the next step is straight from the Woo canon: It's a bogus, sentimental expression of love through the medium of ultra-violence. He goes to see her pimp — Gary Oldman, sporting the best Jamaican posse dreads ever seen on a graduate of the Royal Academy of Dramatic Arts — and exchanges harsh words, blows and ultimately bursts of gunfire. He flees with what he thinks is a suitcase full of her clothes, which turns out to contain $500,000 worth of mob cocaine.

Here's where "True Romance" fumbles. Each character is terrific — tough, vivid, comprehensive, brilliantly acted — except for Clarence. How does this lad who's heretofore been depicted as a sweet, nearly dysfunctional clerk suddenly come up with the nerves and technical skills of a world-class hard boy? Throughout the film, in fact, Slater is enhanced with brilliant tactical abilities that he could only have learned from a graduate level course at an advanced gladiatorial school — that is, a maximum security penitentiary. Tarantino's conceit is dreary and unconvincing: Elvis (Val Kilmer) appears at key moments to walk him through reality. All the other behavior seems solidly rooted in character; Slater's Clarence is a dreamy writer's dreamiest conceit, the poet-killer.

In fact, the movie's best scenes transpire when he's not around. Two are so good they almost blow the picture away. In one scene that recalls John Belushi and Peter Boyle's legendary dueling Brandos from an early edition of "Saturday Night Live," Dennis Hopper and Christopher Walken have a searing encounter in a trailer, as Walken is the chief gangster in pursuit of Clarence, Alabama and the coke, and Hopper is Clarence's dad. Then there's a fight in an L.A. motel room between Alabama and one of Walken's more brutish thugs that's a terrifying ordeal of the physical: tense, violent, brilliant, breathtaking, but more important the perfect expression of her character. Underneath that beautiful body, we've always known there was a hard, cracker farm girl tough as nails.

But for every stroke of brilliance there's a stroke of wanton stupidity. The largest: The movie has no moral compass whatsoever. The $500,000 worth of nose candy is never remotely considered from the standpoint of the woe it will unleash upon the world, but merely as the source of some fast money for the two lovebirds, as they head out to L.A. to sell it to "movie people." The portrayal of movie culture — Bronson Pinchot and Saul Rubinek as, respectively, a venal actor and a sleazy producer — is juvenile but amusing. And Chris Penn and Tom Sizemore are good as two L.A. narcs who stumble onto the brewing deal and decide to take it down.

What isn't amusing is the ending, again almost lifted scene by scene from more of Woo — you might say this movie is from its master's Woo untimely ripped! It involves a mega four-sided shootout in a posh Beverly Hills hotel. Here, Tarantino, amplified by too-slick director Tony "Top Gun" Scott, somehow subtly and unfortunately changes the tone and value of the violence: It suddenly becomes Hong Kong gangster violence, cheesy and fantastic, leaving literally hundreds of bodies strewn about. The bigger it gets, the more meaningless it becomes.

Article:
PULP FICTION GETS REEL: SLICK FILMS GROW FROM SEEDY NOVELS
February 13, 1994

Americans wrote them, but it took the French to figure out what to call them: romans noir, black novels.

Derived from the tough-guy pulps of the '30s and '40s, the American romans noir had their peculiar heyday in the mid-'50s, when mass-market paperback publishing had just been invented. They were the quintessential bus- and train-station book, less than 200 pages long, meant for tired travelers on all-night rides between trunk towns like Memphis and Texarkana. They looked the same: on the cover, a bosomy blonde with a .45 automatic and a cigarette, and on the back a block of copy in red, full of words like "vortex" and "whirlwind" and "web of fate" — but never, ever "literature."

The writers were hacks and could grind out three or four per year, year after year after year, fueled by loneliness, self-loathing and lots of black coffee. They seem to have been men with squalid backgrounds, usually washed out of the newspaper trade and, having failed at screenwriting and PR, almost all with drinking problems and personal lives like unwatched soap operas. One of them was so utterly peculiar that when he lived in Hollywood, he rented not a room but a couch, and traveled the night in an old bathrobe that he represented to people as "Russian fur."

The names were Cornell Woolrich, David Goodis (the couch-renter) and, of course, Jim Thompson (whose "The Getaway" has gotten its second Hollywood treatment and currently is in theaters).

The books were their last stop on the road to hell — usually stories of doomed losers being played by bigger sharks or hot babes, seeking only a provisional redemption in some lonely alley somewhere in an anonymous big city or behind a cow-town diner. "This is a godless world," wrote a British critic of the place, and in it, "Murder is a casual chore."

Of course the French loved them. What can you expect from

a culture that adores Jerry Lewis and Mickey Rourke? Thompson, Woolrich and Goodis were republished in France in Gallimard's Serie Noire and remain steady sellers. Indeed, film versions of the works are just as likely to be French, including "Coup de Torchon," by Bertrand Tavernier, after Thompson's "Pop. 1280," and Jean-Jacques Beniex's "Moon in the Gutter" and Truffaut's "Shoot the Piano Player," both from novels by Goodis. I can recall a chat with the particularly obnoxious Tavernier, who leaned over a table during an interview and announced, with the same congruence of Gallic obstinacy and self-righteousness that might have marked De Gaulle in negotiation with pygmies, "Jeeem Thompson eees a better writerr zan, zay, Weeliam Steeeeronn or Johnnnn Uuuuupdike."

Thompson, born in 1906 in Annadarko, Okla., led a troubled life, variously eking out a living as bellboy, oil hand, actor, burlesque comedian, taxi driver, but most consistently as reporter and detective story writer — all the things writers did before master's programs in creative writing were started. He wrote two "serious" novels, "Now and On Earth" and "Heed the Thunder," to almost no effect. He turned to crime writing in the late '40s and never looked back, all the while fighting the persistent demon of alcoholism. (He was first committed for alcoholism when he was 18.)

In between heroic drinking bouts, he hit the keys: He peddled pieces to the men's magazines of the '50s, including Saga, of which he was briefly the editor. He actually collaborated with Stanley Kubrick on "The Killing" and "Paths of Glory," probably his highest accomplishments. But without Kubrick he was unable to earn a living as a screenwriter and soon went back to the old Underwood and the 2,000-words-per-day regimen. He wrote books with titles like "The Killer Inside Me," "The Kill-Off," "Recoil," "A Swell-Looking Babe" and "After Dark, My Sweet." At the lowest point of his life, he was writing novelizations of "Ironside" episodes and of such dreary screenplays as "The Undefeated."

He ended up with 29 published novels to his credit. He died in 1977, before his celluloid rebirth, a loser to the end.

But rumors of his excellence have been greatly exaggerated,

and where Tavernier claims any sort of greatness for him, he was wrong. Jim Thompson, king of the '50s hacks and revered cult figure of the anti-bourgeois lit set, was a lousy writer. No amount of revisionist bull or reverse snobbery will change that.

In fact, the roman noir gents as a whole were far less accomplished than their immediate predecessors, James Cain and Dashiell Hammett, and their inheritors, Elmore Leonard and George C. Higgins. Here's an exchange from Thompson's "The Getaway" that goes down as one of the most moronic in American letters:

Doc has just blown away Rudy the Piehead, his confederate in a bank robbery, and he turns to his wife and partner in crime, Carol:

"Alas, poor Rudy," Doc murmured. *"But how have you been, my dear? — to move from the ridiculous to the sublime?"*

"We-el—," Carol slanted a sultry glance at him. *"I think I'll be a lot better tomorrow. You know. After I get a good night's sleep."*

"Tut, tut," said Doc. *"I see you're still a very wicked young woman."*

That is Thompson's lame attempt at smutty banter between the outlaw couple, sexually excited by the murder, and it's certainly difficult to imagine either Steve McQueen and Ali MacGraw, or even Alec Baldwin and Kim Basinger, exchanging such inanities in either the 1972 or the 1994 screen versions of the story and not being laughed off the screen.

But the fact that there *are* film versions speaks eloquently to Thompson's true strength, which is story structure, rather than the line-by-line or sentence-by-sentence business. In other words, he was a writer who was good at everything except the paperwork. (I stole that line from Peter DeVries, by the way.)

Thompson had the vision thing down: bleak back roads of underworld America. He had the characters: sociopaths and suckers and nobody in between. And he knew how to put a story together.

Thus it is that his works have enjoyed a better run in the movies of late than anyone this side of John Grisham: "The Grifters," the original 1972 "Getaway" and now the current version, Maggie Greenwald's bleak version of "The Kill-Off,"

James Foley's excellent version of "After Dark, My Sweet." (No one has optioned "A Swell-Looking Babe," to my knowledge.)

Considered strictly as story structure, "The Getaway" is terrific. A professional bank robber, in prison, is paroled after his wife does sexual favors for an influential businessman. In return, the hero-robber is expected to rob a bank to help the businessman out of a jam. The robbery is botched, and one of the robbers betrays the hero, who still manages to shoot him — but not fatally. Then he is betrayed by the businessman, and kills him. He and his wife must deal with the meaning of her sexual relationship — was it a betrayal or an act of sacrifice? — while being pursued by the businessman's cronies, the wounded partner and the entire police forces of Texas, Arizona and New Mexico.

It has a happy ending.

Actually, both versions of the movie have been terrific, but there is further strangeness to report. This is, to my knowledge, a rarity in film culture, but both films employ the same script, which was written by Walter Hill, who went on to become a wonderful director himself ("48 Hrs."). Thus one can see the same scenes being played out to the line by McQueen and MacGraw and between Baldwin and Basinger. Some mild updating has been done — Doc robs a dog track instead of a bank — but the movies are, scene by scene, largely identical.

Except that they aren't. The two are amazing in that they show how influential a director is to the material — how his personality transforms the work. Thus Sam Peckinpah's 1972 version is both more intense and more psychotic than Roger Donaldson's cleaner, more conventional current version. The values Peckinpah injected into the production are absent in the Donaldson version: a worshipful sense of the cult of masculinity, and a concomitant hatred or deep distrust of women.

It should be noted that in bringing Thompson's "The Getaway" to the screen, Hill had to "fix" it. Perhaps his success at doing so, without damaging what was good about the book while abandoning what was ridiculous, indicates how sound its structure was.

Hill had to completely rewire the piece's values. It was Thompson's lame-brained scheme that Doc and Carol McCord, the sexy, romantic, bandit couple, were the bad guys, not the good. There wasn't a lot of conflict in the book: It was simply a case of watching as the charming Doc casually lied to and usually murdered marks. In the climax, as the McCords flee into Mexico (by boat), they are intercepted by the U.S. Coast Guard. Doc lures the sailors in with friendly banter; when they are in range, he pulls his shotgun:

"He got the two of them, almost cutting them in half at the waist with one double blast . . . Carol's shot got the steersman in the face and chest."

The supposedly ironic denouement places the McCords in a mysterious city for criminals run by an exotic Mexican gangster called "El Rey." His pleasure is to bleed them of money, destroy their love and turn them against each other. How dumb is that? This strangeness is typical of Thompson, and, as one critic writes, "This is why filmmakers almost always have to change his endings."

Hill makes the story realistic, setting it fully in the scabby, shifting, mobile culture of tough-guy pro criminals who service larger organizations but do not belong to them — do not, in fact, belong to anybody. He makes them romantic, and it's easy to see an intellectual's most adolescent fantasy at play in "The Getaway": a married tough-boy who outsmarts and outshoots everybody while accompanied by a woman so beautiful and so in love with him that she becomes equally a part of his criminal career.

But Peckinpah, a serious artist with a terrible attitude toward women, gives his movie an evil edge; the subtext is the humiliation of Carol McCord, played with zombie-like lethargy by MacGraw. Peckinpah *loves* to humiliate her: She gets beaten up, deserted pathetically in a train station with her whole life up in the air, dumped into a garbage bin and then a garbage dump. All this happens in an effort to win back the affections of the brutal but very cool McQueen. There's a titillating sense of masochism to it, aided or actually exaggerated by MacGraw's passivity in the role. It's "The Story of A."

Peckinpah's violence is also somehow more terrifying than Donaldson's. He had a psychotic view of the universe, and his gunfights break out savagely, and, with their fast-cutting rhythms, their montage of fast and slow motion, they truly bespeak a universe gone berserk. In that sense, they are the most Thompsonesque aspects of the film.

Donaldson's version feels much less quirky. His gunfights, for example, while extremely efficient (I think his climactic shootout in the hotel is better than Peckinpah's version), lack that sense of true madness. Peckinpah's felt sickly real, while Donaldson's feel slickly professional. They're just as valid, but they somehow strike a different tone; they don't explode your heart, they keep you royally entertained.

And, in this version (same script, remember; these are subtle, non-verbal changes in the texture of the movie), Kim Basinger's Carol is a far more self-reliant character. It helps, of course, that Basinger can do one thing that MacGraw couldn't, and that is act. But it also helps that she's given more weight and strength. Far from being a pitiful victim, she's much more a colleague, and, in fact, in the final gunfight, she's Doc's equal. We see this reflected in strange ways, the most important of which is guns. In Peckinpah's version, Carol carried a little .380, which she used only twice and then meekly. In Donaldson's, Basinger carries the same big-bore .45 automatic as her mate, shoots it very well and, in the climax, uses it adroitly to kill the main pursuer (David Morse).

In the world of the macho thriller, that's liberation! Underneath it all, Donaldson's "The Getaway" is an extended marriage-counseling session with guns.

SEXUAL OBSESSION

"A mad yin-yang of fear and desire"

FATAL ATTRACTION
September 18, 1987

Everybody knows its mysterious power, its capacity to haunt and provoke for days, even years. It's "The Look," when man and woman of no acquaintance momentarily lock eyes across a crowded room and though they occupy different and perhaps unconnectable worlds, they know in a nanosecond that in bed they'd be thermonuclear. Usually, sense prevails; the eyes break off, and they step discreetly out of that queer envelope of public intimacy and go about their business.

But not in "Fatal Attraction," a hot, scary, slick thriller that takes the premise of "The Look" and projects its consequences out into the universe of the psychotic. Built upon the myth of the femme fatale, however, it's still not quite anti-feminine, because its characters stay so specific they never become archetypes.

It begins when Michael Douglas, perfectly cast as a smug Manhattan lawyer of great prosperity but not much self-discipline, shares "The Look" with Glenn Close one night at a book publication party (his firm represents the publishing house; she's an editor there). That weekend James Dearden's otherwise fine script allows them the coincidence of attendance at the same meeting, while his wife is out of town. It's raining; they share a cab, then a drink, then a meal, then each other. It's so easy, the natural gravity of people with glib minds, attractive bodies and un-self-critical senses of morality obeying the glandular pull toward the sack. The sex, as promised, is multimegaton, mushroom-cloud stuff, but in the awkward moments after the last blast, he makes the rules clear: Now is now, tomorrow is tomorrow, and never the twain shall meet. "Gee, it's been great, see ya 'round, and so long."

But no. The steadily advancing horror of "Fatal Attraction" is Close's steadily advancing obsession with Douglas, and the way it encroaches on his life. The progression is almost mathematical: His irritation becomes anxiety and then fright and finally terror. The relationship will not die; she will not let it. He feels trapped, and when he realizes she's capable of violence, he himself becomes savage. It's a mad yin-yang of fear and desire; they goad each other toward terrible violence, and his vulnerable family stands in the middle.

The director, Adrian Lyne, who made his name and fortune with "Flashdance," then almost lost both with "9-1/2 Weeks," brings this one off with a maximum of velocity and style. The result is a film that is as deeply unsettling for its ideas as it is for its big, pulpy thrills. Together, they bring you to your knees.

Two or three of Lyne's conceits really pay off. For one, he uses Douglas almost subversively. The actor, with a slightly puffy face and a streak of callowness under his private school features, carries himself as if he thinks he's the hero of the picture, but he is its goat. What we see is a scared, shallow man unwilling to face consequences and incapable of dealing with them, and ultimately humiliated by his experience. He's not a kind man, either, and never quite sees how desperately ill Close is. Narcissistic to the end, he can't even be the hero of his most severe test: Thank God for his better half. (And thank God for Anne Archer in the role: An appealing, intelligent, very sexy woman, she only makes Douglas's adultery seem all the more contemptible.)

Lyne and Close never quite let her character degenerate into horror-movie stereotype. Even when we hate and fear her and long to see her destroyed, we understand that this beautiful, brilliant woman is a tragic mental case. Close never lets go of the deep core of anxiety and slaughtered self-esteem that is the center of the character's condition. Jason, of "Friday the 13th," she's not; even when she's a monster, she's human.

But the true scoop to "Fatal Attraction" is the skill with which it's been mounted. The most disciplined of the Brit pictorialists who learned their trade in the advertising game — though his compositions can be arch and showy — Adrian Lyne always stops just short of the kind of mannerisms that attract attention to him and away from the story. He's a particular genius at sound, and when silverware clatters on the table or water bubbles from the faucet as Close prowls Douglas's house, the precise timbre of the noise is far more effective than the cliched banshee wail of a Moog synthesizer. It turns your skin to knotty pine. More, it suggests the movie's true meaning and deepest secret: that the real horror in the universe is the horror of real life.

BOXING HELENA
September 3, 1993

It's interesting to speculate on the fate of "Boxing Helena" were its director named Jennifer Chambers instead of Jennifer Chambers Lynch. Here's my guess: A three-night run on one of the lesser pay cable channels.

It's the Lynch pedigree — Jennifer's link to her father, the great and troubling David Lynch — that validates the film and confers upon it honorary membership in the American avant-garde, where it belongs about as appropriately as Norman Rockwell did among the New York impressionists.

In fact, so pitifully and meekly middle-brow is "Boxing Helena" that it runs in panic from the very issues of radical sexuality it conjures up. Out of a grudging sense of fair play, hard to maintain in these days of high paganism, I won't give "it" away — the trick ending, that is. But it's about as cheap as trick endings get.

The film proper is handsome in that glistening, soft-focus, high-quality porn way. It's set in a comfortable universe where every car has been polished to high burnish and the heavy furniture of the mansion that is the principal setting glints with highlights off the mahogany. They must have spent half of Kim Basinger's money on Lemon Pledge!

The story is a cautionary tale: It warns to be wary of geeks bearing gifts, particularly when that gift is obsessive, unrequited love. Sherilyn Fenn plays Helena, beautiful, sexually liberated and utterly dismissive of those who do not advance the agenda of her own pleasure.

Helena's hobby is hurting men: She likes to pick them up, turn them on, make them fall in love with her and then dismiss them airily and move on to another sucker. She's made to order for the kind of man who loves women who hate men.

That particular bloke would be Julian Sands as Dr. Nick Cavanaugh, a gifted surgeon and a very sick puppy. Sands, a British actor who was so good long ago as an ardent romantic in "A Room With a View," has fallen on hard times ever since (he was a flying male witch in "Warlock," one of the most truly ridiculous movies ever made), and this isn't likely to redeem his career. His Dr. Nick is one of your basic-issue weenie boys, self-hating, weak, cowardly, without pride or spine. When he smiles, it says "KICK ME HERE" on his teeth. Seduced and abandoned by Helena, he's been driven not into bitterness or anger but into true dementia. We are given to understand that he in some fashion identifies her with his late mother, who rejected him just as cruelly while she dallied with a parade of lovers. The psychology is definitely on the $1 + 1 = 2$ level.

Though Nick has a flourishing career and a beautiful, ardent fiancée, he can't get Helena out of his mind. He throws an elaborate party, invites her and is humiliated that she chooses to leave with another guest. But she leaves her purse behind. He seizes this object as a fetishist would, and uses it as bait to lure her to his house. There, gloriously, she treats him like a dog (he loves her for it!).

But, trying to flee from him, she is hit by a car. When she wakes up, she's been enthroned as queen of the manse, with Nick as her willing, eager, self-abasing, worshipful servant. Oh, and he cut off her legs.

The movie bears certain resemblances to William Wyler's great "The Collector," in that it's a study of a sexually weak male taking a woman captive and, out of misunderstanding of the physics of love, trying to brutalize her into loving him. But the difference is more significant. Not merely was "The Collector" much better. It sympathized entirely with the terrified young woman; it had a moral center.

"Boxing Helena," however, sympathizes with Dr. Geek; it invites us to feel his pain at rejection and to enjoy his retribution over her sexual humiliation. In a terrible and cheap way, it suggests that she deserves what she gets, as if anyone could deserve that.

Later, he trims her arms and props her in a little high chair in the dining room where he feeds her bonbons and cherries. It's about that time that I got to wishing I could take a shower or something, so grimy was I feeling. Lynch, who is, it must be admitted, an assured technician, films this as a scene of great tenderness, evoking the ways in which she's falling in love with him. Does the phrase "Stockholm Syndrome" mean anything to these kids?

But, even as it dares to address the unthinkable, "Boxing Helena" is also preparing its getaway. In the end, it cops out. You keep telling yourself: "It's not even a movie."

BLUE VELVET
October 3, 1986

If you combined the narrative structure and depth of characterization of "Tom Swift, Boy Detective" with several of the juicier items in Richard von Krafft-Ebing's "Psychopathia Sexualis," you'd get something a lot like, though much better than, David Lynch's "Blue Velvet."

The most appalling aspect of the entire "Blue Velvet" phenomenon isn't the document itself, wretched and seamy though it may be, but the uproar raised by certain critics who've professed to see consistent humor, coherent vision and even genius in this twisted work. (One such critic even claimed that Lynch had "re-invented movies"!)

Excursions into the dark realm of the perverse can be a baroque kick if they're stylish, jaunty and clever; I remember both "Cafe Flesh" and "Liquid Sky" with a great deal of guilty pleasure. But Lynch's picture is a muddy mess, bumbling alternatively among infantile ideas, gee-whiz storytelling, extreme depictions of sadomasochistic behavior and clumsy satire. None of the actors can act worth a bean, and one of them appears to have had his cerebellum pickled in PCP for the duration of the shoot.

The scene is Lumberton, U.S.A., a bright little cartoon-'50s town where radio station WOOD announces the time with the sound of a falling tree, and the DJ announces pridefully that here in Lumberton, "We all know how much wood a woodchuck chucks!" Repeat slowly after me: sa-tire, sa-tire.

But underneath it all, there's a region of savage perversity! Lynch backs this heavy insight with a shot that dips beneath the surface of the green, sunny grass and discovers ants chewing each other to pieces. He thinks he's discovered something. But, like, I mean, they're only ants, after all.

At any rate, the story is a clumsily constructed, boy-detective yarn in which Kyle MacLachlan, late of Lynch's "Dune," discovers a human ear in a field, and, much to their displeasure, gets enthusiastic about helping the police solve the case. Enlisting the daughter (Laura Dern) of the head detective, he makes a quick connection to a torch singer at a local nightspot called the Slow Club.

He follows her home and soon discovers latent perversity awaking in himself. Hiding in her closet, he observes her undress listlessly, then entertain a gangster, who humiliates and abuses her in a scene of flesh-crawling density. The woman is played with bruised, opalescent shock by Isabella Rossellini, Ingrid Bergman's daughter, thereby, via pedigree, intensifying the perversity of the scene. The villain, Dennis Hopper, comes on like one of Heinrich Himmler's Obersturmbann-fuehrers in country-western drag, and the main technical problem with the scene must have been to keep his droplets of saliva off the lens of the camera.

MacLachlan soon tumbles to the fact that Hopper has kidnapped Rossellini's husband and child in order to indulge his perverse impulses. At the same time, this plot is loosely roped into another, involving police corruption, a drug rip-off and a brothel that appears to have been designed by Diane Arbus. Even the film's admirers admit that Lynch is a clumsy story-teller (to keep things straight, he'll replay scenes as MacLachlan reconsiders them) and that the movie makes very little narrative sense, while piling sexual atrocity upon sexual atrocity to very little clear purpose other than numbingly banal truisms and stilted dialogue. ("Life is strange," one character announces.)

In his gropings, Lynch occasionally creates a moment or two of black humor. When he zeros in on a street sign — "Lincoln Street"— and the music billows like a nervous breakdown, it's a funny parody of '40s conventions. When a dim go-go dancer dances lethargically on the roof of a convertible while Hopper and his thugs beat MacLachlan, it has a lyric weirdness to it that's amusing. Dean Stockwell does a turn lip-synching a song that literally has to be seen to be believed.

And the occasional image is arresting; the Popsicle colors and flatness of composition in the "Our Town" sequences are witty. A shot policeman stands in goofy shock, blood gushing down his yellow sports coat, but he will not fall; he looks like a piece of garish pop art.

Still, the movie is almost unendurably cruel. In one grisly scene, poor Rossellini is made to wander naked and beaten through suburbia to the leering amusement of teen-age boys. I never thought the sight of a beautiful woman naked could fill me with such a sense of obscene squalor. Worse, she's given a perverse masochistic personality herself, and her most memorable line is "Heet me, heet me." She likes it, see, and MacLachlan's great self-discovery is that he likes "heeting" her.

But when I got out of the movie, I felt like I was the one who'd gotten "heet."

BASIC INSTINCT
March 20, 1992

About halfway through "Basic Instinct" I was seized with a primordial urge, a spasm of undeniable wanting that arose from deep within my being. I fought it, but what can a man do in the grip of such a demon? I gave in and . . . ZZZZZ-ZZZZZZZZ-ZZZZZZZ!

Overpublicized and underbrained, "Basic Instinct" is a bitter disappointment, worth maybe a 10th of the hype that the media have so obligingly ladled out for its benefit. It makes you feel dirty in the morning. A thin and unconvincing mystery story, it is really driven forward not by plot or character but by the two or three quasi-hot scenes in which highly paid movie stars cavort like Erica and Long Dong in any of a half-million craftless tapes since porn moved to video.

The basic instinct celebrated feels more like plagiarism than sex: In plot, in character relationships, in everything except pleasure and skill, the movie seems a distillation of "Sea of Love" (that's the excellent Al Pacino film, from a Richard Price screenplay, about a haunted detective who falls in love and has Fourth-of-July sex with the prime suspect in a series of grisly sex crimes). The only difference is that Richard Price really solved his mystery; screenwriter Joe Eszterhas, the $3 million man, can't even manage that.

Michael Douglas is no Al Pacino. He's just Michael Douglas, long of jaw and grim of visage, who snarls at everybody. Douglas's San Francisco detective Nick Curran has a "history": He blew away two "tourists" during a drug buy, but has evidently suffered no career ramifications as a consequence. This makes him interesting to Catherine Tramell (Sharon Stone), an icy, blonde, millionaire novelist who collects murderers the way some people collect porcelain collies.

Catherine may be a murderer herself: In the opening moments, we watch a faceless blonde enjoy sadomasochistic sex with a man, then pop him like a balloon with a Kmart ice pick in what is sadly to be the movie's liveliest scene (and it's over 45 seconds after the credits). Learning that Catherine was the dead man's girlfriend and that she had written a novel with such a murder scene in it, Nick and his partner "Cowboy" (played dourly by the normally irrepressible George Dzundza) head out to question her, first encountering her female lover, which, of course, titillates Nick.

When Nick and Catherine confront each other, it's a case of instant hots. She tantalizes him; he tantalizes her. It's only a question of time. In fact, at a police interrogation, she puts on such a show, and he becomes so inflamed, that he grabs his ex-girlfriend, a beautiful police psychiatrist. How do you spell relief? R-O-L-L-I-N-T-H-E-H-A-Y. (The movie's second liveliest scene, by the way.) But soon enough he moves on to the main event, and the movie is crudely designed to derive suspense from the ritual of seduction; as Nick falls deeper in love with Catherine, he becomes more and more vulnerable. He's the fly in the web, and she's the spider-bitch. Meanwhile, she may or may not be counterplotting against him.

For all its fury and sound, "Basic Instinct" signifies naught. The characters are cartoons from a hundred other movies; the overwrought cop, the nymphomaniacal femme fatale, the best-buddy who, as soon as he mentions retirement, is a dead duck. Screenwriter Eszterhas really doesn't do anything well: There's no sense of authentic cop milieu (which "Sea of Love" had in spades) and the dialogue is all generic; there's no genuine wit and the relationships aren't sharply imagined. There's also an ugly strain of misogyny running through the film: The makers deeply hate women.

The director is Paul Verhoeven, a famous Dutch bad boy (he did the wonderfully perverse "The Fourth Man," then moved on to some naughtily violent American hits with the original "RoboCop" and the overdone but amusing "Total Recall"). He has always had a skill for storytelling, however questionable and tasteless the materials; but here he is hopelessly defeated by Eszterhas's talky, slow-moving and derivative script.

CRIMES OF PASSION
November 9, 1984

"Crimes of Passion" is a movie in search of a nervous break-down. Its vibrations are so whacked-out and wobbly, its grasp of its own material so tentative, and its rhythms so unsettling, you keep expecting someone to throw a net over the projectionist.

If it were merely a mess, the movie would be easier to dismiss. Unfortunately, in the confusion, there's a performance too powerful to ignore and a few ideas too provocative to disavow. And like many crazy people, it's wonderfully amusing and charismatic. It seethes with the energy of its own inner conviction, obeying its own privately glimpsed protocols.

The movie, of course, is famous already because it originally earned itself an X rating, and only radical chopping got it its hard R. And it *is* steamy: Kathleen Turner plays a tough-talking streetwalker with a wig of gold Dynel and a heart of sheer genius.

She may be a whore, but she's a good whore, and the movie is therefore full of whore-humor: It's concussive and profane and dirty — but hilarious. Turner says to an earnest suitor, "Look, I'm a whore and you're a trick, so why ruin a great relationship?" And she has a blasphemous but hysterical Miss Congeniality imitation that'll curl your hair.

But she's only half a whore; the other half is a bourgeois dress designer of exquisite taste and dignity but not a whole lot of warmth, and the schism in her personality is the central device of the movie. If this sounds like it's lurching into the lurid regions of the excessive, fear not: The movie becomes even more excessive.

Ken Russell, a specialist in the overwrought, has made a career of excess. His biggest hit matched him perfectly with another excessivist, D. H. Lawrence, in "Women in Love." Since then, however, he's tooted off in one crazy direction or another, first in a series of laughably overdone biographies ("Lisztomania," "The Music Lover") and most recently with the screwball sci-fi screed, "Altered States," in which William

Hurt devolved into an amoeba and was saved not by penicillin or radar waves but the power of love.

This time Russell has really gone around the bend, locating his story in the combat zone between the genders, on that ugly thoroughfare beyond love where lust turns, by the alchemy of rejection, into hate, where sex is an expression of hostility and contempt. This is the sex of power, not passion: These are games people play.

The film appears to be a variation on Luis Bunuel's "Belle de Jour" in that it's about a beautiful woman who, unable to express her eroticism in the context of her "normal" life, has taken on an elaborate fantasy identity, in which she's free to give in to her most private impulses. More important, in the fantasy world, she's able to control what's going on.

Kathleen Turner is the primary reason for seeing the film; hers is an extraordinary performance. In fact, in some sense the performance *is* the movie, since it holds the teetering structure and the melodramatic plot together. There's something remarkable here beyond the performance, however; Turner's pathology — her double life as Joanna Crane/China Blue (the hooker label) — is simply taken as a dramatic assumption. In other words, it's not a sickness, in Russell's eyes, but a fact, following on the human inclination to allow different strokes for different folks.

Instead, the focus of the drama isn't so much on her character but on what she brings out in the two men who manage to penetrate her secrets. In not terribly subtle ways, Russell lets us see that they are the mirror images of each other, each an illumination into the heart of nasty masculine darkness.

With riveting intensity and high style, Tony Perkins plays a nut-case Pentecostal minister who, sexually obsessed with China Blue (and ultimately with Joanna Crane) yet also torn by his own repressions, is dangerously close to violence. This is a figure straight out of Charles Laughton's "Night of the Hunter" or a dozen lesser trashy tales of bogus men of God who dream of grace and rape with the same fervency. But Perkins manages to make the Rev. Peter Shayne palpable by making him funny. Perkins inflates his "Psycho" intensity with a kind of comic irony. The result is something to see: sheer lunacy with veinings of self-aware wit cut through it. On the verge of committing a terrible crime with a terrible murder weapon (it cannot be described in the paper, although Perkins fondly calls it "Superman"), he breaks into a music hall version of "Get Happy." The result is hysterically funny and yet scary as hell.

Alas, in the other part of the triangle, Russell really comes unwrapped. Maybe part of the idea of the film was to create the image of the beautiful hunk, but the actor chosen to represent the "good man" is a disaster. John Laughlin is a hunk, all right, with a great build; he stands about 15 hands high to the shoulder, has strong teeth and looks as if he could count to 10 by stamping his foot in the dust.

Laughlin plays a young married man who, by virtue of some freelance investigative work, begins to keep tabs on Joanna and therefore meets China Blue. Having learned her secret, he quickly takes advantage of it by forking over the requisite 20 bucks. Having thus sampled China, he falls in love with Joanna.

Russell has no luck at all with Laughlin. The character seems unutterably juvenile and callow in comparison to Turner, and her powerful sexual presence just wipes him out. Worse, Russell, a Britisher, comes wretchedly undone in evoking Laughlin's stale marriage and unfulfilling sex life in the suburbs with wife Annie Potts (who was very funny as the secretary in "Ghostbusters" but is merely pathetic here). It's simply beyond his reach, strident and unconvincing. Laughlin's life at home and his life in pursuit of Turner seem not to match at all: It's like they're two separate characters.

But the worse crime comes at the end when, all issues having been ultimately settled, Laughlin gets the girl. But the girl is so much more man than he is. It seems a shame. Joanna deserves more than this musclebound wimp.

THE ACCUSED
October 14, 1988

Crisply made, incisive and riveting, "The Accused" arrives as something long absent from American movie theaters: a film of issues.

I'm not sure "The Accused" quite gets it right, but its passion and the honorable fury with which it argues its position are nevertheless the most impressive things about it. Unlike our fumble-tongued, repetitive debaters, this one goes for the jugular.

Loosely inspired by (but in no sense a re-creation of) a flamboyant case of public gang rape in New Bedford, Mass., the central situation has been amply fictionalized. And perhaps the presence of two eerily beautiful movie stars (Kelly McGillis and Jodie Foster) and a beauty-crazed cinematographer who inappropriately turns a sleazy working-class bar into a night-town wonderland also nudge the film away from being a more persuasive document than it is. The reality — any reality — cannot have been this slick and glistening.

And as its best stroke, "The Accused" is ambiguous toward its central victim. Sarah Tobias (Foster) isn't exactly an innocent baby sitter walking past "The Mill" one fateful night. Ticked at her boyfriend, she poured herself into her hottest outfit, went to a bar where she drank loudly, flirted aggressively, danced suggestively. What started as a lark ended in a brutal rape atop a pinball machine and left her lacerated and bitter, adrift in a largely indifferent legal system.

Another good stroke: Far from the inevitable impassioned feminist, Assistant D.A. Kathryn Murphy (McGillis) turns out to be a wily, squinty-eyed pro, simply interested in hanging scalps on her belt by prosecuting cases she can win, and walking away from the others. Thus, when the men are easily located and the defense attorneys propose a deal, which puts the three away on a lesser charge without a risky trial, she quickly pops to it. No fuss, no muss: American justice at its lazy best.

Everybody's happy, of course, except the victim. The system sees her as a working-class tart who was, after all, really "asking for it." But so incensed is Tobias at everybody's lack of care for her, that she virtually assaults her lawyer. What happens then is the burgeoning of a bond between them, but also something less than a friendship; they never become sorority sisters, it's never upstairs at the Kappa House, and the educated woman's contempt for the uneducated never quite departs the relationship.

But Murphy embarks on a radical legal action when she encounters one of the men who watched and rooted for the rape to take place. She finds a witness who can identify them and decides to prosecute them for reckless endangerment. It's OK to watch and do nothing; but if you pound on the table, off you go.

Legally, I have been informed, there's some basis for such an action, although it's never been attempted and seems to verge in troubling ways toward the Orwellian sin of Thoughtcrime. Moreover, the argument is helped enormously by the portrayal of one of the witnesses (Leo Rossi) as an almost Manson-scale pig. For the sake of the drama, however, it's a great stroke, because it connects with a larger issue.

And that's the whole notion of guilt by omission as well as commission particularly (but not only) as it relates to rape. The movie isn't really interested in the rapists, dispensing with them rather perfunctorily; it goes after the mob, and the crucial scene in the film becomes a recounting of the rape not from Foster's point of view but from the point of view of a witness, the only compassionate (though weak) observer in that circus of cruelty.

I'm a little worried by the way in which the film teases us with the rape. Like Capote's "In Cold Blood," "The Accused" begins immediately after the act, follows investigation and indictment, and climaxes in a grueling re-creation of the event. Even if the rape itself is a terrible act of violence, there's something titillating in the way Tom Topor's script holds it off until the end and derives great, but cheap, emotional power from displaying it.

But the film is exquisitely aimed in the way it punctures one myth, the myth of "asking for it." It begins with the worst-case scenario — a trampy-looking young woman alone in a bar, gyrating in front of a mob of salivating guys — and proceeds from there to the stern moral lesson that nobody is *ever* "asking for it."

Article:
A CLUELESS "BASIC INSTINCT" GLORIFIES MALE VIRILITY, POWER WHILE DENIGRATING WOMEN
March 22, 1992

It's an irony far too exquisite and far too subtle for the makers of "Basic Instinct" to have managed on their own, since they manage no other ironies: The homosexual community is outraged at the film for its negative portrayals of lesbian women as ice-pick wielding murderers.

What is so odd about this is the movie's distance from anything remotely authentic about homosexual life or culture and the filmmakers' basic lack of interest in it. They can't begin to imagine such a thing and have no clue how to represent it. Their "assault" on homosexuals is clearly a smoke screen; it only disguises the true agenda of the film.

Instead, the basic instinct that "Basic Instinct" celebrates is men's hatred of women; it is the most arrogantly misogynistic film to come down the pike since the outlaw oeuvre of Sam Peckinpah, in which raped women repeatedly learned to love their violators. In Peckinpah's defense, he was a great American film artist, if a sick, sick puppy; and he was working before feminism had done much to re-invent the way men think about women.

The makers of "Basic Instinct" aren't artists by a long shot; and, more disturbing, they haven't got ignorance as an excuse. Before it's anything else and after it's everything else, it's the prime mover in what Susan Faludi has called the feminist backlash, an expression of fear and terror toward women, particularly now as they are beginning to assume power in society. Writer Joe Eszterhas, star Michael Douglas, director Paul

Verhoeven: These boys are really scared. (What's the line about men of quality not being frightened of women's equality?)

In fact, "Basic Instinct" is fundamentally a $50-million dramatization of the oldest and ugliest of prejudices that men unleash in locker rooms about the "difficult" women in their lives: "What she needs," they'll say, and I can't pretend I've never said it myself or at least felt it, "is a good ——. A good —— will straighten her out."

The last time I can recall such a thesis being advanced in a mainstream movie was in the benighted year of 1967, so long ago that Sean Connery was still playing James Bond, and as James Bond, an application of his magic powers "cured" Honor Blackman (as "Pussy Galore") from her lesbianism and turned her straight and patriotic to boot. The movie was "Goldfinger," but the golden body part it celebrated certainly wasn't a finger. As absurd as the conceit was, at least Connery had the dark and ruthless magnetism to make such a thing believable . . . but Michael Douglas?

"Basic Instinct" is an encomium to masculine power, and it makes a disturbing connection between sexual power and the willingness to deploy a firearm haphazardly.

Douglas is a hotshot cop who has beaten a rap in which he accidentally — and clearly without remorse — shot two "tourists." Thus, when he's assigned to investigate the brutal ice-pick slaying of an ex-rocker whose body is found splayed and bound on a posh bed, punctured a half-dozen times by an ice pick (note the crude phallic symbolism in the choice of murder weapon), his presence and his history sexually excite the twisted libido of ace suspect Sharon Stone. She likes boys who kill. He responds to her crude come-ons, all of them choreographed as rawly as the set-up scene in a classic stag movie.

This connection has its ramifications: First, it inflames jealousy in Douglas's ex-girlfriend, a beautiful police psychologist (believe that if you will!), and it also ticks off Stone's beautiful female lover. And just to make things interesting and sink the plot into hopeless murk is the fact that Stone and the psychologist once had an affair!

Consider: There are three women in "Basic Instinct," and

each is bisexual, treacherous and violent, and each pines for the Douglas magic as the cure-all. (He should have paid *them* $15 million to play the part!) Male sexuality is held out as the world's most potent vitamin: A shot of vitamin D-for-Douglas can make them feel good all over.

Of course, such nonsense only remains credible in a world utterly bereft of reality, which is why so much of "Basic Instinct" seems to take place in other movies, and why the dialogue has a maddening banality to it, as artificial and unconvincing as the clean part of dirty movies. In other words, it's simply marking time to get to the hot stuff. (On video, this baby will be the champion fast-forward item of the '90s.)

It is therefore both appropriate and inevitable that its vision of "bisexuality" or "lesbianism" has nothing to do with reality. Rather, it's the "lesbianism" of pornography.

It may surprise some readers, but the truth is lesbianism is a constant motif in heterosexual, male-oriented pornography. In fact, a whole subgenre of "girl-girl" tapes may be found in any adult section of any mom and pop video store in America.

Authentic lesbianism, albeit romanticized, is represented in "Fried Green Tomatoes." In that movie, lesbianism was a simple variant on a deeper human condition known as love. It happened to be among people of the same sex, but there was nothing sensational or particularly erotic about it; it wasn't *for* anybody except the participants and if there was physicality involved, it took place off-camera. The two participants — Idgie and Ruth — related in a dozen other ways beyond the sexual.

"Basic Instinct's" lesbianism is display lesbianism. It has no root in character, and it expresses nothing about the participants. It is represented by the mannish Leilani Sarelle, who strikes macho poses and is seen dancing suggestively with Stone. But it has no meaning in and of itself; it only takes on meaning when it's "performed" for Douglas in a nightclub, curiously enough in a posture (front to back) that represents male homosexual practices far more accurately than female ones.

And, of course, it reflects nothing deeper than male fear and classic Freudian displacement: fear of women and fear of one's own possible homosexuality. One degrades women by wishing on them what one fears may be present in oneself, which one cannot face *in* oneself.

Like pornography, "Basic Instinct" is about sex not as communication or affection, but as power: The real question in it isn't "whodunit" (which it bungles, by the way) but "who's-on-top," and indeed one of the sexual subtexts of the film has to do with the politics of position. The ice-pick murderer always slays her bound victims from on top; when she is "made into a good woman" by Vitamin Douglas, she's willing to assume the submissive position. Over and over, in photographing the lovers, Verhoeven arranges the two so that Douglas envelops Stone, his masculinity overcoming and banishing her homosexuality. He has "cured" it.

The ending, too, reflects this power of masculine over feminine, though to be fair I cannot reveal it. But the implication is clear: Douglas, like some Mandrake the Magician, has conquered the woman, beaten her independence out of her and made her dependent.

What these poor boys need is a good ——. That might straighten them out.

"TRUE" CRIMINALS

"Not exactly Rhodes scholars to begin with"

MURDER ONE
October 3, 1988

Maryland has produced many great men of whom it should be justly proud and a few for whom it ought to hang its head in shame. Of the latter category, certainly Wayne Coleman and Carl Issacs, half-brothers and Pure-D scumbags, are the champions.

These two escaped from a work camp at Poplar Hill in early 1973 with a third inmate, a man named George Dungee who had an IQ estimated at "between 64 and 69." They dipped into Baltimore and picked up their 15-year-old brother Billy Issacs, then, in search of beer and gas money, began one of those feckless, pitiful crime sprees for which there exists no sane explanation.

It culminated on May 14, 1973, when they ran low on gas near Donalsonville, Ga., and turned into the driveway of a 67-year-old farmer named Nelson Alday. Over the course of several hours, they killed Alday and five other members of his family, including his 25-year-old daughter-in-law, whom they raped first. In due course, they were apprehended by the West Virginia State Police and now, after several retrials, reside in the Georgia penal system, where Carl labors under the yoke of a triple life sentence and Wayne has a much-postponed date with a deep fat fryer at the end of Death Row.

Now along comes "Murder One," retelling this unappealing story to the last grim detail. The movie, which snuck into three suburban houses without so much as a nod to the local media, without press kits or still photos, boasts one of the vaguest ad lines in movie history: "What happened that night became the most controversial crime in American history." No, it didn't (it didn't even happen at night); it did, however, become the most controversial crime in Georgia history between the murder of Mary Phelan and the trial of Wayne Williams.

The film turns out to be one of those unaffected "true-crime" dramas, set against the tackiest, bleakest icons of the American landscape, primarily fast-food joints, cruddy motels, and along generic highways. In its way and for all its pretensions to an anti-style, it is as formalized as a Japanese Noh Drama. For one thing, the camera placement is always directly frontal to the action, suggesting "impartiality"; and for another, the cinematography, by Ludek Bogner, is drained of brightness, so as to suggest squalor and lassitude. And finally, like Terence Malick's "Badlands" before it, it is narrated by a naif in a listless, unformed voice, meaning to draw horror from the contrast between the banality of his language and the savagery of the crimes he witnesses.

This young man — Billy — is played by a slightly older version of the Henry Thomas who was so lambent in "E.T." a few years back. Although Thomas is the only "name" in the cast and his participation may in fact have gotten the film financed (it's a Canadian job, though filmed mostly in Georgia, with a scene or two in Baltimore), his presence was probably a mistake. Thomas simply carries too much baggage; he's fascinatingly different from, and yet fascinatingly the same as, the boy who told "E.T." to call home, and you're always paying attention to him and not the sleazy story he inhabits.

And he's really not very good, sad to say. Partially this is because Billy is offered as simply a witness (though press reports indicate he may have participated in the killings), which at least provides the audience a character with whom it may make some sort of emotional contact; but at the same time, he's mostly either yawning or whining or standing there looking shocked.

The real fireworks are provided by James Wilder and Stephen Shellen, who play big brothers Carl and Wayne. As a cram course in the human capacity for brainless evil, these two guys are the ne plus ultra. Handsome, coarse, stupid, profane, and without a twitch of human feeling, they goad each other toward trigger time; and when it's over, they forget the murders in a flash. When they see themselves on the tube, they explode with glee, "Hey, lookee there. Damn, we're famous. We're on the TV."

Yes, it's scary stuff. The director, Graeme Campbell, has avoided telling the story in melodramatic terms: There's almost no suspense, and no sense of the noose tightening, or the manhunt drawing closer and closer. Everything is directed flatly, without stress or emphasis, and you provide your own tension.

But what "Murder One" lacks more damagingly is resonance: Campbell and screenwriter Tex Fuller have no theories to explain Carl and Wayne. They symbolize nothing, except the gutter from which they came or the dark truism that "real life" can be a horror show based on no more meaningful a principle than the random distribution of death in the universe. The film is so narrow and claustrophobic that it has no reference to topical issues, such as gun control or theories of incarceration or the criminal justice system.

What, you wonder, are they hoping to teach? Why do they want us to know this? In the end, they provoke nothing except your gag reflex.

BROTHER'S KEEPER
March 19, 1993

Some years back, Truman Capote, that master of self-dramatization, got himself a *Time* magazine cover by coming up with the term "non-fiction novel," which just happened to describe the book he was flogging. The phrase has lingered, even if poor Capote and his book have not, and it's a perfect description of "Brother's Keeper."

This is an examination of a criminal case, real, hopelessly banal and yet unique, that throws a culture into relief, exposing its tics and flaws and surprising strengths (or maybe not). At the same time, it's an examination of mind-sets in conflict: rural vs. urban, them vs. us, prosecution vs. defense, and family vs. others. And it's a hell of a story.

It couldn't have come to revolve around a stranger group of boys.

These are the Ward boys, Delbert, Bill, Lyman and Roscoe, who range in age from 59 to 71. If you ever saw them, you'd probably wish you hadn't. They're dairy farmers, four bachelor brothers in upstate New York who live in utter squalor and self-willed poverty.

You've seen such places from the highway and wondered: Who could live there? The house is ramshackle, the yard littered with junk, and an old school bus has been sunk into the earth to pass for a chicken coop.

At the Wards' farm, the line between animal and human kingdoms has become provisional. The boys don't bathe, they don't change their clothes, they can't talk, they don't even brush their teeth. How do I know? Easy. They have no teeth.

But — do they kill? The state thought so.

One morning in 1990, Delbert, 59, called the police to report that his brother Bill, 64, had died in bed — a bed the four boys shared. The next day, Delbert was arrested for murder.

The state police, after interviewing the somewhat confused Delbert for 12 hours, decided that he had murdered the sickly Bill by suffocating him with his hand, probably motivated by mercy.

In fact, one of the curious strains running through the case is the suspicion that Delbert did for Bill exactly what he would do for an animal in pain: He put him down.

On the day before Delbert was indicted, who should arrive fresh from New York but just-barely-experienced filmmakers Joe Berlinger and Bruce Sinofsky and cinematographer Doug Cooper, with a trunk full of 16-millimeter gear rented on credit cards and a hunger to make the great American movie. And they did.

It was one of those strange cases that caught the public imagination and drove the media bonkers.

Delbert ended up giving interviews to Connie Chung: "Thank you, Delbert." "Thank *you*, Connie."

The story quickly lit up the small town of Munnsville, N.Y. (pop. 499), as the farm community, which had ignored the smelly, semi-literate and near-reclusive brothers, soon came to resent the imposition of "outside" justice.

The filmmakers earned the trust of these people and got them to talk candidly. It's astounding to note how insightful their observations are. And the film shows how the defense lawyer shrewdly manipulates small-town indignation into a powerful force. At the same time, the presence of so many TV news teams, with their stand-ups, their little blazers and their pouffy hair, comes to feel almost like comic relief. The TV boys and girls reduce everything complex and mystifying to hopeless sound bites that make the media seem trivializing.

As the case became more famous, it grew darker. Semen was found on Bill's trousers, opening the possibility of homosexual incest and a lovers' quarrel, which seems unfathomable looking at the squalor of the boys. But still the town stuck by Delbert, even throwing him a dance. There he is with his deer-in-the-headlight gaze, doing a do-si-do with a farmer's wife amid piles of home-baked cookies and pies. Where is Grant Wood when you need him?

"Brother's Keeper" builds momentum like a freight train as it pulls us onto and through the trial, watching the prosecutor and the defense attorney go at it. That final moment when the verdict is rendered is a great movie moment in a great documentary.

THE KRAYS
November 9, 1990

Whatever the Kray twins were selling in the London of the '60s, it wasn't Doublemint gum. Actually, it was protection, and if you didn't buy it, you needed it desperately — from them. They would beat the stuffing out of you, laughing all the way.

Ron and Reggie Kray were two nasty boys from the London slums who rose to pop stardom as gangster-nightclub owners; eventually, they ruled the English underworld, until an indiscreet set of murders undid their empire and brought it crashing down, as chronicled in "The Krays."

They were created by bizarre psychological tides: They were raised, during the Blitz, entirely by a culture of women who lectured them incessantly on the weakness and craven stupidity of men; they enjoyed the peculiar psychic bond so common to twins — an almost telepathic sense of each other; they were also gifted with an abundance of strength and physical courage; and both boys were particularly proficient with fists.

The results are now spectacularly chronicled by British filmmaker Peter Medak, with two brothers from the rock group Spandau Ballet, George and Martin Kemp, as Ron and Reggie. Like "Dead Ringers," this one falls into the genre subset "Twisted Twins." It's a chilling, fascinating movie.

The Kemps manage in the movie to keep the two boys separated, which is a great help. With massive, leonine heads, rugged good looks and sleek, panther-like body language, they could blend into one character easily enough. As the film has it, however, Ron was gay and slightly smarter and greatly more charismatic, and Reggie straight, more loyal, dumber. Ron pretty much could twist Reggie any which way, except romantically. When Reggie fell in love, it was with a simpering, thundering crash. But he knew how to give love only as he had gotten it: His claustrophobic, oppressive version drove his wife to suicide.

The movie traffics in weirdness, much of it relating to Billie Whitelaw's presence as Mama Kray. Whitelaw is a powerhouse actress, and that power has never been better deployed. She encourages her boys, while at the same time building a kind of cozy, twisted world in which no fresh air is allowed, and that leads to all sorts of craziness. The underleaders of the gang check into the house, take their shoes off, chat banally with Mum, accept tea and crumpets from her, then go upstairs to the meeting world and decide whom to kill. It's the juxtaposition of smothering domesticity with the hardest of urban violence that gives the movie its shuddering creepiness.

In this sense, it recalls the great Cagney film, "White Heat," in which our crazy hero's love for his nasty mom drove him forward to more and more irrational violence; in the act of being gunned down by a police sniper, he could bellow to his mentor, "Ma! Top of the World!"

The Krays found their own top of the world when they blew their cools and tracked down two surprisingly small fry on whom to perform rather public executions. The Godfather would never have been so stupid, which may be why there are going to be *three* movies about him, and only one, *this* one, about The Krays.

THE THIN BLUE LINE
September 9, 1988

Poor Randall Adams; his fate makes Job's look like a bad day at the office.

Adams is the central antagonist in Errol Morris's compelling non-fiction film "The Thin Blue Line." Not exactly a Rhodes scholar to begin with, he was an Ohio drifter headed toward California who took refuge in Dallas, where he'd gotten a temporary minimum-wage job pounding nails. One day in 1977, headed back from this interesting career, he ran out of gas.

What happened next is very difficult to account for in a meaningful universe, where cause and effect rule; rather, it suggests the random whimsy of a psychopathic god. Adams was picked up by a young Texan named David Harris; the two had a few beers, went to the movies, and smoked a joint together. Harris, who was driving a stolen car, dropped Adams off, and some hours later apparently shot and killed a policeman who had stopped him because his lights were out.

When Harris was apprehended some months later after bragging to friends about his kill, he quickly changed his story, blaming the man he'd picked up. And thus Randall Adams ended up on Death Row, and, after a ruling by the Supreme Court on a technicality, with a life sentence.

Knowing this miscarriage of justice to be the material of the film, you expect certain things: a conventional marshaling of the facts delivered in a tone of liberal outrage after the fashion of "60 Minutes"; a conventional northern liberal fricassee of southern conservative justice; a conventional movie, in other words. What is so astonishing and beguiling about the movie is how assiduously it avoids the conventional. Morris calls it a "non-fiction feature" rather than a documentary, and he proceeds in a way no documentary has ever proceeded.

For example, Morris completely avoids a narrator; the viewer is, in a sense, his own narrator, or more appropriately, his own detective. The movie sifts through a series of carefully ordered documents, interviews and diagrams — it's like reading a particularly interesting police file — in which you track two increasingly diverging phenomena: the case against Randall Adams and the truth.

The film also has a "Rashomon"-like quality to it, as it returns, over and over, to the fatal five seconds when someone pumped five .22s into Patrolman Robert Wood while his female partner sat drinking a milk shake in the patrol car. Morris diverges completely from the documentary tradition by "re-enacting" the shooting; we see actors shooting and dying and speeding off into the night, in the lurid cinematic vernacular of the '80s-style police thriller, complete to slow-motion and those ubiquitous close-ups of the muzzle-flash blossoming like an orchid of light from the barrel.

Sometimes Morris can't quite control the film's sense of irony. The film is at its weakest when it is most arrogant — when, for example, Morris pokes fun (as if with a cattle prod!) at one of the self-serving "surprise" witnesses who condemned Adams at his trial. The woman is clearly — pardon my French — scum, and it comes out quickly that she made a deal with prosecutors to have charges against her daughter dropped in exchange for perjured testimony. But as she gives a transparently ludicrous account of her motives — "Ah've always injoyed halpin' them polices" — Morris cuts to some sequences from a 1940s Boston Blackie serial with a girl detective. It's just too cute.

Where Morris is at his best, curiously, isn't in the re-enactments of the killing but exactly where you would think he'd be dullest: in the interviews. There's something penetrating about his interviewing technique (though he's edited out most of his own questions): He leads his two entwined antagonists deeper and deeper into self-revelation, one toward dignity, the other toward confession.

Adams seems somehow purified by his suffering; he's acquired a kind of angelic pallor and a translucent skin tone; his eyes are so intense they're almost spiritual; like Kafka's "Hunger Artist," there's not an ounce of spare flesh on him. And yet in some sense the movie is a lesson in the power of appearances: In photos taken in 1977, Adams was the archetypal American nightmare figure, a wild-haired, wild-eyed piece of white trash. He was tailor-made for the fall, and the Dallas cops and D.A.s were there to help pitch him over.

Meanwhile, little David Harris looks like a Mouseketeer. One of those cute blond kids, he has and had the demeanor of a choirboy and the radiant smile of a boy model. Again, on appearances, you can understand how the cops, perhaps unconsciously, yearned to believe him, even when the facts didn't support his story.

Morris finds him stunningly open about his past and "that night"; yet, even as he is working the kid toward a confession in the 10th year of Randall Adams's incarceration, and even after he has discovered the kid's criminal escapades in California, there's yet another stroke of complete absurdity. Harris, during the making of the film, burglarized a Dallas apartment, kidnapped a woman and shot a man to death — and ended up on Death Row himself!

"The Thin Blue Line," which is the thin blue line between the way things usually happen and the way they *can* happen, is a completely fascinating look into the gutter. It's a chronicle of America at its worst, driven forward by a raging musical score by Philip Glass, and made more tragic and depressing by the irony and detachment of its tone.

And, one can say of it something one can say of damn few other movies: It may actually get an innocent man out of jail. It may not just make people feel good. It may actually *do* good.

HENRY: PORTRAIT OF A SERIAL KILLER
October 31, 1990

If you're going to do it, this is the way you have to do it. The question is, why do it at all?

But John McNaughton didn't worry about that; he went ahead and did it. His "Henry: Portrait of a Serial Killer," a Halloween treat for bad boys and girls, is deeply unsettling and very scary. It's a still life, with weapons, of one of those spectacularly misconfigured human mutants who occasionally blow into the headlines, make us tuck our children in every night for a week, and then vanish into legend.

Henry kills because he kills. The movie conjures up the usual blather as theory, and it's certainly believable: The son of a prostitute, he was abused in all the ways a boy can be abused until, at 14, he took up a bat, a gun or a knife — his own accounts vary — and did his mama in. He's been killing in her name ever since, mostly prostitutes, but generally anyone who wanders into his view when he's in one of his moods.

Actor Michael Rooker's vacant stare and vaguely courtly manner call up the image of a man beyond explanation. Clearly inspired by the ravings of confessed serial killer Henry Lee Lucas, Rooker's Henry is a killer at once both horrifying and commonplace.

The movie rides the very thin line between art and trash, between exploitation and illumination. It's true, certainly, that it takes one into a universe of such moral squalor that one feels tainted afterward: In one key scene, we watch as the thorough Henry industriously beheads a victim, the better to dispose of the remains. And there's a desecration of a family, as viewed through the cracked prism of a video camera viewer, that's very close to being the most appalling sequence of images captured in an American movie.

But it's also true that McNaughton makes choice after choice to avoid shock for the sake of shock. He shows very few actual murders, preferring to discover Henry's victims after the fact. He never sinks to the slasher-film level, where, through the genius of the empathetic camera, you become "The Killer," enjoy the killer's power during the stalk and walk away having made the kill yourself.

Rather, McNaughton's technique is yoked to the sensibility of his subject: The movie is deadpan, gritty, sordid, sleazy, miles from any sense of glitz or "style." McNaughton slams us into what might be called drifter-culture, as bereft as possible of the majesty of the psychopath as imagined in conventional movies. Henry and his pal Ottis (Tom Towles) aren't Jason or Freddy; they're trashy parolees living with roaches and dirty dishes on Chicago's dreary North Side. They are unlettered, illiterate, borderline dysfunctional, formed by the dreary litany of abuse and incest, and ready to pass on their grief to any and all who come before them. If you saw them, with their dead eyes and slack mugs and tatty, greasy clothes, bells would go off: You'd stand aside, you'd vacate the area quickly.

One constant theme is society's helplessness to such casual beasts. Gun laws are no help at all: "One phone call and I can git a gun," says Henry. The "system" is almost invisible, represented by one self-deluding, inattentive parole officer. The police simply don't exist.

The "plot" concerns Henry's one brush with normalcy: Ottis's sister Becky (Tracy Arnold), fleeing her trashy husband, comes North to spend some time with the boys, even as Henry is slowly initiating the slovenly Ottis into the rituals of murder. She likes Henry, even as her brother "likes" her. Her presence, ultimately, is the catalyst that drives the two apart and that sends the movie toward its dismal, resonant ending.

Why do such a film? One reason is to suggest the chaos that lurks in the universe in a way that movies seldom can. This one suggests that if the smiler with the knife shows up, there's nothing to do but die.

HORROR

"In the moist and ferny jungle of the id"

THE SILENCE OF THE LAMBS
February 14, 1991

Valentine's Day may never be the same.

Jonathan Demme's powerful "The Silence of the Lambs," opening today in a grand gesture of macabre taste, is rose-red with blood and blue-black with bruise; it's chocolate candy for the reptile part of the brain.

Working from Thomas Harris's shocking and very scary novel, Demme goes straight to the heart of madness. The movie is at its queasy, mesmerizing best as it explores the world of the sexually disturbed sociopath who wants not merely to kill, but to obliterate with the baroque flamboyance of a Picasso.

The plot is simple enough. A grotesque monster named "Buffalo Bill" has killed and flayed five women. Conventional investigatory techniques lead nowhere, but the one authority who might be able to decipher the clues, psychiatrist Hannibal Lector, won't assist the FBI. Why? Because he's psycho, too.

Thus the FBI, ably represented by actor Scott Glenn, selects a trainee to go interview Hannibal, on the ruthless theory that the killer may somehow be enchanted by this nubile, defenseless young thing.

The young agent is played by Jodie Foster, and Dr. Lector by Anthony Hopkins. Their odd-couple show is the most stunning asset of "Silence of the Lambs."

He's an ugly little toad with bright eyes and a mind as gifted as it is liberated from conventional morality. The terrible thing is that in his seething brilliance (and this is the film's queasiest assertion), he's a rather attractive person.

For her part, Foster is brimful of willingness to face the unfaceable. Demme gives her considerable psychic baggage of her own. In her own quest to save the "lambs" from the slaughter, she's willing to undergo the ultimate debasement; it's inherited from a father, a cop who caught a bullet for his troubles.

Doctor and student; father and daughter; master and apprentice; voyagers through horror. The relationship is a terrible journey toward terrible knowledge, and Demme manages to infuse it with the kind of messianic geekiness that is as fascinating as it is repulsive. We feel the slow process of envelopment and seduction.

The melodramatic devices that surround this central conceit are efficient. Buffalo Bill has kidnapped a senator's daughter, and since he starves his victims for three days before the atrocity, that 72-hour time frame drives the movie.

As good as this movie is, I can't say it is any better than Michael Mann's "Manhunter," based on another Harris novel. Both flourish to the degree they are able to re-create the mindset of their malformed characters; it's a swell place to visit but you wouldn't want to live there.

MANHUNTER
August 15, 1986

"Manhunter" is an eerie, persuasive thriller that will probably appeal to two kinds of people: those who are admirers of "Miami Vice," and those who are psychopathic killers. Those who are both will be in pig heaven; those who are neither had best stay away. The film, derived from Thomas Harris's eerie, persuasive 1981 novel "Red Dragon," tells of the hunt by a weirdly gifted FBI agent of a hideous psychotic killer. The movie was written and directed by Michael Mann, who has achieved great fame for developing and supervising "Miami Vice," and the movie bears all the hallmarks of high "MV" style: snazzy compositions; silky, mesmerizing camera movements; an astutely calculated color range, and over-reliance on rock music for emotional impact.

If these staples of "Vice" have grown irksome from over-imitation on a host of lesser shows (and also from "Vice's" less than smashing second season), they are well deployed here. What Mann is interested in doing, and what he does well, is etch a terrifying dreamscape in which psychological monsters prowl for each other. We very much feel that we're in some moist and ferny jungle of the id where intellection and impulsive savagery are entwined in a deeply frightening way. Mann creates an extremely unsettling sense of psychoculture: The movie could be said to take place not in the belly of the beast but in his brain.

William Petersen, the intense, young actor who made his debut in "To Live and Die in L.A.," plays Will Graham, the title character. Graham is an investigator who specializes in serial killers at considerable risk to his own body and mind. His personality is familiar, but his technique is unsettling. A conventional burnt-out cop, he's seen too much too soon and is discovered staring moodily out to sea like the pouting Achilles outside the walls of Troy, unsure whether he'll join the hunt again. But he's too good to sit this one out.

The crime that draws Graham from retirement — he lives on the beach in Florida with wife Kim Greist (of "Brazil") and son — are the murders, during consecutive full moons, of two families. The deaths and subsequent mutilations of families in their beds at night are extremely heavy stuff, but fortunately Mann is a glib enough technician to evoke these crimes just vividly enough for dramatic purposes without ever seeming to dwell on them. Besides showing a keen sense of style, he shows something even rarer for so visually oriented a director: good judgment.

But the real fascination in the film is watching Graham work. Evidently possessing a rare gift of psychic empathy, he likes to visit crime scenes and re-create the crimes in his imagination as he traces the killers' steps and thereby inspires in himself intuitive leaps in logic. Mann chronicles this process with extreme believability, particularly as Graham draws near to the final revelation that unveils the killer (neatly handled here as it was in the book).

Another tactical triumph of "Manhunter" is the way that Mann keeps track of the investigation. Where "Miami Vice," particularly in its later incarnation, all too typically pursued style at the expense of meaning, Mann labors mightily here to keep the story of the investigation moving forward and grounded in the realities of modern forensics. (Mann himself, in an unbilled performance, plays a lab technician.) There's an awful lot of convincing police procedure, helped in no small amount by Dennis Farina as the extremely believable FBI supervisor.

Sometimes Mann tries to cram too much in. I was unsure, for example, how Graham made a key connection between Hannibal Lector (Brian Cox), a creepy psychopath he had previously caught, and the "Red Dragon" killer-at-large, by way of a secret communication between them. But the air of menace is so complete and so compelling, it's easy to forgive this gaffe.

The movie also includes one of the book's more unusual gambits. In the second half, we meet the killer, played with ghastly geekiness by Tom Noonan. Harris worked the killer up in some degree and insisted on portraying him with some sympathy: He's a giant, ugly man, with a cleft palate, who was savagely abused as a child. In his strangeness he has taken to — this is muted in the movie — an over-identification with the poetry and art of William Blake, particularly with the painting "The Red Dragon and the Woman Clothed in the Sun."

This is fascinating but somewhat intrusive, particularly as we watch the killer become involved with a blind woman and seem almost to discover love. Frankly, it somewhat violates the ritual of the hunt. Do we want to understand these people? Isn't the satisfaction of the moral tidiness of movies, as opposed to the messiness of real life, the pleasure we take in blowing those people away?

Needless to say, the plot soon reverses itself, putting Will Graham and the Red Dragon at opposite sides of a room, and a .44 Magnum between them. It's *one* of those rare cases in which shooting first and asking questions later seems not only prudent but just.

THE HITCHER
February 21, 1986

No one is likely to confuse "The Hitcher" with a work of art — or even, come to think of it, a real movie. Still, this glitzy little thriller, despite its overwrought pretensions and its underwrought grip on probability, really hums along.

The film begins with a strictly take-it-or-leave-it proposition: the premise that the menacing figure standing by the roadway is not just a bad guy, but the Bad Guy Himself, old Scratch, Beelzebub, Shiva the Destroyer, Loki, Set the Egyptian God of Night, Zul from "Ghostbusters," Jason out of Friday the 13th, and so on and so forth.

And if anyone can sell the notion, it's Rutger Hauer. The hulking Dutchman, with his scruffy yellow hair and his malevolent blue eyes, looks so creepy standing there in the dark, he could be all of the above, and more. As for lone teen-ager C. Thomas Howell's decision to pick him up, that's another story. He picks him up for a very good reason: If he doesn't, there won't be a movie.

In fact, the movie's most irritating flaw is that its screenwriter, Eric Red, just hasn't worked hard enough, and all the way through, the malevolent Hauer and his quarry-cum-executioner Howell continue to act in ways for which the only meaningful justification is that if they didn't, the movie would have to stop right there.

"The Hitcher" is thus primarily an exercise in style, not sense. If anything, it's most reminiscent of Steven Spielberg's astonishingly kinetic movie debut (for TV), "The Duel," with Hauer in the role of the truck. And it's got some brilliant stylistic flourishes going for it. Robert Harmon, who directed, is an ex-cameraman, and the film is beautifully composed, with a cold, slick, haunting look. It is set against an almost desolate Texas landscape where, now and then, a gas station that looks familiar from an AC/DC album cover will put in an appearance. A few weathered-looking lawmen and other isolated citizens show up, are slaughtered for their trouble, and thereby return the film to Howell and Hauer.

Harmon also appears to have studied George Miller's "The Road Warrior." The true stars of "The Hitcher" are the car wrecks, which he choreographs with amazing grace and vitality. Harmon has worked out some stunning ways to slam vehicles into each other, ways that feel completely original; one such, which might be called the Waltz of the Dodges, sends two police cruisers bounding in parallel tracks in the road shoulder with such delicacy that they look like the dancing hippos in Disney's old "Fantasia."

And the two actors are extremely believable, if almost nothing they do is. One of the real pleasures of "The Hitcher" is its creepy, icky feel. Although the attraction that Hauer has to Howell is never spelled out, it's clearly of a dimension unusually charged for an American action film. It's a perverse blend of contradiction, partly sexual, partly paternal, partly simple human need, completely inexplicable, and it gives the film an almost European texture — as if Hauer's old pal Paul Verhoeven, he of the sublimely kinky "The Fourth Man," were calling the shots.

But as much license as you grant the movie in exchange for its thrills, it always wants a bit more, until finally it wants too much. OK, so Hauer is somehow "mythic evil" and can kill in mysterious, spookily silent ways. But does that justify a scene in which he shoots down a helicopter with three pistol bullets? Later, he is in chains, on his way to maximum security; clearly he has the power to escape, yes? Yes, but why can't Harmon work out a way to *show* him escape, instead of checking into the sequence after he's burst from his cuffs?

THE STEPFATHER
May 29, 1987

What's so terrifying about Jerry is the emptiness of his face. He has the bland mug of someone raised in a Holiday Inn at an interstate exchange, a generically American set of features that could have been composed by one of Norman Rockwell's less gifted assistants. To see him is to think you know him, which is a big mistake, one that people around him keep making. He's all chipper-pep, organization, go-getterism. He's a salesman, a family man, a regular small-town guy with a homily for every occasion, and when he gets irked, he has the odd tendency to slaughter his family, then go out and get another one.

Jerry is played with chilling authenticity by Terry O'Quinn in Joseph Ruben's chilling "The Stepfather," which opens today, trailing a wake of brilliant out-of-town reviews. And for once, the advance word is dead on: This one's a corker. Call it a masterpiece on a very small canvas and compare it to such compelling and queasy classics as Noel Black's "Pretty Poison" or Hitchcock's Mother's Day Card from Hell, "Psycho." Not for majority tastes, of course, hard-edged and darkly comical, finally unspeakably violent, "The Stepfather" is still a feast of astonishments.

Jerry's thing is perfection; he's been poisoned by 1950s sitcoms like "Father Knows Best" and he wants each new family to match the tube's idealized version of harmony and love. When they don't, it becomes the night of the long knives. One of the sharpest things about "The Stepfather" is that it never stoops to explain him — he can't *be* explained — even as it creates him with such a miniaturist's brush of reality that you're made to believe him completely.

Part of this sense of conviction is O'Quinn's astonishingly well-modulated performance; and part of it is the shrewd script by old-time mystery writer Donald E. Westlake; and still another part is director Ruben's extraordinary sureness of balance as he guides the film between the nightmare comedy and the nightmare. But still another part — and the most potent part — is the way the thing feeds on its audience's own mesh of guilt/love/hate/fear/loathing/pain, etc., as directed toward the families we find ourselves in. Jerry has a kind of mythic quality to him; he's every parent's aggressive instincts unleashed and given James Bond's license to kill.

As a technical exercise, Westlake's script is extremely well plotted; just as he seems to be laboring to set up conventional developments, he double-crosses you. A righteous avenging angel, for example, on whom your hopes come to rest, becomes dead meat in seconds — and it's the most vulnerable of victims who ultimately gives the devil his due. At the same time, the film never seems overtly mechanical; nothing happens arbitrarily, but out of causes and motives (except for a lamentably gratuitous nude sequence near the end).

The movie begins with Jerry blandly cleaning up after a massacre, pausing to straighten a picture on the wall while the blood coagulates on the carpet, then heading into the sunlight while whistling "Camptown Races." It's made more powerful by the Teflon ease with which Jerry slips into a new family setting, as husband to widow Shelley Hack and stepfather to teen-ager Jill Schoelen. The central tension is between stepdaughter and stepdad, for Stephanie, as Schoelen's character is called, senses in an instant that there's a worm crawling in her dad's brain. The angst between them is like a rancid vapor; it suffuses the cute house, curling through the floorboards, all the more vivid for mom's brainless refusal to sniff its presence (Shelley Hack, a former "Charlie's Angel," has gotten quite good at playing self-delusion). Stephanie catches on to Dad's real weirdness when she sees him flip out in the basement. The scary thing about it is just how close his psychotic rage is to normal rage; it just goes that little degree further, into madness. And it's made more horrible because the film has made us the only witnesses to Jerry's madness.

In fact, all the way through, the movie plays mercilessly with double-entendres, as when Jerry says smugly, as a private joke, "Father knows best." The words seem utterly normal to everybody but us. Meanwhile, Westlake is feeding us tidbit after tidbit of information as various people draw closer and closer to understanding just who he is.

I suppose if one were cruel, one would have to say that "The Stepfather," no matter how resonant, is Just A Psychological Thriller. Yes, that's all it is. But the middle American homily it most ardently expresses is the coda for the thriller business, the pro's oath: "If a thing is worth doing, it's worth doing well."

A NIGHTMARE ON ELM STREET
January 18, 1985

Wes Craven's "A Nightmare on Elm Street" is absolutely the last thing one would expect from the maker of 1974's ultra-disgusting "Last House on the Left" — one of the first true splatter flicks — and the brain-dead, oafish "Swamp Thing" of two years back.

It is, Lord help us, a literate, clever, witty, imaginative horror film, just when, after the accumulated outrage of so many dreadful slasher items, the genre seemed as bankrupt as a 1929 savings and loan. It is certainly the best horror film to come this direction in many a full moon; it may be the best horror movie since David Cronenberg's eerie, disorienting "The Brood."

In fact, like Cronenberg, Craven displays a talent for imagery that is unusually provocative, not for the sheer gore it displays, but far more for the idea it expresses and the visceral jolt the idea detonates in the pit of your stomach. His storytelling skills falter a bit at the end, but the movie is nevertheless a riveting experience.

Craven builds his film around a classic device: the nightmare itself. It seems that someone — some strange, unknowable thing — is killing the teens on Elm Street and implanting in the surviving kids' heads terrible, terrible nightmares. It is Craven's vision of these voyages through hell that gives the film its special, chilling power. And within those satanic fever dreams, it is the details that have particular brilliance.

The nightmares simply bleed into real life, without (or so it seems from Craven's subjective point-of-view) the formal intervention of sleep; the sleeper, remember, never *knows* she's asleep. In one nightmare, for example, the heroine, a teen-aged girl named Nancy (extremely well played by Heather Langenkamp), is bathing; suddenly, a hand reaches up from the tub and pulls her down and down and down. There's something primordial about this idea in and of itself: Being abruptly denied the relative solidity of the porcelain upon which one is sitting — the very foundations of rational stability itself — is extremely unsettling. Then, far beneath the surface, she glimpses up in her liquid terror to see — Oh deliciously clever detail! — the ovoid shape of the tub admitting a halo of green light far above, like a hole in the ice. Everything else is terrible blackness.

Furthermore, it's not that she awakens, choking and spitting water in the tub to discover, in classic movie fashion, It's All Been a Dream. That's the point. It has been a dream, but a dream like no other: Someone has tried to kill her from within it.

Or consider the terrible scene in which Nancy flees up the stairs, but the stairs themselves suddenly become infirm, and her feet sink with aching slowness into them, gummy and leaden with some kind of crud. As in an authentic nightmare, the authentic world has become unstable; the rules of physics no longer obtain.

Nightmare motifs, of course, are not new to movies and not new to horror movies in particular. However, they're almost always irritatingly used as red herrings, as in the end of "Carrie" or in "An American Werewolf in London," that is, to goose a cheap shock out of the audience at a slack moment in the narrative but to no serious dramatic purpose. Craven's idea is different: The nightmares aren't part of the story, they *are* the story.

As it turns out, the literal explanation of the goings-on is somewhat unimpressive, given the power of the movie. It seems that, many years earlier, the parents in the neighborhood had secretly murdered a child murderer whom the courts had let free because of sloppy police procedure. Now, still scarred from the gas in which they doused him, and wearing a slouch hat, he has returned somehow to enter the minds of their children and — from within the dreams — murder them.

The movie provides a good dose of shocks. Perhaps the best thing about the movie, however, is that it never surrenders to the staple sequence of sleazier efforts: the long stalking motif in which the terrified and usually nubile female victim's every twitch and feeble gesture are observed with contemptuous disdain by the killer — that is, by us, the audience — and the final stroke is milked for its sexual connotations.

The teens in "A Nightmare on Elm Street" are well-developed as characters, rather than as bodies, and a steady performance by old pro John Saxon as Nancy's father, the town sheriff, is equally welcome in a genre in which adults routinely are depicted as complete ninnies.

THE EVIL DEAD
April 5, 1984

Since its premiere at the Cannes Film Festival in 1982, and a subsequent rave review appearing in *Twilight Zone* magazine by Stephen King, Sam Raimi's "The Evil Dead" has acquired a cult reputation as a terrifyingly original low-budget horror picture, and it has virtually made the career of its 23-year-old director.

There is abundant precedent for such an event. In 1968, a Pittsburgh director who specialized in commercials, George Romero, imprinted himself instantly on movie consciousness with the crude but completely convincing "Night of the Living Dead" and went on to the multimillion-dollar "CreepShow." Similarly, "The Texas Chainsaw Massacre" established Tobe Hooper; he went on to "Poltergeist" for Steven Spielberg. David Lynch enjoyed a parallel breakthrough, when his grotesque "Eraserhead" attracted attention on the midnight movie circuit; he moved on to "The Elephant Man" and is now directing the $25 million "Dune" for Universal.

And so it has been with Raimi, who, on the strength of "The Evil Dead," is now firmly ensconced in Hollywood and working on his first "major" film for a mainstream producer.

Except in this case, to paraphrase Gertrude Stein, there is no there there.

What's always scariest in horror is the concept, not the spectacle. Romero, Hooper and Lynch all built their films out of an insidious but nevertheless inspired central idea; their movies somehow addressed or tapped into subconscious fears. Romero, for example, used the notion of the authentic, urban dead — winos, old people, victims of accident — as a terrifying device to evoke a sense of a world gone absolutely berserk; the most powerless had suddenly become the most powerful. The graphic displays of gore, the assault on the sensibilities, the final numbing triumph of death over life that followed — all were merely expressions of this idea.

"The Evil Dead" has plenty of gore, it assaults your sensibilities like the D-Day invasion force and it buries you in corpses up to your eyeballs, but it has no central idea. It has no idea at all. Knock, knock, who's there? Nobody.

The — you should pardon the expression — "story" is as follows: Three college girls and two college guys show up at an obscure Tennessee cabin for no reason that Raimi ever bothers to establish. There's not much chemistry among them; none of them really has a personality. They're not even there, in prime movie sleaze traditions, for the illicit pleasures of sex and drugs. They appear to have driven into the wilderness at great effort and expense merely to die for Sam Raimi.

The occult angle is laughably thin; it seems that a "professor" had previously used the cabin as a site for experiments with the "Sumerian Book of the Dead," bound in human flesh; however, when he called up the snoozing demons of the earth — for some reason they were snoozing not in Sumer but in Tennessee — they made chicken fricassee out of him and his wife. Our heroes find the volume — it looks like a coloring book smeared with pizza — and a tape recorder on which he has helpfully left the correct chants. They press the Play button, and presto, guess who's coming to dinner? Or, rather, guess what *becomes* dinner?

As this translates into actual practice, each of the possessed girls becomes a hideous she-demon, obligating the two men to beat, burn, rip, dice, shoot, gouge and ultimately chop them to death several times apiece. ("Dismemberment is the only protection," warns the professor.)

Unfortunately, the makeup applications that transform the women into demons are hopelessly amateurish. They don't look frightening at all, merely like rejected dancers from the Michael Jackson video "Thriller." You keep waiting for them to boogie.

Or you keep *hoping* that they will boogie, to provide the film with a leavening smidge of wit (it has none) or life (it has very little).

The characters — though perhaps quotes should be added to "characters" to indicate Raimi's limp grasp on the notion of personality — help turn themselves into stomach-turning goo by behaving with numbing stupidity. Even after they understand what's going on, they persist in wandering off alone to help Raimi's primitive sense of plot possibility.

"The Evil Dead" is so primitive it's essentially a home movie — but from a very sick house.

DAY OF THE DEAD
July 19, 1985

The dead are back, and they want to party.

That's the theme, the spine, the style and the spirit of George Romero's "Day of the Dead," which opens today at a number of area mausoleums. (It's also a rip-off from the ad line of an upcoming "Dead" parody called "The Return of the Living Dead.")

It is a movie to goof on, a movie that invites its audience to partake in dialogue with the characters on-screen, and a movie whose stupidity and shameless, hustling eagerness to show the unshowable somehow grant it dispensation from the outrage one ought to feel.

In this case, "Day" doesn't quite follow "Night" — that is, "Night of the Living Dead," Romero's cult hit of 1968; there's been an intervening "Dawn of the Dead," in 1979. "Dawn" lacked the crude horror of the first, which was a queasily terrifying movie, but it had a spirit of sarcasm that was something to behold, featuring, as it did, zombies breaking into a Pittsburgh shopping mall and boogieing to the Muzak as they ate any living thing they could get their slimy mitts on.

"Day," in turn, exchanges satire for claustrophobic intensity and incredible ingenuity in special effects. It is set in the same world — a kind of Yoknapatawpha County of corpses — in which the human race has been infected by a virus that rots the brains of its victims, turning them swiftly into cannibalistic crazies; at this point, the zombies are definitely winning. The odds, reports a scientist, are definitely in their favor, at 400,000 to 1.

Thus "Day" transpires in an underground lab where a ragged team of scientists tries to domesticate the beasts on the principle that if you can't lick 'em and you don't want to join 'em you can at least employ 'em. Meanwhile, their complement of army guards is freaking out on the pressure of the solitude and the pressure of the encroaching zombies up above and in the pen.

Of course all this is pretext for the real stuff. The real stuff is mayhem and slaughter in excruciating detail. Ninety minutes in this movie are like a year in medical school. It isn't very pretty what a zombie without pity can do.

There is, in fact, no civilized defense for Romero's work, and that is part of its appeal. Romero is an outlaw artist; he's working so far beyond the limits of what is permissible, you tend to be drawn to him in the same way that you'd be drawn to a merry, avuncular Mexican road agent. He's irascible and infantile at once. And, damn it, he's not without talent.

First, he's an exceedingly competent director, very good especially with actresses. Both Gaylen Ross in "Dawn of the Dead" and Lori Cardille here function as centerpieces. Both are heroes. Both are strong, competent and admirable. Both completely out-perform the male characters. And, huzzah, huzzah, both survive.

Romero is also an extraordinary imagist and action technician, and he's able to put together his various slaughterfests with about as much grace and style as can be managed. He plays expertly with tone, knowing exactly when he can bring you to the point of giddy stupidity at the outrageousness of it all, and exactly when to bring you to the vomitorium.

On the other hand, he lets his soldiers ham for the camera endlessly; I could have done with a good deal less shrieking on the part of Joseph Pilato as the screwball Captain Rhodes and

Jarlath Conroy as his second in command. They were easy to tell from the zombies because they were so loud.

JASON GOES TO HELL: THE FINAL FRIDAY
August 17, 1993

"Jason Goes to Hell: The Final Friday" proves that the road to Hades is strewn with bad intentions.

Is there a morsel of energy left in the old stalker formula? If there is, director Adam Marcus sure doesn't find it, instead settling for a rehash of the customary whackings and dicings appended to a plot of stupefying banality, held together by a skein of logic that might be regarded as subneanderthalian. This one is strictly for the entry-level trade.

The big news, if you're a connoisseur of such things (and you shouldn't be), is that Sean Cunningham, who wrote and directed the original "Friday the 13th" 13 years ago, has returned to steward the last edition out of existence. But the film takes on the irksome ambience of a vanity project, with producer Cunningham splashing self-referential strokes about, most notably setting the infamous Crystal Lake, in the undiscovered country of "Cunningham County," on all the police cars and uniform patches. Who does this guy think he is, Hitchcock?

That irritation aside, little sustains "Jason." Even the old shhh-shhh-shhh-ah-ah-ah on the soundtrack seems to have less zing and too much echo.

Cunningham's writers, Dean Lorey and Jay Huguely, completely reverse the premise that has buttressed the series by revealing that it's really Jason's heart that was driving him; it has a life and will of its own, like an alien creature. Thus, when Jason's body is literally blown to pieces by a government SWAT team (where were these guys when they were needed at Waco?), his surviving heart re-enters the body of the coroner and takes him over, to launch yet another reign of horror. So why didn't this happen back in 1984 or '86?

Soon, necking and fornicating teen-agers are being turned inside out all around Cunningham County, as Jason's heart trades up in body-shells until at last he is born again in toto. It looks like the worst possible news for a while. Maybe we're going to be stuck with nine more movies! But then, for some obscure reason, it's revealed that one of his relatives can finally and totally kill him. See, it's a . . . relationship movie.

Literally nothing is new, except that possibly the camera lingers upon the actual killings a few seconds less than in earlier editions and the premise is slightly more connected to science fiction than brainless horror, though there's no science and it's still brainless. Two things would have marginally helped: A theory that at last unified the data of Jason (I mean, other than: "Cash from debauched suckers is good!") and a final money shot of Jason entering the dark place. We needed an image of him burning up far below; instead, a bunch of garden-gloved hands pull him into what looks like a swimming pool excavation.

As for the statement in the title "The Final Friday" — promises, promises.

And finally: Hey, exhibitors, what about enforcing that R-rating? The theater in which I saw the picture was jammed with kids under 18 and I didn't see their moms anywhere in sight.

Next time, I'll name names.

SLUMBER PARTY MASSACRE
September 6, 1982

What lover of rotten movies could resist a film with a title like "Slumber Party Massacre," especially with its camp ad slogan, "He's dressed to drill"?

With a title and a come-on like that, the film, now playing at a shopping center and a couple of drive-ins, sounds like a parody — and indeed, it may have been conceived as such.

Written by Rita Mae Brown, the lesbian-feminist author of "Ruby Fruit Jungle" and "Southern Discomfort," and produced and directed by Amy Jones, the film throws so many of the hallowed cliches of the hey-let's-slice-up-some-girls genre at you in the first few minutes, you have a good deal of difficulty taking it seriously. One suspects that Brown and Jones may have had in mind that most difficult of all stunts: to create a parody of a genre that also totally and satisfyingly fulfills its requirements.

But either as parody, or taken literally, "Slumber Party Massacre" never wakes up.

The ingredients of the genre have been repeated so many times that they're almost as formalized as a recipe and can be expressed as such:

<u>Slaughtered Teen Casserole</u> *(serves any number)*
1 mad killer
6 dumb, nubile teenage girls
1 isolated house
1 set of parents away for the weekend
1 nosy little sister
3 dumb, wimpy teenage boys
3 phony subjective-camera stalking sequences, and
2 real subjective camera stalking sequences
Slice, dice and perforate, adding large quantities of blood; cook at 350 degrees for about an hour and a half.

To this conventional concoction, Brown has added a few mild feminist spices, but not so that you'd taste them unless you were looking for them.

For one thing, she's provided her mad killer with the most ominously phallic weapon yet for such guys: He carries a huge power drill with a bit about 2 feet long and 2 inches thick.

The constant visual motif of the violence in the picture, then, is an ugly stylization of the sex act.

Jones demonstrates this concept vividly: Though she has trouble putting together action sequences that create any real energy or generate any real power or suspense, she usually contrives to have the offending victims on the ground, in the posture of submission, with the drill (and the driller) looming above them.

And Brown also provides the driller with the most pristine statement yet of the anti-feminine ethic of the berserk male id, which is the catalyst in all these films: the notion that women in particular and victims in general somehow *need* to be debased. As he stands above Chris (Michele Michaels) and holds the instrument up the instant before the plunge, he purrs, "You know you want it. You love it." His name, by the way is Ross Thorn. *Thorn.* Get it?

And she has decreed that the power of womanhood shall triumph over the intruder, rather than male rescue. Thus the men in the picture — the two wimpy teen-age boyfriends, an innocuous neighbor and a delivery boy toting a pizza with olives and mushrooms — go to their deaths with a minimum of fuss but a maximum of sound effect.

The noise of the drill grinding through human flesh and bone is the one technical achievement of the film: It sounds like a moody New York method actor saying *Buzzy Buzzard is a busy Bozo* real fast, with a mouthful of dry peanut shells, while somebody in the background gargles syrup.

But the killer isn't nearly as impressive as his tool — one of the main problems with "Slumber Party Massacre." In a similar (and much better) film, "Visiting Hours," Michael Ironside made a fabulously charismatic villain, a dark, muscular, brooding presence and a much more convincing synthesis of mythic, male evil.

By contrast, Michael Villela seems like a retired English teacher who's taken up slaughter as a hobby. Thin, gray-haired, mild-looking, almost wispy, he generates no terror, no sense of power.

What the movie suffers from most of all, however, is a lack of craft. Its ambitions lie beyond the grasp of its director. Amy Jones must be very young; surely she's never directed a major feature before.

The movie never seems polished or accomplished in any way. It's jumpy, and its camera set-ups are clunkily conventional. She never gives the movie much in the way of style, and in no way does she recharge or re-invigorate the cliches.

When John Carpenter made "Halloween," he used a shrewdly muscular style. The film had such a sense of motion to it, such unremitting pace, that you never noticed its absurdities.

Jones has a few clever ideas, but they're so random they don't help the movie much. She plays a nice game with blood imagery: red fluids swirl through the film in a variety of ways, establishing, visually, the mood. A particularly nice conceit is built around a cloud of cherry Kool-Aid floating through a pitcher that precisely predicts the killer's demise. Floating in a swimming pool, his blood billows cloudily around him in the water. And the one convincing action sequence uses the theme of parallels: As a victim dies outside the house, simultaneously another dies inside — but on the TV.

Brown's script also fails almost completely to create convincing characters; one had hoped for something much better from a novelist of her gifts. These are more teens of the "raunchy" variety so popular to filmmakers these days, but her girls never come alive until they die.

"Slumber Party Massacre" proves that the knife may be sharp, but it cuts both ways.

Article:
HISTORY'S PSYCHOPATHIC KILLERS PARALLELED BY FILM MONSTERS
February 24, 1991

Now and then a psychopathic killer comes along so spectacularly malevolent that you can but wonder at the presence of an evil that transcends the concept of scale. And they have been around for a long time.

The original Bluebeard, for example, was a French nobleman named Giles de Rais, who, in the 15th century, is said to have murdered not wives, as the folk tales insist, but boys, in the hundreds. The original Dracula, on the other hand, was a 14th century Rumanian nobleman known to history as Vlad Tepes, or Vlad the Impaler. He skewered thousands on stakes the size of telephone poles as a melancholy testament to his thirst for carnage; he landscaped his castle gardens with crucifixions.

But the psychopathic killer, the twisted creature who kills not for profit or gain or survival but out of sheer need, and over and over and over, really hit it big in modern times in the year of the triple eights, 1888. Calling himself Jack the Ripper, that one murdered and butchered five London prostitutes, led Scotland Yard on a merry chase through the warrens and alleys of the slum called Whitechapel over a few months' passage and then receded into the mists of time and curiosity forever.

The movies have not been slow to claim the psychopathic killer, with the latest wave unfurling these days in the form of "Sleeping With the Enemy" and "The Silence of the Lambs." Their antecedents can be found far back, particularly in German films. An early version of a man so misformed by evil was contained in the German silent "The Cabinet of Dr. Caligari," a movie made entirely in the fractured universe of the nightmare, where the creeper was a haunted zombie with death-blackened eyes. Shortly after the coming of sound, Fritz Lang made what is still a great movie, "M," with Peter Lorre starring as a helplessly warped child killer so driven that he's as pitiful as he is horrifying. The thrust of the movie, still watchable after all these years, is the momentary coalition between the underworld and the police so that the monster may be removed from the world and business can proceed as usual.

In our time, one can certainly see the attraction of the creature to low-end filmmakers: A "psycho" villain needs no personality or psychology — his galvanizing presence is enough to hang a wisp of a story upon, and far too many times he's been merely masked in a hockey faceplate, given an assortment of bladed weapons, and sent forth to slay teen-agers.

The conceit of the classic slasher film is to make the camera — that is, you — the slayer. Its secret appeal is to give you the thrill of the kill without the risk. In deeper terms, however, the psycho is simply the blank force of the irrational in the universe: He kills without meaning, like a turnpike blowout or a rooftop sniper or an icicle falling off the roof. He's simply an emblem of the universe's cruelty if it discovers you in the wrong place at the wrong time. He's always scary but never interesting.

But "Sleeping With the Enemy" and "The Silence of the Lambs," both involving outsized psychos, go a bit farther into the syndrome than mere exploitation, making at least an honorable attempt to give name and face and reason to the mayhem. Almost too programmatically, they represent the two traditions of screen psycho, a tradition that in fact reflects the ego and the superego and their struggle for control of the conscious mind.

In "Sleeping With the Enemy," Patrick Bergin, his Irish accent suppressed but not his natural silkiness, plays a prosperous investment banker who to all the world is a massive success, but who, in the privacy of his home, is a monster. He's the classic superego maniac: His civilizing restraints sit like a hat atop his violent instincts, and he uses that tension creatively to advance himself. He's the abusive husband, cubed and squared, but the curiosity about him is that his proclivity is not to violence, but to order; the violence is only incidental.

Director Joseph Ruben has worked this theme before, more terrifyingly, in "The Stepfather," in which Terry O'Quinn played a man who so wanted his new families to be perfect and happy that when they failed him by being merely human, he felt impelled to destroy them and start over again. His is the dangerous weirdness of icy control. He's not over the top; he's under the bottom, a portrait of repression as agent of violence as it bends a sick man toward the unthinkable.

Bergin is particularly menacing in the psycho role, with glowering, romantic eyes and such total self-control. A key moment comes when, with his fearsome will, he silently bullies his wife into validating his sickness. She tells him, under the subtle threat of beating, that he does this not because he enjoys it but because it's necessary; his actions come from a "need to correct." If he enjoyed it, of course, "he'd be a monster."

The antecedents to Bergin hail usually not from horror movies but from military films; he's the original of Ahab, a ship captain whose icy competence hides the fires of true craziness. You can see him again in two other legendary officers: Bogart's

Captain Queeg, limited in mind and charisma but nothing more than the sum of his rigidly held disciplines, who begins to shatter under the pressure of crises; and, most classically, Alec Guinness's Colonel Nicholson in David Lean's great "The Bridge on the River Kwai." Nicholson's rigid discipline is the stuff of unbelievable fortitude but also the tragedy of military catastrophe because of his inability to adjust to a radically new situation: Commandos come to destroy the bridge that is his monument and, obeying laws he cannot begin to fathom, he conspires to destroy them.

In civilian guise, he appears only once, but famously. That's in Hitchcock's "Psycho," in which the pressure of the savage instinct has so benumbed Anthony Perkins's Norman Bates that it has actually shattered his personality into distinct halves. He's Norman, the weenie geek clerk and mama's boy, fearful, obedient, a creature of rigid self-control and all-consuming guilt. But he's also Mama, who in his dead mother's clothes sets out to destroy those women who have sexually excited poor Norman and thereby threatened the sanctity of her bond to her precious little son.

Dr. Hannibal Lector, in "The Silence of the Lambs," is of the other variety. He has simply given in to his instinctual drives, however misformed, and shaped his whole life in order to accommodate them. In a curious way, he's the most well-adjusted man in movies. He accepts who he is, even revels in it. He's the ego killer, whose sense of "me-ness" demands the obliteration of a sense of "otherness" from the universe. Even in prison, where he's given to merry disquisitions on the anthropology of sociopaths and amuses himself by playing anagrammatic games with various law enforcement agents who seek his advice, he's always plotting in service to the secret agenda of his needs.

And in another curious way, he's almost always attractive, simply because he's dynamic. He knows exactly what he wants and moves directly to get it. He has no doubts or qualms, nothing causes his trigger finger or sword arm to halt. His actions are usually so direct that in a medium that revels in kinetic action, his behavior comes to seem heroic, because it is so direct and consequential. And in the fascinating way in which he rationalizes his convictions, he's always somehow charming.

Lector, the psycho killer in excelsis, comes from a flamboyant line of development. He has a touch of Jack the Ripper to him, particularly in that he's a psychiatrist and rumors have long persisted that the original Jack was a mad surgeon or a royal (at any rate, someone who had an ironic self-awareness of his deeds). The one letter to Scotland Yard felt to be authentic from the authentic Jack is a chilling document, as much for its merriness of tone as for its grisliness. It's exactly the kind of clever clue that a Dr. Lector would have enjoyed planting.

We see this type also in Hitchcock's great "Strangers on a Train," in which, with an amoral glee, Robert Walker's chilling seducer tries to cajole a young tennis player (Farley Granger) into committing a tit-for-tat murder.

A contemporary psycho to Walker's is James Cagney's brilliant Cody Jarrett in the classic film noir, "White Heat." Criminal mastermind, macho gangster, prison yard stud, he's also a mama's boy (like Norman Bates). But unlike Norman, no spirit of repression haunts him; if he sees you and he doesn't like you, he shoots you.

In this sense, Cody has a kind of rugged integrity, and there's a note of elegy to his death when the nominally heroic but actually duplicitous federal agent Riordan (Edmond O'Brien) brings him down with a sniper's bullet, using the kind of sneaky, safe killing that Cody would have spat upon as sissy stuff. At least Cody looked you in the eyes when he shot you.

As Dr. Lector goes on to what will almost certainly be great popularity, viewers should bear in mind that what's so attractive about him is exactly what's so dangerous — what he wants is what he gets, and it's usually a piece of meat with a person attached.

Article:
HORRORS! WHAT ARE MOVIES COMING TO?
October 31, 1982

"THE HORROR! The horror!" Mr. Kurtz cried in Joseph Conrad's "Heart of Darkness."

Contrary to rumor, there's no evidence to suggest he had just emerged from a screening of the soon-to-be-released horror film "Creepshow."

Still, he was clearly expressing a basic human fascination with things macabre — with death and decay, with murder and violence, with the darker colors of the spectrum of human behavior — that find their most obvious and profitable reflection in horror movies.

The horror film, as the poet R. H. W. Dillard once observed, "is, at its best, as thoroughly and richly involved with the dark truths of sin and death as any art form ever has been."

This isn't news. The horror movie has been around for years, has undergone high periods and low periods, but has never really relinquished its grip on the blacker regions of the imagination.

The news is that the horror film, once a part of Hollywood's sleazy underbelly, loved only by pimply cognoscenti and almost thoroughly ignored by critics, has slouched toward and finally entered the mainstream.

On Nov. 10, for example, Warner Brothers will release the $12 million "Creepshow," a concoction of gory tales modeled on the old "Tales of the Crypt" comic books and assembled by two of the largest names in the horror field. Stephen King, author of such low-brow, high-sales novels as "Carrie," "The Stand" and "Cujo," has collaborated with George Romero, the director of such mega-horror-hits as the classic "Night of the Living Dead" and "Dawn of the Dead," to produce what some industry observers believe will be the first runaway hit of the fall season.

Early returns are exceedingly promising; the film played a four-week test engagement in Boston in the late summer and did brilliant business. If the film is a hit, it will surely spawn, as do all hits, a rash of quickly conceived and sloppily made junior versions.

Other big-budget horror pictures that have arrived in the past few years include "Poltergeist" (re-released last Friday), directed by Tobe ("The Texas Chainsaw Massacre") Hooper under the supervision of Steven Spielberg; "Cat People," Paul Schrader's visually stunning remake of the 1942 Val Lewton classic; "The Thing," John Carpenter's remake of the 1951 Howard Hawks classic; "Ghost Story," John Irvin's version of the Peter Straub best seller; and "Alien," Ridley Scott's sci-fi gripper, with its famous chest-busting scene.

Still others are planned. David Cronenberg, a Canadian film director who has made such cult hits as "Scanners" and "The Brood," has an expensive, studio-financed film due out in the spring titled "Videodrome." And even the normally benign Walt Disney studio is preparing a version of Ray Bradbury's "Something Wicked This Way Comes."

"The B product," says Romero, an independent filmmaker who's always gone his own way, "has been the A film since the early '70s."

He dates the beginning of big-budget horror back to the success of William Friedkin's "The Exorcist" in 1973, which demonstrated that horror had the clout to galvanize large numbers of people into lines at the box office.

Still, in the outer environs of Hollywood, the lesser movie mills continue to churn out cheapie horror pictures at an alarming rate, and it's a rare week in a big city when some off-the-wall indie — "Maniac," "Incubus," "Dr. Butcher, M.D. (Medical Deviate)" and "Evilspeak," to name a few of this year's dubious treasures — doesn't come slithering along.

The reasons for this are partially economic and partially psychological.

Economically, movies that go boo seldom go bust. Horror films remain, for marginal production companies, the safest, surest investment. They usually don't involve expensive special effects, experienced professional casts or elaborate settings. A few gallons of Karo syrup, the standard industry stand-in for blood, splashed on a former pizza waitress in the producer's living room will do. And their methods are so primitive, yet so convincing, that it doesn't demand a great deal of skill to bring them off.

Most important, they almost always return their investments and frequently turn a profit, confirming H. L. Mencken's dark insight that nobody ever went broke underestimating the American public.

In fact, a scheduling coincidence — engendered, no doubt, by the occurrence of Halloween on a weekend — makes it possible to study, in the privacy of your own home tonight and tomorrow night, the two most notorious low-budget, high-profit splatter films ever made.

Tonight at 9, ABC is broadcasting the original "Halloween," John Carpenter's shrewdly made, riveting story of "the night he came home," *he*, in this case, being your typical psychopathic murderer who sets out for obscure reasons to eliminate a group of teen-agers on Halloween night.

What distinguishes Carpenter's work from the dozens of clones that came afterward is nothing so much as high technique. "Halloween," called a classic in some quarters, is sheer trash, but it's exceptionally well-made trash. It knows what scares you.

One need merely compare it with tomorrow night's midnight screening on Channel 45 of Sean Cunningham's "Friday the 13th" to see the difference. Where Carpenter's camerawork is fluent and elegant, his sets well dressed, his sense of timing exquisite, Cunningham's are crude to the point of vulgarity.

"Friday the 13th" is really just an excursion into the back room of a butcher shop. It showed audiences things only a meat cutter had seen before but, because it was backed by a major studio (Paramount), it crept by with an R rating where clearly an X was called for. Thus, it was opened up to the lucrative teen-age market and became the surprise hit of the summer of 1980. (A similar ratings scandal occurred this summer when the Motion Picture Association of America awarded "Poltergeist" a PG rating, to the shock and dismay of thousands of parents who took their children to the exceedingly intense film. In fact, some state and municipal film boards tried to apply their own R ratings to the film.)

But both films make excessive use of the technique that can easily serve as a demarcation line between high terror — fright — and low horror — shock. They use the subjective camera, which has the unsettling effect of putting the audience into the brain of the murderer and enabling it to watch the act of murder through his or her eyes, and feel the vicarious mastery of slayer over victim.

For whatever the excesses of the George Romero works — and they were legion, particularly the use of explicit gore — he never made killers of his audience.

This effect, by the way, was only made possible by a technological development, the Panaglide. This is a portable camera held on the cameraman's body by an elaborate harness, as with any one-man unit; but it remains magically steady and level no matter how swiftly the cameraman moves because it's gyroscopically stabilized in its casing. It gives him extraordinary freedom of motion.

One can't help but wonder about the future of this innovation. Like the 3-D techniques of the early '50s, it seems fatally linked with the most exploitative of films, and whether Panaglide shots will become a part of the vocabulary of more normal movie-making is a question yet to be answered.

The psychological aspects of horror movies, which trouble many parents who watch their children take in a steady diet of the things, are more problematic. One has to ask not merely why, but why *now*? Why, in the past four or five years, has there been such an abundance of horror while other, more traditionally American genres, such as the western and the detective story, have almost completely lost their box-office clout?

Ron Kurtz, a former Baltimorean who rewrote "Friday the 13th" and wrote "Friday the 13th Part II" — and isn't particularly proud of it — acknowledges the cynicism in the process.

"The kids have the discretionary income now. And what they want is simple. They want something they can't get on TV. And gore seems to be the only thing that reaches them."

But Stephen King, the master of horror, as his millions of readers can testify, believes the appeal of horror is universal.

"I think we're drawn to it because we're mortal, and we keep trying to fit our minds around this concept of dying. A lot of what horror is for me is a contemplation of the things that could go wrong."

He believes horror and humor appeal basically to the same feeling. "Humor and horror are close together, because they're both from the same oppressive impulse. In both cases, we're happy because it isn't us. In many horror movies, the reaction is that people laugh afterwards."

But King goes further. He believes the appeal of horror pictures to the collective imagination is cyclical.

"Horror movies are more popular in times when people are afraid. In the movies, anyway, the cycles that run in tandem are scary movies and funny movies. In times when people are scared and frightened, they turn to horror material like it's a home."

A brief survey of the genre bears him out.

The first horror movie is generally acknowledged to be the 1908 15-minute version of "Dr. Jekyll and Mr. Hyde," the first of 11 versions of the story. (The 11th is about to reach us, a parody version starring Baltimore's Bess Armstrong and titled "Jekyll and Hyde . . . Together Again!")

The first real burgeoning of the genre was, perhaps not surprisingly, Germanic. In the chaos of post-World War I Germany, there came three landmark films, all of them dark with Teutonic shadows and Wagnerian grandeur. The first, in 1919, was the extraordinary "The Cabinet of Dr. Caligari," an avowedly "expressionistic" film, full of crazy angles, tilted hallways and corridors, and a lurking ghoul. It was followed by Paul Wegener's "The Golem" and F. W. Murnau's "Nosferatu" (recently remade by Werner Herzon with Klaus Kinski in the title role). These two films established the archetypes that continue to dominate the genre: the monster and the vampire.

The next high period for horror was the early '30s — high noon of the Depression — when the American classics "Frankenstein," "Dracula" and "Freaks" were made in three successive years.

In the early '40s, in the depths of World War II, Val Lewton, a Russian-born producer, made a series of low-budget, high-imagination pieces, at least three of which are remembered to this day: "Cat People," "The Leopard Man" and "Bedlam."

The 1950s were primarily concerned with horror themes on a grander scale, in which the subgenre of monster pictures dominated, and it's difficult not to believe that the motif of mighty beasts or insects trashing major American metropolises — "The Beast from 20,000 Fathoms," "It Came from Beneath the Sea," "Them" — didn't extract its imagery from similar notions of nuclear destruction. (Although this genre has all but disappeared, hard-core horror fans may take some delight in the approach of a rare exception to that rule, the first true monster picture in years, the sublimely loony "Q," about a flying serpent that nests in New York's Chrysler Building!)

Now, however, in the early '80s, horror movies have become much meaner.

"There's not a big place in the world for gore," says Stephen King, "but I think there is a place. Every now and then you can hit somebody with something like that (a graphic exhibition of violence). It doesn't do to overdo it, like the slice and dice films, because you just make people vomit."

But King also thinks the era of the bloody movie is drawing to a close: "I've noticed a wide attendance cut-off in the real gore movies. One of the signs that the films are not working as well as they used to is that gimmicks have begun to creep in. The last 'Friday the 13th' picture was shot in 3-D."

Romero, whose films are excessively violent, says he, too, has thought a lot about violence and gore. His two most famous films — beloved by some critics and by midnight cult followers the world over — are set in a world in which, infected with a space-borne virus, corpses have risen and become brainless, voracious cannibals. In "Dawn of the Dead," as lurid a movie as has ever been made, three people find refuge in a shopping mall and build a new society. But every night, the zombies break in and march about to the programmed Muzak. The

movie is frequently brought up short on scenes of dismemberment and decapitation, including one scene in which a motorcy-
clist, affixed to a coin-operated blood-pressure machine in the
mall, is literally ripped to pieces before our eyes, while the
blood-pressure readings go from high to higher to highest.

King contends that horror stories and movies must work the
same way *any* story or movie works. "I think the idea of genre
can be misleading. At bottom, a bad horror story is a bad story,
not because of the horror but because of the story. And if it's a
bad story, it doesn't have any right to live."

WISE GUYS

"Can the family that slays together

stay together?"

GOODFELLAS
September 21, 1990

I like a movie that takes a moral stand. Martin Scorsese's "GoodFellas," a violent look at the authentic Mafia, focuses exclusively on the deadly tools of the trade. It makes the clear and resonant point that Italian sausage should be banned.

Before and after every hit, these swarthy, laughing tribal barbarians settle down to a hearty meal, a curly tube of dead pig smothered in glops of tomato guts, shreds of pepper, basil, oregano, garlic slices, fennel, fried onion, some Chianti, and wads of bread soaked in butter. The meals look like massacres, but they send you out of the theater on a beeline to Little Italy.

In other words, food, as much as violence, is the leitmotif of "GoodFellas," and perhaps the surest way to explain both its ample delights and its strangeness of tone. To these men, food is just as meaningful as murder; they can kill and eat in the same hour, and with great gusto at each. They've never heard of either cholesterol or punishment. Food and death are equal parts of life, of course; and "GoodFellas" wants to look at the Mafia as life — or, as culture.

The movie, rich in detail, teeming with incident and character, a bit cluttered with "documentary" affectations, over-narrated and, perhaps in the end, somewhat skimpy in drama, is more like an ethnography than a story.

Based on journalist Nicholas Pileggi's "Wise Guy," with a script by Pileggi and Scorsese, it's an anthropology of the streets that follows the adventures of a low-level gunsel and hustler of mixed Irish/Sicilian heritage named Henry Hill over a 20-year cavalcade from boyhood errands for the neighborhood wise guys to his final enrollment, at the far end of a gaudy career, in the federal witness protection program.

Hill is played by Ray Liotta, and some people who expect more of Robert De Niro may be disappointed to learn that his is the supporting role. Liotta, however, is just fine. So scary in "Something Wild," so dewy in "Field of Dreams," Liotta is both scary and dewy in "GoodFellas." His Henry is a combination of innocence and craven amorality. He's a sycophant who puts loyalty to peers higher than loyalty to society. He loves the life, and recalls the early days, the pre-drug days, as a kind of Camelot, when the Knights of the Crooked Table sallied forth into the Big Apple to enjoy the fruits of crime that nobody had the guts to prevent them from harvesting.

Liotta is the center of a mock family. His two brothers are pals Tommy DeVito (Joe Pesci) and Jimmy Conway (De Niro); their "father" is the solemn Mafia sub-lieutenant Paulie Cicero (Paul Sorvino). The news here is that Pesci, known primarily to audiences from his superb comic turn in "Lethal Weapon 2," is the truly frightening character in the movie.

His Tommy is stone-cold nuts. Small and vain and stoked on testosterone to his eyebrows, he lives on the giddy edge of homicide. Any tiff can explode into murder; he is a lethal weapon, and when he shoots a gofer for giving him lip in the middle of a card game, it's a terrifying, unsettling moment.

De Niro is much smarter and more controlled. When he kills, he kills for a purpose, not because he can't help it. But, as with all of them, "whacking" (the vernacular) has no moral meaning; it's done routinely, as a solution to certain business problems and by certain rules, and when those rules are broken (Tommy breaks one), accounts must be settled (Tommy's account is settled).

But the movie isn't just about "crime": as an ethnography, it expands to take into consideration the larger community, and Scorsese is fascinated with the world of hoods, from soup to nuts, and including spouses and children. In fact, at one point he splits his narration between Henry and his wife Karen, a nice Jewish girl played by Lorraine Bracco, who is drawn into the culture by her love for Henry and his exoticness (she likes his gun and the fact that he beats the starch out of someone who's insulted her). Her astonishment at the gaucheries of the alien Italian culture provides the movie's highest comic point.

And it is a comedy, despite the frequent episodes of stomach-churning violence. Part of the humor is the contrast between the deadpan flatness of Liotta's narration, its affectless ho-hum tone, and the vivid crimes he describes. Also, like the Mafia itself, there's a wild strain of nihilistic outrageousness to it. These guys aren't on the edge, they *are* the edge; they'll go to guns in a split second, and from the other side of the camera, it has a wicked amusement to it.

If the movie falters at all, I believe it's in Scorsese's overreliance on documentary techniques. Far too often, he'll go to freeze frame, while Henry numbingly narrates the orchestration of the moment. And like any movie that spans decades, it's both too rushed and too short. The hijacking of a Lufthansa payroll at Idlewild Airport is a key moment in the drama, but Scorsese doesn't have time to dramatize it; it passes in off-screen narration, and thus the violence that ensues—as one of the triumvirate tries to isolate himself from the crime by killing everybody he's hired to pull it off—seems unrooted in the story, simply arbitrary.

And Henry's surrender to reality and his exile to "real life" — these are punishments designed in hell — somehow lack the impact they should have at the end of so long an enterprise (two hours and 15 minutes). But it's a grand movie, almost completely convincing and viciously unromantic — even if you believe that when sausage is outlawed, only outlaws will have sausage.

PRIZZI'S HONOR
June 14, 1985

The case for "Prizzi's Honor" is being made in the highest precincts of the culture, and it's not a bad argument. This new John Huston film, you will be told, is dark and funny simultaneously. It features brilliant performances (particularly by Jack

Nicholson). It has the density of a renaissance drama under the glossy surface of the most recent "Miami Vice" episode. It offers a range of sensations not usually found in a summer movie. It is literate, grown-up, quirky.

All true. All beside the point.

The point is, "Prizzi's Honor" is not very good. Tedious, self-important, almost perversely designed for maximum box-office flameout, it feels most of all like the last indulgence of a once-great director whose storytelling skills have eroded conspicuously. Worse, it is a movie that is almost wholly bereft of the sort of pleasures that might ensure it any kind of wide public success.

It is, in short, a very big movie made for a very small audience.

Derived from a dense Richard Condon novel, whose torturous plot it follows far too closely (perhaps because Condon co-wrote the screenplay), the movie tells of various professional confusions and complications in the life of one Charlie Partanna, Mafia hit man and underboss. The gimmick is that Charlie's problems in the underworld mimic, in a dark way, the problems of the overworld. Specifically, like any yuppie couple, he and his wife Irene are trying to make a two-career marriage work. It's just that the careers are murder. Can the family that slays together stay together?

When Charlie first spies the elegant, Waspish Irene Walker (the elegant, Waspish Kathleen Turner, who has played more interesting characters) at the wedding of Don Corrado Prizzi's granddaughter, it's love at first sight. How's a not terribly bright guy like Chuck supposed to figure she's a freelance popper herself? This is a sort of Spencer Tracy-Katharine Hepburn comedy of the '80s: It's "Adam's Rib," played with guns and blades instead of barbed wits.

The real drama of "Prizzi's Honor," however, isn't really yuppie-angst. Rather it's a drama of the inside vs. the outside. Charlie is the quintessential insider, chosen from birth to play an important role in the affairs of his clan, the Prizzis, America's leading Mafia aristocracy. But he has found subtle ways to rebel against his fate: For example, he's abandoned Maerose

Prizzi (Anjelica Huston in a wonderful performance), with whom the family prefers that he bond. And when he marries Irene, it's an act of independence almost too radical to be accepted. And when, furthermore, Irene refuses to sit home and raise bambinos, but insists on keeping her career going, the pressures and complexities grow almost intolerable for everyone. An insider has married an outsider, and the struggle of the movie is to restore him to his sense of loyalty.

With this promising theme and this great cast, why isn't the film any better? It really starts with the screenplay (Condon was assisted by Janet Roach), which is as loyal as any Prizzi gunsel to the intricacies of the original document. Alas, the form of the feature movie cannot as gracefully accommodate the weight of exposition as can the novel. Curiously, what makes Richard Condon such a delight as a novelist — his arcane details, his endless trivia, his blissful exposition — dooms him as a screenwriter. Within the original situation — the marriage of Charlie and Irene — there are at least four subplots involving murders, kidnappings, competition from another family, competition among other Prizzi underbosses and a complicated casino swindle that Irene has evidently masterminded. It's a case of too much being not enough: For much of the time, nothing is happening, except that someone is explaining some dense plot that is never dramatized. ZZZZZzzzzz.

Then there's the issue of the rules. The rules say — don't ask me who wrote them, but they are nevertheless inviolable —that hoods can kill in the hundreds, they can slaughter in the thousands, and still enjoy our sympathy, as long as they only kill their own kind. Jimmy Breslin's "The Gang That Couldn't Shoot Straight" attests to this, and even early in the film, Jack Nicholson can ice a thief without much in the way of trouble. But the movie utterly dies on the screen when, during an attempted kidnapping, an elevator door opens, a perfectly innocent woman steps out, and Kathleen Turner shoots her in the face.

And it turns out, furthermore, that Huston simply doesn't have the resources to sustain a tone as delicate as black humor over the entire run of the film — it's never quite as inventive and outrageous (and purely hilarious) as such black classics as Tony Richardson's "The Loved One" or Carl Reiner's "Where's Poppa?" At the same time, the plot is so sluggish it doesn't quite work as a thriller; its satire isn't sharp or focused enough to provide satisfactions there, either. But worst of all, after alienating the audience, Huston never wins it back, and the ultimate destinies of Charlie and Irene come not to matter a great deal, even when the movie ends in a moment of grisly, intimate violence that again confounds the tone and seems so uncharitable that it leaves you cold in the belly.

Nicholson is very close to camp in his Charlie. It looks like his upper lip has been pickled in anti-freeze and like he's grown a subcutaneous layer of fat around his temples. When he thinks, it's with the effort of a shotputter; you can see the thought penetrate his skull through the eyes and work its slow way through the capillaries to the center of his brain where, several minutes later, it is reacted to. All right: dumb. Dumb as hubcaps. And brilliant, in a sly way, another dazzling Nicholson coup. The problem, however, is that Charlie and Irene never make a lot of sense as a couple and, failing to believe in their affection, one cannot particularly believe in their *dis*affection.

The movie shows there's such a thing as too much loyalty — to a novel that was something less than a classic. That's fool's honor.

THE GODFATHER, PART III
December 23, 1990

In "Godfather III," the circle of corruption that was America widens and widens to include the Catholic Church and, ultimately, the whole world. This is clearly a cynic's view, but Francis Ford Coppola, who has buried a son, perhaps has earned his cynicism the hard way.

But, because of that cynicism, Coppola's somber, riveting, "Lear"-like "Godfather III" tale is far from perfect and represents a level of storytelling magic a few notches shy of the first two "Godfather" films.

Still, it is painfully genuine, the most corrosive film since Akira Kurosawa's equally bleak "Ran," which shares the common link to "Lear." Some of the story details may be blurry, but you feel Coppola's full engagement at the emotional level.

Al Pacino's Michael Corleone is Coppola's sick and tragic king. The year is 1979; Michael, the weight of his immoral choices graven into the fallen flesh of his face like the imprints of paws in the snow, is seeking escape from the guilt of his past (notably the murder of his brother, Fredo) in the bosom of the church. The film opens at one of those ironic family celebrations that marked the first two films, where honest joy and dirty business go hand in hand with the rhythms of the tarantella.

Michael is essentially trying to bribe his way into heaven by thrusting huge amounts of cash on the Vatican, and for his efforts is rewarded with a high church decoration, which is the cause of the party. But he has not lost his business acumen; at the same time, in exchange for the charitable donations, he expects Vatican support in a ploy to take over a European conglomerate, which will completely remove the Corleone family from the nasty trade that earned it its power.

The film moves through three acts: in an early maneuver, we see Michael forestalling the challenge of a flashy mid-level gangster named Joey Zaza, well played by Joe Mantegna; in a central section, Michael retreats to Sicily to recover his health (he's diabetic) and to contemplate the obstacles to his course; and in a final act, he moves swiftly and with authority to destroy his oppressors, but at tragic cost.

After the fashion of the first two movies, the plot dovetails with events in the real world, notably the financial scandal that rocked the Vatican in the late '70's and the short reign of Pope John Paul I.

In the plot, we see themes that were expressed more forcefully in the first two films: the visionary Godfather opposed by a seemingly unworthy enemy who's actually fronting for a much slyer and more sophisticated opponent; the terrifying calculus in determining what is "family" and what is "business"; the coming of a swift young hero out of nowhere, his rise, and at what expense; the development of tender young love, and its betrayal.

But "Godfather III" is never quite as sharp as its predecessors; its plot turns are muddled and the complex financial conspiracy that underlies the story never quite becomes clear, at least upon a first viewing. And, somehow, it never acquires the urgency that the first two films had.

And yet it's a wonderful movie. Pacino is simply magnificent; what a piece of work is man, and Pacino's soul-sick Michael is the species in microcosm, the injured king, bruised with regret, desperate for redemption, yet ever the wary warrior, the inspiring leader and the tender, devoted father. Without this icon of central charisma, there's no movie, and there's plenty of movie.

The younger generation is represented by Andy Garcia, as Vincent Mancini, Sonny Corleone's illegitimate son (we saw his vertical conception in the opening moments of the original "Godfather"). Garcia has been a star waiting to happen for about three years: Now he's happening, and how. His Vincent is tough and smart and Garcia shows him growing; we watch him shift from angry street punk to smooth choreographer of family business. Garcia is fire and ice — he has Sonny's toughness and temper, but he learns, over the movie's three hours, Michael's gift for control.

Others in the cast are also superb, particularly Diane Keaton, reprising Michael's wife Kay — it's her best role and performance in years. Eli Wallach is appropriately avuncular as the endearing Don Altobello, behind whose chummy smile there may lurk other agendas. And Talia Shire does an excellent job as Michael's tough sister Connie, who has grown into a true mafioso's persona.

Coppola's most controversial decision was to cast his own daughter, Sofia, in the role of Michael Corleone's daughter, also named Sofia, after Winona Ryder dropped out of the production on the first day of shooting. It is difficult to condemn a man for loving his daughter too much and attempting to give her the world; but the melancholy truth is that Sofia Coppola is not a professional actress. The camera sees what her father cannot: an untrained young woman never completely comfortable, and extremely awkward in the intimate moments, as when she and Andy Garcia are purportedly in love. If you let this ruin the picture for you, my sympathies. I did not.

But the best thing about "Godfather III" is that, with the same stately rhythms and burnished cinematography (Gordon Willis, the cinematographer, is brilliant), and the same sense of ritual and destiny, the movie returns you to what is paradoxically the darkest and the brightest of worlds; the darkness of crime and conspiracy and bitter failure, and the brightness of art and humanity and the pulse of life itself.

BUGSY
December 20, 1991

Think of Fitzgerald's Jay Gatsby, a romantic egotist to the end. Think of his wonderful shirts. Think of his clothes, his charm, his charisma, his American hankering to be better, to climb in society, to hang out with the swells.

Now think of him pulling a snub nose and blowing a sucking chest wound into somebody, and you have "Bugsy."

Warren Beatty's best film since "Bonnie and Clyde" and possibly Barry Levinson's best film, period, "Bugsy" is set squarely in the increasingly hard-to-find Neverland of adult movie-making. Literate, witty and completely entertaining, it's the best film of the Christmas season. It's a meditation on the dark places that romantic American yearning can take a neighborhood boy, and the answer is: dead on a couch with a bullet hole where your eye used to be.

Give Beatty the credit that's due him. He found and nurtured the project and was willing to play a character ominously close to all the evil things that people have been saying about Warren Beatty for years: His Bugsy is vain, sublimely aware of his own beauty, manipulative, not terribly intelligent but terribly driven, completely amoral, an indefatigable womanizer and social climber. And a beautiful dresser.

Levinson, working from a script by James Toback, has come up with an addition to the canon: the gangster as flake. The Bugsy of the film isn't the urban hard case of earlier gangster movies or the solemn, pope-like patriarch of the Coppola version (though yes, Alex Rocco's Moe Green in "Godfather I" was a version of Bugsy Siegel); this gangster wears hairnets and asks waiters if his tan is fading. He stares endlessly at his own screen test (arranged by boyhood chum George Raft), and the fascinating contents of no mirror escape his close attention.

When he runs — he's always in a hurry, like his movieland analogue, Sammy Glick — he looks particularly ridiculous, all that beauty and dignity and vanity held with such rigid stiffness as he pitter-patters along, an image, amid all the guns, of essential innocence.

But of course, he's "bugsy." As in, nuts. As in, uh-oh. The guy was, by all indications, born without fear or doubt and was very, very tough. Whether his bravado was Nietzschean will power or simple craziness, no one can say: But he killed, it is estimated, more than 30 men, and didn't have a problem with putting the gun close, pulling the trigger and watching the light go out of his victim's eyes. He also liked to hurt people with his hands.

Beatty gives Bugsy's violent edge an almost feminine hysteria: It's shrill, girlish violence, like a cat fight with guns. It seems to come from nowhere, stealing over him in a black fury of an instant. In that respect, it's truly frightening and it goes a long way toward diffusing the charge that the movie makes gangsters and molls glamorous.

The movie somewhat telescopes the authentic Benjamin Hymie Siegel's last 12 years of life on earth to about three. An East Coast mob star, he's sent west by his bosses Lansky and Luciano on the Twentieth Century Limited to horn in on the very mild mob activities going on in the City of Angels. This he accomplishes with a few harsh words, and by bringing in the rogue loner Mickey Cohen (Harvey Keitel) as his enforcer.

That easy triumph cleared the way for the main matter of the end of his life, his love affair with a bit Hollywood player named Virginia Hill (Annette Bening). This is one of those old-fashioned guys-and-dames knock-down drag-outs from the fabled days when men were men and women were also men. Hill, from hardscrabble Alabama (the movie strangely gives her a New York accent), was as tough as brass bushings herself and fights him tooth and nail — the suggestion is that all that anger made the sex very, very good. She and Bugsy were the Kate-and-Spence of the Tommy-gun set, famous for the typhoon-like quality of their brawls.

But like many a poor boy, Bugsy is brought low by his dreams. He looks into the desert and sees . . . Viva Las Vegas! The consuming obsession was his vision of a mob city in the desert that existed to milk money from rubes. He began the process by building the Flamingo (Hill's nickname). In fact, a little of "Bugsy" connects with one of Beatty's better movies, the too quickly forgotten "McCabe and Mrs. Miller," in which he played a western dreamer who fell in with a hard woman and tried to build an oasis of vice in the wilderness, fell out with the hard boys and paid with his life. So it is with Bugsy, who, to finance his dream, ended up stealing from the mob. It was not amused.

The movie isn't faultless. A long farce-like interlude in New York in which Bugsy desperately tries to balance the elements of his life — the mob, his family and Virginia — becomes too quickly ridiculous and shows. Joe Mantegna, who ought to make a perfect George Raft, doesn't; in fact, he barely registers. But Ben Kingsley is a wonderful Meyer Lansky and the late Bill Graham is forceful and frightening as Lucky Luciano.

Still, the movie is like a trip to the West Egg of gangster movies: romantic and poignant, funny and sad, the story of a man who was great with a gat but, like so many poseurs, ended up dead.

SCARFACE
December 9, 1983

"Scarface" is a corrosive fable of avarice and violence on the model of "Macbeth," tracing the rise and fall of a charismatic mobster. For a time, it seems to be on its way toward greatness; but then — perhaps reflecting the descent of its protagonist — it tumbles into mediocrity.

It's electric, after a fashion, and certainly powerful, particularly in its evocation of the world of cocaine merchants (which seems the most primitive of Darwinian jungles) and of their language (which consists of one word repeated so often, as so many parts of speech, it's almost a mantra). But its characters become, by the end, such one-note stereotypes and its plot sinks under the weight of such leaden conventionality, that it becomes difficult to care. You just want it to be over.

"Scarface" is at its best in the beginning, when, like its hero, it is hungry. When we meet him, Tony Montana seems a creature of extreme craft and cool. His little eyes dart about as if radar-directed; his will and self-regard are ironclad, his reflexes extraordinarily agile.

As the scene begins, Tony — Al Pacino, his face sexily mutilated to provide the necessary decoration for his nickname, his accent thick as dark Cuban coffee — is being interrogated by immigration officials. They don't quite buy his story of political victimization at the hands of the commie-fiend Castro, who has just exiled him and 25,000 others of various degrees of moral turpitude to the United States. It's a great scene, shot brilliantly, that calls up (not accidentally) the opening scene of "The Godfather." The camera circles Tony but stays low. We see only the sitting Tony being assailed by an orbiting patrol of thick-torsoed, faceless interrogators; and we watch Tony play them expertly.

In time, Tony is allowed to return to the wire enclosure where the exiles are stored as they await release into society-at-large; it becomes immediately clear that Tony has a cynic's sure confidence in the corruptibility of the system and of his fellow man. In mere minutes of screen time, he's arranged to kill a former Castro official for a wealthy, vengeful family in exchange for his freedom. And when Tony kills, director Brian De Palma sets the hit up in such a way as to explain his soul to us: The strike is quick and ruthless and efficient. He leaps into the frame like a bolt of lightning.

Thereafter, it doesn't take Tony long to make connections with a sleazy cocaine merchant — Robert Loggia, avuncular and jolly, but the first of many stereotypes — and to begin at the bottom. He's a payoff man, essentially a gofer, and his first job dumps him in a cheap motel with a grinning Colombian to make a pickup. It is here that "Scarface" enjoys its brief flirtation with greatness.

What ensues is certainly the single most exciting and convincing action sequence of the year, but more important, it has great dramatic energy. It tells the story, it tells us about Tony, and it tells us about cocaine racketeering. The Colombians are ruthless crazos, and they've set up a rip-off; Tony has been sly enough to outguess them, and the result is a terrifying, out-of-control tango of violence that is all the more horrifying for the casual way it spills out of the hotel room and into the streets.

Yet curiously, after this moment, the movie begins its inexorable decline. The episode establishes Tony in the business, but at that point De Palma and the script by Oliver Stone seem really to lose interest in his professional life. In fact, a whole hour goes by before we again see Tony in the practice of his career.

Rather, the movie becomes a tedious, condescending study of Tony's vulgarity: Tony is a monster, De Palma and Stone seem to agree, because he has such bad taste in clothes and interior decorators. De Palma is so busy scoring cheap points off Tony's polyester taste and woolly-headed insensitivity that he fails to interest us in Tony as a character; the strain of condescension runs through the movie like a rancid odor from a broken sewer.

"Scarface" gets progressively less interesting as it continues; it loses its originality and conviction. Worst of all, it fails to dramatize consistently what is special about Tony. He's a violent, vengeful punk, but the world is full of violent, vengeful punks. What is it about this one? What shrewdness of calculation, hardness of spirit, and vision of destiny propel him to win out over the others?

Pacino's performance, so electric in the early moments of the film, ultimately becomes a kind of catatonia; Tony's decadence is communicated by his leaden eyelids and slack jawline. Tony seems to maintain his grip on the top by dumb animal luck.

A perfect example is an attempted assassination in a garish nightclub. Tony's original boss has imported two shooters with machine-pistols to blow him away; from a range of about 15 feet, they open fire. What happens? They miss.

Tony has been wide open to their assault and, by all that's plausible in this world, he should be one cooked goose; but miss they do and Tony adroitly drops to the floor and pots them both with two shots from his automatic. There's no sense of the laws of the real world here: He hits, and they don't because somebody wrote it that way.

The movie also suffers from a curious inheritance from Ben Hecht's original 1932 script. In that film, the Capone-like Paul Muni enjoyed a crazy, nearly incestuous relationship with his sister. Thus is Tony Montana suddenly presented with a sister (Mary Elizabeth Mastrantonio) and a whole, unsuspected closetful of obscure longings. Unfortunately, De Palma and Stone don't do enough with this to make it convincing; it seems cobbled-in awkwardly and undeveloped.

Like Tony, "Scarface" hasn't any brains. No ideas perk through the cursing and the violence. In "The Godfather," Francis Ford Coppola was arguing for the legitimacy of the Mafia as a reflection of American business. Right or wrong, that's an idea. "Scarface" is about machine guns and cocaine. It's also about an hour too long.

THE UNTOUCHABLES
June 3, 1987

Brian De Palma's new film, "The Untouchables," is full of terrible beauty — but like many another specimen of beauty, it's only skin deep.

It gives us a Chicago toddling in blood, which spreads in evil, satiny puddles across the pavements and linoleum. The excess plasma is a necessary byproduct of the violent conflict between Al Capone and his henchmen and a small, elite unit of federal law enforcers led by Eliot Ness, who fought each other like rival cowboy gangs in the Dodge City of the 1880s.

And in fact, the traditional western, the western of the '30s, seems far more in evidence as an influence than the traditional gangster movie; all the way through, De Palma discovers his men in heroic poses after the fashion of a John Ford film; they fondle their weapons with the ritualistic intensity of gunslingers. (The movie has the feel of an African click-song with all those oily bolts being thrown!) And even Stephen Burham's photography sees the city as a kind of Monument Valley, full of imposing vistas and mountainous architecture, rather than displaying the more customary images of the spidery, shadowy nightmare city of crime melodrama.

But the real connection between De Palma's film and the western is psychological — or rather, in the lack of psychology that underlies both this movie and the more innocent westerns. De Palma, working from a script by Pulitzer Prize-winning playwright David Mamet, has envisioned Chicago 1930 as a morality tale, pure and simple. It's a classic good guys vs. bad guys scenario, completely bereft (or, depending on your point of view, thankfully free) of irony, revisionism, pathology, elaborate motivational theorizing, and critiques of capitalism or communism. Its characters are necessarily larger than life, but that also makes them lighter than air. In the past, particularly in such films as "Body Double" and "Blow Out," De Palma has been accused of being almost decadently hip; here, he's so square you could draw a chart by his angles.

I also should point out that the movie bears no resemblance

to, or pays no homage to, the extremely stylized television show of the same name of the late '50s and early '60s, in which the solemn Robert Stack played an Eliot Ness with all the gravity of a figure out of Kabuki drama, as narrated in stentorian monotones by Walter Winchell. No one affiliated with the movie appears to have seen the television show. Or perhaps they've seen it and decided to head in the opposite direction with a vengeance.

So instead of grit we have gorgeous golden photography; and instead of a grave-voiced papa figure for an Eliot Ness, we have Eliot the true-blue kid. Played by an appealing Kevin Costner, he's as boyish and enthusiastic, if unformed, as Brandon De Wilde in "Shane," and as eager for a father figure. Everything about him is stylized in slathers of innocence: His wife and darling babe, for example, are photographed in the pearly pink shades of a Madonna and Child. And he's after Capone not out of passion (though it becomes that) or personality, or out of neurotic need (he has no neurotic needs, because he has no neuroses), but for a simple reason: Capone has broken the law, and the law is holy.

De Palma tracks Capone's crusade from bumbling innocence to utter savagery. He becomes a vicious killer as he toughens up under the conflict and begins to take losses. Yet, De Palma never makes much out of a self-evident irony: To destroy a savage, Ness must *become* a savage. And when Ness acknowledges such at the end of the film, he does so without guilt. It was worth it, he says almost smugly, because he got his man.

After a first failure, he recruits a team — Sean Connery as a wise Chicago beat cop, Charlie Martin Smith as a cute accountant, and Andy Garcia, the least vivid, as an Italian-American who takes Capone as a personal insult. These four, using Connery's inside info as their guide, put together a merciless and increasingly violent campaign to get Capone the only way possible — for his violation of Internal Revenue Service laws.

The real core of the film is its action sequences. No one has a greater gift for this kind of show-stopping bravado than De Palma, and he puts together a few that knock your socks off. One witty sequence features a thwarted assassination of

Capone's bookkeeper in the bowels of Chicago's Union Station that manages to be an astonishment in and of itself even while poking a great deal of fun at Eisenstein's great Odessa Steps sequence from "The Battleship Potemkin" (surely the most parodied scene in movie history), complete to the image of a runaway baby carriage in the middle of exploding mayhem.

The performances vary considerably. Connery, bull stud and given all the brawny he-man lines, nearly steals the show. Smith is so appealing that you know in a second he's doomed. Garcia, who was brilliant in the poorly distributed "Eight Million Ways to Die," is oddly muted.

But the real disappointment in the film is Robert De Niro's bombastic Al Capone. As he was in "The Mission," De Niro is way out of his range here. An actor who excels at depicting psychotic states in lonely, little men (Travis Bickle in "Taxi Driver," for instance, or Rupert Pupkin in "King of Comedy"), he has the distressing tendency to get smaller as the part gets larger. His Capone is all showy ham; we never feel cunning and brains behind the scars on his fat little cheeks. The performance is so loud to begin with, it has no place to go, and soon tires.

HARLEM NIGHTS
November 17, 1989

It would be easy to dismiss Eddie Murphy's new "Harlem Nights" as infantile twaddle if the movie weren't so seething with pernicious values, cruelty and smugness.

But it's more than infantile twaddle: It's *evil* infantile twaddle, irresponsible, ugly, nasty, brutish — and long.

Here's a movie that begins with a 7-year-old boy blowing a bullet through a man's head. The movie doesn't view this as tragic necessity or ugly bravado: It sees it as cool. Great. Not 40 miles from here, whole sectors of the District of Columbia have been turned into a mini-Beirut by teen-age gunmen in the employ of, or who themselves are, crack dealers. And now we have the repulsive spectacle of the most successful black entertainer in America telling these dangerous, dysfunctional and tragic youths that guns are cool and that he who shoots first is the coolest of them all.

But Murphy's real problem is with women. Get this young man some professional help. He's sunk so far into misogyny he's hardly human anymore. In the world according to Eddie Murphy, there are three categories of women: whores, good whores and bitches.

A good whore is loyal, feisty, hardworking and obedient; when she gets uppity, of course, she's got to be butt-kicked a bit, and there's a scene, meant to be amusing, in which Murphy actually fist-fights fat old Vera (Della Reese) in a back alley. He ends the fight by shooting off — oh, witty stroke! — what he calls her "gnarly, crusty, ugly, little black toe."

The bitch is Jasmine Guy as Dominique La Rue, who, under the urging of her lover-boss, mobster Bugsy Calhoune (Michael Lerner), invites Murphy up to her pad, makes scorching love to him, then, in post-sex relaxation, reaches under the pillow for a pistol to kill him. But he's not called "Quick" because he's slow.

As for the run-of-the-mill whore, that's Sunshine (Lela Rochon), the origin of whose name can't be explained in a family newspaper. She has three scenes, all played in the key of High Lip-Licking Wantonness, where she seduces, then abandons, a mobster; then the movie abandons her.

And that's the entire female population of "Harlem Nights," with not even a nod to the millions of strong, brave black women who have held families together on nothing more than guts and love.

As a piece of film work, "Harlem Nights" is almost unbearably primitive. Murphy, who also wrote and directed (sort of), hasn't come close to penetrating the mysteries of the craft. He has no idea what to do with extras, for example, and no sense of how to create on film the squirming hubbub of urban reality. Thus the movie, nominally set in the Harlem of 1938, is in actuality set nowhere but on a barren studio back lot. The scenes, particularly the crowd scenes, are all dead; the extras stand around posing uncomfortably in the background with stiff looks on their faces waiting for someone to tell them they can relax because the camera's off.

Murphy steals his plot from a variety of sources, including a little bit from "The Cotton Club," but mostly it is an enfeebled rip-off of "The Sting," which follows as after-hours night-spot owner Richard Pryor (a bland performance in a role that's nothing but sainthood) works up a caper to prevent Lerner from taking over his club by setting up a betting scam, then heisting the money pickup. As for Murphy's Quick, mostly he just hangs around modeling clothes and hogging camera time.

Only infrequently does "Harlem Nights" stir to vitality, and inevitably the life-giving elixir is hostility. Murphy has no skill at revealing personality through dialogue or action, but when he writes lines that are reflections of his skills as a stand-up comedian and depends for their effect on the blitzing density of their profanity and their anger, the stuff can be very funny. And it is, for a while. But does *every* joke have to turn on some colorful pronunciation of the 12-letter synonym for the fellow who gets lucky on a date with mom?

"Harlem Nights" is a sad and dilapidated movie, a dispiriting filmmaking debut for the most visible and powerful minority star in Hollywood. He owed everyone more and better.

COPS-R-US

"A lot of wrecked flesh around"

LETHAL WEAPON
March 6, 1987

No case can or should be made for the excessively high-octane "Lethal Weapon" as any kind of great movie-making. In its exultation of macho aggressiveness and in its celebration of both the mind-set and firepower necessary to leave a lot of wrecked flesh around, it might even be irresponsible. That nod to the grown-up part of my own brain and the grown-up part of the general population having been made, however, I must also state the following harsh truth: This sucker is flat-out terrific and nearly undeniable in its appeal to your worst instincts.

It's another in a recent genre phenomenon, the black-white cop movie (as opposed to the black-*and*-white cop movie, a different kettle of grunions altogether) that surely had its origin in "48 Hrs." and was represented last summer in "Running Scared." Scriptwriter Shane Black has come up with a new wrinkle in this very small cloth, however. In past films, it's the black partner who, fueled by exposure to racism, seethes with anti-social impulses and the white who's the force for conservatism and control. Black pulls the switcheroo: The very fine actor Danny Glover plays Los Angeles detective Sgt. Roger Murtaugh as a family man, a conservative, a bedrock of stability, a wearer of herringbone sportcoats and striped rep ties. It's his new sidekick, Martin Riggs (Mel Gibson), who's the full-tilt bull moose looney-tune.

One look at Gibson and you know he's trouble: With his batty blue eyes flicking about to the rhythms of a chimpanzee playing bad ragtime on an out-of-tune piano, his lush hair flying about as if combed out by Jackson Pollock, his tight jeans, rumpled shirts, off-white cowboy boots and baseball hat, he's your all-American (if Australian-raised) death-wisher, your psycho cop on the very, very edge of forever and gone.

His massive commitment to nihilism is expressed in his own lethal weapon, which happens to be the formidable 16-shot Beretta 9mm automatic; at any given moment, he's liable to turn the universe into Swiss cheese like Fearless Fosdick on a gin toot. Guns talk in this movie, by the way. Glover's conservatism is expressed in his modest Smith and Wesson revolver, a .38 special.

Richard Donner is one of those directors with a great deal of technical facility and not much personality, which actually pays off here. You don't feel the director's neurosis getting in the way of the actors or in the way of the action. The movie is told, not felt, and tightly controlled for extreme speed and maneuverability.

Still, Donner has his flourishes. There's a moment where Glover cowers as the villains around him fire into the desert floor; the size of the bullet strikes is enormous, like tactical nukes, and we feel totally Glover's vulnerability.

The plot of "Lethal Weapon" ultimately becomes absurd, and the final scale of its violence is a little outsized. From an initial murder, which turns out to be connected to the main plot in dubious ways, we journey not into the small-time world of crooks and cops, as in "48 Hrs.," but onto the track of a Ludlumesque cartel of ex-Special Forces troopers which—under the leadership of a charismatic general—is importing heroin in industrial quantities. This conspiracy is so gigantic it would have to include everybody from the CIA down to the Cub Scout Pack 15 of Herndon, Va. And — especially after five or six of the most brilliant action sequences since "The Terminator" — I was a little disappointed by the climax, which exits wholly the reasonable and enters wholly the crazed, when Gibson chucks away his Beretta and goes mano-a-mano against head villain Gary Busey in a martial arts kickoff on Glover's front yard. It just seemed unnecessary.

But if its plot doesn't quite compute (neither did that of "48 Hrs.," for that matter), what does compute is chemistry. Glover and Gibson click: They hum, they purr, they squabble like Oscar and Felix, they rip like George and Martha, they bop like Stan and Ollie. But they care: You feel the affection building underneath the locker-room shoving and the jock-like needling. Ultimately, it's through their bond that our bond to the movie arrives; the film is worked out much more neatly from an emotional point of view than from a narrative point of view, in that, while the formal story may not hang together, the psychology underneath it does. It's through his love for Glover that Gibson is able to re-enter the human race, which is a nice note to strike amid the carnage.

LETHAL WEAPON 3
May 15, 1992

I've always considered the bottom-feeders of the American film audience to be those dim souls who wander in five minutes or so before the climax and stare at the screen in utter bewilderment. But that trick won't get them into any trouble with "Lethal Weapon 3," which has a starting point and a stopping point but no true beginning, middle or end.

The movie is made up of modular components — action sequences, seduction sequences, banter sequences — that are arbitrarily arranged. You could reorder them totally, you could scramble them in a Cuisinart or bounce them down the steps in a basketball, and it wouldn't make a bit of difference.

It's not a story, it's a circus: an arrangement of death-defying acts and comic high-jinks in a variety of rings for our viewing enjoyment. Nothing builds, but some of it is great fun. Particularly amusing is a scene in which Mel Gibson's battered Martin Riggs goes scar for scar and bullet-hole for bullet-hole with Sgt. Lorna Cole (Rene Russo) to the point where the splendor of all that bare, ruined flesh turns them on so fiercely that they jointly jump each other's bones. (It's also the movie's idea of "tenderness.")

But some of it isn't much fun at all. Too many times our boys respond to danger with the same kind of macho, slap-happy festival of fists and clubs that won Daryl Gates's authentic LAPD world-wide opprobrium. In one sequence, Gibson punches a handcuffed suspect in the jaw, then utters a quip to his pal. I think Chief Gates would like "Lethal Weapon 3," and I don't mean that as a compliment.

It is rumored that the movie has a plot. I could find no corroborating evidence. The proceedings seem to be generated by a certain problem: A corrupt former policeman has stolen 15,000 confiscated guns from the department and is redistributing them on the streets, using the profits to sustain a real estate venture in the desert. That last stroke may seem inane, but it was fitted into the movie because Richard Donner, the director, won permission to torch a housing project abandoned in the S&L scandal. Equally inane, the movie begins with a sequence in which Riggs and Danny Glover's Roger Murtaugh flee a skyscraper just seconds before it implodes and seems to sink into the primal muck. It's neat as all get out. Never mind the fact that the skyscraper was actually located in Orlando, Fla. And never mind the fact that it has nothing to do with anything else in the movie.

The Gibson-Glover shtick is also wearing a bit thin. This time, Glover's Murtaugh is nearing retirement — his eight-days-and-out countdown gives the movie its only shape — and Gibson's Riggs nevertheless keeps thrusting him into the line of fire, with that callous psycho disregard. So the two spat and spit like the Kramdens. It's funny, but it's a reprise, not an advancement. And what is Joe Pesci even doing in the film? He's like a guest comic on the Carson show, doing a routine, not a performance. Only Russo really registers, a karate-kicking, Beretta-blasting Internal Affairs investigator every bit as violent as Gibson. (In fact, *he* becomes the nurturer.)

The action sequences boast an empty spectacle, but they've come to feel almost robotic: It's slapstick with automatic weapons. Stuart Wilson's villain isn't vividly imagined enough to compel interest in his ultimate demise (as opposed to Gary Busey's spooky bad guy in the first installment), and his henchmen are all ciphers.

The movie also traffics in a kind of hypocrisy regarding

firearms: It sees no problem when the good guys respond to every crisis by hosing down the immediate area with 9-millimeter hollow tips, and it doesn't have a second thought about offering the handgun as the immediate solution to interpersonal problems. At one point, in fact, Gibson pulls his Beretta to scare a jaywalker. But at the same time, it affects a fig leaf of liberal outrage at the proliferation of guns in the black community, and their easy obtainability under laws that are hardly stringent. When is Hollywood going to learn that kids want guns because they see them in movies? The first two "Lethal Weapons" probably sold more Berettas than all the ads in *Guns and Ammo* combined.

Critic Pauline Kael once reduced the movie formula to "kiss, kiss, bang, bang"; "Lethal Weapon 3" is a further de-evolutionary step: it's "bang bang bang bang."

48 HRS.
December 8, 1982

"48 Hrs.," Walter Hill's sensational slam-bang action picture, is set over two hectic days, but it only takes about 20 minutes to make a star out of Eddie Murphy.

It also may revitalize the sagging careers of several others affiliated with it, including Nick Nolte, a brilliant actor weighed down by a string of flops, and Hill himself, a brilliant but flawed director who's yet to deliver a completely good movie.

Murphy's big moment is all his own, however. As Reggie Hammond, a shrewd convict whose help has been enlisted by Nolte as a San Francisco detective tracking down two escaped killers, Murphy takes his $500 Giorgio Armani suit and, more important, his 5-inch-thick armor-plated *attitude* into a sleazy country-western bar full of fat-necked crackers, and proceeds, on sheer intensity, to turn the joint inside out.

Murphy, the most consistently hilarious (one might say the *only* hilarious) actor on the "new" "Saturday Night Live," seems to represent a new figure in American movie representations of blacks: He's not quite the macho-tough black-exploitation stud from an earlier era, like Jim Brown or Fred Williamson, who's all sexual power and coiled, ugly violence. He's too shrewd, too weaselly tough. What he's got — and what the bar scene is contrived to exploit — is a furious sense of *will*. His eyes glitter with street-smarts; he's all angles and jive and con, and he's almost got the pimp's power to get inside the heads of the people he wants to dominate.

Scrawny, almost pretty, Murphy's Reggie has such impregnable self-regard it seems made out of Kevlar, the nylon padding that stops bullets. Murphy is a walking flak-jacket; nothing touches him. He's cool and bad. And when he looks a man three times his size in the eye and orders him to turn and spread or he'll put his *@(#%^|\ ass in a %+*<&* sling, he makes the whole audience believe it. (Incidentally, the movie features some of the most pungent, vivid profanity of the past several years; if you're disinclined to admire the creativity of street English, you'd better stay away.)

But "48 Hrs." isn't just a one-man routine; what gives it its edge and bite is the way Nolte and Murphy play together. Nolte's cop is big, brave and a little stupid. He's not quite what you'd call a liberal. Hill and Nolte let us know that Jack Cates likes to hurt people a little too much, and maybe likes to use his big .357 a little too often. The other cops know it, too, and so the shaggy, grumpy Cates is a kind of Conan the Cop, a loner, an outsider.

But when Nolte and Murphy connect, the circuit is complete: The movie is totally electric. There's so much racial hostility between the two, it's so edgy, furious, jived-up and hip, so raunchy-profane, that it's utterly convincing; it has the jittery feel of something that's improvised.

The story follows the traditional trajectory of such exercises with economy and logic, though perhaps not a great deal of originality. The bonding of Nolte to Murphy is neatly accomplished by a convergence of need: Nolte needs Murphy and Murphy needs Nolte because the two killers (James Remar and Sonny Landham, both quirky, terrifying visions of urban evil) know where Murphy has stashed the $500,000 that he ripped off a drug dealer. And thus Nolte contrives to get Murphy sprung from the penitentiary where he's serving a three-year sentence, and the two trek into the urban wilderness.

Of course, the secret theme of all this — like so many good American pictures — is male bonding. The real course of the narrative isn't Murphy and Nolte closing in on Remar and Landham, but Nolte and Murphy closing in on each other. It is a love story of the repressed, masculine kind, where a glance or a grunt or a snicker or a needle is far more tender and meaning-ful than anything that passes between a man and woman. In fact, all of the women in the picture are prostitutes, except for Nolte's girlfriend Annette O'Toole. She's a bartender.

The movie also has a wonderful sense of the city; the urban wilderness is almost an abstraction, and Hill loves to show green fluorescent shine on gleamy-wet streets, or abstract jig-gles of neon color in the blurry night. According to the produc-tion notes, Ric Waite, the cinematographer, shot the film in an exceedingly fast new Kodak film stock that's able to make un-precedented use of available light; it makes the night seem as vivid as a symbolist poem.

Another trick Waite and Hill cook up is to film at exceed-ingly long range, using a telephoto lens; the effect pays off doubly. First, it gives the action a kind of grainy, wobbly texture. Secondly, it foreshortens the relationships between objects, slightly exaggerating the actors against the background and giv-ing the composition an oddly surrealistic sense. Waite, inciden-tally, has collaborated with Hill before. It was his green-tinted imagery that gave Hill's second-to-last film, "The Long Rid-ers," its lush, plush, Garden of Eden look.

But then Walter Hill's films have always looked terrific; like Paul Schrader, he's one of the young directors who believes that a movie must *look* to be, and his work is all stylized and glossy. He's also mastered the vernacular of the action pictures in a way that few directors his age have. Something of a Peckinpah acolyte, he loves violence and he's always depicted it (in "The Warriors," "The Driver," or his last, muddled film, "Southern Comfort") with a great deal of conviction and dramatic impact.

But he's always been dogged by a sense of the pompous. He

doesn't want to make movies, he wants to make myths. He's always insisted on conferring on his actors and his actions a kind, blankly solemn, symbolic half-life: There are so many archetypes in his films there isn't room for any people.

Perhaps because Murphy and Nolte are so good together or perhaps because he had to work so fast (start to finish, seven months on "48 Hrs."), the film lacks that doughy solemnity. It's all sinew and style and roaring excitement and good fun, which, it seems to me, make the highest art of all. It's certainly Walter Hill's best picture.

BLUE STEEL
March 16, 1990

Director Kathryn Bigelow has fearlessly walked where others of her sex have feared to tread. She hit the mini-big time with a stylish, bloody horror movie called "Near Dark" that won her a great deal of attention; now, complete with stars and a multimillion-dollar budget, and the whole city of New York as a backdrop, she moves farther into boyland: the urban cop thriller, subset psycho drama, sub-subset gun movie.

So give her A's for audacity, N's for nerve, S's for style, and I's for incompetence.

What's it spell? Antsy — more or less — which is how you'll feel at the movie's halfway mark.

Jamie Lee Curtis plays a rookie cop who, first day on the job, faces every cop's nightmare: armed, destabilizing perpetrator in a crowd, no time to think or maneuver. She trusts her instincts and blows the sucker away, a righteous shooting all the way except for the fact that the guy's .44 Magnum, delivered into midair by the force of his dead finger's letting go as he falls in the inevitable slow motion through the inevitable plate glass window, comes to rest an inch from yuppie stockbroker Ron Silver, cowering on the floor. In the ensuing confusion, Silver makes off with the revolver. One touch, one fondle, and he's gone around the bend.

He then becomes a psychopath, his evil drawn out and given focus by the weapon's power, though he's equally mesmerized by his weird attraction to the policewoman. He begins to stalk people and pump them full of lead, leaving empty cartridge casings with her name engraved upon them.

In trouble because she can't prove the man she killed was armed (Silver has the gun, remember), she's pulled out of suspension and handed over to homicide dick Clancy Brown to hunt the killer down. At the same time, from an oblique angle, Silver has re-entered her life and is now romancing her.

The movie never quite makes its mind up about a great many things, but the biggest of them is guns, which is its central difficulty and keeps it from coming into focus of any sort. It begins with the idea of the gun as demon; one touch, and almost supernaturally, mild, nice-guy Silver is turned crazo. OK, maybe that's a fair premise: About 30,000 people a year can't handle the responsibilities of firearms and kill themselves or someone else. So it's an anti-gun movie. Fair enough.

But no. This movie *loves* guns, particularly long-barreled Smith & Wesson revolvers. It caresses their satiny skin, is fascinated by the orchestration of cartridge sliding into cylinder, cylinder snapping into frame, hammer clicking back and then the big ka-boom! It loves to photograph people in heroic or determined postures built around gun handling or gun fighting; it's like an animated gun magazine.

It also has a desperately icky fascination for affiliated fetishes of power, like leather belts, epaulets, cartridge loops, bullets, badges; it loves to study Curtis as she slides into her uniform, buckling her buckles and tying her shoes and setting her cap just so upon her head. Achtung! Women in uniform!

But exactly as it's apotheosizing hardware and software, it's deconstructing at the plot level. The script, as written by Bigelow and Eric Red (who wrote and directed the much nastier, swifter "Cohen and Tate"), is pitifully short on invention. Most absurdly, the two writers can concoct no sensible way for Curtis and Silver to interact for their final shoot-out, so they settle on the absurd: Curtis simply walks around New York until she runs into Silver. There may be 12 million stories in the naked city, but I doubt this is one of them.

Lots of ink will be spilled on Bigelow's alleged "talent" — but not by me. The movie seems composed mostly of the kind of bombastic new-movie cliches that grew tiresome about 1982: big slow-mo vistas, excessive back-lighting, precious design strokes that demand attention at the expense of the story.

In all this showing off, there's not much the performers can do, but poor Silver, so radiantly alive in "Enemies, a Love Story," seems particularly betrayed by his participation. Lacking the capacity to express any motivation, the script dithers desperately as it tries to invent a personality for him, and settles for a higher form of silliness that feels almost plagiarized, word perfect, from the works of the sublimely geeky horror novelist Thomas Harris, who wrote "Red Dragon" (it became "Manhunter," whose stylizations it apes) and "The Silence of the Lambs."

Harris's talent is that he can really put you inside the smoky, fervid brain of the psycho, show you mind systems so alien they are awesome. This is something poor Silver attempts manfully to do, as guided by Bigelow and Red, in a number of soliloquies that sound as if they were written by Harris. I hope they're paying the novelist royalties; he certainly earned them far more than Bigelow or Red.

THE DEAD POOL
July 13, 1988

Can Dirty Harry be mellowing? Is he turning into Slightly-Smudged Harold?

By my count, Inspector Harry Callahan of the San Francisco Police Department only kills 11 guys in "The Dead Pool." That's not even two cylinders full of .44 Magnums, and it has to be some kind of low, since the hallmark of Clint Eastwood's last three Dirty Harry pictures has been escalating, nonsensical violence, an endless cacophony of gunfights, car wrecks, flying glass and shattered story lines.

Not only is the body count significantly lower, but Harry seems somehow less irked than before. The chip on his shoulder has dried up and blown away, leaving only crow's feet near the eyes, a bristle of gray through the hair and a scowl of bemused cynicism. Eastwood's own performance is easily the best thing in the picture, and it's basically one long amusing sigh of irritation: You sense that somehow he's so comfortable with the character — this is his fifth outing — that he's relaxed completely. Gone, thank heavens, are the character's sanctimony and ingot-heavy self-pity that, commingled with neurotic fury, made Harry such a pain in the butt in the blood-sodden, moronic "Sudden Impact."

Finally, and most radically, the movie actually makes sense. Not much, but a little.

Despite Harry's reputation for butt-kicking, the film turns out to be a reasonably traditional mystery — a first for the Dirty Harry movies, it's actually got *clues*! — about a serial killer who uses the making of a horror movie as a pretext for pulling off several flamboyant murders. When it's discovered that the director of the film and several of the key people — out of a sense of debauched amusement — were running a "dead pool," wagering on the demise of celebrities, and that several of those celebrities have died, the case becomes a media sensation.

The movie even has room for a sense of humor, something completely new to the Dirty Harry series. It has elements of parody: a radio-controlled plastic car chases poor Harry and his new buddy Al Quan (Evan Kim) down the hills of San Francisco in humorously small-scale allusion to the great car chase in Peter Yates's "Bullitt." And the work-up of director Peter Swan's "oeuvre" as horror meister is baroquely overdrawn and quite amusing.

The Irish actor Liam Neeson appears as Swan, No. 1 suspect and a kind of inflated version of David Cronenberg or George Romero, and you can feel in Neeson's roaring exaggeration and self-seriousness the low-key Eastwood's icy contempt for such men, their posturing and their movies, although the Big Guy is on pretty shaky ground here, both morally and aesthetically. In his career as film director and actor, Eastwood has killed quite as many as Cronenberg or Romero has, and in ways just as graphically violent.

Then there's the press. Clearly Eastwood views the Fourth Estate with something less than affection. Again, reporters are played as ravening dogs, baying for anything that will help them advance their careers at the expense of larger concerns, and this is the only issue on which Harry returns to his tiresome self. (A movie critic is even killed!) In fact, the subtext of the film is a variation on this theme: A young television reporter (Meryl Streep look-alike Patricia Clarkson) gets close to Harry for a story, is ultimately drawn into his life, is shot at by gangsters and almost killed by the villain, and becomes the object of a media hunt herself, which sickens her. The last image makes this obvious: She and Eastwood walk defiantly away from them; the media are hooting and seething like Visigoths at the gates of Rome.

Good character work is turned in by both Clarkson, as the reporter, and Kim, the new partner. But I'd still have to classify "The Dead Pool" as diverting rather than distinguished.

For one thing, the plotting feels quite mechanical and isn't nearly clever enough to sustain the pace of the film, which is actually a bit draggy in places. Harry and Quan's "investigation" is laughable; mostly it consists of Harry saying gruffly, "Check with MVA," then sitting down to open his mail. It's also a shame that the Quan-Harry relationship, as pleasing as it is, really doesn't go anywhere; the partner is dropped in the last third of the film.

Although Eastwood didn't direct this film, neither, evidently, did Buddy Van Horn, who gets the credit. It completely lacks any personality; it feels like it was directed by the Invisible Man. The action sequences — particularly three early gunfights in which Harry does a 4, another 4 and then a 2, without missing a shot — are so perfunctory they seem to arrive by telegram (and have scant little to do with the story proper, merely being an excuse for Harry to flash the gun that made him famous). This is a shame.

The first of the Dirty Harry films was crafted by the brilliant genre meister Don Siegel near the end of a distinguished career in the B leagues. Characteristically, it moved with snap and brio and when the guns came out, the movie became almost heartbreakingly exciting. No director since — not even Eastwood himself — has been able to get that kind of wattage out of the stories. "The Dead Pool" isn't a dud pool, but it's still a long way from the kind of blazing summer entertainment it could have been.

IN THE LINE OF FIRE
July 9, 1993

You thought "Jurassic Park" was about dinosaurs? "In the Line of Fire" is the great dinosaur movie of the summer: It's about that most ancient and near-extinct of beasts, the hero who places his life on the line out of a sense of duty, honor and country.

And at the same time it represents another vanishing species: the Hollywood thriller crafted brilliantly — tight, logical, completely believable and yet emotionally resonant. It's certainly the best movie of the summer.

It's also Clint Eastwood's best movie as an actor since — well, since Clint Eastwood started acting. His Frank Horrigan, a magnificent creation, is a lion in the winter of age and in the winter of his discontent. He's a Secret Service agent with a past: He was the No. 1 boy oh so long ago in a different world, in Dallas, Texas, on Nov. 22, 1963. A rifle was fired. He had 5.6 seconds to get from where he was to where the brain-shot would hit. It was within his powers to do so. Obviously, he didn't make it.

So Eastwood stalks about like T. Rex, his demons dancing visibly behind his eyes, his commitment to duty nearly as intense as his confusion about a world that's changing rapidly as he tries to, but cannot quite, adapt. This makes him a thorny problem for his younger superiors and an intriguing enigma to

agent Lilly Raines (Rene Russo). But his partner (Dylan Mc-
Dermott) knows the truth: Frank may be old and politically
incorrect, but he's the flat, cold best.

And he'll have a chance to prove it. In the fall of 1992,
during a heated presidential election, another lone gunman is
going hunting. The difference: This one's no screwball with a
mail-order rifle and a four-buck Japanese scope, but a pro —
an ex-CIA cowboy with a fund of endless bitterness and the
technical resources of a Steven Spielberg. Played with preening
intelligence and a core of steel-will violence by John Malkovich,
Mitch Leary is very bad news indeed.

In fact, what's so engaging about the movie is the infinitely
textured relationship between these two archetypes. When I
heard that Malkovich was playing this part, it irked me that
such a great actor would go slumming like John Lithgow in
"Cliffhanger" or James Earl Jones in "Conan the Barbarian."
But Malkovich brings his considerable intellect to bear on the
part: He's like a fallen angel, a Lucifer, himself once a member
of the choir who has toppled so far that only the vilest debauchery can express his rage. Yet, he's drawn to Horrigan, whom he
acknowledges as a member of the same killer elite. The two of
them are like Ahab and the whale, or Holmes and Moriarty:
They need each other to define each other.

Thus, "In the Line of Fire" joins a great tradition of cat-and-
mouse assassination thrillers, such as "Rogue Male," "The Day
of the Jackal," "The Eye of the Needle" and one or two others I
could name. Like its distinguished predecessors, it gets the details right. The script, by Jeff Maguire, pays attention, and the
Secret Service's enthusiastic cooperation has helped provide a
technical milieu of great authenticity, as it re-creates the culture of Protection Details working their craft at the very highest
level. One small touch will show how much care has been taken.
For years movie makers have been blithely using "plastic guns"
as a plot device for defeating metal detectors, forgetting, of
course, that the bullets that such plastic guns would carry are
still metal. But "In the Line of Fire" deals with this issue in a
solid, creative, low-key way, getting the metal bullets *around* the
detector, rather than through it.

The script also pays attention to emotional details: All of the "business" — the subtext of jokey, needling banter between actors — works, and each of Frank's relationships — with Russo and McDermott, with Gary Cole as his immediate boss, with John Mahoney as the head of the outfit — has a vivid, amusing texture. We feel lives really being lived, relationships awkwardly growing by fits and starts.

The director is Wolfgang Petersen, famous for "Das Boot," and, since he moved to America, nothing. He's another dinosaur who won't die; he hasn't worked at this level since he surfaced. The film reminds me a great deal of Fred Zinnemann's low-key and brilliant "Day of the Jackal": There's no sense of phony heat, as extra-narrative devices like visual pyrotechnics, thumping music or Cuisinart editing schemes are deployed to make the piece more frenetic. It just builds, relationship by relationship, detail by detail, clever stroke by clever stroke, taking you in and making you its own. It ought to wear a sign: "Danger, Professionals At Work."

Article:
HOLLYWOOD'S SHOOTING STARS
March 22, 1987

A director famous for his focus on "real people" sums up the state of the film business in a single word, which he utters through his nose with the disdain of a young prince describing the odor of a broken sewer, and in a sense, he has: "Cops!"

"Can we have a break please?" he laments of the American movie hero. "He's either a cop or with the CIA. Or he's an ex-cop. Or it's a father-and-son thing, except the father is a cop. Jesus, can't we get away from that? Can't we deal with some *normal* people?"

The answer, Barry Levinson, is no — or at least only occasionally, on special movies, like your "Tin Men."

Look at the box office, the secret polling place of the American public. Levinson's wonderful "Tin Men," in its first weekend of national release, checked in with a very healthy per-screen average of $5,858 nationally (and $8,184 in Baltimore), for total box office receipts of $4 million. But "Tin Men" is still three places behind cops.

The cops in question happen to be the dashingly nutty Mel Gibson and the warmly healthy Danny Glover squabbling like Lucy and Desi as they litter the L.A. landscape with well-perforated bodies in the film that looks to be the mega-hit of the early spring, "Lethal Weapon." In fact, the movie has become the rare film to make significantly more in its second week than its first — $9.8 million over $7.1 million. Though there are specific reasons for the success of "Lethal Weapon" — Gibson's sexiness, the dazzling action sequences, and the swiftly told story — the movie might also be taken as just the latest evidence that the cop has become the primary fantasy figure of the American subconscious.

He is the vessel into which we pour our contradictory feelings about society; our angst over a perceived breakdown in the rule of law, and the dichotomy between our respect for his courage and our queasiness toward his sanctioned violence. He can be a figure of sympathy: at the mercy of a petty bureaucracy, swamped by red tape, unappreciated by his superiors, loathed by the media, misunderstood by all but those few others in the brotherhood of the badge. He can be a figure of fright: guts-macho with a satin-steel .357 and the batty eyes of a killer. Now and then, we even require — Eureka! — that he be "sensitive."

However, his presence at the center of our fantasy lives is, culturally speaking, a relatively new development: As recently as 1954, the great film critic Robert Warshow could write, "The two enduring creations of the American cinema are the westerner and the gangster: men with guns." Both those archetypes have vanished — or more properly, have been absorbed — into the cop.

Critics have been slow to pick up on this. Perhaps it's the very ubiquity of the cop, who goes on and on while other figures flourish, then perish, which keeps him largely invisible to the scrutiny of paid watchers. He's like the wallpaper or the green shade of paint in a government office; always there. While there have been plenty of studies of film noir, in which cops figure on the periphery, or the gangster movie, which again pushes them to the outside of the story, almost no one has paid attention to the formal cop movie: No one has tracked its evolution and tried to interpret its deeper meanings.

One such meaning, surely, is the way in which the Hollywood cop functions as a litmus test of wider feelings toward authority. For example, the Depression era of the 1930s was, not surprisingly, the heyday of the classic gangster picture, in which the Horatio Alger parable was played out, though in subversive form, in tales of rags to riches. All charisma accrued to the criminals who defied the system, rather than the men who caught them and protected it. Think of the three great gangster pictures of the '30s: "Scarface," with Paul Muni; "Public Enemy," with James Cagney; and "Little Caesar," with Edward G. Robinson.

It's no surprise that the films made stars of each man, but try to recall the names of the policemen who opposed them — an anonymous legion of functionaries. The gangster in those films was the figure of tragic romance, and in his ambitions, his rise and fall, the true meaning of America was played out. Cops were little scurrying regular guys — they were exemplars of the hated Rest of Us, obscure servants of the mistrusted state. Their real purpose was to represent the hypocrisy of a society that admired the flashy gangster's rapacious hunger and willful scramble to the top but that could not officially sanction such drive, no matter how perversely attractive it was. One of the rare times cops were permitted an identity came in 1935's "G-Men," also with Cagney, which portrayed the gangster as scum and the cop — federal agent, in this case — as hero. Part of the impetus for this picture came from J. Edgar Hoover himself, who was anxious to see the FBI apotheosized and to see Hollywood turn away from romanticizing the gangster.

In the early '40s, the romantic spotlight moved off the gangster, but shifted not to the cop. Instead, it illuminated another outsider: the private eye. Again, cops were part of the machinery of society, almost always corrupt or at least grim, and not terribly bright reps of "the system."

In 1941's "The Maltese Falcon," for example, it's the great Bogart as Sam Spade who represents the force for moral order in the universe; the two cops played by Barton MacLane and Ward Bond are simply Irish police beef: hulking emissaries from "downtown," openly hostile to the quicker-witted Spade and utterly incapable of solving the mystery.

A rare police hero came in Otto Preminger's "Laura," in which Dana Andrews was the investigating officer who solved an intricate crime. But Andrews's triumph was equivocal to say the very least: He was clearly a neurotic loner who became absorbed in the case not out of any commitment to society but because of a passionate and pathological commitment to the victim, Laura (Gene Tierney) herself. He was an interesting but not really significant character: cop as geek and voyeur.

By the late '40s, and throughout much of the '50s, the documentary tradition had taken over the crime melodrama, and the police, even then the focus of dramatic attention, became examples of corporate America; they were invariably portrayed as part of a quasi-scientific "team," remorseless but largely impersonal in their pursuit of criminals. You see this in the mock-documentary "T-Men," the breakthrough film of the gifted Anthony Mann, which watches as two cops take on criminal colorations to penetrate a mob of counterfeiters. Rather than questioning the pathology of men who could play criminals so completely that even other criminals were surprised or wondering about their own grasp on their identities, the film holds their impersonation up in a light of wonder and awe as a kind of poster-simple examination of How Our Government Works to Protect Us.

A similar documentary spirit pervades Raoul Walsh's "White Heat," wherein federal agents use a bunch of scientific gizmos to track James Cagney's completely psycho Cody Jarrett. When T(reasury)-Man Edmond O'Brien penetrates the mob to betray Cody, the act isn't viewed as betrayal or courage and it's not done out of outrage or vengeance; it's simply beyond passion, curiously neutral, as if O'Brien is simply another instrument like the radio-ranging devices that track Cody's car. The TV show and 1953 feature film "Dragnet" are perhaps the perfect example of this documentary impulse.

However, a spirit of dislocation did begin to slip into the police in the mid-'50s. In Fritz Lang's "The Big Heat" and Joseph L. Lewis's "The Big Combo," the detectives — Glenn Ford and Cornel Wilde, respectively — are obsessives who take their passions to pathological extremes to ensnare particular gangsters. This tendency toward the instability of the policeman really blossomed in the next decade.

The '60s, that halcyon era of anarchy and rebellion, saw the full-throated, bushy-tailed emergence of the bad cop. (There had been, as the title of a 1953 Robert Taylor melodrama suggests, such a figure as the "Rogue Cop," but he was clearly an aberration, not a symbol; the system always brought him down.)

As the movies pandered to a baby-boom audience high on its own suddenly achieved power to bring a war to a stop and a society to a halt, they tended to honor young rebels and portray cops as killers, emblems of the larger corrupt society. Two repulsive examples spring to mind: In "Cisco Pike," honorable drug dealer Kris Kristofferson is pursued by evil cop Gene Hackman, who wants to push heroin himself; then in Karel Reisz's "Who'll Stop the Rain?," derived from Robert Stone's National Book Award-winning novel "Dog Soldiers," noble heroin smuggler Nick Nolte is pursued through Southern California by evil federal narcs led by Anthony Zerbe. Clearly films of this ilk reflected the perception that it was society that was corrupt and the outsiders, the romantic rebels, who were its salvation.

And yet the next development in the treatment of the American cop was almost a radically reactionary shift; now the system was seen as *too* permissive, its will lost, its strength eroded by liberal reforms in police authority and judicial procedure such as the Miranda ruling. Now the American film pushed the idea that it was the policeman who was our lone champion, and his enemy was just as surely liberal reformists as it was drug dealers and punks, and this perception freed the policeman from his normal constraints. He was no longer part of a team; he despised the team.

The purest example of this idea was the notorious Clint Eastwood film of 1971, "Dirty Harry." It was clearly a worst-case scenario of conservative fears regarding liberal reforms and pandered to working-class audiences which feared that the "system" had been wholly subverted and now coddled criminals while handcuffing cops.

Eastwood plays an honest, incorruptible and thoroughly direct San Francisco police officer on the track of a vicious psychotic. When he catches him, he applies unnecessary force to pry information out of him — the location of a kidnapped girl in an underground coffin with a vanishing air supply. The girl dies anyway; the killer is released because the snooty D.A. (from Berkeley no less!) rules that Harry compromised the psychotic's rights. When the killer performs his next atrocity, society is defenseless and only Harry has the spine left to stand up to the guy with a .44 Magnum (guns are a big deal all the way through the film; the phallic imagery of Harry's having the biggest one is almost too banal to be commented upon).

Now the cop had become a righteous barbarian; by the rights of the wilderness, he'd inherited from his dim antecedent, the western hero, the moral authority to shoot first and kick his opponents where the sun didn't shine (unless they were nudists). There were dozens of pictures in the tradition of the barbarian cop; artistically, the best was probably the hard-charging "French Connection," in which Popeye Doyle's pursuit of an elegant French drug king was clearly pathological but so single-minded that it had a perverse charm to it. The films had a patina of reality in that they reveled in the image of the city as wilderness where anything went, but of course their portrayal of police procedure and the latitude of permissible force was almost comically exaggerated. We see this formula carried to almost cartoon-like purity in the ludicrous Sylvester Stallone cop movie, "Cobra," which was one of the rare big-budget cop-movie failures.

By the '80s, a new element had been added: that of race. Understanding that blacks comprised a large part of the audience for the urban thriller, Hollywood now brought its newest wrinkle to the genre: the bonding of black and white (or representatives) as a kind of fantasy image of racial cooperation. The best example of this is Walter Hill's dynamic "48 Hrs.," in which detective Nick Nolte makes an honorary deputy out of con Eddie Murphy and the two of them track down two vicious killers. A new film due out shortly, "No. 1 with a Bullet," similarly teams Robert Carradine with Billy Dee Williams.

What is so fascinating about "Lethal Weapon" is that not only is it a pretty sensational cop movie on its own, but it astutely combines a little of all cop movies, becoming the mega-, the ultra-cop movie. Within its narrative, it manages to entwine the two traditions of the cop movie and the two modes of heroism in cop movies — the yin and yang of the cop tradition, as it were.

It's more than just the black-and-white racial mix, though the movie clearly profits from that; there's a psychological understructure that's quite interesting as well. Glover is clearly the life force. What's impressive about him, and deployed very carefully for the audience, is his commitment to his family, which stands for the wider society. He has connections, friends; he is man, the social animal. He's the logical descendant of the late '40s and early '50s, when the police were a revered pillar of social order.

Gibson, on the other hand, is the maverick, psycho cop, the heir to the tradition of Dirty Harry and Popeye. He's the cop as loner; the cop as bitter, frustrated, violent and pathological personality, without a good grasp on himself.

Yet it's significant that the movie, while it deploys the outer manifestation of these characteristics, is also careful to keep them from being society's responsibility. The theory behind Gibson's wackiness is the death of his wife in an auto accident, not his bitterness over "the system" or any larger social connection. His looniness isn't offered with any social reverberations; he's just cuckoo.

The drama that really holds "Lethal Weapon" together isn't the rather feeble business about a drug ring composed of ex-Green Berets, which never makes much sense anyway, but the way in which the two traditions of American cop respond to each other and eventually form a team. The two guys' love and the reconciliation of the opposing forces they represent give the movie such a giddy, flavorful force and, despite its violence, such a cheery personality.

So why cop movies? Because Cops-R-Us.

ACTION-
ADVENTURE

"The myth of masculine force"

DIE HARD
July 20, 1988

Probably no slicker, more astutely engineered thriller will come along all summer than "Die Hard," the new Bruce Willis film. To watch it is to ride a roller coaster with a quart of nitroglycerin in your lap, a bad hangover in your head and a Sony Walkman turned up to 9 banging "The Anvil Chorus" up against your eardrums, and that's putting it mildly.

The movie is basically pap as it trafficks through a number of pulpily familiar themes — fancy guns; earthy, working-class heroes; suave, elegantly hypocritical terrorists. But it illustrates a key principle in the realm of melodrama: If it's fast and gaudy enough, and if it beats you to oatmeal efficiently enough, you're willing to throw out all your doubts, sit back and suck up the excitement. Its true title should be, "Cliches Die Hard," but for this much fun, who cares?

The movie will almost certainly make Bruce Willis the big-screen star he no doubt wants to be. Willis is perfectly cast as John McClane, a New York detective who finds himself trapped on the upper floors of a Los Angeles high-rise with 35 hostages — including his estranged wife — and 12 sublimely efficient terrorists, who among them have more high-tech weapons and communications gear than the Delta Force carried into Iran.

Willis has at last found a role fitted to the charms and strengths he brings to his television performances on "Moonlighting." Unlike the passive stiffs he's played in "Blind Date" and "Sunset," his McClane is an attractively vigorous personality: He's human enough to be likable, brave enough to be admirable and funny enough to be laughable. Muscled up, grimy and bloody, he's like some kind of hero-rat, scurrying up ladders and down chutes of the building as he stalks and is stalked. But best of all, he's not quite a superman: You can feel his palpable fear as it writhes against the pull of duty. He's no Rambo, declared impervious by screenwriter's decree to enemy bullets. He's the reluctant guy who has to do what he does because there isn't anybody else there to do it.

And the movie has two other key ingredients absolutely essential to its success: two great villains. The British actor Alan Rickman, in his first film, makes a silky Hans Gruber, terrorist with a heart of gold-greed. Gruber is the rankest cliche: elegant, suave, reekingly hypocritical, a terrorist in a tailored suit. Yet Rickman, who reminded me a bit of the young Jose Ferrer, manages to build the character out of something quite attractive: a lack of sentimentality and a keen self-awareness.

Then, as his No. 2 man, the former Soviet dancer Alexander Godunov, for many years a kind of good guy (as in "Witness"), is simply great as a hulking, psychotic gun freak who declares special enmity toward Willis when Willis's first kill happens to be Godunov's brother.

As an orchestration of special effects, stunt work and fluid camera skills, the film is brilliantly guided by John McTiernan.

In other respects, "Die Hard" isn't quite so lucky. Surrounding the skyscraper drama are coarsely imagined subplots: One of them involves the bureaucratic skirmishing among the first sergeant on the scene (well played by Reggie VelJohnson), an officious assistant chief (over-played by Paul Gleason), and two overaggressive FBI agents (Robert Davi and Grand L. Bush). This squabbling simply overwhelms credulity, but it's there for a reason: It's a conceit of the film, clearly meant to pander to the teen-aged audience, that Authority, like Father, doesn't know best and is, moreover, corrupt, incapable of meeting the challenge and, finally, quite ridiculous to the point of humor.

Then there's an irritating business of yuppie-bashing, in which junior executive Hart Bochner, who has committed the treason of making a pass at Willis's estranged wife (Bonnie Bedelia, again in a part that underuses her considerable talents), attempts to schmooze his way into the favor of the terrorists and is promptly rewarded with a bullet in the nose. There's something repulsive in the class-baiting underneath all this: This upper-middle-class guy is, of course, a slimeball in the crunch, whereas the stoutly working-class Willis — complete to plaid shirt and tattoo — is a stud. And, as usual, television news people are dismissed as glossy swine.

But there's one subplot payoff that provides the movie's best surprise. As it's set up, the film appears to be a variant of the taming of the shrew. Willis has gone out to L.A. to win back his high-flying, newly successful wife (who is personal assistant to the CEO of a Japanese multinational corporation). You know how the lesson will proceed: In combat, he'll prove himself so much the better man, and she'll see that in putting her career ahead of his, she's been a jerk, and will immediately agree to revert to the Good Li'l Woman all of us feel we so richly deserve.

But the script has a nice twist on this old lemon: It's that his ordeal doesn't change her so much as him. He may be the best man, but he learns who the best woman is. It's a sweet moment in a movie otherwise most conspicuous for its firepower.

THE TERMINATOR
October 30, 1984

Is this a movie or a bumper sticker that reads "Honk If You Love Guns"?

You got a Franchi SPAS (Special Purpose Automatic Shotgun) in 12 gauge.

You got an AR-18 with a 40-round magazine.

You got a long-slide .45 automatic with a laser-beam sighting device.

You got an Uzi in 9mm.

You got an Ithaca 37 pumpgun, also in 12 gauge, with a cutdown stock.

You got a chrome steel .44 Magnum.

You got Arnold Schwarzenegger in chains and jackboots and a New Wave wardrobe kicking in doors and hosing down people with some of the above and being hosed down himself with the remainder.

You got somebody named Michael Biehn trying to keep Arnold from killing somebody named Linda Hamilton.

You got car chases, gunfights, murders, massacres, beatings, smashings and other fun.

You got "The Terminator."

This high-tech, gun-crazy nightmare is calculated to drive pointy-heads, secular humanists, wimp-liberals and other quiche-eaters apoplectic with rage, while yanking in millions at the box office.

And at this humble goal, "The Terminator" will probably succeed. It's mindlessly violent, a gas, a hoot and a toot. It's as stylish as "Miami Vice," this season's other cheap thrill, and it features the best action sequences to come down the pike since "The Road Warrior."

Give it to James Cameron, who directed and co-wrote: He'll never win either the Nobel Prize for Literature or Peace, but he knows how to turn an audience on. A superb action mechanic, Cameron delivers a sense of rocketing pace and terrifying plausibility that keeps the film flying along even when its plot permutations are absurd or predictable. And cinematographer Adam Greenberg's gloriously vivid, lurid night photography gives the film a nightmare hue that's impossible to forget.

The idea is simple: Forty years in the future, after the nuclear holocaust, the machines have taken over and are busy trying to eliminate the human survivors in a campaign that Cameron works up in homage to George Pal's 1954 classic, "The War of the Worlds," if not Adolf Hitler's 1942 anti-classic, "The Battle of Stalingrad."

The machines' most effective opponent, however, seems on the verge of working out a way to beat them, so they send a cyborg — a flesh-covered, computer-controlled killer robot — back through time (to the L.A. of 1984) to murder the young woman who would have been his mother (Hamilton). The humans find the time travel machinery, and send back a young guerrilla soldier (Biehn) to stop him.

Thus the battle of tomorrow is being fought in the alley-ways of tonight.

Some viewers may see this as the mirror image of 1979's clever little gem, "Time After Time," in which the killer — Jack the Ripper — went forward in history from the Victorian '90s in H.G. Wells's Time Machine and was pursued by Wells himself. But the similarity stops quickly enough: "Time After Time" charmed by virtue of its wit and performance, "Terminator" on the basis of its skull-crushing, spine-snapping grandeur. One was light, the other dark; both are thrilling.

Schwarzenegger plays — or rather "is," because acting skills are not quite demanded — the killer robot. It is the rare role that isn't beyond him, although the movie never bothers to explain why a 21st century post-human robot would have a German accent. But put him in a punk outfit with the Franchi in one hand and the AR-18 in the other, and you have a terrifying movie creation — Frankenstein with two fistfuls of fully automatic firepower.

One of Cameron's cleverer ideas mandates that after each explosion, spray of gunfire, or detonation into flame, Schwarzenegger's hair becomes more like Billy Idol's, until at last he looks like he's about to burst into "Eyes Without a Face."

As for Biehn and Hamilton, they are not nearly as bad as they might have been for this sort of movie; in fact, they are really rather good. Biehn, recently the "bad rookie" on "Hill Street Blues," is lithe and athletic, but I wish the character had a touch more depth: Why doesn't he ever look around at the civilized world, which he's never seen, and scream out in pain for what would happen to it?

Hamilton is the real surprise. She was similarly manhandled — or rather, kid-handled — in "Children of the Corn," her other starring role, and appeared briefly in "The Stone Boy." Here, hers is the key role and she fills it nicely.

Cameron may overdo his climax a bit — it's a variation on the "Friday the 13th" theme of the Dead Killer Who Just Won't Stay Dead — but he really delivers on one of the ritual requirements of the genre, which is the perfect squelch line at the ultimate moment of the villain's destruction. The perfect squelch is especially pleasing here, because the demise involves a perfect squish. Pronounced with just the right tone of righteous fury and emotional release by Hamilton, it gives the movie the proper exclamation point of violent exhilaration on which to end.

"The Terminator" is as violent as a cockfight, but of its sleazy kind, it's terrific, a new trashclassic.

TERMINATOR 2
July 3, 1991

He said he'd be back and he meant it.

Caparisoned in black leather, encapsulated in shades under a punk brush-cut, carrying enough firepower to devastate the entire LAPD, and possessed of the same remorseless will, the big guy with the erector-set endoskeleton and computer-chip brain presides over $80 million worth of frenzy in "Terminator 2: Judgment Day," which is the biggest, loudest damn movie of the season.

If it shoots, burns or can be blown up, it's in this film.

Director James Cameron's follow-up to the astonishingly resonant "Terminator" of 1984 cost roughly 13 times as much as the original and it's not quite as good, but it's nevertheless a powerful, thrilling document, combining a driving story and an impassioned concern over nuclear war with a vivid dosage of movie-style mega-violence, tough-guy romanticism and special effects that are literally unbelievable.

Set a couple of years in the future, it picks up the story with Sarah Connor (Linda Hamilton) having turned into the complete woman warrior and being sent, for her troubles, to the nut house. Meanwhile, after the genocidal machines incinerate 3 billion or so of us, her 10-year-old son John (Edward Furlong) is fated to lead the surviving humans against the machines. He's Peck's bad boy, San Fernando Valley style, in his foster home. But Skynet, the computer grid that is to become the nemesis of the future, hasn't given up its plot to eliminate its enemies by sending an assassin back through time to destroy, as a child, the boy who, as a man, is fated to destroy them (or it).

The time-travel shenanigans don't bear thinking about unless you like that sort of thing. I think they are based, ultimately, on a paradox that makes them as impossible as an M.C. Escher perspective; when I tried to think them through, I got a big headache.

The gist of the picture is beyond paradox, however. It's that this time, two Terminators descend from the future. One of them is very nasty and one of them is very good, and for a few minutes Cameron replays the game of ambiguous tag that got the first film off to such a start, in which, as these two characters circle their intended victim and protectee, we're not quite sure which one is the good one and which one is the bad one.

Can I be giving too much away to let you know that Arnold is the good guy? Don't you already suspect the unlikelihood that the highest-paid movie star in the world is going to star in an $80 million movie in which he's a child murderer? In fact, one of the amusing strokes in the picture is the way in which Cameron uses his story to recapitulate the Schwarzenegger career — we watch Arnold begin as that granite block of Teutonic absolutism and gradually thaw into something less formidable and even lovable. He even gets a joke.

The plot trick that sets this up is laughable. It seems that sometime in the future, bad Terminator Arnold was captured and blithely "reprogrammed" by the humans, after they learned that the fearsome T-1000 had been sent through time to destroy the Connor boy. But if you can wink at that, you're on your way through a gigantic chutes-and-ladders game on the theme of escape and evasion, as the bad guy gets close, time and time again, and, like some wicked parody of the nuclear family, the machine, the pistol-packing mama and the little boy not only try to survive but to work out a way to save the world from its own approaching obliteration.

T-1000 is played by a blank, cat-like young man named Robert Patrick, recently a killer in "Die Hard 2." Though he's sleek and lithe, he's not particularly impressive physically (in human form, that is), and you wonder how he'll measure up against the Michelin Man physique of Arnold. But Cameron's best trick is soon to come: It's that T-1000 isn't a machine but some sort of intelligent "liquid metal" — in other words, he's a lava lamp with an attitude problem.

The cinema technology that brings this off is extraordinary; the apparition isn't optically matted-in with that tell-tale blue line, and it never looks animated or fake. The illusion is complete: a palpable, quivering blob of quicksilver that undulates into, and then out of, human form. When it's shot, the bullet courses through him as if it's tunneling through lead gelatin.

Yet as astonishing as Patrick and his technical manifestations are, I still miss a real personality, of the sort that Arnold provided to the original. Here he's a force of future nature, but he's always a force, not a mind.

What works in the film isn't just the world-class fireworks, the set-piece escapes, invasions and gunfights. Curiously, amid the blastings, there's more than a few tender moments — between the mother and son, and the son and his new "father." Yes, hideous as it sounds, they do become a parody of a family. In the end, the movie turns out to be about small parental things such as sacrifice and love, and it achieves a grand power in its last moments. It pulps you, and then it moves you. Resonant and sweet, as well as thunderously violent, "Terminator 2: Judgment Day" is terrific.

FIRST BLOOD
October 22, 1982

Nobody plays the noble savage any more nobly or savagely than Sylvester Stallone, and his new film "First Blood" seems hell-bent on getting him into the state of nature before the second reel.

In a certain sense, the movie is built of heroic, romantic, Stone-Age imagery. Director Ted Kotcheff loves to watch Stallone, his biceps bulging, his eyes buggy and haunted, his lips purple and pursed, slither through the underbrush, scramble over the rocks, or hunch shivering and dirty before a fire, chewing a haunch of meat. Stallone looks like the young Victor Mature in "One Million B.C."

Except that where Mature carried a club, Stallone ends up with an M-60 machine gun. The movie is not set in the Stone Age but what might be called the new Ice Age — post-Vietnam America. It argues that the greeting for a generation of soldiers has been pretty chilly.

And when "First Blood" keeps its mouth shut, it's not a bad little picture, tight, trim, tense, haunting.

Based on a novel by an English professor named David Morrell, "First Blood" features Stallone as a former Green Beret A-Team trooper, a Medal of Honor winner no less, named John Rambo, now footloose and full of emptiness, wandering the land. A chance encounter with a thuggish small-town police chief in the Northwest leads to an arrest for vagrancy, and before you can hum "A hundred men we'll test today, but only one will wear the Green Beret," Rambo's been beaten, debased and humiliated, and in retaliation sets off on a one-man rampage of retribution.

To its credit, this is the rare action movie that, after all the shooting and bashing, ends with a man crying: Stallone, in an extraordinary moment, howls in hysterical rage over his betrayal, his pain, his emptiness. It's his best scene, and a rare expression of sympathy for that classic American chump, the Vietnam combat vet, who has now been thanked for his trouble by a monument in Washington that looks like an unfinished foundation for an insurance office.

But the movie could just as honestly be accused of exploiting the very tragedy it seeks to examine. While it seems to aspire to *understand* the anger of the vet, at the same time it loves the visual and emotional spectacle of the berserk man. It loves the idea of revenge. It traffics in that cruelest of all stereotypes, the image of the vet as the gun-crazy, trained killer, ready in the flash of a second to revert to the jungles, ready for — perhaps *hungry* for — action.

And it suffers from an excess of pretension. "First Blood"

arrives with a freight of allegorical sanctimony that pins it to the ground in spots.

It could never be accused of being subtle. Its ironies are so primitive they seem Neanderthalian. For example, did the county in which the small Oregon town is located have to be called "Hope County"? Do the police officers have to strip poor Rambo, crowd him into a corner and, laughing maniacally like redneck nitwits, shower him down with a blast of water from a fire hose? The visual allusion to jailhouse rape, and its echo of a raped generation, is so explicit it's almost pre-literate.

And, visually, the movie evokes continual comparisons between Stallone and that other American martyr, the Indian. It's no coincidence that Stallone quickly puts on head band and loin cloth, nor that blood marks his skin like warpaint; it's also a cheap shot.

A curious figure in all this is Brian Dennehy, the police chief who arrests and "pushes" Rambo and who becomes enmeshed in a dangerous mano-a-mano with him. Perhaps the most significant factor in the movie's faltering tone is the way it deals with him.

In the first place, the selection of Dennehy for this part is an odd choice. True, Dennehy is big and blond and burly and in all outer respects a typical slab of police beef; but he's an unusually intelligent actor — you may remember him as the bartender in "10" or the sergeant in the TV version of "Rumors of War." He gives the cop a thoughtful dimension that's technically quite accomplished, but may do the movie no good. He's almost too smart for the role he's asked to play.

Richard Crenna is another miscalculation. He almost destroys the movie. The fault here may lie with the concept of the character, not the actor (and we can be thankful that Kirk Douglas, originally signed for the part, backed out). Crenna, as "Col. Traut," Stallone's C.O. and team leader in Nam, is that most wretched of concepts, the "intellectual, ironic" officer.

In fact, the whole movie comes close to coming apart under the force of its predilection for stereotypes. If the cops are a tribe of redneck crackers more appropriate to a Smokey and the Bandit film, then the National Guard troopers hunting Stallone in the woods are buffoons out of "Li'l Abner." "First Blood" would have been much better if it had been more naturalistic, less inclined toward exaggeration.

I wish, too, the film had been a little more tightly edited: Its action sequences are thrilling but never stunning (except for a great stunt leap by some guy who should have been paid half-a-mil for the risk he took). In this one, they don't build and leave you pulpy and panting the way, say, George Miller did in "The Road Warrior," or Don Siegel used to, before he hooked up with Bette Midler.

At its best parts, "First Blood" is almost a silent movie; the silence is golden, and when the movie talks, it turns to untarnished brass.

RAMBO: FIRST BLOOD, PART II
May 22, 1985

Designed to make you re-up, Sylvester Stallone's jingoistic "Rambo: First Blood, Part II" will probably have almost the opposite effect: It may make you *throw* up. It reconfirms the sensible notion that patriotism is the last refuge of the scoundrel.

And it certainly finds new meanings for the word "shameless": In fact, it's so slavish in its obsequious need to satisfy the audience's basest prejudices that it ought to be arrested for pandering. It goes beyond shame into craven, abject, slobbering repulsiveness, an orgy of rabble-rousing commie-bashing the likes of which haven't been seen since the McCarthy days.

When Stallone, who co-wrote with James Cameron (who wrote and directed "The Terminator"), isn't sure what to do, he kills somebody. Or he tortures somebody — himself, usually, as he seems unhealthily drawn to inflicting pain upon himself in public; or he gives a self-serving little speech, laying claim to emotions he has no right to express. Let the Vietnam veterans — none of whom he consulted — talk about Vietnam: It's their war; they bought it with blood. What is most repellent about the whole thing is that Stallone helps himself to their suffering and cloaks himself in their dignity and valor without paying any kind of price. Perhaps it needs to be said, but not by Rocky.

The difference between "Rambo: First Blood, Part II," at $15 mil, and Chuck Norris's tacky "M.I.A." at about $500,000 is about $14.5 million. Other than much higher production values, prettier photography, bigger explosions and a more elaborate array of weaponry, the movies are virtually identical in both their numbskulled politics and their narrative crudity: They both represent the triumph of primitivism.

I actually like Norris's a little better: It wasn't so pious, it didn't award itself so many points for its nobility; it wasn't quite such an exercise in star vanity as "Rambo." It was schlock movie-making that had the good sense to acknowledge its own schlockiness in every ricky-tick frame.

A much more revealing comparison, however, is with Ted Kotcheff's excellent "Uncommon Valor," which told the same story, but stayed within the framework of the feasible and drew its power from its sense of documentary accuracy and its sense of military culture — and from excellent performances by Gene Hackman and Fred Ward.

The story in the Stallone version is standard to the genre: Rambo, ex-Green Beret and Medal of Honor winner, is discovered pounding rocks on a chain gang (what is this, 1923 in Georgia?) and is freed in the first few seconds of the picture in order to go on a POW recon "Somewhere in Nam." He goes, finds a crateful of guys, frees one, and then at the key moment is betrayed by a lily-livered bureaucrat and captured by the Cong. They kill his girlfriend even! (You can tell this is a documentary: She's a world-class model running through the jungles in mascara and eyeliner and speaking a dialect known as Sioux Princess.)

Bad news, Cong! He escapes, kills every yellow thing on the horizon and a few white things — Russkie special forces guys in gray-black camouflage tunics, just the thing for refighting the Battle of Stalingrad, but not too cool in the green jungle.

Then he goes back to base camp and hits the bureaucrat in

the nose with his purse! Well, no, he doesn't, but it would add the final lunatic touch to this nonsense.

The movie's chief shrewdness is what is so repulsive about it, and that is the single-minded way in which it sets about to milk the audience's most primitive prejudices. It seems calibrated on the smug assumption that the lunatic fringe is no longer a fringe at all, but the heart of the heart of the country. It makes no statements, it only confirms what the Great Unwashed know without proof to be the case:

• We didn't lose the war in Vietnam, but were betrayed by cream-puff liberal bureaucrats hiding in the sanctity of Washington who wouldn't let our boys do what they wanted.

• One white man is worth a hundred, a thousand, off-white men.

• The Vietnam vet is the biggest martyr in American history, unloved by his country, unhonored by his peers; and the draft-dodgers got all the pretty girls.

But "Rambo" isn't a bad film because its politics are revanchist and its sentiments are cheaply held or because it's irredeemably vulgar. It's a bad film because it's a bad film: All the way through, it's undone by ludicrous touches. There's a torture scene in which Stallone, strapped Christlike to the wall, is pumped full of juice but won't cry out. He's too tough for the Red scum. Then there's the wondrous sequence in which a Vietnamese officer lets fly at the Rock with an automatic pistol: The Red bullets won't bridge the distance. But Stallone, armed with a fiber-glass, pulley-assisted bow, is so righteous that his high-moral dudgeon provides him with the strength of thousands: He's able to fire an arrow farther than a pistol can fire a bullet, and blow the Red rat to commie-hell.

Perhaps the movie went implacably wrong when James Cameron came aboard as a co-writer. Of course, it's difficult to know who is really responsible for what in a film production, but it seems clear that one of the ideas in "Rambo" is to turn Stallone into a good Terminator. In fact, the strategy backfires.

Like David, he kills in the ten-thousands and, like Arnold, no man can stand before his wrath, particularly one of Marxist-

Leninist persuasion. But this, of course, reduces the movie swiftly to circus.

RAMBO III
May 25, 1988

"Rambo III" may be the first movie in history in which an AK-47 gets an Oscar nomination for Best Supporting Actor, but, like any proficient commando, it's an evasive target: It stays low to the ground and there's just not a lot of it there to hit.

Perhaps stung by the critical fury generated by his smug, holier-than-thou "Rambo II," with its cancerous back-stab theory of the Vietnam War, Sylvester Stallone has dialed the sequel's ideological content down almost to nothing. To join up for this crusade, you merely have to accept one proposition: that it was a Bad Thing for the Soviet Union to invade Afghanistan, and since even Russians now accept this argument (though for different reasons), it's probably not asking too much for America's movie critics to join up.

What remains is action: "Rambo III" is a 90-minute fantasy, painted in garish primary colors, crude, boisterous, loud, rather insane and certainly energetic. It has almost nothing to do with war and everything to do with war comic books.

Kids from the '50s may remember the phenomenon of Sgt. Rock, the larger-than-life figure who dashed through enemy automatic weapons fire dispensing justice from the barrel of his Tommy-gun, improbably impervious to the physics of the battlefield, accompanied by red-inked sound effects that crackled off the pages: BUDDDA-BUDDA!!! ZING! KA-CHOW!!! Well, that's "Rambo III."

The set-up is just the barest whisper of a story: Rambo, now working in a Buddhist monastery in Thailand (!) and doing some recreational stick-fighting to raise money for the monks, is approached by his old pal, the Special Forces ace, Col. Trautman (Richard Crenna). Trautman is going into Afghanistan, to set up a delivery of some Stinger missiles into a troublesome district where a particularly nasty Soviet commander has all but closed down the resistance.

But Rambo begs out, his droopy eyelids perhaps too heavy to drag into combat one more time.

"John," the colonel says, "you've got to face who you really are."

Then Rambo speaks four of the nine words that constitute his speaking part in the film; unfortunately, I could not understand them.

The colonel is captured by Soviet gunships, taken to an evil mountain fortress and there tortured by a Russian colonel who looks like Max Von Sydow with a hangover. And Rambo goes in after him.

The rest is gunfire, explosions and macho sentimentality.

Still, there are things to be grateful for. The action is crisply choreographed if somewhat bombastic, and first-time director Peter MacDonald brings off a couple of stunning sequences. There's a gun-ship assault on a high mountain village that feels terrifyingly like the real thing and displays how utterly vulnerable people on the ground are to the modern machinery of high-tech war.

And there's a dazzling sequence in which Rambo takes shelter in a series of underground caverns and is pursued by a Soviet spetsnaz team (their Green Berets); in the eerie half-light, our guy takes out the big bad Reds one at a time, moving, of course, with the Zen-like precision and authority of a Ninja.

Emotionally, the movie is also dialed down. The inevitable Afghan orphan boy bonds to Our Hero, but the film never milks this moo-cow of an idea with quite the same shamelessness of "Rambo II," where the sacrificial "bossy" was a beautiful Eurasian model who spoke Sioux-princess dialogue ("Me want go America, Rambo") and who was picked off by a sniper the second her lips touched his. KA-CHOW!

The Russian-baiting is a bit tiresome, but it is so generic and characterless it probably won't bring us any closer to nuclear war. One sly touch I appreciated: The Soviet colonel is at least allowed a portrait of wife and kids in his quarters, suggesting that he's not so much an evil psychopath as a lonely soldier trying to do a thankless job in a terrible country.

And the torture sequences, also inevitable, aren't quite the pseudo-pornographic orgies of crucifixion imagery they were in the last "Rambo"; moreover, it's not Rambo himself who is turned into a modern martyr, but poor old flaccid Richard Crenna, and even then the Russians seem not to have their heart in it. I mean, how much fun can it be to beat up Walter Denton?

In keeping with its sense of emotional minimalism, the movie also lacks that lugubrious sense of self-pity and noble suffering that so contaminated "Rambo II." There's no underlying, invidious theory of betrayal to give it that piquant edge of hysteria — no "This time, do we get to win?"; no treacherous liberal State Department coward, lying and sniveling and groveling. It's just plain, primitive action built along "us-good/them-bad" lines. At the same time, the movie is so dead-on, it has no room for irony. It never occurs to Rambo that the roles have been reversed from his last war: He's now fighting with agrarian peasants against a puppet regime supported by a sophisticated superpower. Only Trautman remarks on the vice of this versa, and he appears not to understand it either. Still, to require irony from Stallone is to require song from a pig. It's a waste of time, and it annoys the hell out of the pig.

As for the performances, there's not much room for them amid the explosions. It's a shame that the film does so little with Kurtwood Smith, who was so chilling as the villain in "RoboCop." He disappears after the first few minutes. Crenna is an old pro doing his best to keep the leaky tub afloat and to keep his toupee from catching fire in the various pyrotechnics; Sasson Gabai is lively as an Afghan scout.

Stallone is almost never at rest, and to criticize him as an actor is almost beside the point. It's more like a dance performance than a dramatic one; bulgy-bloated with muscle, his doggie eyes drooping like a beagle's in a sauna, his hair flopping all over the place like Geronimo's, he's not a man so much as a symbol of untrammeled macho aggression, at home only on the battlefield. It's a ridiculous adolescent posture, but Stallone almost sells it: Nobody looks better in a tank top and Apache head band than this peculiar bird.

TRUE LIES
July 15, 1994

In "True Lies," Arnold Schwarzenegger is stirring, never shaken: He's James Bond with the bratwurst pecs of Mr. Universe, one of Herr Glock's devilish 9mm Model 19s in a shoulder holster, and a feathery-light quip on his amused lips, who blithely sails through hell without cracking the shellac of mousse that holds his hair in place.

What compels this hoary '60s superagent cliche to our attention is the stunning dynamism with which it is delivered. Arnold is only Arnold, but a good director, such as James Cameron, is a smoke. Cameron did both "Terminators" and the second "Aliens" and he knows how to stage action better than anyone in the world with the slight exception of John Woo. But he's really not engaged at any level here except the technical. The film has the soulless but carefully engineered texture of a Summer hit, which it will be, rather than a Real Movie, which it isn't. Cameron's slumming. But boy, can he slum!

The plot, borrowed from a much slighter French farce, is a flimsy platform by which to get from one action sequence to another. Arnold plays Harry Tasker, a suburban Washington computer salesman, who is solid, decent, evidently prosperous and, alas, rather boring, much to the disappointment of his wife Helen (Jamie Lee Curtis). We are given to understand that such boredom extends to that marital demilitarized zone known as the bedroom.

But what Helen can't know is that Harry is actually the No. 1 operative for "The Omega Sector," a super-secret CIA offshoot that combats nuclear terrorism. We first meet him stepping out of a hole in the ice in a frogman's wet suit, which he sheds to reveal a dapper tux. He then slides with a lizard's grace into a glittering party in Switzerland. Rigging explosive distractions, he penetrates a computer network, drinks a glass of champagne, dances a tango, then shoots and body-surfs his way out and down the snowy slopes — all with the wry detachment of an English poet holding forth on the art of the simile.

The party sequence is merely prelude. It sets Harry up in pursuit of a mad (but purely generic) Arabic terrorist named Aziz, played by Art Malik, who has come into possession of four Soviet warheads. He means to detonate them in America, because that's the sort of thing terrorists do (the portrait of Muslims is borderline offensive, by the way). To nab Malik, Harry must track him through the offices of the de rigueur femme fatale, an art importer played with icy elegance by Tia Carrere, who seems a little young for the part, though she dances a mean tango.

One of the film's best gags is almost totally irrelevant to the story. Harry turns the tables on assassins in Georgetown in a men's-room shootout that deconstructs the world into Swiss cheese. He ends up chasing the motorcycle-mounted Aziz through Washington on a police officer's horse, through streets, hotel lobbies and ultimately up elevators and onto rooftops. It's one of those astonishing, completely unbelievable but mesmerizing set pieces at which Cameron excels, its unlikelihood campily playing off its sheer sense of dazzlement. You wonder, "How can he top this?" But he always does.

Then Cameron (who also wrote) stops the film and turns it into a somewhat bizarrely configured Hepburn-Tracy number. The frustrated Curtis becomes the objet d'amour of a sleazy used car salesman (Bill Paxton) whose method of seduction is to tell his targets he's a secret agent; that, in fact, he's Harry! But Harry, who has no appreciation for irony, finds out about it and utilizes the full force of his agency to squash the affair and the little man. Then, ickily, he further twists his power to play an elaborate and extremely sadistic prank on his poor wife, blackmailing her (through a secret guise) into taking on the role, and performing some of the degrading acts, of a prostitute. Jim, it's not very '90s! What it is, is very kinky stuff. But this gambit provides the structure for what follows: Harry and Helen, suddenly kidnapped by the terrorists, must save the world. We realize, however, that something much more than the deaths of millions of people is at stake: their marriage.

Then Cameron notices it's been nine minutes since anything exploded, and off we go again.

Tom Arnold does a nice job as Arnold's mild sidekick, but the true breakout performance is turned in by a Marine Harrier jump jet. This aircraft, much beloved by our leathernecks for its ability to stop on a dime and to set down in a parking lot like a helicopter, is commandeered by Arnold (who just happens to know how to fly it) and hauls ass to Miami to deal with the terrorists who A) have an atom bomb, and B) have his daughter. Now, time for some big-time critic's insight: What a cool plane! Where can I get mine?

This next sequence is literally unbelievable. The plane drifts in midair around the skyscraper like a Chris Craft floating in a swimming pool, while Arnold and Malik scamper about its dangerous contours for control of the bomb key. A stunningly authentic illusion, done entirely on camera (no computer morphing) by using an actual airplane suspended from a crane 30 stories up, the sequence must stand as one of the best pure adrenaline hits of all time.

I must have turned to a buddy 10 times during the film and gasped "Un-be-lievable!" The movie is relentless in its hold on certain parts of your anatomy. You may dislike it for its thinness of plot, its odd, ugly sexuality, or its sleazy rendering of Arabs. But I defy you to deny its power.

Article:
GUNS ARE GOLD ON TODAY'S SILVER SCREEN
June 8, 1986

"The two most successful creations of American movies," wrote the film critic Robert Warshow in 1954, "are the gangster and the westerner: men with guns." That is no longer true. Today, the equation, although it uses the same components, has been rearranged subtly: the most successful creations of American movies are guns with men.

Close attention to the gun as physical object is certainly one of the hallmarks of the modern action film, and it distinguishes the genre movies of the 1980s from the movies that came before. As never before in film history, directors are featuring guns, gun lore, gun love and even gun worship as the centerpiece in a certain kind of male-oriented action-adventure film.

Currently, two "gun movies" are blazing away on the screen. The first is Sylvester Stallone's "Cobra," which features numb performances by the actors and brilliant performances by a Finnish Jati-matic 9mm submachine gun with a laser sighting system, and by a .45 automatic with special etched ivory handgrips. Each displays considerably more personality than the man who carries it. The second is the just-opened "Raw Deal," with Arnold Schwarzenegger as an unfrocked FBI agent who has taken on the Chicago Mob. Schwarzenegger wears designer clothes and the latest in firepower, chiefly the Heckler & Koch 9mm MP-5 machine pistol, which lately has supplanted the Uzi and Ingram MAC-10 as weapon of choice for Hollywood spray shooters, as well as the Smith & Wesson .357 Magnum.

Other recent films that were principally built around the iconographic usage of firearms have included "The Terminator," probably the best gun movie ever made, and "Commando," both Schwarzenegger vehicles; the two Rambo films, with Stallone, built around the American M-60 light machine gun; the Clint Eastwood "Dirty Harry" films, with their ever-present Smith & Wesson .44 Magnum; the "Death Wish" films, particularly the most recent, in which Charles Bronson sported a .44 Magnum Wildey automatic; and several of the Chuck Norris films, which increasingly feature firearms over karate, such as "Invasion U.S.A." and "Delta Force."

By contrast, it's interesting to watch a filmmaker with no interest in firearms whose imagination is not provoked by them. In "Hannah and Her Sisters," Woody Allen features himself as a neurotic who, at one point, attempts suicide with a firearm. To Allen, the gun is meaningless, except as it extends the story: He features no close-ups of it and never even places it at the center of his frame.

On the other hand, a firearms fetish can be deployed in such a way that it actually subverts the narrative thrust of the movie. Such is the case in the high lunacy of "Cobra." There's a sequence in which Stallone's character, police Lt. Marion "Cobra" Cobretti, is on the run with a model (Brigitte Nielsen), pursued by a vaguely defined gang of psychotic killers. Hiding in a motel room, Cobra opens a case he has been carrying and lovingly assembles his submachine gun. The camera studies this process to such a degree that the film loses all contact with its story and becomes almost purely abstract, a study of bolts clanking into tubes, springs being compressed into coils, screws being turned, cartridges being threaded into magazines, all to the tune of pulsing, bleating, bad rock-'n-roll. Of course it's all absurd: Why would Cobra, in intense jeopardy, carry this formidable piece around *unassembled*, except for the convenience of the cameras?

The reason — other, that is, than that Stallone also wrote the movie and knows the bad guys won't attack until after he tightens all the screws — is that it's art of the ritual. In its form, the gun movie has evolved into something as rigidly circumscribed as a Noh Drama. It features, at its purest, at least four of the following six elements:

• The gun it is built around must be exotic, preferably a fully automatic weapon, although short-barreled pump shotguns increasingly are favored (the Franchi Spas-12, an elaborate Italian weapon that looks like a laser cannon, is a current hot item).

• The gun must be identified and described at some point in the story.

• It must be lovingly assembled.

• It must be fondled, cocked, rubbed, clicked, checked and patted frequently.

• It must be used, but, more important, its special features must be factored into the climax.

• Its qualities must jibe with the qualities of the man who carries it, until each is an extension or reflection of the other.

It must be, in short, a character in the drama, a co-star, if you will.

"We deal in lead, friend."
— Steve McQueen in "The Magnificent Seven."

Clearly, Hollywood filmmakers have been fascinated by firearms, their effects and their emblematic significance for some time. In fact, the most provocative image in what is generally conceded to be the first feature film involved, as Warshow said, a man with a gun. This was the opening sequence in "The Great Train Robbery," Edwin S. Porter's 1903 western (filmed in New Jersey). The movie ends (in a complete non sequitur) with a mustachioed cowpoke firing point blank into the camera, much to the consternation of members of the audience, who frequently ducked. In a sense, audiences continue to duck 83 years later, but now there's far more lead in the air.

Still, the history of the gun in Hollywood films is curious. If weapons were ubiquitous, they were never quite at the center of focus in the early years of westerns. The legacy of the firearm as a totem clearly dates from the western serials of the 1930s and 1940s when, in order to differentiate the heroes, directors took to giving them fancier weapons than the run-of-the-mill Colt Peacemaker. The Lone Ranger, for example, used silver bullets and a chrome-plated Peacemaker; Wild Bill Elliott carried his two silver Colts backwards in his double holsters, with ornate horn grips on the weapons to make them stand out even more. The ne plus ultra of this direction in weaponry probably was the long-barreled, pearl-handled silver Colt carried by Alan Ladd in "Shane," the ultimate "good guy's gun" in the ultimate "classic" western that shuffled through its western icons with the self-conscious solemnity of high mass.

At the same time, gangster pictures were enshrining another weapon in American legend: This was the Thompson sub-machine gun, the classic gangster firearm, that was featured in such films as "G-Men," "Little Caesar" and "The Roaring Twenties." The six-gun and the Tommy gun were the first two

high-concept weapons: They accrued such an immediately recognizable set of traditions that they instantly communicated
information about their users. The guns became the men; they
became highly charged communicative objects, almost what
some linguists call a non-verbal micro-language.

The gun remained dramatically important in violent, melodramatic stories, but, with these two exceptions, was generally
unstressed visually. The first film that featured a powerful modern weapon and that was built around its potential for extreme
damage may have been either "The Killer Is Loose" or "The
House of Bamboo," both released in 1955.

In the former, Wendell Corey plays a psychopath attempting
to murder police officer Joseph Cotten's wife with a .357 Magnum; in the latter, psychopathic Robert Ryan used a German
9mm pistol, the P-38, to enforce discipline in his mob of ex-GIs
who had formed a crime syndicate in Tokyo. Both films featured, in prototypical form, the distinctions of the modern gun
movie. The weapons were identified and demonstrated, and
expressed the character of the men who carried them. The two
guns were seen as expressions of their characters' mental unsta-
bleness and ruthlessness. By helpful contrast, it's interesting to
note that the classic "psycho" movie of the age, Raoul Walsh's
"White Heat," attaches no particular visual or associational
importance to the guns that James Cagney used.

*"Being as this is a .44 Magnum, the most powerful handgun
ever made, you have to ask yourself if you feel lucky, punk. Well?
Do you, punk?"*
— Clint Eastwood in "Dirty Harry."

In 1969, what might be called the ultimate gun western appeared, even as the western itself was dying. This was Sam
Peckinpah's "The Wild Bunch," which featured a motley collection of professional killers fighting a last glorious battle against
modern times. But "The Wild Bunch" itself had to some degree
been coopted by the coming of those modern times. Peckinpah's pros used Colt .45 automatics, 12-gauge Winchester

pump guns and, in the delirious Armageddonesque finale, a Browning .30-caliber, water-cooled machine gun — pointedly avoiding the traditional Colts and Winchester 94s of western iconography, which lay undisturbed in their holsters.

The movie had many meanings, but one was clearly contained in the weapons, which were the implements of trench warfare; it was that the old traditions of individual heroism were being subverted by technological improvements in the killing game, and that courage was becoming obsolete, or meaningless, in the face of weapons that fired hundreds of bullets.

As if to argue the opposite side to this position, Don Siegel's "Dirty Harry" arrived two years later. Here the western had been transferred to an urban environment, but most of its classic traditions remained intact: It still was a lone man with a six-gun standing against the uncivilized hordes.

But quelle six-gun! Eastwood's revolver was the massive Smith & Wesson .44 Magnum. It had been added to the script by gun-fancier John Milius, in an uncredited rewrite, as a means of giving Harry — originally to be played by Frank Sinatra—the same kind of distinction that Wild Bill Elliott derived from his fancy rig. But here, under Siegel's furiously fast-paced direction and a powerfully and ingenuously argued right-wing platform, the identification of man and weapon reached its zenith. Eastwood simply *was* the long-barreled, ultra-powerful man-killer, an absolutist in a world of relativists.

At the same time, another tradition was feeding into the Hollywood mainstream. This derived from the James Bond films, espionage fantasies set in a world of exaggerated comic villains and expressive of what might be called a cult of equipment. The Bond films were always, at some level, a celebration of gear; they went to great lengths to specify exotic hardware, firearms especially. It was conspicuous consumption at its most flamboyant. Even today, nearly every schoolboy knows that Bond packs a Walther PPK, which is looked at as an extension of his suave cosmopolitanism. The gun is a sleek, compact European model that fits snugly into the breast pocket of a tuxedo, without distorting the hang of the lapels; it draws smoothly.

"(Give me) the 12-gauge auto-loader, the .45 long slide with laser sight, a phased Plasma rifle in the 40-watt range, and the Uzi 9-millimeter."
— Arnold Schwarzenegger in "The Terminator."

Still, neither the western heritage nor the Bondian cult of expertise could quite explain the exponential growth of weapons-fixated films of the 1980s. What does explain "Rambo: First Blood, Part II," for example, which zeroes in on the M-60 machine gun with a gynecologist's clinicalness; or "The Terminator," which boasts a wardrobe of exotic weapons not seen in normal life this side of a SWAT-team's vault?

First of all, the development must be seen in terms of larger social trends. One of them reflects a curious and largely unreported-upon tendency: the growth of an exotic-weapons cult, which manifests itself in a variety of ways, of which the movies are but one. Another is the fact that gun manufacturers, who for years turned out hunting, target-shooting and self-defense weapons, have found in the past decade a new market for exotic weapons. Thus, many of them manufacture semi-automatic versions of the hard-core automatic weapons previously limited to military and police usage. It now is possible to buy a semi-automatic Uzi or MAC-10 or AK-47 or M-16 in virtually any gun store in America, and there clearly are buyers for such weapons.

Another manifestation of this tendency is what might be called the exotic weaponry press: Whereas 10 years ago there were but three or four magazines that covered sporting and target shooting, now there are dozens of magazines that concentrate on exotic weapons, such as *Exotic Firepower, S.W.A.T., Soldier of Fortune, Magnum Handguns, Combat Shooting, Gung-Ho, American Eagle* and the like. These three industries — the gun manufacturers, the magazines and the movies — clearly interrelate in their willingness to serve and profit from this audience.

Gun buffs may not form a significant part of the American film audience numerically, but they are passionate about their loves; they go to the movies, they buy the magazines and they buy the firearms to see the guns shoot. Film companies realize this, and frequently use the specialized-firearms press as a way to target this specialized audience by permitting special access to the gun magazines, which in turn will run admiring and noncritical articles. In the current issue of *Guns*, for example, there's a cover box announcing, "Exclusive Interview: Jack Lucarelli and Jameson Parker talk about guns in their new film 'Jackals.' "

But perhaps the deeper point — leaving aside the conventional Freudian reading of all this phallic-oriented machismo — is that the implements of war tend to be most fascinating when the wars are far off. During the early 1970s, when American exhaustion with the Vietnam War was at its peak, a number of movie traditions died, chief among them the gung-ho war movie with its stress on leadership, team play and superior firepower. Now, however, Vietnam has eroded in memory. The reality of its tragic consequences has slipped off into ether; what remains are bittersweet sensations of loss and betrayal of the war that, in movie mythology, Our Boys Weren't Allowed to Win.

The gun — particularly the Vietnam-era M-16s and M-60s that, via television, are intractably bound up in the collective consciousness of that war — therefore is useful to filmmakers as an icon of national will, an expression of American superiority that should have been unlimbered more fully in Vietnam.

There also are clear class and sex implications in "gun movies." A gun movie is aimed at an exclusively male audience — indeed, it has the power of discouraging feminine participation, which is not a byproduct, but, one supposes, the end product. It's also aimed, like gun sales and gun magazines, at a predominantly blue-collar audience.

And still a deeper meaning lurks within "gun movies." One suspects that at heart the gun movie is an assertion of male will against the confusions of a baffling world, including feminism and what may be perceived as the breakup of society as exemplified by rising crime rates. In this way, the gun, particularly the automatic weapon, harks back to its own imperial-age origins as an implement primarily meant to be used against primitives. As the sardonic Hilaire Belloc wrote, "Whatever happens, we have got/The maximum gun and they have not." He was, of course, talking about Hottentots, Dervishes, Zulus and others who fell victim to the white man's war machine. But the message — although it's now become a fantasy — remains the same in a new age of barbarism.

As John Ellis notes in "The Social History of the Machine Gun": "In many ways, then, the machine gun has become something of a contemporary icon. The sheer violence of its action, and the indiscriminate deadliness of its effect, has made it a useful symbol for expressing modern man's frenzied attempts to assert himself in an increasingly complex and depersonalized world . . . The machine gun has now become personalized, itself the means by which men desperately try to make their mark on the world in which they feel increasingly powerless. In the fantasy world at least, technology has turned against itself."

Article:
ALL FIRED UP OVER BIG GUNS: HOLLYWOOD'S STILL PROMOTING MYTHS
June 13, 1988

Guns, guns, guns!

Even as Maryland and other states struggle to come up with some kind of sane, fair handgun policy, what comes banging into town on successive Wednesdays but two el primo, big-bore gun movies?

Legislators are trying to ban Saturday night specials, but who's doing anything about Saturday Night at the Movies?

You have only to look at the advertisements to realize that, as firearms problems, fueled in most cases by narcotics problems, multiply in a complex society, and the right to reasonable public safety seems to be locked in an insoluble dilemma with the mandate of the Second Amendment, Hollywood is still selling the same old lie.

Here's Clint Eastwood in "The Dead Pool," released last week, where the weapon — a Smith & Wesson Model 29 in .44-caliber Magnum with an 8-inch barrel — is the central icon to the myth.

And, in a film that should make him a star, here's Bruce Willis, bare-chested and shoeless but nonetheless cloaked in a wardrobe of firepower that's considerable, including, again as the central image in the advertising image, a Beretta Model 92 9mm automatic. The movie is "Die Hard," a kind of combination of "The Towering Inferno" and "The Wild Bunch."

And more gun movies are coming out. Friday, "Midnight Run" opens with Robert De Niro as a modern-day bounty hunter trying to escort prisoner Charles Grodin back across country, but being pursued by various Mafia and FBI functionaries. De Niro's choice of arms is the ubiquitous Beretta, the current "hot" gun in the fantasy game.

Then, in August, "The Young Guns" arrives, one of the rare pure westerns of our decade, with Emilio Estevez, Lou Diamond Phillips and Kiefer Sutherland — among others — as a gang of renegade youths raising hell in the frontier of the 1880s. The film certainly plays with our most ferocious social problem: not men with guns, but something far more menacing — *young* men with guns. The trailer, at least, makes the film appear as a kind of homage to the design art of Samuel Colt and Oliver Winchester.

In "The Dead Pool," as it turns out, there's significantly less gun love than the movie ads and stills might indicate. There's no formal identification of the weapon and its gaudy capabilities (though by this time, perhaps none is necessary). In the original 1971 "Dirty Harry," probably the quintessential "gun movie" of all time, screenwriter John Milius made an explicit connection between his hero's moral and tactical potency and his handgun, then (but no longer) "the most powerful handgun ever made."

Anyone who saw it can remember the Eastwoodian sneer, hard as frozen steel, as it loomed contemptuously over the seemingly immense muzzle of the revolver: ". . . . but, being as this is a .44 Magnum, the most powerful handgun ever made, you have to ask yourself one question, punk. Do you feel lucky today? Well? Do you?"

The final score: .44 Magnum 1, Punk 0.

In one sense, this connected with an ancient tradition: Warriors, particularly since the Middle Ages, somehow were their weapons. One has only to venture to the armor collection of the Metropolitan Museum of Art in New York to realize that men who depend on weapons in battle can make mystical, perhaps neurotic, connections to them: The blades of the Middle Ages were loved and respected like especially obedient, handsome children, shined to murderous glare, burnished, polished, inscribed, absorbing the full flower of a craftsman's creativity in service to his master.

And there was something knightly from the beginning about Dirty Harry; his big gun, an Excalibur for our times, was only part of it. Equally potent was his place in time — 1971 — at the tail end of the dizzying spin through history known as the '60s, and its compulsive insistence on finding new codes of behavior — not better codes of behavior, just newer ones, almost always involving styles of personal and pharmacological liberation. The venue, of course, was San Francisco, the Gomorrah of New Times. Against that background, Harry and his big gun stood for conservative virtue, strength, absolutism in a period of moral relativism; he was the old nobleman whose skill at arms vanquishes a treacherous enemy, who, in the first film, was a psychotic wearing a peace button (he was a viperous flower child played with chilling vividness by Andy Robinson).

In this new Dirty Harry adventure, however, the considerable heat generated by the weapon has vanished, as has, unfortunately, most of the skill and wit with which the original was put together. The movie doesn't boast a bit of the sinewy grace and power of the first, being, in the end, a torpid mystery about a serial killer who is part of a film crew making a horror movie in San Francisco. The few action sequences involving the gun are pretty standard stuff by movie standards and Harry — good heavens, can this be real? — even gives up his gun, when an explicit theme of the original film was his unwillingness to do the same. It represented a concession to the forces of evil and stood, symbolically, for the liberal lack of will for combat and hunger for appeasement that were at the center of Harry's idea of What Was Wrong With America.

Nevertheless, Warner Bros. had no difficulty in choosing the image of the gun as a central icon for the advertising campaign of the film, whether or not that icon fairly represented the film. In this, the studio returns to the old meaning of the gun and to its old power, and confirms one of the central difficulties of firearms in society: Whatever horrors they are capable of inflicting when used meretriciously or sloppily, guns are beautiful, potent symbols, high-concept in the truest meaning of that term in that they instantly convey notions of glamour and danger.

Then there's Willis, posed melodramatically with his high-capacity Beretta, in "Die Hard." In this one, Willis and his Wondernine — gun culture term for such a slick automatic — take on 12 terrorists in a Los Angeles high-rise office building.

The film is explicitly a gun movie in the classic sense; for one thing, it sports a variety of weaponry that should do any SWAT team proud. For another, in the tradition of the classic sense, it uses the guns to identify the various characters, for good and bad. The characters *are* their guns, and each one has a specific weapon that expresses his personality (this is the secret language of movie guns).

The head terrorist, brilliantly played with an abundance of sleazy charm and ghoulish irony by Alan Rickman, carries a Heckler & Koch P7, a radically designed, very au courant, very expensive European 9mm pistol that clearly expresses his fundamental hypocrisy: Ostensibly a believer in "the people," he has aristocratic tastes in guns, clothes and crimes.

Villain No. 2, played by the former Soviet dancer Alexander Godunov (who's also very good), carries another racy European weapon, a Steyr AUG (the German acronym, unraveled, translates into Universal Army Weapon), which is a slicker version of the M-16 that's entirely shrouded in plastic and has what's called a bull-pup configuration. The magazine housing is behind the grip and the whole thing looks like some kind of reverse vacuum cleaner of death.

Then, finally, there's Willis's Beretta, which has become the ubiquitous "duty" gun of the '80s, ever since the U.S. Army adopted it as its sidearm in 1983. Ugly, squat, fat, somehow decent, the gun has become the heir apparent to the old six-shooter as an emblem of the lawman's might of right. It's the Peacemaker of the '80s.

Indeed, the subtext of "Die Hard" is explicitly western, even though the weaponry and the setting are extremely high-tech; the head terrorist contemptuously dismisses Willis as an "American cowboy" who has seen too many movies; Willis dubs himself "Roy" — after Roy Rogers — in his radio conversations with higher command; and the climax of the film plays itself out in "High Noon" fashion, complete to the classic fast-draw mechanism of a thousand B movies.

The problems with the gun movies don't really begin with their inaccuracy, though that is considerable. Dirty Harry has been a joke from the start. To begin with, no urban police department would sanction one of its officers carrying the .44-caliber Magnum. Its big-game round travels at over 1,500 feet per second and it's far too powerful for city use apt to penetrate its target, go through three walls, bounce off a window sill and wound a child three blocks away. Then there's the item of marksmanship. Every time Eastwood fires (one-handed, no less), he hits, displaying gun skill of a caliber found only among a handful of world-class action shooters today, who use extensively modified, delicate firearms costing thousands of dollars. By contrast is the harsh real world. In the Great Miami Shootout of 1986, between FBI agents and two fleeing, heavily armed bank robbers, the federal agents, under heavy fire themselves, fired over 200 rounds at their targets, for a total of 18 hits, only three or four of which were solid.

In the Willis movie, it seems that nobody has heard of ricochets; bullets never bounce with catastrophic consequences as they do in reality; they never go through walls and kill the innocent. The officers never take any safety precautions; they fire indiscriminately, and when they shoot someone, it's a completely non-traumatic experience. The corpse is carried away, they repack their pieces in their holsters and they walk away for coffee and doughnuts. (There's also never any post-shooting investigations to make certain the force was legitimately employed, as is the case in the real world.)

But even if the movie-makers don't quite get their facts right — or even care much about the facts — there's something even more disturbing. That's the attitude toward the weapons that the movies foster, an attitude that can reach out into society, particularly into the skulls, otherwise thick, of the teen-age boys who constitute the key action audience. It's the old myth of the frontier. And the myth? The myth says that a man is his gun, and the bigger the better. It says that shooting fast and well takes the place of not shooting. It sells, further, the idea that all problems can be solved in a blaze of gunfire, when reality teaches — as say, it recently taught Carl Rowan — that a blaze of gunfire simply makes for more problems.

It's begun to occur to me that maybe it's not the guns themselves that are evil so much as the ideas that surround them and the ways they are used to make large amounts of money for small groups of men. The guns, after all, have always been there; what's new to the system — in the past two decades or so, beginning more or less with "Dirty Harry" — is how we think about them, thanks to a species of movie that celebrates the gun as something beyond a tool or a toy, but as an icon of machismo or an item of fashion. And the next question is even more provocative: What's the point of banning certain categories of guns if at the same time up on the screen the gun is identified as a potent symbol of masculine force, the key to a whole identity, and the man who uses it becomes the central figure in what amounts to a religion of force?

Certainly, for both gun-haters and gun-lovers, much of our neurotic energy toward guns comes from the movies (and to a lesser extent, from television). Both shooters and non-shooters should be able to agree that gun deaths aren't going to be lessened until gun myths are; maybe a good place to start is Hollywood.

THE WILD, WILD WEST

"Death comes all at once, and how!"

UNFORGIVEN
August 7, 1992

"Unforgiven" tells the story of how the West was lost. It was lost, as was the East and the South and the North, to pointless, ugly violence, men with guns who couldn't imagine the pain their bullets would cause and who had no capacity to conceptualize the vacuum of loss they created when they killed.

It is, in short, the antithesis of all those heroic gunfighter movies and that national anthem of "killer as hero." Its characters aren't knights but mean and squalid psychopaths, as cagey as they are obdurate, bitter as snakes and ugly as sin.

Only in its final minutes does it somewhat squander its grip on the moral imagination, in a climax that seems oddly to undercut all that's come before and returns us to the hallowed sense of violence as cleansing, which so animates the world's true killers.

Clint Eastwood, who produced and directed as well as starred, plays William Munny, a reformed gunslinger or, in the argot of his times, assassin. The movie makes it clear he's less than a paragon: He was a heller with a gun, a back-shooter, unfazed by moral qualm. He could kill anything. Now, reformed by his late wife, he's taken up hog farming on a mud pie of a place somewhere on the vast and dreary prairies of the West, his killing all behind him.

But the hogs are dying of fever and his prospects are narrowing and he isn't getting any younger. When a young cowpoke calling himself the Schofield Kid (for the Smith and Wesson revolver he totes) comes along and tries to sign Munny up for a job of murder and $1,000, the old coot says yes, rounds up a chum (Morgan Freeman) and heads out. Their mission is to kill two cowboys who one night sliced up the face of a prostitute out of sheer cussedness.

What Munny discovers is nothing new to him but everything new to us: that when mortal matters are invoked, everything becomes murky. In fact, Eastwood's visual conception of the West is an expression of the moral funk of his universe: the press of leaden skies on a desolate mud flat where a town has been put, all of it rendered in the sepia of old photos and undistinguished soup.

Nothing is clear. The villainous cowboys don't seem quite so villainous, the sponsors of the reward don't seem quite so noble, and that paragon of morality, the sheriff, isn't quite so incorruptible. Eastwood's idea of law and order is founded on the principle that men who have been beaten to a pulp are unlikely to break the law.

The movie is definitely old-fashioned, not only in its choice of materials but in its storytelling methods (it was written 18 years ago, before the coming of today's hyperkinetic cutting rhythms). So it sometimes just seems to mosey along, exploring highways and byways, not nearly as sprightly as, say, Eastwood's own "The Outlaw Josey Wales." Its sense of narrative drift somewhat reflects the futility of the mission that its central trio has embarked upon.

So lax is the pace that the movie is continually discovering oddballs. The most charming and least relevant is Richard Harris as English Bob, a gunfighting dandy who shows up to claim the reward while radiating disdain for the rowdy colonials. It's a great pirouette of a performance, all foppish style and camera-hogging antics. But when English Bob meets Sheriff "Little Bill" Daggett (Gene Hackman), just as Harris the actor meets his match in the indefatigably avuncular Hackman, "Little Bill" lays such a whipping on English Bob that it sends the poor boy all the way back to Mayfair.

Bill Munny receives a similar drubbing. And so does his friend, Freeman. But Eastwood doesn't go home. He just decides to kill everyone.

This is the most troubling aspect of "Unforgiven." For two hours of its running time, it's an exercise in demythologizing.

Great gunhawks are revealed to be fraudulent; golden deeds of the past are shown as bunco jobs; courage turns out to be either a function of too much alcohol or not enough IQ (or both). The whole fable of the West is nothing more than an evil scam.

And the biggest scam artist of them all is Bill Munny, who snipes at a wounded, pleading man in one instance and then covers as his partner blows away another man perched on a toilet seat. "High Noon" it isn't; it's more like the darkest midnight of the American soul.

Perhaps the audience's blood lust has been engaged, and the weight of Eastwood's man-killing past is too powerful to deny. But it does seem to me that the movie finishes in a flourish that endorses rather than denounces the pulling of guns, making it seem cool rather than futile. In other movies that have studied the outlaw spirit — "Bonnie and Clyde," "The Wild Bunch" and even "Thelma and Louise" — the bad boys, no matter how lovable, have followed the dictates of their melancholy profession, taken their wages, and died.

The Eastwood solution is to yield to box-office formula in a demonic explosion of gunfire that feels straight out of the oldest and most unreflective B-westerns. It's a gunfight at the "I-am-not-OK Corral," and the movie ends on its most troubling note.

DANCES WITH WOLVES
November 21, 1990

"Dances With Wolves" is a bebop with revisionist history, an epic of smug hindsight. Exasperatingly, it's also wonderful.

How much easier if the movie were crummy and could be dismissed. But, damn its smarmy soul, it is beautifully watchable, a return to the visual vernacular of the western epic and all its old-fashioned scenic values sweeping, romantic, adventurous and enthralling.

It's almost a fable-pure account of a journey to a heart of lightness, the story of a man who discovers redemption exactly where it shouldn't be, among the people his own kind has declared savages.

Kevin Costner, who also directed in a pitch of high storybook lyricism, plays a young union cavalry officer, wounded and decorated late in the Civil War, who requests a trip west to see the frontier before, as he says, it vanishes.

That's anachronism No. 1. In 1864, the year of the story, the frontier had been the central fact of American life since 1620 (when the frontier was Massachusetts!). In 1864, the idea of its "vanishing" was literally inconceivable, as vast tracts of land were still unsettled, unpenetrated, and largely unknown. Costner gives his character an extremely convenient eco-visionary's sensibility about one century before such a mind-set existed on the planet.

That, in fact, is the method of the film: to judge the past by the standards of the present and to find it wanting. It's a marvelous platform from which to tell a story, and Costner struggles to keep it from becoming a pulpit. Yet, at the same time, it's somewhat disorienting and it diminishes the movie's deeper meanings with cheap pop sanctimony, '90s-style. It's particularly easy to be "against" Manifest Destiny in 1990, having benefited from its results for 90 years.

In any event, traveling westward to the Dakotas, Costner's Lt. John Dunbar encounters a rogue's gallery of insane or repulsive whites, including a suicidal post commander and a flatulent, repulsive, filthy wagoner. Then, by mysterious occurrence unexplained by the movie, he finds himself not only in command of an outpost but its sole inhabitant. He becomes the 7th Cavalry's resident Thoreau, his Walden a slatternly lean-to on the ocean of the prairie, his only companion an inquisitive wolf — anachronism No. 2 in the pragmatic hunting culture of the frontier — whom he bonds with rather than shoots.

The main thrust of the film, however, chronicles his adventures with his nearest neighbors, a tribe of Lakota Sioux. Much has rightfully been made of Costner's vision of Sioux culture and much is about to be made of it again. By far the best and most pleasing aspects of the three-hour-long "Dances With Wolves" cover the young officer's gradual absorption into the lives of the Indians. It has the purity of a boy's adventure fantasy to it.

Costner's Sioux may be romanticized, but they're not quite mythologized. As noble and photogenic as he lets them be, he never quite paints them as saints. He makes it clear, in the film's most thunderous passage, that they live by killing — and his account of a mounted buffalo hunt captures not only the explicitness of the ultimate stroke, but also the exultation of the hunt, and the sheer pleasure to it.

And he doesn't obscure or rosily tint their savagery: They are an iron age people, living in a world in which prisoners are rarely taken but scalps *always* are.

Reverentially, the script allows the actual Lakota to be spoken on screen, and the translations (the film is nearly two-thirds subtitled) reveal a language of subtlety, irony, wit and almost poetic precision. No cowabunga spoken here, Buffalo Bob. But more to the point, the Indian performers are brilliant. A romantic subplot involving a captured white woman, played by Mary McDonnell, sounds like it fell out of a time capsule from the '50s, but it works out well.

The other surprise is how funny "Dances With Wolves" is. In this regard, director Costner knows that his best resource is actor Costner. As Dunbar, Costner is the quintessential boy-man, a dreamer, achingly vulnerable, so desperate to be liked he seems more a Holden Caulfield than a John Wayne. He gets a great deal of comic mileage over the dignified reserve of the Sioux and their own sense of ethnocentricity as they attempt to comprehend the loony doings of this earnest bumbler (even his Civil War heroism is presented as a kind of lucky bumble rather than an explicit act of military heroism).

Unfortunately, blather takes over in the last reel. When the thoroughly assimilated Dunbar once again encounters white soldiers, he's shocked to discover what horrid, crude apes they are — a ludicrous stroke, since he's been in a combat army for several years.

Of course, these men soon reveal themselves to be the inevitable homicidal maniacs, and quickly cuff the officer — who, after all, has only deserted his post and given guns to the enemy — and haul him off for interrogation and trial.

The moral equation only works if it's pitched in hyperbolic absolute: If Indians are all noble and sweet and innocent, and whites are all despicable and violent (except for our hero), then there can be no doubts about the rightness of Costner's actions; but neither can there be any complexity, ambiguity or irony. Thus, leaving the imaginative zone for the political zone, it ceases to be a work of art and becomes a work of ideology. A shame, but not enough of a shame to ruin an otherwise wonderful experience.

POSSE
May 14, 1993

Mario Van Peebles didn't just want to make a western. He wanted to make *every* western. And in "Posse," he gets about 90 percent of them.

The movie is insanely ambitious, completely captivating and maybe only six plot twists too incoherent. It has style to burn; too bad it didn't burn a few pages of script somewhere in the process.

The curiosity is that Van Peebles, son of legendary Melvin Van Peebles of "Sweet Sweet-back's Baadassss Song," is much more interesting as a director than as an actor. The movie is constructed around his own screen presence, in the way that Eastwood built "Unforgiven" around himself and his ragged, steel-eyed, rat-trap of a face. Yet, as an icon, Van Peebles doesn't really have the smoldering force, the riveting sense of interior drama, to moor the piece. His main character, Jesse Lee, remains a remote and impassive center of this three-ring circus of a movie. Somehow you don't *feel* Jesse Lee, you only see him.

Jesse Lee is a buffalo soldier, an African-American infantryman with lots of plains service behind him, who finds himself in the middle of the Spanish-American War of 1898. Literally in the middle: The film opens in a huge battle, with palm trees exploding and Spanish bullets cutting through the high grass. He and his unit are sent by a cynical white officer (Billy Zane) to steal a Spanish gold shipment behind the lines. Only when they succeed (rather too easily) are they themselves ambushed. But they survive, manage to reach America from Cuba, and set out for the West, to right some past wrongs.

There, with his gang (the "Posse" of the title), he finds himself fighting against greedy interests, on the side of black settlers in a free town founded by his father (Robert Hooks). It sounds like a black-white kind of thing, but Van Peebles is too crafty to reduce issues to pure race, particularly where it may dilute box office. He appends a token white to the good black gang (Stephen Baldwin, who is very vivid) and he appends a token black (Blair Underwood) to the bad white gang. Is this progress or what?

That aside, Van Peebles the director clearly has a sense of history, both filmic and American. The movie is a kind of pick-hit of great moments from great westerns. He's particularly enchanted by the Italian Sergio Leone, who invented Clint Eastwood in "A Fistful of Dollars," and the movie is full of Leone's trademark moments of visual bravura, extremely formalized shots that reduce western themes to arrangements of totems: A favorite shows a close-up of boots scuffling in the dust and, in long focus, we see a gunfighter's opponent readying himself for slap-leather time.

But others have their moments, too: Van Peebles re-creates almost exactly — one might call it a quotation — the famous slow-motion shot from Sam Peckinpah's "The Wild Bunch," in which a slain gunman collapses through a plate glass window. Then there's a scene set — for no reason other than homage — in Utah's Monument Valley, which stood in the work of the great John Ford for just about every state west of the Mississippi except Hawaii, and if Ford had lived long enough, he'd have gotten to that.

At the same time, "Posse" aspires to restore a lost figure to historic status — the African-American cowboy. In this, the film is less than successful. In fact, as a goal, however estimable, it's almost contradictory to the film's showboaty style. The movie is so determinedly a movie, an artifice, that it seems to have nothing to do with any sort of reality. It's such a pastiche, an essay in visual bravado and fantasy, that it can have no other effect but to trivialize its very subject. It's a fantasy of a western, complete to a cast that's so hip-hop "cool" that it's hard to take as anything except a goof.

That's part of the insane overreach of the film. Still, the players are all good, although the movie is so crowded with faces that it could have used a few more characters and a few less moments of "hey, isn't that . . . ?" Among the "Isn't that's" are Pam Grier, Reginald VelJohnson, Tone Loc, Nipsey Russell, Isaac Hayes, Robert Hooks, Richard Jordan and Paul Bartel. Every time you see one of them, it takes a second to get back to what's going on in the story.

Van Peebles may have failed at rewriting history, but he's made a good stab at redefining folklore.

TOMBSTONE
November 24, 1993

With his handlebar mustache and high-Victorian wardrobe, Kurt Russell looks amazingly like the authentic Wyatt Earp, the architect of the gunfight at O.K. Corral in Tombstone, Ariz., in 1881. But that's where the authenticity in "Tombstone" stops — at the facial hair and morning-coat level.

A generally bad but quite entertaining revisionist romp through the saloons and brothels of the town too tough to die, "Tombstone" has great fun mixing styles, facts, wise cracks and archetypes in new and generally unrecognizable ways.

Wyatt, for example, is now a far cry from Henry Fonda's stately, taciturn icon of respectability in John Ford's 1946 "My Darling Clementine." He's that new guy thing, the "Paralyzed Male." In fact, indecision, regret, reluctance and confusion cloud him; he doesn't even want to make the long sloughing march through the dust to the corral where the drunken

Clantons are waiting. He hopes they'll sober up and go away. What, has he been dancing around the firelight with Robert Bly? Does he think it's the I'm-OK-you're-OK-corral?

In the Earp nuclear family, as "Tombstone" has it, the role of warrior male has been passed on to older brother Virgil, played by the stately, taciturn Sam Elliott as an icon of respectability. In fact, of the various cowboys and gundogs of "Tombstone," only Elliott would have been welcomed on a Ford set. All the others would be dismissed as Nancy Boys.

The movie is full of outlandish touches of the sort that would never have been permitted in the more austere and earlier incarnations of the genre. My favorite was a scene in which Doc Holliday (Val Kilmer) and Johnny Ringo (Michael Biehn) hurl Latin epigrams at each other in a flurry of erudite one-upmanship. It's a delicious conceit: gunmen as fallen intellectuals, Poe and Rimbaud, each on a course of glamorous Nietzschean self-destruction. Why is Johnny so bad, the dull Earp asks the poetic Holliday. He's getting revenge for the day he was born, responds Doc, who was evidently not a mere dentist but an M.D. and Ph.D. fresh over from the University of Vienna and his residency under Herr Doktor Freud.

Actually, Holliday and Ringo (first conceived as antagonists in John Sturges's "Gunfight at the O.K. Corral," with Kirk Douglas and John Ireland in the roles) are the main hoots of the film. Kilmer especially has a high old time. He plays Doc not as the consumptive, embittered alcoholic, but as a kind of ironic, poetic boulevardier, with drop-dead comedic timing and a golden boy's fascination for the flame. With his rolling, Virginia aristo-accent, he's more like a gallant young poet-officer heading out to the Western Front to kick the ball at the Hun while making merry quips.

Biehn's Ringo is a wild boy, with piercing eyes, world-class grace and the same nihilistic fire burning within. When he and Doc finally face off for the big gundown, it's one of the movie's few genuinely felt moments.

The rest is pretty much wreckage. "Tombstone" uses good actors promiscuously; it has a brilliant cast, much underused. There's Stephen Lang doing a Gabby Hayes imitation as Ike

Clanton. Powers Boothe dandies up his impersonation of Curley Bill Brocious to an alarming extent, as if he's afraid no one will notice him; Bill Paxton is sadly meek as Morgan, youngest of the Earps; Billy Zane has an incomprehensible turn as a kind proto-Brando who wanders among the shooters offering tragic profiles and meaningless sighs; Dana Delany is from the wrong planet; Jason Priestley is negligible; and Robert Burke (he was "RoboCop 3") is so low-profile I didn't even figure out who he was.

The gun violence is equally all over the map. For example, the famous corral shootout is pretty accurately re-created (at the halfway, rather than climactic, point). It was men in a space about as large as a rowhouse's back yard shooting at each other without bothering to take cover. Maybe a total of 30 shots; maybe a total of 10 seconds.

But then it becomes an Italian revenge job, and the blood and thunder inflate to operatic dimension, becoming not more dramatic but more ludicrous. John Ford would have thrown up.

WYATT EARP
June 24, 1994

It's as if they remember it wrong. Baby boomers, Kevin Costner and Lawrence Kasdan included, have the lyrics to a hundred mid-'50s TV series theme songs inscribed in their cerebellums, but somehow, when those two were calling up the last line from the hokey chorus to Hugh O'Brian's "Life and Legend of Wyatt Earp," they didn't remember: ". . . and long may his story be told."

Oh no. *They* remembered, ". . . and may his story be told long."

This may explain why the extreme length of "Wyatt Earp" pushes it beyond the merely mediocre and into the realm of the ordeal. In the packed theater where I saw it, the walk-outs began halfway through the first hour, and by the third hour — it's three hours and nine minutes long — women and children were being cavalierly trampled by bored men trying to beat it to the parking lot.

The first hour is junk. Really, wasted time: You'll do better, much better, if you check the starting times and show up an hour late. Young Wyatt, growing up on a farm in Missouri; Wyatt the buffalo hunter; Wyatt the married man; Wyatt the mourning husband (his first wife dies of typhoid; he burns the house down); Wyatt the drunken Arkansas horse thief.

Not merely does director Kasdan fail to weave these unrelated episodes into a theory of character while at the same time over-mythologizing them (assisted by the Big Important musical stylings of James Newton Howard), but he can't seem to get the story started. Nothing is happening, there's no real drama, other than the question: What will Kevin Costner do to his hair next? The episodes tell us nothing about the man Wyatt is to become; he seems born anew when he gets a job as a deputy marshal in Wichita, where his tactic of clobbering the bad boys first and only inquiring later as to whether or not they were really bad begins to earn him a reputation for controversy.

But the key question Kasdan never answers is: Why should we care? Costner isn't much help, either. His Earp is glum, oppressive, self-important, a dire presence. Contemporary accounts suggest that the real Wyatt had two extraordinary strengths: He was always deadly calm, and he was one of those rare men who was quite literally fearless. He'd just stand there, aim and fire, no matter the lead whizzing in the air. He himself expressed it most eloquently: "Take your time — fast."

The movie begins finally to find some shape when Wyatt, by then the unacknowledged Earp brother CEO (but why?), moves himself, his common-law wife and his brothers and their wives to Tombstone, Ariz., in 1880, in search of the entrepreneurial freedom to make money. What they found, of course, was another kind of El Dorado: The famous gunfight on Oct. 26, 1881, at Fly's Photographic Gallery. (A fact: the O.K. Corral was next door.)

This part of the film works largely because it's very difficult to screw up a gunfight in a movie. You have guns, you have men, you have shooting, what else do you need? But Kasdan comes very close to screwing it up. It was an enormously complex event, essentially involving the Earp boys, plus Doc Holliday, against two other clans — the Clantons and the McLowrys — as seen through a prism of intensely tangled municipal politics in a city that had two competing units of law enforcement — City Sheriff Johnny Behan (Mark Harmon) and U.S. Deputy Marshal Virgil Earp (Michael Madsen). Why did the fight happen? Kasdan has no idea. Who were the Clantons and the McLowrys? Don't ask Kasdan.

In fact, none of the many movie accounts of the famous fight, including the pulp "Tombstone" of last year, "Gunfight at the O.K. Corral" (1957), and "My Darling Clementine" (1946), has so completely botched the telling of the story and mangled the context so thoroughly. Thus, other than as an event of some compelling action dynamics, the gunfight has very little dramatic meaning. Who *are* these guys anyway?

I must say that to the degree that I understand it, the actual event is re-created authentically: Ike Clanton *was* unarmed. Billy Clanton *did* fight heroically; Wyatt *did* kill Frank McLowry and Doc *did* kill Tom McLowry with Virgil's shotgun. It was over in about 30 seconds; three men died, two (Virgil and Morgan Earp) were maimed for life, which in Morgan's case wasn't to be much longer. And no, contrary to the Burt Lancaster-Kirk Douglas version, Johnny Ringo, who had taken up with Doc's paramour, Kate "Big Nose" Elder, wasn't there.

As did "Tombstone," "Wyatt Earp" somewhat hastens through the aftermath of the fight, itself the subject of a movie (John Sturges's "Hour of the Gun"); and its last gunfight, a crazed shootout in a gulch, doesn't make a lot of sense and seems perfunctory. Doc kills Johnny Ringo in this one, but we have no sense of the drama between them; Wyatt also kills Curly Bill Brocious, an event unsupported by the historical record.

As is usual in these cases, it's Doc who gets all the good lines, though Dennis Quaid's lines aren't as good as Val Kilmer's in "Tombstone," nor is he as dynamic as Kirk Douglas in "Gunfight at the O.K. Corral." He's so gaunt he looks as if he's made out of bone china; I worried that one of his more complex epigrams would shatter his delicate bones.

Nothing really works. The sleepily dangerous Michael Madsen is lost as Virgil, JoBeth Williams and Catherine O'Hara never get a chance to do much but pout and simmer as various Earp brothers' wives, and Joanna Goings, as Wyatt's third wife, Josie, has far too contemporary a face and attitude for a period piece like this.

"Wyatt Earp" certainly never acquires the majesty, the thunder or the resonance of "Dances With Wolves" or even "Gunfight at the O.K. Corral." It's a myth in search of a man.

THE WILD BUNCH
April 2, 1995

One of the more amusing follies of the past several weeks has been America's film critics trying to come to some kind of terms with Sam Peckinpah's "The Wild Bunch," the newly restored "director's cut" which has just been released 26 years after its original, shocking arrival in 1969.

Most agree: It's a great movie. One even called it the greatest American movie ever made. But no one seems quite to understand why. There's a lot of blather about how it's really "anti-violence" and how it shows the logical consequences of violence, etc. etc. etc., blah, blah and blah. But none of it is convincing.

That's to be expected. "The Wild Bunch" is a confounding piece of work, and one could argue that its very greatness lies in the contradictions it so happily endorses. It's a movie that young people adore, but it's about old men. It's theoretically anti-violent, but it is clearly one of the most violent movies ever made; more troubling, its fundamental attitude toward violence is enigmatic, possibly unknowable, certainly inexpressible in the bromides that, then as now, pass for public discourse. It struggles with the issues of loyalty to brothers, or loyalty to a larger "code" that underlies not only the American West but the

American East as well and all of Hemingway and his clones, the boy-division in American literature; but unlike Hemingway and his clones, it comes to no clear conclusion.

It does not, really, endorse anything healthy. In fact, it bubbles with delight in making a fetish of America's most dangerous pathologies; gun worship, the will to violence, tribalism. It is aggressively racist; it is incidentally sexist. Its heroes are scum, and the lawmen chasing them even scummier.

It is the ultimate chasm movie. If you like it, your passion for it goes beyond words, a fact brought home by the reality that it is one of the most visually influential movies ever made, and one sees echoes of its imagery in hundreds of other movies. There isn't a director alive who doesn't wish he made "The Wild Bunch," with the possible exception of Nora Ephron. (Possibly somewhere there are women who care for it as powerfully as men do; I've certainly never met any.)

For those who hate it, no critic can salvage its reputation, no argument can resurrect it, no theory can justify it. It is simply an unspeakable object, an outlaw work. It might be the beginning of the tidal wave of vulgarity that has overwhelmed the American motion picture and the culture in general. It's the original and best pulp fiction, obsessed with the impact of bullets on flesh, that proudly beats out its anthem of anarchism throughout, reaching a last act Gotterdammerung of carnage the likes of which had not been seen before and has not since.

All this from a western?

Yes. "The Wild Bunch," to reduce it to genre, is of the set western, subset caper picture, sub-subset Mexican division. Its tone, in legend, derives from the fact that director Peckinpah was once talking to a genuine old-timer who informed him that the gunmen of the West weren't the paragons of virtue played on the screen but mean and bitter as tomcats — and that's one of the film's radical values, the way in which it clearly reinvents the image of the western hero by *inverting* it.

Its melancholy spirit, however, derives from another fact. It's a road picture, but a subset therein also — it's the best end-of-the-road picture ever made.

The road is the road of the American frontier, which illuminated this country's imagination for a century, bright with hope and possibility, full of freedom for personal expression, but also nascent with that fundamental American promise, which no European country could ever offer its common citizens: the freedom of room, of space.

But in 1913, the room is running out. The frontier is closing down, and like Vikings or Samurai, two other doomed warrior classes, the professional gunmen at the center of the movie are at least self-aware enough to realize it, even if they can't quite articulate it. They are caught between epochs, caught, as it were, between two kinds of .45s.

Pike Bishop, the outlaw chief, carries a Colt single action, the beloved six-shooter of 50,000 cowboy movies, the gun that Gene Autry and Roy Rogers and the Duke himself carried. But he also carries two .45 automatics, the Army 1911 model, which was much faster to shoot and reload. You laugh at a critic's obsessions with firearms? Fair enough, but in "The Wild Bunch," the firearms are more articulate than the men: They put Pike and the Bunch right on the cusp of the romantic old days turning into the mean new ones, as the movie, with its machine guns, trench shotguns and hand grenades, looks forward to a modern world where personal honor is impossible.

Led by shrewd, brave Pike (William Holden, whose once beautiful face by 1969 wore the imprint of several decades' saturation in expensive bourbon and looked like a Spartan shield after a long day at Thermopylae), the Bunch sets out on a futile last crusade for a big score, which ends up riding them straight into oblivion. They go down with guns in their hands, under the impression that that's what's expected of them and that they had no choice; and, to put it mildly, they do not go gently into that good night. Ask the Mexican Army at Agua Verde; they knew them well.

Pike's right-hand man is Dutch, an amiable killer played by Ernest Borgnine at his most avuncular. Dutch also is the mystical custodian of "the code," consistently issuing rulings on what is and what is not permissible, which the Bunch just as often disobeys as obeys. Two others are nasty, feral Texans, Lyle and Tector Gorch (Warren Oates and Ben Johnson, both superb);

there's the *de rigueur* old man, Eddie Sykes (Edmond O'Brien in his last great role); and finally a Mexican youth, Angel. He's played by Jaime Sanchez, a true surprise who stepped off the set of the cornball TV show "The Real McCoys," on which he played Pepito to Walter Brennan's crusty Grandpa McCoy; yet, in this movie, he's instantly sexy and dangerous. Why he never became a star is one of "The Wild Bunch's" eternal mysteries.

The first of the movie's moral switches opens the film. When first we see them, the Bunch rides into a west Texas town in the olive drab rectitude of the United States cavalry. Of course, they're not gallant soldiers; they're robbers, come to steal the payroll from the railroad, that font of capitalism and tyranny. Meanwhile, up on the roof, lurking in the shadows, is what might be nominally described as the other side of the moral equation, but is in reality another force for anarchy: a band of degenerate hillbillies, dismissed even by their own leader (Robert Ryan, another with a beautifully ruined face, in a late, elegiac performance) as "egg-sucking, chicken-stealing gutter trash." This mob has been hired by the railroad to gun down the Bunch; anybody who gets in the middle is out of luck.

That first sequence, utterly shocking, establishes the tone of the film to come. It's a gun battle that becomes a massacre in which the combatants don't give a gob of spit for anybody who passes between them. Men, women and children go down spastically. It also establishes the movie's prevailing image of a universe of fragility, apt at any moment to erupt into grotesque and unstoppable violence. Here and in subsequent sequences, Peckinpah pretty much re-invented the way violence was portrayed on screen, with excessive use of new "squib" technology, electronically detonated capsules of ersatz blood that replicated — or exaggerated — the impact of bullets striking the body and, occasionally, passing through and leaving it.

In fact, no film more convincingly dramatizes the body's vulnerability to gunfire, the sense of penetration and violation. One feels, as one never had, the passage of bullets through body, a metaphorical allusion not to being tagged but to being skewered. But Peckinpah also shot with multiple cameras at varying speeds and knit his action footage together in a terrifying rush of sensation driven forward by an incredibly sustained rhythm. To see the film is somehow to sink into the very essence of chaos. (In fact, several times more, Peckinpah brings us to the tippy edge of hell, as we struggle for balance. And in the last segment, he lets us fall.)

If it is a universe without physical stability, it is then, metaphorically, a universe without *moral* stability too. Most radically, there's no equation between virtue and courage, a new device in a movie culture that routinely portrayed evil as craven and cowardly. Pike and the Bunch are essentially tribal murderers, like marauding Goths, who have no empathy for those outside the group; Pike can callously reach down and peel a woman's bloody shawl off his stirrup, picked up when he trampled her to death. Yet they are almost unbearably brave. They take on overwhelming odds, confident in their courage and valor to vanquish them. And they have other virtues and defects of the warrior class: incredible cunning, lack of wider political allegiances (they glibly sell out their country), passionate tribal bonds and a willingness, finally, to face the consequences of their actions.

But what is so interesting about them is how confused they are. They stubbornly cling to their code. One problem: They have no idea what that code is. "We gave our word," Pike insists at one point.

"It's not that you gave your word," Dutch ripostes, "it's who you gave it *to*."

They squabble constantly over the issue of honor and behavior, lurching around for justifications of what their limbic systems compel them to do nevertheless.

If there's a value at the center of "The Wild Bunch," it's a love that dares to speak its name. It's nihilism. Somehow "The Wild Bunch" lingers and tantalizes because, way down in its medulla, in its ancient brain, it's in love with the terrible beauty of death. This will never be politically correct, unless you're a Nazi, and a psychiatrist would certainly have a great time with Peckinpah on the couch, exploring whatever tics and twitches drove him so self-destructively. Clearly, genius though he was, he never hugged his inner child.

But with nihilism comes another odd state of being: It's called liberation. The reason the movie is so invigorating is that it postulates a freedom from fear. There comes a point when the Bunch, or what remains of it, gives it all up.

"Let's go," Pike says to Lyle.

Lyle squints, and what passes for thinking flashes electrically through his tiny brain; and then he says, "Why not?"

He and Pike step outside, where Dutch and Tector wait. They lock and load, fiddle with their gear, and start a long, shuffling walk toward what they know will be their own deaths. Unlike the heroic mannequins who customarily inhabit the center of the Hollywood movie, these are truly believable characters, not so much warts and all as *all warts*, but the film sells the freedom they feel as powerfully as any movie has sold any emotion.

They don't walk into hell: They *are* hell, come for breakfast. You may not love them — indeed, if you do, you're probably pretty sick yourself. But the movie invites you on that long walk into the last fight, and it invites you to face the ugly truth that your inner child may be a nasty little brute with a .45. It's like other great works of profound and bitter misanthropy, such as "Lord of the Flies" or "Day of the Locusts" or "Death on the Installment Plan," except that in its coils, death comes all at once, and how!

THE FUTURE

"Smiling through the apocalypse"

TOTAL RECALL
June 1, 1990

What if you woke up one day and remembered that you were
somebody else? And what if, as soon as you started to remember, people tried to kill you? That's what happens to Arnold
Schwarzenegger in "Total Recall."

"Total Recall" is no standard-issue Schwarzenegger epic,
though its co-stars might be said to be guns and death. Instead,
it issues from the same distinctly ungentle imagination of the
Paul Verhoeven who was last represented on screen with the
astonishing "RoboCop," after a distinguished if equally ungentle European career. Thus, Verhoeven's "Total Recall" is of the
same powerful brew of violence and intellect, violence and originality, violence and mordant humor, and violence and perversity that marked "RoboCop." (Also, the movie is very violent.)

Schwarzenegger, an Earthbound construction worker in the
totalitarian year 2084, with a stable job and a voluptuous wife
(Sharon Stone), finds himself troubled by dreams of experiences in the Martian colonies. This is strange, as he's never
been to Mars and the place is an unlovely land, where a greedy
mining combine controls and exploits its workers, selling them
the very air they breathe while requiring slavelike efforts to
retrieve a profitable ore necessary for war back on Earth.

When he makes an effort to discover the source of his mal-
ady, and the large angry men with guns attempt to kill him,
Schwarzenegger makes a further discovery: Not only does he
seem to be somebody else, but he has somebody else's nasty
skills, and with terrifying swiftness, he manages to kill four men
in close-quarters combat.

It turns out — or so he thinks — that he's the Martian rebel
Quaid, a lieutenant in the underground struggles against Mars's

dictatorial boss Cohagen (Ronny Cox). He's been captured, and his mind has been (inefficiently) erased, and he has been given the new wife and the new identity. On the run, he meets a new confederate: himself. Or rather, the self he was before the mind erasure, in the form of a videotape in which Old Quaid briefs New Quaid on what to do and where to go. This is an interesting science fiction theme, used by Kurt Vonnegut as well as Philip K. Dick, whose original story suggested the plot of "Total Recall": a former self, much more learned, addressing a new self, with instructions. In this film, Schwarzenegger really does learn how to be his own best friend.

Everywhere Quaid goes, Verhoeven shows us miracles. He also shows us why this movie cost over $50 million, and why it might have been worth it. Earth, for example, looks like a large junior college in California; Mars is a cheesy, rude, underground frontier town, where strippers and whores and dope dealers do what they can to distract from the misery, but overhead, a "cheap dome" doesn't quite keep out the intense sunlight, and genetic mutations are common.

Verhoeven's sense of humor is subversive. He gives us a moment when a beautiful woman gets shot point-blank in the head and we cheer. He invites us to laugh over the humorously grotesque mutations. He makes us giggle with horror when we meet the legendary Quato, the leader of the resistance. This baby has to be seen to be believed. And he gets great mileage out of Sharon Stone, heretofore merely a nubile presence in a few undistinguished movies. Stone, far from the dim Stepford wife she seems in the first few minutes, soon reverts to her own identity as a highly efficient security agent who's quite capable of going one-on-one with Arnold — or with anybody. And her treachery sets up the film's best line — about instant divorce. You know Arnold — always making mit dose visecracks.

But there's a curious irony to "Total Recall" involving Schwarzenegger. The film wouldn't exist without Schwarzenegger, who found the script and battled for it, who encouraged his producers to hire Verhoeven on the strength of "RoboCop," who quite decently allowed the director his vision of the film, and who clearly did not insist on being at the center of every scene.

The movie would not exist without Arnold Schwarzenegger, and yet Schwarzenegger's limits are exactly what limit the film. Unlike "RoboCop," which featured a gifted actor like Peter Weller, Schwarzenegger is never quite able to bring Quaid to the kind of duality of mind the film seems to require of him. Basically, this is a $50-million "Dr. Jekyll and Mr. Hyde" remake, and its deepest moments represent the age-old fight in a man's soul between his good and bad selves — the movie's best surprise is the other self in Quaid. But Schwarzenegger, so physical a presence (he looks great running, jumping and shooting), just hasn't the skill to bring out the richer dimension of theme.

Arnold's presence guarantees that it could be made, but also guarantees that it remains a great thriller, not a great movie.

ROBOCOP
July 17, 1987

Imagine the Tin Man from "Wizard of Oz" with Dirty Harry's outlook and Rambo's machine-pistol, and you'll get a pretty good feeling for "RoboCop."

Bloody, sarcastic, clever, set in the funky-junky-punky retro future just around the rusty corner, the movie is paced more swiftly than the several hundred speeding bullets that rattle through it; it's a great, ugly comic strip of urban angst. It represents, moreover, a peculiar and beguiling union of sensibilities. In its glossy, high-tech look and flamboyant special effects, it represents the very best of big-budget American movie-making; but in its mordant darkness and sense of the fantastic, it displays the kinky ethos of the Dutchman Paul Verhoeven, who has made his mark with such eccentricities as "The Fourth Man" and "Flesh and Blood."

Verhoeven has seen the future and it doesn't work. (He's also seen "Blade Runner," "Brazil" and "1984.") Crime in

"Old Detroit" has gone berserk, and gun-happy gangs roam the urban wilderness, shooting holes in every thing and every body that gets in the way, including policemen, 32 of whom have died recently. Even though the police department has been taken over by private industry, things haven't changed much. As the movie begins, a new young officer named Murphy (Peter Weller), for one, is assassinated rather routinely by a sadistic gang of cutthroats.

But the OmniConsumer Corp. has wider plans, hoping to replace all policemen with a large mechanical chicken, armed with 20mm cannons, that is known as ED-209. Except the ED-209 accidentally blows away a marketing executive. Oops! And when ED-209 is put on the back burner, a hot young exec sees his chance and sells the corporation on the RoboCop concept, which takes the body of the dead cop out of cold storage, re-animates it with state-of-the-art electronics, drop-dead hydraulics, a computer program and full-automatic firepower capacity, as designed by someone who spent a childhood looking at Buck Rogers comic strips. The result is something that looks like an art deco Transformer with a human chin who moonwalks when he does the locomotion — and who kicks ass.

As conceived by screenwriters Edward Neumeier and Michael Miner, "RoboCop" has at least three sardonic levels of plot to it. In the first of these, the man left in "Robo" struggles to come to terms with the machine that is most of him, as poignant memories of home and family, supposedly destroyed in a mind-wipe, keep flooding in. In still another, the corporation is the battleground, as the hot young exec (Miguel Ferrer) finds himself in mortal struggle with his immediate supervisor (Ronny Cox) for the favor of the chairman of the board; and in still a third, the gang that shot straight into Murphy finds itself being shot at, with a vengeance, by RoboCop.

Verhoeven manages to keep these three stories whirling along, and in the end also manages to unify them into a coherent, ironic and very funny whole; as a plot, "RoboCop" is pop pulp at its most pulpily pop. Yet, "RoboCop's" enormous sense of humor — particularly as it scores points off the rampant careerism that has turned the American corporation into something nobody could have imagined — isn't quite funny enough to blur the impact of its considerable violence.

Verhoeven happens to be drawn more to evil than to good, which may explain why his villains (Cox and Ferrer and gang chief Kurtwood Smith) are so much more vivid than Weller. It's not merely that Weller spends a full four-fifths of the film encased in his RoboCop suit and is therefore denied access to the actor's means of expression, such as voice, face and eyes. Rather, it's that when he's not shooting bad guys, Robo isn't that interesting, and Weller, who seems somehow squirrely and evasive, can't find enough texture for the role.

But the movie is deeply amusing in all other respects. As a piece of design work, it's enormously clever, particularly as production designer William Sandell gets modern Dallas to stand in for next year's model of Detroit. And Sandell, or whoever imagineered ED-209, has a great gift for witty machines: ED manages to be scary as hell and hilarious in its bumbling literalness. And there's a terrific sequence in which Murphy's reincarnation is miraculously presented from his point of view, as a TV screen flicks on, has trouble focusing, then locks in: presto, life!

In all, "RoboCop" is pretty special, walking the line between the tacky, the profound, the bloody, and the hilarious with great adroitness. It's more fun than a barrel of mechanical monkeys.

THE ROAD WARRIOR
August 20, 1982

When the Australian director George Miller yells "Action," he isn't just whistling "Waltzing Matilda" — he means it.

And if you're a purist and believe a movie is first of all motion and energy, then you're led to one conclusion: "The Road Warrior," Miller's new film, is some kind of wild masterpiece.

This is exactly the work of soaring, billowing spirit and crackpot genius that John Milius was trying to achieve with his oddly leaden "Conan the Barbarian." But where "Conan" was self-indulgent, sluggish, peculiarly pompous, "The Road Warrior" is swift, lean, and brilliantly conceived.

It imagines and makes real and internally consistent a whole, ugly world; it fills that world with believable, albeit exotic, characters, about whom it seduces us into caring intensely, and it sets them in motion in a story that moves like a punched double-barreled 420 GTO across a salt flat.

Set 15, maybe 25 years in the troubled future, it depicts the world "after the gasoline wars." Society has come unraveled; small groups of people forage together across a barren landscape (which is, but doesn't have to be, Australian) and try to avoid marauding bands of punk killers, predators who roam in garish outfits aboard garish vehicles. Gas is more precious than life itself; gas *is* life.

Clearly, aside from certain technical details, the setting could be just as easily anywhere in the troubled past: in the West, say, in 1868, after the Civil War; or in Japan after the fall of the Shogunate in the 16th century, when roving bands of Samurai fended for themselves; or even long, long ago in a galaxy far, far away. Miller has universal archetypes in mind; and without laboring the point excessively, it's self-evident that he conceives of storytelling on a kind of primal level: These aren't romances he's spinning, but myths.

In this wasteland, we discover a lone, resolute but typically cynical hero. Max, with his tired dusty leather, knee brace, and burnt-out but still wary eyes, has something of the gunslinger to him, something of the Samurai and something of Sir Percival. But he feels all new. He's the post-industrial man, just as he's also a little prehistoric. Max (whose early life was sketched in "Mad Max," Miller's first film) comes across a small fortified settlement besieged by punk guerrillas. When he rescues some fleeing survivors and earns entry, he learns of the treasure the settlers have accumulated: They've distilled a tanker-full of gasoline.

From there issues a story so basic it's almost primitive and is told almost wordlessly: The settlers ask Max to help them get the gas out and themselves to a better life. He agrees, for a price. But as he performs, he finds himself drawn deeper and deeper into their community; and at the end, Miller has you understanding how much more is at stake there than a tankful of juice.

Max, played by Mel Gibson (of "Gallipoli," as well as "Mad Max") with crackling toughness and authenticity, is only the first of a whole gallery of unusual and enchanting characters filling "The Road Warrior." There's the Gyro Captain, a throwback to the aviators of the 1914–18 war, who flies an autogyro and wears a leather pilot's helmet, leather coat and puttees; the feral boy, speechless, filthy but clever; and the Humungus, leader of the marauders, with a Mr. Universe body and hideously scarred face hidden behind a hockey mask (echoes of Darth Vader).

But Miller's most spectacular creation is Wez (Vernon Wells), Max's special nemesis and perhaps one of the most flamboyant movie villains since Jack Palance shot his way through "Shane." Wez is all punk. With shrieking mohawk haircut and tattered leathers and bulging bare arms, he's got a malevolent athletic grace to him, a fury that radiates. Wells is an extraordinary physical actor. He moves with great precision and force, and although the part is conceived on a grand, almost operatic scale (as is, indeed, the whole film), his performance never becomes sheer, narcissistic hamminess. He always finds ways to communicate Wez's low cunning, his intelligence.

As a director, Miller has studied his predecessors well. He has John Ford's sense of landscape — he gets Australia to look like Ford's fabled Monument Valley — and also Ford's feeling for the heroic composition. When his lone, bleeding hero, like a tired athlete, stands silhouetted against the twilight, his face grim and drawn, it's like seeing John Wayne as the Ringo Kid in "Stagecoach" all over again. This shot is so formal it's almost a cliche; what enables Miller to get away with it, to revise and revive it, is his wonderful sense of detail and Gibson's physical authority.

Miller has Sergio Leone's talent for texture. There's nothing bland and clean about Max's world, as there was nothing bland and clean about the world of the Man With No Name. Miller makes you feel the grit and the dust almost down to the individual particle; he makes you feel the wind pushing across the desert, and the give and spread of the old leathers the characters wear. (His cinematographer Dean Semler must be a genius.)

But what gives "The Road Warrior" its special sizzle are the action sequences, and there's perhaps no better director with cars in the world today than Miller. His climax follows Max as he breaks loose from the settlement in a huge tractor trailer, hauling the gas. As he penetrates the lines of the besiegers, they leap to follow him, and what ensues is an epic, almost 30-minute pursuit across the desert, as, one by one, the punks come at Max and one by one he battles them off.

Miller choreographs dozens of vehicles in this sprawling, high-speed combat, sweeping, swirling, choking on dust; man leaping from car to truck and back again, punching and shooting. Miller's talent is for *timing*. He keeps building and building, cutting away, splicing together pieces of film in an extraordinary symphony of motion. (His stunt crew deserves medals for its work.)

A subtle touch helps hold it together — a soundtrack whose basic thrust is a steady, humming road, to suggest the power and drive of the vehicles, with other refrains built on top of it.

Charlie Chaplin once said that only chases and fights were pure cinema. By that standard, "The Road Warrior" is so pure it's sanitary. This is storytelling through pictures raised to the level of art.

It may be narrow, and nobody would say it has much of a brain in its head, but it's a little like an athlete: You don't expect ideas from it, you expect performance.

"The Road Warrior" performs — and how!

ALIENS
July 18, 1986

If you can imagine a film equally loved by subscribers of *Ms.* and *Soldier of Fortune*, then you can begin to appreciate the appeal of James Cameron's "Aliens."

This new movie might be looked at as "Wonder Woman vs. Them!," pitting an extraordinarily forceful woman against an insectoid enemy in a battle to the death. But it's also a demonstration of the flexibility of genre; it shows how forms can accommodate new meaning.

Ridley Scott's original "Alien," of 1979, was nominally a science-fiction film, but in execution was closer to a slasher movie, chronicling with escalating horror the methodology by which a psychotic killer zapped one by one the inhabitants of a haunted house (all right, it was a spacecraft) until only the virtuous woman remained. So is this sequel nominally a science-fiction film, being set in the future and deploying the icons of science fiction; but it's really a war movie, chronicling the methodology of a Marine platoon off on a heavy-contact combat mission.

And in case I'm sounding too much like a college professor (God help me), then let me be absolutely clear about one thing: "Aliens" is one hell of a movie.

It opens 57 years after the close of Ridley Scott's film, with Ripley (Sigourney Weaver), the sole survivor of the space freighter Nostradamus, at last being picked up in deep space. She's not a day older because she's been hibernating all this time.

After making her report, she's asked to return to the planet of the space killers, where, in the interim, a colony has been set up, along with an oxygen-generating system, which means James Cameron's gyrenes do not have to wear Ridley Scott's cumbersome deco space helmets. She is asked to accompany a Marine probe of the place since all communication has been lost.

For reasons that don't make sense but don't really have to make sense, she agrees; once there, it's war day.

As he demonstrated in "The Terminator," Cameron is a terrific action director. As a vigorous and adrenaline-pumping orchestration of escalating thrills, a more powerful movie has not been put together since "The Terminator" and, before that, "The Road Warrior." The climactic sequence, in which Weaver, with the assistance of a fabulously designed "lifter" — that is, a pneumatic exoskeleton that turns her into a kind of superwoman — goes one-on-one with the meanest mother (literally) of the alien species, is one of the most extraordinary action sequences ever filmed.

Cameron also is witty. He's got a great sense of the wisecrack, and of the jostling macho Marine platoon culture (although the platoon is coed). He's capable of playing games with Scott's signature, the atmosphere seething, however illogically, with smoke. (His frame, however, tends to be less crammed with information.) But there's something subtler, a little bonus for movie mavens. Scott, it is widely acknowledged, borrowed a lot of his imagery from Mario Bava's 1965 "Demon Planet." In the same way, Cameron makes use of a '50s horror film, Gordon Douglas's feisty "Them!," borrowing particularly the imagery of a rescue of an endangered child through dangerous corridors; and, secondly, the imagery of the burning of an egg chamber deep in the center of a nest.

Yet, as much as I admire "Aliens" and as much fun as I had, it still strikes me as somewhat a lesser accomplishment than either "The Terminator" or "Alien." This is because each of those films had something that Cameron has chosen to exchange for mechanical spectacle: intimacy.

What gave "Alien" its terrible power was a sense of claustrophobia in the sweating chambers of the ship; what gave "The Terminator" its juice was the passionate hate between Arnold Schwarzenegger and Michael Biehn and the passionate love between Biehn and Linda Hamilton. Underneath all the ultraviolence, there beat a romantic heart.

In "Aliens," the relationships are pretty much pro forma, as are the personalities; even Biehn, billed as co-star, is a hazily imagined regular guy without a lot of specificity to his character. His relationship with Weaver is a major unrealized asset in the picture; they josh like guys, but there's no passion at all.

The real passion in the movie, at least in theory, is between Weaver and Carrie Henn, as a young child and the one survivor the platoon finds on the planet. In an early cut of the picture, Weaver was revealed to have been a mother whose daughter grew up and died during the 57 years of her snooze; thus the Henn-Weaver relationship was designed to take on even more powerful overtones.

The core of "Aliens" is that it's a mother picture. Unfortunately, Henn is Cameron's biggest mistake. He has no ability to write the tender dialogue between them, and the exchanges always ring false. Secondly, he uses the kid as a chipper little morale officer and gives her a lot of wisecracks and funny business, all of which ring patently false.

Still, it's the maternal subtext to the picture that gives the climactic sequence such power. Besides the sheer transcendent believability of it, it also has an extraordinary resonance. Both contestants are female and both are parents; we very much have a sense of two moms squaring off to determine the destiny of the universe. It's Earth Mother vs. the Grandma from Another Planet.

BLADE RUNNER
June 28, 1982

Ridley Scott's brave new film, "Blade Runner," shows the future — and on the whole, I'd rather be in Philadelphia.

Scott's ambitious, dense and stylized detective thriller, set in an incredibly detailed Los Angeles of 2014, may be this year's doomed dazzler, a film that's brilliant and magical, but utterly incapable of generating the kind of mass audience response it needs to justify its $30 million price tag.

If you go expecting to see "Star Wars III" or "Raiders of the Lost Ark 2," you'll be bitterly disappointed; worse, you'll be bored. It's more like "Chinatown in Tomorrowland," or "Sam

Spade Visits Alphaville," tracing its lineage back through Polanski and Goddard to hardboiled, shadowy classics like "The Big Sleep" and "The Maltese Falcon." But it's also only itself, as it defines and explores what must be a new genre altogether: high-tech sci-fi film noir.

Based on a novel by Philip K. Dick, "Blade Runner" seems to be set in a future that's projected from 1940s culture and is filled with '40s memorabilia: trenchcoats, big automatics, shadows on the walls, laconic, hooded dialogue, diamond-hard existentialism, a cast that's at its most eloquent with its eyes, and some of the best movie smoking in years. Like a '40s thriller, it's got a story that twists tortuously, demanding that you master a specialized vocabulary in order to follow it. If you go for popcorn, you may as well head for the car.

No American film has yet looked (or I'd guess *will* look) this good this year. Scott, whose first film, "The Duellists," was also a feast for the eyes, packs his frame with details: In fact, the movie is so visually rich it really requires a minimum of two viewings before the fretwork ceases to dazzle enough so that you can really concentrate on the story, which may be its fatal flaw in the marketplace.

Art director David Snyder and production designer Lawrence G. Paul, guided by consultant (billed in the credits as "Visual Futurist") Syd Mead, have collaborated on a vision of the future that is at once instantly weird and instantly familiar. Their key concept is "retro-fitting," which means, basically, that the future has been built in and around the rubble of the present.

Sleek, mile-high skyscrapers rise above tawdry, neon-bleary, garbage-strewn streets. Old buildings sit like mushroom stalks among the roots of the newer structures. Pipes bleed steam or smoke into the air; it's always raining, it's always crowded, it's always spooky. The special effects, by Douglas Trumbull, who worked on "2001," are spectacular, but the controlling imagery may be derived from Heavy Metal comics, particularly those by a gifted French artist who calls himself Moebius.

Cinematographer Jordan Cronenweth, who shot the distinctive "Cutter's Way," films all this in a palette of inky-shadowed blue-violet, with the neon signs showing like bright gashes in the night. (There seems to be no day at all in 2014.) The prevailing fashions are punk and media: Ads blink or beep or wiggle everywhere. Cars (called "spinners") whizz through the thick, damp air, and giant, light-spangled blimps sail above, broadcasting advertisements for the joys of the "Off-World."

But the streets remain mean — and street talk is an ugly patois of Japanese and Spanish. Another of the key ideas is that American culture, at the lowest level, has been somehow "Nipponized," and when Harrison Ford, as an ex-cop named Rick Deckard, prowls the alleys of L.A., he could be lost on the Ginza Strip.

Deckard packs what looks like an .83 Magnum and wears a trenchcoat that covers his shoe tops. He needs a haircut and probably hasn't brushed his teeth in a month. When we discover him, he's sitting in a pile of garbage in the rain, reading a wet paper, looking for work.

"They don't advertise for killers in a newspaper," Deckard tells us in voiceover, mimicking the tough-guy style of Philip Marlowe's clipped, poetic narration, "and that was *my* profession."

Work finds him, in the form of his ex-boss, Captain Bryant of the Rep-Detect squad of the cops, who wants him back on the team.

It seems that four replicants — genetically engineered humans built for hazardous duty in planetary exploration but lately mutinous — have commandeered a shuttle and landed in the city. Deckard is an ex-"blade runner" — a replicant hunter. His job is to "retire" them: in short, to blow them away.

Why kill the reps? The answer is left unstated: Presumably, because of their superiority, they would quickly infiltrate and take over society if left unchecked.

What follows is a morally complex double-hunt (with romantic complications) as Deckard stalks the four replicants while they in turn try to get close to the genius, Elden Tyrell, who designed them, in order to solve the mystery of their own destiny. But Deckard falls in love with Tyrell's assistant, Rachel (played by Sean Young, who appeared in "Stripes"), and it gives nothing away to reveal that Rachel turns out to be a replicant herself.

The four replicants are led by Roy, played by the Dutch actor Rutger Hauer. Hauer, who is given a stylized diction that approaches blank verse, is a frightening concoction. With snow-white hair and electric blue eyes, he's a commanding figure: more than human. Yet the maturity and ambiguity of the story demand that he be *only* human in his quest for survival, and in great anguish over the deeper contradictions of his situation. It's a remarkable performance that never veers into parody: He could ruin the film if he came on like a Batman villain. He never does.

Young isn't bad in a somewhat limiting role — both Daryl Hannah and Joanna Cassidy as other replicant women register more flamboyantly — and her part seems tailored out of old Joan Crawford bits; her broad-shouldered wardrobe is pure Crawford, too. But she has a wonderful moment — stolen, no doubt, from a dozen '40s movies — when she undoes the pins that hold her hair in place, and the stuff falls about her lovely face and speaks of erotic abandon more eloquently than all the writing and pumping in "Behind the Green Door."

Scott's camerawork is slow and majestic and his editor has put the film together in a pace that might be termed stately, rather than kinetic.

But "Blade Runner" has something no other big film of the summer has — it's got the nerve to expect you to come to it, instead of its going to you.

It will fail, for just that reason, and for just that reason, the failure is noble.

WAR

"The charisma of brutality"

FULL METAL JACKET
July 10, 1987

Put simply, "Full Metal Jacket," Stanley Kubrick's devastatingly brilliant new film, is about turning boys not into men but into bullets.

A "full metal jacket," in the argot of small-arms ammunition, is a lead-cored 7.62mm bullet sheathed in copper for the M-14 rifle. The lead provides density for kinetic energy, while the copper provides hardness for penetration. The result is something that flies with terrible swiftness where it is pointed and, when it lands, does massive damage — if it hits its target.

To pursue the ballistic analogy, as I believe Kubrick intends, the movie watches as the density of individual personality is sheathed, however imperfectly, in hard copper by the rigors of Marine boot camp; then it continues as the young boy-bullets are fired at the enemy in the battle of Hue City, in South Vietnam, during the Tet offensive of 1968. The results, as with any high-powered round, are terrifying, a little awesome and finally sickening: Some hit, but most are wasted pointlessly, to fly off and disintegrate in little puffs of far-off dust. (The profligacy of gunfire, as storms of wild bullets lash out to tatter the world, underlies one of the visual motifs of the film.)

Yet so analyzed, the movie sounds traditional and embittered, a sort of "Platoon II." Not so: Kubrick is not a traditional storyteller, and he resists providing viewers with simple attitudes. His goal — he achieves it magnificently, though at some risk and high cost — is to provoke and confound. The movie leaves you in turmoil. He is not merely saying, "War is hell." He is saying, "War is hell, and yet men love it and it is somehow a profound and absorbing human experience. What does it mean?" In the end, for Kubrick, war is like the black monolith at the center of his most famous film, "2001": It is dense and impressive, yet ultimately unknowable. In fact, the two movies might be seen as companion pieces: In the first, Kubrick looked off the earth to man's fondest hope, the stars, and could fathom nothing; in the second, Kubrick looks into the earth at man's darkest folly and discerns the same terrible mystery.

I suspect, for that reason, that those caught up by the tidal gush and flow of emotion, and by the glibness, of "Platoon" will be disappointed in Kubrick's rigorous, almost ascetic approach to Vietnam. He's not an in-your-face filmmaker; he doesn't rub your nose in the is-ness, the there-ness, of the experience. And indeed the film is at its worst when it's trying to make "Apocalypse Now" style points about the absurdity and surrealism of it all. Rather, even at its most intense, the movie insists on remaining cool and composed. At every step of the way, Kubrick is hovering on the edge of abstraction, and the movie is so formally beautiful, like an austere, symmetrical French garden, that it's an astonishment to experience the pain and trauma it finally delivers.

The film begins in an almost operatic 45 minutes set on Parris Island, S.C., during the terrifying initiation into Marine Corps culture known as boot camp. Kubrick, economic and focused, simply plunges into the center of the process and therefore duplicates the recruits' terror and disorientation. It's as if they've just been born into a horrible new world, and their obstetrician is gunnery Sgt. Hartman, the drill instructor, as formidable a man as ever strode to the center of a screen.

Hartman is played by a former Marine drill instructor named Lee Ermey, who also served in Vietnam and helped Kubrick invent the James-Joyce-like dense patois of scatological profanity that defines Hartman and corrupts the air. His is a terrible yet profoundly attractive character. You sense his heroism just as you sense his cruelty, his ruthlessness. At the same time, he has an extraordinary sense of humor; not to make it sound like a comedy (though in a fashion it is), but these long 45 minutes at boot camp are just as nervously hysterical to watch as they must have been barely endurable to survive. Yet Hartman's terrible beauty is somehow the key to the film: He is Father

War, war itself, terribly cruel, terribly charismatic, terribly fascinating, a widow maker and mother crusher and yet a god to boys. (It's a great performance, by the way.)

Gradually, the boys, like new-born chicks flicking bits of shell and yolk out of their eyes, begin to focus, and as they do, they come *into* focus. The two most closely observed are Joker (Matthew Modine), the barracks ironist and intellectual, and "Gomer" Pyle, the barracks fool. Pyle, played with animal passion and pain by Vincent D'Onofrio, is a large, soft, stupid boy who attracts hurt like a human magnet. He becomes Sgt. Hartman's special project — there's one in every platoon — and he comes to absorb the sergeant's fury: His lumpy lead is particularly difficult to sheath in hard copper.

And then, of course, because the most terrifying thing about the system is that it works, Gomer literally *becomes* a bullet. His story ends with the bang rather than the whimper, and leaves viewers staggering and disoriented. Cut to Vietnam, some months later.

I think one brilliance of "Full Metal Jacket" is Kubrick's refusal to join the two halves of his story together neatly. A lesser filmmaker would have been more didactic in the connection, tidier. Kubrick, however, leaves the connection rough and suggestive and allows us to fit together the pieces by our own theory. He seems to pick up his themes and re-deploy them, and yet he's never terribly explicit about this, just as he wasn't explicit in joining the ape sequence to the space sequence in "2001."

We discover, in the film's weakest, middle third, that Joker has become a marine combat correspondent, writing bland agitprop for *Stars and Stripes* while cultivating a fashionable antiwar attitude. Here, Kubrick slithers about, and one can feel the influence of co-writer Michael Herr, who wrote the hallucinatory memoir "Dispatches" and co-wrote "Apocalypse Now" for Francis Ford Coppola. There's a lot of black humor about cynical media coverage, visiting movie stars, pompous colonels, psychotic door gunners: It's all familiar, and it was much more pointed in earlier incantations. There are even a few sad moments when Kubrick seems to be ripping off the black sensibility of his great "Dr. Strangelove."

But soon enough, "Full Metal Jacket" finds its way again; the
movie settles in for a terrifying account of a Marine patrol
through the ruins of Hue, when Joker and his photographer
attach themselves to a platoon to get some "trigger time," as
they refer to it cynically. But the result is anything but cynical.

There's something weirdly transcendent about these final 45
minutes. Yes, that's Hue, those are demonstrably Marines, and
that's definitely a Vietnamese sniper; but as these men stalk
and slay each other in the maze of the wrecked city, the scene
takes on the imprint of an ancient ritual, losing contact with the
specific and blurring into the universal. It's not merely that the
grunts become all grunts, as this war becomes all war; rather it's
a sense that war is the most profound expression of the basic
evil of humanity. Kubrick ties it all together in a climactic moment, when the hated enemy stands before the gun-mad boys,
and we feel their rage — and a deeper horror at the world's
excess of pain.

The final brilliance is the way Kubrick inverts the meaning of
the point-blank gunshot that climaxed the earlier section; in a
mad world, murder can be the inevitable consequence of a
hideous system. But it can be — is this a final grace note amid
the rubble? — a mercy.

Kubrick isn't and never has been an optimist, and the movie
ends with a bleak image: His Marines, having survived the caldron and surrendered on all human fronts, are left with no big
concepts to celebrate, only their own sense of rampant selfhood. It's chilling but it's terribly real, and if nothing else sums
up the waste and slaughter of the Nam, it's that one last moment. The guys sing, "M-I-C K-E-Y M-O-U-S-E!!!"

PLATOON
January 16, 1987

The accolades for "Platoon" have been piling up like bodies in front of a machine-gun position. And there's much to praise: The movie has the certitude of utter conviction. It's like a long year in hell, a harsh and convincing evocation of war at the grunt level, as fought by the reluctant troops of the 25th Infantry Division in 1967.

As a portrait of bad soldiers in a bad unit led by bad officers in a bad war, it's a scorching examination of what went wrong in Vietnam. (Its answer is, everything.) As a vision of the human capacity for evil, it's terrifying. As an orchestration of sensations, it's brilliant. As a work of small-group sociology, it's illuminating. As a piece of archaeology, it's first class: It's got the details all right, from the slouchy insouciance of the teen-agers festooned with weapons to the constant staticky crackle of the radio chatter, in its opaque, laconic language, which almost serves as a Greek chorus to the unfolding tragedy.

Yet underneath all this, there's a corrosive irony. Exactly as the war it chronicles was conceptually flawed by the chronic problem of fighting 1967's battles by 1944's tactics, so is "Platoon" flawed by its decision to make 1987's movie by 1957's structure. Attempting to transcend the genre of the war movie, it fails, returning always to the conventional. Underneath its gaudy '60s cultural precision, it's achingly familiar. It may make the point that war reduces man to stereotypes and that all wars are more similar than they are different; but that doesn't change the point that we're still dealing in stereotypes and similarities, and that it really hasn't found a new way to encompass the unique weirdness that was Vietnam.

The story itself is an old one, familiar from "Attack," "The Naked and the Dead," "The War Lover" and any of a dozen others that push the line of the Army-as-corrupt-institution. This is the chestnut about the sensitive soldier torn between a saintly leader and a satanic leader, inspired by one and debased by the other.

Charlie Sheen plays Chris Taylor, a young college dropout

whose tour with the 25th forms the spine of the story; Taylor also serves as the alter ego of writer-director (and ex-25th Infantry Division grunt) Oliver Stone. Charlie, who's a little "sensitive" for my taste, is given to the melancholy-romantic narration that would sound more appropriate in the mouth of a betrayed lover in a film noir, and there's no indication that Stone means this banality as irony.

Upon reaching the 25th, he's quickly assigned to Sgt. Elias's squad: Elias (Willem Dafoe) is the saint, a benevolent scarecrow who, between search-and-destroy operations, mellows out in a fog of grass smoke in his Haight-Ashbury-styled bunker. In war, he's a lion; in peace, he's a pussycat. But there exists considerable tension between him and Sgt. Barnes (a ferocious Tom Berenger), the senior platoon sergeant. Barnes is your basic-issue, Pure-D, mean, redneck cracker, whose natural home is war. Anybody who was in any army will recognize this guy in a flash, but was it necessary to give him a face scarred like a tangle of barbed wire, to stand for the scars on his soul? Subtlety is not Stone's strongest point.

The conflict between Elias and Barnes explodes in what is probably the best sequence of the film, a searing foray into a village. The emotional mathematics of it are scary. Put a group of not terribly bright American teen-agers loaded down with guns, jangled with stress and fury and exhaustion, with no clear goals except survival, and no clear leadership except a psychotic hillbilly, into a village of sullen peasants, and you've got the components of massacre. The guys are a blink away from blowing away everybody — men, women and kids — and Stone directs the sequence at high operatic pitch. You feel the rage rocketing through the squad; it's pretty hairy. Then Elias comes dashing in, jumps Barnes as he's about to shoot a little girl, and the battle between them turns ugly and ultimately violent.

But from here the story begins to feel more like a war movie than a movie about war. It's hard to believe that one career sergeant (Elias) would file charges against another (Barnes), or that the officers would leave them together on missions, waiting for the inevitable continuation of the feud. And Stone doesn't quite play fair. Although the movie has been told from Sheen's point of view, he makes it clear that Sheen doesn't see the ugly crime that results. For narrative convenience, Sheen, by "reading" a man's eyes, knows what's happened, setting up a confrontation that will strike some as powerful but struck me as unduly melodramatic.

What we end up with is a movie about war in which form and content are the real combatants. The cultural details, the seething atmosphere, the sense of physical despair and fatigue, and the total, numbing presence of the fear ache with reality. They could have come off NBC News in the late '60s; the familiar dramatics from any Warner Bros. '50s movie.

THE KILLING FIELDS
January 18, 1985

"War," a famous '60s bumper sticker reminds us, "is unkind to children and other living things."

Just *how* unkind is the principal subject of "The Killing Fields," an extraordinary journey to the elemental places in the soul. One is tempted to haul out the melancholy Pole's most shopworn line to describe the ultimate destination of Roland Joffe's film, which is based on *The New York Times* magazine article by Sydney Schanberg: into the heart of darkness.

The heart of darkness is Cambodia under the Khmer Rouge, an Auschwitz for our times.

Yet Joffe does not get there immediately; rather he describes, in careful stages, the process by which the seemingly placid and remote Asian country became first a combat zone and then a death camp. I can't think of a film — not even Coppola's "Apocalypse Now" or, going way back, Lewis Milestone's "All Quiet on the Western Front" — that so brilliantly depicts the sensations, the visceral terrors, the sense of the world having gone completely mad that seems to be the essence of war. "The Killing Fields" feels so real you want to take cover.

Joffe's ability to convey both the terrible beauty and the terrible waste of war is nothing short of remarkable. Clearly, he and his production designer, Roy Walker, and his cinematographer, Chris Menges, have studied the look of the war in Indochina and duplicate it here with chilling accuracy: the grandeur of a formation of Hueys roaring in over the tree line, the almost boyish postures of the young Asian soldiers dwarfed by their bell-like pot helmets and shiny new black plastic M-16s, the wary grace of the professional soldiers ("Made in the U.S.A.," says one Aircav adviser proudly). But unlike tidy war stories that treat combat as a kind of glorified football game, the fighting here is sloppy and crude, terrifyingly random and terrifyingly wasteful — and it uses up children like firewood. It kills them, and when it fails to kill them, it turns them into killer robots shorn of remorse.

For this reason — the reason of the density of the suffering it portrays and the slaughter or psychic destruction of the children, which is its real subject — "The Killing Fields" is sometimes almost impossible to watch; yet, having watched it, it is almost impossible to forget.

As a narrative, the story is remarkably simple. It's so simple it follows the classic romantic recipe of meeting, losing and getting, although the topic is friendship, not love. (Well, it is love, but of a special kind.) It chronicles the relationship between *New York Times* correspondent Schanberg (played by Sam Waterston) and his Cambodian associate Dith Pran (Haing S. Ngor, who is actually a Cambodian refugee), who meet, work, bond, are separated and are finally reunited.

Schanberg, as the film portrays him, is a go-getter of the first order; he may even be a little neurotic in his eagerness to get the story and to beat his competitors. Danger is meaningless; the story is everything. An early adventure portrays his and Pran's risky and officially opposed journey upriver on a patrol boat (whose crew had been bribed) to the city of Neak Luoung to learn the truth behind government reports that a few bombs had fallen on the wrong target, causing minimal damage. What they find is that an entire flight of B-52s, through navigational miscalculation, has dropped tons on the place; the devastation is appalling. For their efforts, Schanberg and Pran were arrested and spent an uncomfortable night with the rock-and-rollers of Cambodia's ragtag army. Also for their efforts, Schanberg and Pran brought the Western world the first reports of the bombing's extent and violence.

It's a little hard to like Schanberg in the film, even though he is played by the extremely likable Waterston. In fact, his colleagues didn't much care for him (though they respected him immensely and, in some cases, almost worshipped him as a hero) because he beat them so regularly. Joffe makes the point explicitly at Schanberg's hotel: The wiry, intense correspondent (who routinely screams at U.S. officials) always sits alone. The others come to him; he almost demands this. Only a freelance photographer, Al Rockhoff (played with edgy intensity by John Malkovich), treats him with any ease, presumably because he is so high so much of the time.

Schanberg's obstreperousness becomes more advanced as the military situation deteriorates and the Khmer Rouge's ring around Phnom Penh grows tighter. When it becomes clear that the Western-backed forces of Lon Nol are losing, it never occurs to Schanberg to leave the city; it never occurs to him to require his assistant to leave (as did Pran's family and many of the Cambodians who had worked for Westerners). In fact, it never occurs to him to do anything but his job. Thus the two men find themselves in the center of a holocaust.

The Americans — the film is blistering in its indictment — had no idea of the dark currents of violence welling under Cambodia's placid exterior and therefore had no idea of the forces they were unleashing when they casually violated Cambodia's neutrality and began the process that ultimately led the country to take sides against the Communists. The American military wasn't really interested in Cambodia except as a way to get at the North Vietnamese. As Waterston says early in the film, and as the British journalist William Shawcross put it in his devastating expose of American policy and how it affected the country, Cambodia was definitely a "sideshow." What nobody knew was that for the Cambodians, bizarre violence had been a dirty little secret for hundreds of years.

But even knowing that, a cultural anthropologist would have had a hard time predicting what the Rouge did. The film is vivid to the point of fever in its depiction of a world gone mad: a world ruled by psychotic teenagers with AK-47s and exceedingly peculiar ideas. To be educated was to die. To question was to die. To have fought against them was to die. To have been a government official was to die — and to have all of one's family die.

But the Khmer were also possessed of a malevolent strain of agrarian purity. They "emptied" the cities, turning the population out into the fields — to work at subsistence-level agriculture, or to die. (Estimates are that 2 million may have died.) It is into this maw that Pran — after a stay at the French Embassy, where the other Westerners were taken for protection — is dispatched, there to disappear, seemingly forever, into the horror of a culture literally eating itself alive.

For Schanberg, the separation was a kind of modern intellectual's self-inflicted hell: a crucible of guilt and self-doubt that almost cost him job and family. It's clear that he blamed himself for being unable to come up with an excuse or a gambit by which Pran could survive.

Yet here the movie is perhaps at its weakest. Though it is convincing in its vision of Schanberg's stateside torment and his self-hate, the cross-cutting scheme of the film can't help but suggest that Schanberg's ordeal was somehow the "equal" of Pran's. This is guff, of course.

For Pran's hell was the simple, physical terror of living on the edge of extinction and starvation in a Khmer Rouge "work camp," where life hung on the fragile whim of the dead-eyed teen-aged guards. That he survived and escaped (when so many did not) is a tribute to his resilience, his cunning, his extraordinary grace under pressure. Schanberg may have won all the prizes and been the wunderkind of American journalism, but one knows, of course, which of the two really had something on the line.

To the movie's credit, Pran is played by an extraordinary Cambodian physician who had actually undergone worse torment than Pran himself, and who escaped under just as terrifyingly dicey circumstances. Dr. Ngor may not be a trained actor, but he is certainly a natural one. And as the story ceases, really, to be Sydney Schanberg's and to become Dith Pran's, Dr. Ngor grows in stature until his luminous, humane, fundamentally decent soul fills the movie. It's a brilliant job.

Also to the movie's credit is its insistence on being fair. Far from a left-wing screed in which all the characters on the "wrong" side of the political spectrum are thugs and louts and all those on the "right" side are saints, wits and martyrs, "The Killing Fields" looks at a human tragedy and sees not good guys and bad guys but just guys: small, frightened men, some brave, some not, all human, alone on the darkling plain, while the ignorant armies all around them clash by day and night.

So if "The Killing Fields" is a document that chronicles man's inhumanity, it is saved from bleakness and despair by virtue of its chronicle of Pran's humanity. Flawed, like the men it portrays, it's still a great movie.

CASUALTIES OF WAR
August 18, 1989

Brian De Palma's "Casualties of War" may turn you into a casualty of film.

It's a spectacularly unpleasant movie that draws its undeniable power from the charisma of brutality. It makes you the sixth member of a five-GI, long-range recon patrol that goes on an odyssey of rape, torture and murder. Based on a piece of reportage by Daniel Lang in *The New Yorker*, the movie is so punishingly claustrophobic, it numbs you. You're thinking, we gotta get outta this place if it's the last thing we ever do.

David Rabe's screenplay is certainly astute in its comprehension of the psychology and politics of rape. The angry boys who so desecrate their victim aren't ipso facto evil, and Rabe and De Palma do an extraordinary job of placing the events in context. They make you see how the war itself is the prime rapist, how the spirit of violation is so universalized that what the soldiers finally do is less an aberration in individual behavior than an inevitable consequence of a system that puts very young, very heavily armed men into a culture of violence without any responsible supervision whatsoever.

The young soldiers hunt an enemy they can never find, who kills them without mercy, then vanishes. While their friends die, they fire at shadows. The villagers whom they are ostensibly there to "liberate" sell them Pepsi by day and sell them *out* by night. The movie may lack the spectacle and accurate grunt anthropology of "Platoon," but it does get at the crushing weight of the soldiers' frustration.

And the men themselves are well-defined — and brilliantly performed. The prince of all this disorder is Sgt. Meserve, a street- and jungle-savvy New Yorker whose natural aggressiveness and piercing commitment to self-preservation, as much as the chevrons on the shoulder of his boonie fatigues, make him the natural leader. Sean Penn has never seemed so darkly charismatic and so full of rage and power. And, to complicate the complexities of the issue, Rabe and De Palma and Penn make it clear to us that Meserve is the best soldier. In a moment of brilliant improvisation, he fires the shots that save new boy Michael J. Fox's bacon.

But Fox, playing the true hero of the piece, a Midwestern draftee named Sven Eriksson, is the one member of the squad who, life saved or not, won't yield to Meserve's cult of personality. He wants desperately to be a good soldier, but he wants even more desperately to be a good man. And between the two moral opposites are the three men of the patrol, a lumpy gamut of Everymen, including a suck-up corporal, a dim transfer and an eager-to-please fatboy. Among the three of them, they don't have the spine of a single worm.

The poor victim, played with heartbreaking vulnerability by Thuy Thu Le, has committed no crime except the crime from which, in war, there is no reprieve: wrong place, wrong time. What follows after the abduction is barbaric — not a single act of violence, but a long, teasing ritual of humiliation, a slow dance to the ultimate act, where the power is more aphrodisiac than the sex. In fact, sex has little to do with it: The true motivation for each man is the fear of seeming less tough or more sensitive than his buddies.

Through all this, Eriksson does not participate, but he vacillates wretchedly. His indecision costs the young woman a chance to get away. Yet, as the men go further and further, it becomes apparent to them that they cannot permit the victim to escape — and they begin to wonder about Eriksson. In the murderous opportunism of combat, it's easy to dispatch her. The irony is that for all of this, their mission is a success; they intercept a VC supply route, call in an air strike, and engage and destroy the enemy from the high ground.

Despite Fox's believability and boyish charm, he's the least developed character and the least credible one. From somewhere, the authentic Eriksson (a pseudonym; Daniel Lang never revealed the soldier's real name) found the courage to struggle against the military tradition of going along to get along, even when his company officers advised him to take a hike. But it's as if De Palma and Rabe somehow don't get him; they can never explain his moral courage in the way they explain the others' moral cowardice. (In fact, he was deeply religious, which they chose to ignore.)

And the movie, as gripping as it is while it's in the field, simply hustles through Eriksson's dilemma, his solution to it and the remarkable court-martial that followed in completely unconvincing movie shorthand, compressing what must have been a year's worth of complexity into a two-minute montage. Perhaps worse, the film is presented in the awkward structure of flashback as Fox recalls the traumatic episode after having seen a young Vietnamese woman (the same actress) on a bus in San Francisco. This leads to an almost embarrassing moment of deliverance in a park, where she seems to remove the curse of remembrance from his tormented young skull.

But there's a deeper problem that has more to do with mercy and forgiveness than film aesthetics. And that's simply . . . why? It took about 15 years for those of us who stayed at home to come to terms with those of us who went, to remove them from their far exile of having lost a war we didn't want them to fight but didn't want them to lose, either. So why make a film that focuses on the tiny percentage of men who served without honor rather than the millions who served with it?

Article:
CHANGING FILM IMAGES OF VIETNAM
August 27, 1989

It was magnificent, but was it war?

Seven brave American special forces soldiers — lean, laconic, hungry for a fight — venture to a foreign village. Laboriously they train the peasants in the art of self-defense, nobly they strive to win hearts and minds; earnestly, they lecture on modern firepower, perimeter defenses, ambush and counter-ambush.

Then one day the village is attacked; the fight is bitter and lasts several days. Like many a battle, it waxes and wanes, attending its own terrible tidal rhythms. At last, when the gun smoke has lifted, the villagers have triumphed. The surviving Americans limp from the village, having won the day.

No, it wasn't war: It was "The Magnificent Seven," a 1960 western, starring Yul Brynner and Steve McQueen. Coming two years before our first advisers ever packed up their M-1 carbines and steel pots and began to wander the boonies among their reluctant Vietnamese advisees, it should have had nothing to do with Vietnam. But it seems to have everything to do with it. The movie, even though distilled from a far more complex peasant-samurai epic by the great Japanese director Akira Kurosawa, has always struck me as the first chapter in the movie history of Vietnam.

It was an almost dream-pure, myth-deep expression of American hubris and the fierce professional confidence of the early '60s , when a few brave men could do anything. It was the theory, and Vietnam was the practice, at the cost of 56,000 U.S. soldiers killed and a national nightmare that seems, even 29 years later, never to have ended.

It certainly returned in big-screen color this month with the arrival of Brian De Palma's scorching account of an American atrocity, "Casualties of War," based on a 1969 *New Yorker* piece about four infantrymen in a long-range recon who abduct, rape and murder a Vietnamese woman, and are turned in by a fifth.

Certainly, the distance between "The Magnificent Seven"

and "Casualties of War" is immense. One is confident and ennobled; the other dark and crippled. One is untainted by ambiguity; the other is a portrait of national neurosis, worked out in microcosmic terms. And one is a pure tribute to male courage and the old virtue of grace under pressure; the other locates the darkest of hearts in the bravest of men and finds a link between heroism and sexual pathology.

It's tempting to draw a straight line between the naivete of "The Magnificent Seven" and the cynicism of "Casualties of War," and interpret the distance as representative of some higher moral progress. But it seems to me equally possible that "Casualties of War" is an anomaly, that it arrives as if from a time machine, and the radical rage that imbues it is more meaningful and truthful to the America of 1969 than the America of 1989. It may be a movie that should have been made then; and it may be a movie that should not have been made today.

But as "Casualties of War" and a dozen other films in the last few years flood down upon us, a conspicuous irony cannot be avoided. During the war, we could not face direct images of it; now, 20 years later, we cannot seem to evade them.

This turn of events may be dated with the precision of carbon-14. It originated in the ludicrous failure of the first — and last — of the big '60s Vietnam epics, John Wayne's preposterous "The Green Berets." Conceived as a patriotic anodyne to the mounting anti-war sentiment of 1968, as well as an elaboration of American policy — a kind of ersatz "Why We Fight" — it quickly earned the contempt of nearly everybody who refused to see it.

At this late date, no movie in history is less worth trifling with, except in a larger sense. In a curious and again ironic way, the Duke's overproduced Nam epic failed in exactly the way that the overproduced American war effort was to fail: It never really understood the enemy and it insisted on applying the formulas of the last war to this one.

Vietnam, as a subject, seemed almost to disappear from the screen after the collapse of "The Green Berets." It was in part due to the surfeit of Vietnam imagery that poured into American living rooms courtesy of the most intimate television coverage of a war in history. It was also because of the deep national depression after the embarrassment of the Tet offensive. But Vietnam, of course, had not disappeared. It had simply adapted camouflage.

The later '60s and early '70s were very much the era of the un-Vietnam Vietnam war film — that is, the film that was not about Vietnam except, of course, that it was.

Usually, these movies were westerns, that helpful vessel of the American folk id. There were many — "The Hunting Party," "Soldier Blue," "The Wild Bunch" — in which themes of the war were worked out against a western landscape. Certainly, however, the most notable and obvious was Arthur Penn's "Little Big Man," a radical critique of the search-and-destroy policy of the Westmoreland strategy as echoed precisely in the campaign of the 7th Cavalry under Lt. Col. George Armstrong Custer in the Valley of the Little Big Horn in July 1876.

Taking Thomas Berger's picaresque and almost completely apolitical novel of the mythic old West, Penn came to focus almost exclusively on the highly mobile forces of the cavalry — striking on horseback rather than, as their successors would in Vietnam, in helicopters — as they moved across the plains and committed what amounted to My Lai-scale atrocities against the Indians. As the TV news cameras slow-motioned napalm bursts into slowly blossoming orchids of death, so Penn located the beauty of flashing sabers and raging horses and fleeing women. The film was designed to work you into such frenzy that by climax, you were cheering the deaths of your own soldiers at the Little Big Horn.

With the total Vietnamization of the war by 1973 and the withdrawal of U.S. troops, the Vietnam War movie went into perhaps its most loathsome phase: the brief era of the Vietnam veteran as psychotic gun-crazed loner, in earnest films like "Who'll Stop the Rain?," based on Robert Stone's "Dog Soldiers."

Of course, the ne plus ultra of the crazy veteran genre was Martin Scorsese's brilliant and troubling "Taxi Driver," in which Robert De Niro courses the steamy summer streets of New York City in his bright yellow Checker, wearing his Vietnam jacket, sinking further and further from reality and reaching toward the lessons that only the military could have taught him, the lessons of violence. In fact, the film is meant to be sarcastic: It took our biggest bogeyman of the minute, the crazed vet, encouraged him to his greatest madness, then took perverse, ironic pleasure in contriving circumstances by which his massacre of street low-life (after a failed presidential-candidate assassination) turns him into a hero. The irony is more piquant because his service had earned him anonymity and contempt; it was his craziness that invented him, exactly as it was the "craziness" of the vet that invented him for the larger society.

Vietnam proper returned to the screen in 1978's "Deer Hunter," a murky allegory so full of technical blunder and racism it seems remarkable that it convinced anybody, including the members of the Academy of Motion Picture Arts and Sciences, that it could be best picture; it wasn't even a *good* picture.

It was followed quickly in 1979 by "Apocalypse Now," Francis Ford Coppola's troubling and vast film that seemed to take its tone from Michael Herr's hallucinogenic reportage from in-country called "Dispatches." More than anything, "Dispatches" was about the language of Vietnam, that dense, acronym- and irony-rich patois of the lyrical and the practical that immediately identified its speaker as one who'd been there. In that same sense, Coppola — using Herr as screenwriter and his incandescent prose as a visual guide — tried to re-create in images the surrealism of the whole thing.

Those two films pointed the way to what might be called the imagist school of Vietnam filmmaking — that is, elaborate work-ups by self-styled artists who, of course, found it impossible actually to go to Vietnam as grunts and who made films untroubled by a sense of technical accuracy because, of course, they were far more interested in the war as an elaborate literary metaphor than any kind of on-the-ground reality. Stanley Kubrick's "Full Metal Jacket" seems to be the most perfectly developed version. It was such a dedicated artifice that it could actually be filmed in London!

But it's the '80s movies that have moved into the most peculiar ground, and to hear them is to hear David Byrne's refrain in your head, "Same as it ever was, same as it ever was." They are formed by the tense dialectic between those old antagonists, the left and the right. Not in the streets, but certainly in the movie theaters, it's beginning to feel a lot like 1969 again, although this time nothing is symbolic, nobody is using horses for Hueys: These are the movies that nobody had the guts, or could get the backing, to make back then.

In some cases, they're genuine artifacts, such as Oliver Stone's "Platoon." Stone actually wrote the screenplay to the movie in the '70s, when he returned from a tour as an Eleven-Bravo — an infantryman — in the 25th Infantry Division. So the language and the astonishingly authentic infantry culture all had the sense of arriving, in 1987, from a time machine.

On the other hand, the right has certainly contributed its share. At the purely fantasy level, the bogus refighting of the war in the Rambo and Chuck Norris "MIA" pictures is standard-issue commie-bashing and flag-raising, calculated to feed on bedrock conservative working-class perceptions of a liberal "sellout" in Vietnam and to provide a satisfying sub-text of the war as it could have been fought.

Perhaps more to the point — and certainly more honorable — was John Irvin's "Hamburger Hill," an old-fashioned "unit tribute," meant to celebrate a platoon of the 101st Airborne as it made 11 assaults up the murderous slopes of Hill 881 in the Ashau Valley. It held to a professional's code: Politics is the province of politicians; we are soldiers who do our duty, follow our calling, take our wages and die. The operative metaphor here was of battle as weather: an all-consuming climate that mulched everybody into the mud and milled out individual differences. In the end, when a few haggard survivors made it to the barren top of the hill, you couldn't tell who they were. That wasn't a mistake, though some critics thought it was. That was the point, the whole point, the only point — that individual heroism was dead and that only concentrated team effort could carry the hill, not only on the small scale but also on the national one.

Thus it is that "Casualties of War" feels very much more like 1969 than 1989. It's an avowedly pointed film that goes to great lengths to establish that the boys who commit the atrocity are by no means aberrant, but are rather the outcome, the necessary result, of a system that is in itself corrupt. That is its final equation: Corrupt policies beget corrupt systems that beget corrupt soldiers.

This may be true; then again it may not. What is especially unfortunate about the film, it seems to me, is its blast of radical fury at a generation of Americans only recently returned from exile. It is true that four men did rape and murder a young woman in Vietnam; but it's also true that 400,000 did not. So which is news?

There's something terribly smug and sanctimonious about isolating the bad boys, then unleashing the full power of corporate movie-making ($23 million worth) to dramatize their badness, particularly because the men making the movie, of course, couldn't have been troubled to accompany their less fortunate, less educated and less lucky peers to the Nam. It was an old leftist telling the working-class schmucks that he was right, after all. And telling their sons and daughters, too.

When I saw the movie, it irritated me. As I thought about it more, it enraged me. Now, when I consider its invitation to join a crusade of pious finger-pointing and righteousness, I can't help but think, "Hell no, I won't go."

BORN ON THE FOURTH OF JULY
January 5, 1990

For about an hour, "Born on the Fourth of July" seems determined to become a great American movie. It's the old, sad story of how Johnny got his gun: the young man of the working classes who buys into the most cherished of national myths and marches off proudly to do his part.

Of course, he comes back in parts, the top part alive, the bottom part dead.

Oliver Stone's screech of rage at what happens to young men's bodies in the maw of war has classical antecedents: The Great War poets denounced the theory behind the slaughter as "the old lie" — Dulce et decorum est pro patria mori — and the movie is aware of its anti-war heritage. It works on the principle of contrast — among the soft illusions of life before war, the cruel shock of war and the wretched process of adjustment after war. Thus the slow dance toward the bullet that shatters the hero's spine feels as if it's snipped from the pages of *Life* and the *Saturday Evening Post*.

Stone's camera has the lyric conviction of a patriotic jingle: It swirls in and out and around the life of Ron Kovic, of Massapequa, N.Y., who is spoon-fed on cliche and begs for more. War, sports, church and family: These bright threads entwine into a tapestry of an unquestioning American boyhood. The kid who prowls the forests of the 'burbs with a squirt gun and a plastic helmet will necessarily be the same one who finds himself enacting the ritual for real in the paddies and dikes of Nam just a few years later.

The camerawork here is particularly revealing; Stone has adopted the visual vocabulary of the romantic epic. He loves to sweep and track, establishing the theme of motion as symbolic referent to hope. Occasionally he'll revert to slow motion to elongate moments of particular passion. The brilliant cinematography by Robert Richardson insists on finding magic innocence in such American rituals as prom night, wrestling matches, joshing in the cafeteria with the guys, and first kisses. Tom Cruise, playing Kovic, has just the right shadings of ardency and secret ambivalence of the self: His Ron Kovic believes in God and country but not quite in Ron Kovic.

However, Stone's intentions are not romantic but ironic: The icons of faith and patriotism, the gung-ho spiel of a manly Marine recruiting sergeant, the strident exhortations of Kovic's rigid mother, who emerges as a kind of Catholic Medea of Long Island, her patriotism devouring her oldest child, are all subtly exaggerated until they become like floats in the Macy's Thanksgiving Day parade.

We notice all this; Cruise's Kovic doesn't until it's too late and he's shouldering an M-14 as a Marine platoon sergeant on his second tour of Vietnam.

Stone, of course, is on solid ground in re-creating the chaos of the war. He has been there before as a grunt himself and as a movie-maker. And his true talent as a filmmaker has always been his raging sense of the ugly nitty-gritty — again, he takes us into the platoon-level mayhem and horrifying sloppiness of battle by re-creating moments when Kovic and his squad, in a fire-fight, throw rounds into a hooch, then enter to find dead women and children; when Kovic hits a target on the crest line who turns out to be one of his own men; and when Kovic himself receives his spine shot.

The aftermath is horrifying. Veterans' hospitals are pits, and again Stone's ability to create the sensation of experience is particularly intense. He takes you far into paraplegic culture, to the intimate ordeal of life as lived by young men whose bodies are half-corpse and whose sex lives will be only torturing memory.

Kovic still never says die; then, finally sprung, he returns to find his parents queasy (his mother particularly) in his presence, his brothers distant and his culture, by now having changed its mind about his war, disinterested, even embarrassed. It's no wonder that Kovic felt so seduced and abandoned.

In a terrible sense, "Born on the Fourth of July" is a coming-of-age movie: Its methodology is to locate the steps by which Ron Kovic found a place in America where his rage didn't exile him but ennobled him and where his self-pity wasn't an embarrassment but a badge of honor. But where "Born on the Fourth of July" begins to fade is exactly where Kovic himself evidently began to find himself: in radical politics. In the anti-war movement lay his salvation, as he made a religion out of his betrayal and constructed a new identity from it.

Unfortunately, Stone is at his shakiest in trying to find a way to express this idea, particularly since, by this time, the movie is closing in on the two-hour mark and he knows he's running out of time. He closes on an odd trope that is not only unsettling but somehow manages to trivialize that which has come before.

The movie ends in a hurry by contrasting Kovic's experiences at the 1972 Republican Convention and the 1976 Democratic Convention, one of which boots him out when he tries to commandeer it and one of which invites him to speak.

Why does this seem such a cheap shot? Partially it's Stone's insistence upon reverting to political meanings in the narrowest frame of reference, as if the war in Vietnam were a phenomenon of Republicanism rather than Americanism (hmmm, weren't there some Democrats involved in sending the guys over there, too?), and failing to note that the America of 1972 was a far different place than the America of 1976, which had more to do with Kovic's receptions than the virtues and evils of the two political parties. And it's the cheapness of the execution, in which Republicans are smug little blond yuppies with smile-button faces knitted up in infantile rage, and Democrats are a richly multihued texture of America the beautiful. In its last moment, the movie feels like an election-year advertisement.

As for Cruise, he's brilliant and heartbreaking; his core of essential goodness and his dogged insistence on doing the right thing, if only he can figure out what it is, make "Born on the Fourth of July" work.

GLORY
January 12, 1990

It was said by a poet of the "noble six hundred," the brigade of British cavalry who rode blissfully into the Russian guns at Balaclava in 1854, that theirs was not to reason why, theirs was but to do and die.

The same, however, was not true of another wild-charging, immeasurably noble 19th century unit, the 54th Massachusetts Volunteer Infantry. They got the doing and the dying part right, perishing in the hundreds in a futile charge against a heavily fortified Confederate position; but *they* knew the reason why.

The reason was that they were free black men in the first all-black unit raised in the North; now, unbelievably and in defiance of 20 years of film-industry marketing wisdom, their story has been told in "Glory," which is — now let's get this straight — a 1940s movie made in the 1980s about the 1860s being shown in the 1990s. It feels, therefore, to use Kurt Vonnegut's memorable phrase, as if it's come unstuck in time.

It's certainly the first straight costume drama to arrive in American theaters in many and many a moon. It's also, fundamentally, a World War II-style "unit tribute," in which the true hero is the organization, and the individuals are heroic to the extent to which they sublimate themselves to the larger purpose.

It is, furthermore, stiff, clunky, sterile, leadenly earnest and somehow — yes — great.

No amount of critical fancy-dancing can obfuscate the fact that for its first hour, "Glory" is a deeply wretched exercise. Matthew Broderick, playing the heroic young officer Robert Gould Shaw, who formed and led the 54th, is hopelessly overmatched by the rigors of the part and seems at a baby-faced loss trying to breathe life into a figure so remote from our century: a patriotic idealist hungry to throw himself and his men into battle and willing to sacrifice all for the cause.

It doesn't help that director Ed Zwick, the "thirtysomething" creator whose second feature job this is, has no luck at all giving the past a sense of spontaneous reality. He uses ex-big name actors in cameo roles (Jane Alexander as Shaw's mother and Raymond St. Jacques as Frederick Douglass), and they're as stiff as plaster mannequins leaning in the corners. Worse, it's as if Zwick has never seen "Tom Jones" or Richard Lester's "The Three Musketeers," or Arthur Penn's "Little Big Man," all of which managed to portray the past as the felt present: a dirty, seething, teeming happening place. Zwick's "past" is a formal, prettified, almost Disneyfied 1863, full of gaily costumed dress racks.

And the piece is conventionally imagined. Every cliche kid from "A Walk in the Sun," and "Bataan," "The Fighting Sixty-Ninth," and "To Hell and Back" checks in: Wise Old Sarge,

Dumb Country Hick, Fresh Young Kid, Attitude Problem and Romantic Intellectual.

However, after an interminable time in crinolines and in bayonet drill, the movie slouches like a rough beast to its true subject, the waging of war and the spending of young men's lives. And here, wonderfully, it is reborn; "Glory" seems to transmogrify itself into another dimension.

By this time, of course, the actors have had a chance to bring a higher level of specificity to their coarsely written roles. Morgan Freeman, for example, plays the older enlistee whose quiet wisdom gets him promoted to sergeant major. The role is as much a stereotype as "Fast Black," the pimp the actor played in "Street Smart"; yet, just as brilliantly, he's able to give it such complexity and believability that the concept somehow transcends its origin in the pulp imagination.

Thus it is that, by battle time, one has wholly connected with the men of the 54th and their willingness to pay the ultimate price. And thus it is that the movie's depiction of their slaughter is heartbreaking. Whether Zwick or a second-unit director is responsible, I don't know; what is clear is that the movie takes you to the center of the thick-and-fast that was combat in the black-powder and bayonet era, and it's not a pretty place, nor one you'd care to visit. The battle is like a horrifying hailstorm, except that what it pelts it kills and the bodies stack up like threshed wheat. Yet, unlike virtually the whole canon of war movies since 1968, this slaughter isn't viewed as futile, and its victims aren't suckers.

"Glory" means its title literally; it argues something rarely felt or expressed in American films anymore — that in certain wars, for certain causes, it is truly an honor and a privilege to fight, because there are bigger, more important things than living forever.

Article:
THE PATRIOT GAME: TWO NEW FILMS TAKE OPPOSITE VIEWS OF WAR
January 14, 1990

Ron Kovic and Robert Gould Shaw never met each other, being separated in time by almost exactly 100 years. But by the
whimsies of the American motion picture industry, you can
meet them on the same evening or at least the same weekend:
They arrive to our attention together, almost as if it were
planned that way.

Ron Kovic, played by Tom Cruise, is the central (indeed
only) figure in Oliver Stone's scorching "Born on the Fourth of
July," and William Gould Shaw, played by Matthew Broderick,
is the young Boston infantry officer and abolitionist who leads
the black 54th Massachusetts Infantry in "Glory."

And what could these two very young men who passionately
believed in their country, right or wrong, have to say to each
other and to us? Though one was an officer from the upper
classes and one an enlisted man from the lower, they have
much in common. Raised to duty and responsibility, they ea-
gerly joined great crusades, embracing them with the totality of
their being and giving them all they had. One died, at the age of
27, in a blizzard of scrap iron and musketry that decimated the
Civil War unit he led; the other, on a scrub hill in Vietnam, felt
at 21 the horror of a high-velocity, full-metal-jacket bullet clip-
ping his spine, murdering the lower two-thirds of his body.

One ended up on a bronze plaque on the Boston Commons,
on which the pigeons defecate and by which the citizens passed
unmindful until along came a movie; the other, in the wreckage
of his body and an all-encompassing bitterness, managed somehow to resurrect his personality and to define a new life, one
just as passionately committed — but this time to the concept
of My Country, Wrong.

What both movies are about, finally, is the price a country
can sometimes demand of its young men; and both probe its
right to make this demand. And this seems a particularly propi-
tious moment to be asking such questions, as 23 other young

Americans in the Persian Gulf have given their lives for either their country or their country's vanity (results not yet in) and scores more now languish in veterans' hospitals. The movies are about what the British war poet Wilfrid Owen called "the old lie" — patriotism and its inevitable subtext that it is an honor to die for one's country.

Owen knew of the idea's duplicity more than most: That was to be his fate, too, on the Western Front on the day before the armistice in 1918. Yet, however hollow the exhortation may sound now in an era of moral provisionalism, certainly one man who believed it literally was Robert Gould Shaw.

In fact, literalness — or lack of it — is the key to the two movies. It begins with title. "Born on the Fourth of July" is ironic; it is derived from George M. Cohan's jingoistic-jingle from World War I, "Yankee Doodle Dandy . . . born on the Fourth of July." This is taken to sum up Kovic, who was actually born on July 4, 1946; it's also an indication of the cartoonish, infantile allure of the patriotic delusion.

It is the thrust of the movie that Yankee Doodle Dandies end up in body bags or steel chairs for their ardor; and, more generally, that the whole substance of the war and the notion of sacrifice to the greater good is cruelly meaningless. Indeed as Kovic has it, as abetted by Stone, he only recovered his manhood when he declared himself in opposition to the war and forged a new identity as anti-war protester.

On the other hand, the word "Glory," the full title of the Broderick film, is not used at all ironically, but dead-on literally. "Glory" argues that the men of the 54th Massachusetts, and Robert Gould Shaw in particular, died as heroes in a wild charge that calls up not the poetry of Wilfrid Owen but that of Alfred Lord Tennyson, musing on another wild charge in another war: "When can their glory fade, noble six hundred?"

And that, perhaps, is why Shaw is such an uncomfortable figure to an age that expects cynicism and despair in its heroes (and why Broderick has so much trouble playing him). Shaw's ardent Victorian patriotism was entwined with his progressive belief in the cause of abolition and his sense of equality of men. He had no doubts and was eager to prove his beliefs — both for himself and for the black soldiers he led — in the crucible of battle. In the film, he's seen to volunteer himself and his unit for the most dangerous position of assault on the heavily forti-fied Fort Wagner.

As for the men, they too have no doubts. It is one strength of a film whose first half plays as stiffly as a performance at the Hall of Presidents in Disney World that it really begins to come alive when its superb black cast is given the room to etch vivid portraits of soldiers. These aren't generic brass figures from Boston's bas relief; they're scratchy, twitchy, complicated, re-sentful, stupid, cunning men, themselves the object of scorn, themselves doubted and feared. But what they have in cruder form is the same thing that Shaw has in more refined essence: a willingness, an eagerness, to risk a violent death to advance a cause larger than themselves.

The movie's most moving victory is its ability to recall this long-lost sense of romantic sacrifice that used to be the staple of patriotism, but was also, in its darkest issue, the fuel on which empires fed — the enthusiasm of young men for hazard in search of honor (or markets) for the nation.

And that is also why "Glory" feels so much like an icon out of time. It's like a monument to what was once the secular religion of the United States, a belief in its place in the world and its essential moral goodness among the other nations. If it reminds a viewer of anything, it's not Civil War costume dramas (all of them fundamentally ridiculous), but that generation of ardent World War II movies known as unit tributes, which all followed the same course.

It went like this: A bunch of green recruits is gathered, al-ways a country bumpkin, a city slicker, an attitude problem and a kid among them. They bond through the ordeal of basic train-ing and the irritation they engender in already tested units. There's always a deserter who comes back to see the light (Jimmy Cagney in "Fighting Sixty-Ninth," Lloyd Nolan in "Ba-taan," Denzel Washington in "Glory") and a tough Sarge (John Wayne in "Sands of Iwo Jima," Morgan Freeman in "Glory"). There's the speech, in which some lesser character explains what it is they're fighting for. Then, of course, we end in the crescendo of the big battle where it all pays off, except in the case of the 54th it didn't, as Fort Wagner was never taken. (There's no sense in the movie that the black troops were "betrayed" by venal white superiors.)

Taken together, the two films seem to sum up a history of movie patriotism. In "Glory," patriotism is conceived without rancor or irony. When Denzel Washington takes up the banner and races up the hill, only to be blown away by Johnny Reb's guns, his sacrifice is heroic and meaningful; the flag he carries isn't a joke.

The patriotism that sends young Ron Kovic to Vietnam is still built around flag worship and a young man succumbing to the romance of heroic deeds in far-off places under a star-spangled banner. But when the young Ron stands on the curb watching the veterans march proudly by under that banner, his vigorous belief in it seems tragic, as though he has been gulled.

Even the great "patriotic" scenes in movies from a less sophisticated era now play as camp. The famous flag-waving musical number in "Yankee Doodle Dandy," the Cagney biography of Cohan from '42, was meant literally. But today it plays ironically, a goof on the patriotic impulse that is seen in liberal circles as "right wing."

For more years than not, it was held both by government and motion picture industry that one of the movies' primary tasks was to build patriotism, to get the boys to sign up to do their bit. This didn't begin to crumble until the mid-'50s.

The first film suggesting that authority might be corrupt was Robert Aldrich's "Attack" of 1956, the first movie for which the Army refused to provide equipment (which, in pre-budget-conscious days, was a routine operating procedure that spoke for the oneness of purpose between film industry and government).

"Attack" starred Jack Palance as an embittered second lieutenant in a Battle of the Bulge infantry company whose hated, cowardly commanding officer kept betraying his own men in battle, leaving them to die for nothing. It ended with the men of the company shooting him on the stairway as he climbed to surrender to the Germans. But it pulled one punch: It suggested that the captain (played in full weasely snivel by Eddie Albert) was an "aberration" rather than an inevitability.

World War II didn't really provide a good background for movies questioning the authoritarian impulse that is usually patriotism's most vivid subtext, since nearly everyone agreed that it was a "good" war. Not until Joseph Heller published "Catch-22" in 1961, with its radically hilarious portrait of higher ranks and scheming opportunists, was that war fair game. But Vietnam particularly opened the floodgates.

How quickly it changed! John Wayne tried to make a "conventional" war movie about that unconventional war, complete to the kind of exhortations that had worked brilliantly in his World War II films, and he was virtually hooted off the screen. Telling young men that their "country" demanded their deaths for a greater good lost its cachet by 1966 — only the young Ron Kovic, of Massapequa, Long Island, was slow to learn the lesson.

The melancholy legacy of the Vietnam debacle has been the replacement of one set of cliches with another, an old lie with a new one. The films of the industry's first 50 years were routinely respectful. They sold, without introspection, the ideas that authority, like father, knew best and that the flag was an icon to be cherished; today's movies are routinely *dis*respectful.

"Casualties of War," in which American soldiers rape, brutalize, then murder a Vietnamese girl, is pretty much the "conventional" movie of the post-Vietnam era. It argues that authority is ipso facto corrupt by the very nature of its mandate for aggression: Those who would make war would also make rapists and murderers, that's all.

The natural position, therefore, of the movie industry is that authority is always suspect and rebellion is always innocent, spontaneous and pure-hearted. A movie like "Glory" feels like a museum piece, whereas "Born on the Fourth of July" is strictly state of the art, politically.

It has been said that patriotism is the last refuge of scoundrels, but, in truth, it has been one of the first refuges of the motion picture industry. Now, for better or for worse, with an occasional exception such as "Glory," contempt for patriotism is.

SCHINDLER'S LIST
December 24, 1993

In 1981, the film critic of this newspaper wondered in print about a young director's apparent ignorance of the past as demonstrated in the glibly amusing "Raiders of the Lost Ark," with its cartoon Nazis: "The film," he wrote, "is absolutely nailed into a certain time and place in its textures and details, yet still manages to lack a wider and tragic sense of history . . . It's as if Spielberg has never heard of the Holocaust."

Twelve years later, the same critic can write of that same director: "He *has* heard of it, indeed."

Steven Spielberg's new film, "Schindler's List," is an unblinking vision of that firestorm. It looks, without ever averting its gaze, at the darkest of the dark: executions, beatings, mass murder, the consignment to night and fog of a whole people, the reduction of a culture to ashes. But it's also a story of redemption as a man learns that it profits him not to gain the whole world if he loses his soul in the bargain. Working from a non-fiction novel by Thomas Keneally, Spielberg tells the astonishing story of Oskar Schindler, Nazi war profiteer and wannabe Krupp, who set out to exploit the Jews and ended up their savior. A businessman and not a soldier, he fought the Third Reich with the only weapons available to him: his charm, his backslapping and glad-handing, and his underlying shrewdness.

Indeed, Schindler is a strange hero, and Irish actor Liam Neeson seems to play him like a movie producer: a charmer and bon vivant, the guy who's always calling out "More champagne, garcon," while trying to get his mark to sign on the dotted line. Like a producer, he doesn't really *make* anything; his real skill is finding people who can make things and putting them together with people who want things made, while scraping off all the profit for himself. Thus it is that this all-too-common bourgeois greedhead is as astonished as anyone else when, during the razing of the Krakow ghetto in 1944 (the tragic event that is the centerpiece of "Schindler's List"), the little mouse says, "This is wrong," and it begins to gnaw at his heart.

It's a great story, and it makes a great old-fashioned movie-movie. As sheer narrative, "Schindler's List" just roars along, creating a world, peopling it with believable characters and following them through the crises of history to their own fates. It watches as Schindler negotiates the survival of "his" Jews, the 1,100 he's commandeered to work in his factory. Alternatingly charming and bluffing, he becomes a dynamo of nerve, of sheer will preventing the Reich from its agenda of execution, even to the degree of getting people *out* of Auschwitz. In the end, it costs him everything.

But standing in counterpoint to Schindler's burgeoning discovery of virtue is a darker presence — the Lucifer, as it were, of the Holocaust. In "Schindler's List," this demonic figure takes the form of SS Obergruppenfuhrer Amon Goeth, commandant of the Plaszow Forced Labor Camp and architect of the "action" against the Krakow ghetto ("action" being the Nazis' euphemism for massacre).

For years, this nasty boy was a stock figure in World War II movies and books, but the British actor Ralph Fiennes manages to bring dimensions to him as yet unseen. Fiennes's Goeth is a kind of intellectual lout, lazy and corrupt (we watch his pot belly grow), debauched beyond redemption, and yet somehow a strangely compelling figure. Fiennes gives him shadings of self-doubt and vulnerability; it's as if, as the film continues and Goeth gives full vent to his reptile brain (he loves to shoot people), his flesh itself becomes somehow mottled or clouded with corruption. He's a strange figure, who, however much one may want to see him as the personification of Hannah Arendt's "banality of evil," insists on being its opposite: the *charisma* of evil. That most very troubling character, the monster with the human face, he clearly fascinates some secret part of Spielberg.

It's a mark of Spielberg's growth that he has put away childish things. Gone are the Spielberg hallmark shots, the swooping crane moves, the blissful camera glides, the night sky apile and aglow with stars and metaphorical possibility. He's even abandoned that most obvious foundation of the imagined story, color, in favor of a black and white that carries the thought: "This is real."

But it shouldn't be said that he puts aside technique. There's not a single artless shot in the film and in fact sometimes artlessness itself is used artistically. In an early scene, in which Goeth and Schindler meet for the first time, Spielberg seems to glory in the prosaism of the setup. Occasionally, one will get up and wander off screen, then wander back, violating every convention of feature filmmaking with the utter untidiness of it all.

In the early going, Spielberg shoots in a mock German expressionism. When Schindler first arrives in Krakow and begins to seduce the Nazis into giving him war contracts (he takes over a Polish enamel plant to produce messware utensils), the film has the glistening, G. W. Pabst patina of German expressionism to it, so that the action seems almost to take place in a dream state of dark shadows and dazzling highlights. This is the soul of high Nazism: all theater and champagne and ringing, evil confidence.

But when he moves to the bitter reality, Spielberg abandons expressionism for the banal feel of cinema verite: the jittery camera jumps and roams, never framing its subject professionally but seeming to discover new shocks with each pan. The film's stock is slightly overexposed, giving it a bleached-out quality — as if the tragedy itself is too powerful for the emulsion to record on celluloid.

Still, he's not beyond "touches." The last act in the Krakow ghetto action, for example, was a nighttime hunt for stragglers; squads of SS killers roamed through the buildings, shooting those they found. Spielberg builds this sequence around the incandescent flicker of gun flashes — the composition bears a haunting resemblance to those famous star-jubileed "night skies" he portrayed in "Close Encounters of the Third Kind" — and pulls back to reveal a night cityscape illuminated by starbursts of machine-gun fire.

I wish, at the end, Spielberg had resisted a last burst of speechifying, in which Schindler expresses baldly that which the film had expressed symbolically. And I wish a sentimental coda, during which the actors appear with the actual survivors they played, had been avoided; it has the feel of a curtain call, entirely too show-bizzy for what's come before. But "Schindler's List" is American filmmaking at its highest and most passionate apogee. Spielberg is the rare man among us who has gained the whole world *and* found his soul.

SHOAH
November 24, 1985

To see "Shoah" is to die a little. It's to hear the dogs and smell the excrement and sense the despair when the shower room door is locked and Cyklon B is released in the darkness instead of water. It is to sense that you are the answer to someone's perfectly logical final solution — to be the germ that someone quite logically has decided to sanitize out of existence.

Yet it is never to see these terrible images, which in any visualization veer toward the pornographic and the sensational.

But to see "Shoah" isn't quite to be blind to the vision of hell: This isn't the radio of tragedy. Indeed, the majesty of the 9-1/2 hour film is the way in which the director, Claude Lanzmann, has conjured imagery that conveys the meaning of the Holocaust without exploiting its icons. This is the Holocaust in reflection: its traces, its almost unendurable burden of grief, its excoriating memories.

The 9-1/2 hour evocation — documentary is not quite the appropriate word — has been playing to extraordinary response in New York for a month now and has just opened in Washington, where it is being exhibited in two halves that may be seen on different days. It asks much of its viewer: not merely an investment in time but an investment in strength. No one should see it who is not prepared for it.

This caution isn't issued because the film is shockingly

graphic — indeed, it is almost bucolic in its imagery, which is very much the source of its power. But the film also works in curiously muted ways, taking much of its meaning from its radical length and from the steady accumulation of details. It is like a stalactite of anguish: It slowly builds, over the long minutes, accumulating force and majesty, though at no one moment can you point to it and say, "There, there, that's it."

This is the movie's initial brilliance; to show no film from archives. Those images, when first unleashed on the world with the liberation of the death camps in 1945, were so potent in their grainy black-and-white shadings of the unbelievable, that they were disorienting. But now they have been hammered flat by repetition: They have become banal, perhaps meaningless, as any bit of information repeated over and over again must ultimately become.

Lanzmann, a French World War II veteran and journalist who conceived the epic project and has spent 10 years on it, understood from the start that "to show" was to trivialize. Or, as Terrence Des Pres put it in his brilliant "The Survivor, An Anatomy of Life in the Death Camps": "Extremity makes bad art because events are too obviously symbolic. The structure of experience is so clear and complete that it appears to be deliberately contrived." Thus Lanzmann has designed a film that works in subtle ways, avoiding the obviously symbolic, and the clumsily contrived. The movie works through the intellect first, before reaching and destroying the heart, and then lodging forever in the memory.

But to begin with a description: "Shoah," which is the Hebrew word for annihilation, is a series of interviews with survivors of the Holocaust — that is, from the victims and from the victimizers, and from the witnesses. It operates on a ruthless principle of truth, and its central device is the very long interview. As these men speak, recollect, re-create, nudged by the continual on-camera presence of Lanzmann if necessary (sometimes ruthlessly), the camera cuts away to the locality of actions they are describing and in the most seemingly perfunctory manner explores them, almost like a travelogue through hell.

The contrasts are sometimes extraordinary: As one of the

two survivors of the death camp at Chelmno (where 400,000 perished) speaks, Lanzmann's camera penetrates a lovely Polish wood, ripe and sweet with the flavors of autumn. It comes as a shock to realize that this is it, the blasphemed ground, the killing field.

And other times, they are not extraordinary at all. Lanzmann has an extraordinary feel for the nuances of landscape, almost like a great painter, and he can imbue the most seemingly inane vista with terrible, terrible meaning.

It seems clear that at some period over his long ordeal, Lanzmann studied the photography of the Holocaust with a great deal of attention. Thus he is able, almost, to quote from the pictures without ever resorting to showing them. This is most evident at Belzec, a primitive death camp in southeastern Poland, where the effort to kill was in the pioneering spirit ("It was the laboratory," says a Nazi). There are no monuments: We see a sandy, useless, completely commonplace patch of European soil. Yet by some stroke of genius or luck, Lanzmann has discovered a woodpile at Belzec; his camera studies its nuances and textures, its uncountable objects. Of course, anyone who has read the accounts of the discoveries of the camps by Allied troops in the late spring of 1945 will be aware that the soldiers almost always compared the thousands of desiccated bodies they found to pieces of wood; the visual connection between the dead wood and the unseen but ever-present dead bodies detonates like a bomb in the skull.

At another time, Lanzmann hurls the camera down the seedy little forest road that leads to the killing ground at Treblinka: It is at sunset, a particularly lurid sunset, and the camera sees the hot blaze at the end of the road, looming through the trees. It's just a sunset — or is it? No, it's the ovens, burning horribly and unstoppably in the distance. And still another stroke of visual brilliance is his use of railway imagery — he actually puts his camera on a flatcar and pushes it through the Auschwitz gate — which expresses the inescapable fact that the Holocaust was primarily a phenomenon of railways.

But these are all background subtleties; in the foreground are the survivors themselves.

They are extraordinary men, but what is even more extraordinary is Lanzmann's treatment of them. He's not a coddler, a sympathizer, but a seeker after the larger truths: almost a fascist of truth. He bullies and cajoles, his pitiless camera keeps humming away, yielding up, with almost horrible accuracy, the sense of penetration to a dark core of memory. The men always begin the same: a monotone. They have trained themselves to numbness; they tell their stories like automatons, meaning to go once over lightly, and be done. Then the questions begin.

"Was the road asphalt?"

"What color were the crematorium walls?"

"Was it cold?"

He forces them to start over, at the tiniest, most accessible level. The nuts and bolts of slaughter. And gradually, he breaks them down: We watch the memories flood over them until they are crunched and weeping. Of these, perhaps the most affecting is an account by Jan Karski, a Pole, who during the war was a courier between the Polish underground forces and the West. He was taken into the Warsaw ghetto and shown the worst, and was the first man to carry the message of the Holocaust to the largely indifferent Western world.

Karski, now a Georgetown University professor, sits in his elegant study in front of the icons of civilization (books, sculptures, and paintings fill the wall behind him) and attempts to recollect for the first time in years what he saw. Yet, before he can get a word out, he is a broken, shriveled man: The memories are too raw.

Karski is significant, because, unlike the others, he is somehow Us. That is, he is not really a victim himself, but a witness; his testimony is by far the most eloquent (it is the emotional climax of the film, coming late in the eighth hour); he symbolizes the empathetic experience.

As for the Germans, some secretly filmed, they are rather pathetic. You almost wish that Lanzmann had found a few proud old SS men who'd be willing to look into the camera and say, "Yes, I did it because I believed in it," whose evil was somehow commensurate with the immensity of the crime they inflicted. Instead, he's unearthed a sad collection of dissemblers and delusionary personalities who have mastered the gentle art of slithering away from responsibility. These guys are very apologetic, but of course they "didn't know and were shocked!" Gently and insistently, Lanzmann unravels their pretensions; his camera studies dispassionately the befuddlement in their eyes as their interrogator reduces their arguments of innocence to utter pulp, exposes their melancholy self-pity to the contempt it deserves and skewers their dismal vanities with the grace of a lancer. ("Mr. Lanzmann," protests one gravely, almost insulted by a suggestion he's made, "we never processed 18,000 in a day! It was more like 12 to 15,000. And we had to work halfway through the night!")

In no sense is "Shoah" a history: It advances no argument, it leaves vast sections of the process uncovered (the Aktioncommandos, who ranged through Eastern Russia in the first few months of the Russian invasion, machine-gunning millions in pits, are not dealt with; nor are the millions of non-Jewish victims of the Holocaust). It has only a slight interest in larger context.

In fact, critics have had difficulty finding a word for it. It's a threnody: a song of lamentation for the dead, a monument where there are no monuments. Its most powerful image is one that I think will stay with me forever. Above the sandy soil at Belzec, the birch trees gleam. There's just enough wind to flick the leaves, which play in the sun, an endless, dense ripple of green light somehow seething with life. It's hard to look at all those leaves tossing in the push of the wind, and not understand that they are the traces of souls, now aflutter in the breeze of memory.

SOPHIE'S CHOICE
January 21, 1983

"Sophie's Choice," Alan Pakula's long-awaited version of William Styron's memorable novel, is so powerful it may give you nightmares — it has the voltage to jolt.

Yet nagging doubts remain: It may be *too* powerful, too ambitious, too loyal to its source, and all these too's don't quite add up to a satisfying sum. Rather, they suggest that being powerful isn't quite the same thing as being good.

The novel, as most of its readers will testify, was a great, rushing, word-mad thing, hurled ahead by Styron's glorious (or, occasionally, gloriously bombastic) prose style; in fact, its language was a character almost as important as Sophie. The book was as ambitious as the universe itself in its quest for the Big Themes of love, lust, betrayal, guilt, madness and genocide. And it was expansive enough to accommodate meditations, essays and soliloquies from its self-indulgent author. Edgily perched somewhere between greatness and glorified hackdom, it was, whatever else, a great wallow.

Pakula clearly loves it, and his reverence and care are evident in every second. For example, he goes to a great deal of trouble to keep his compositions in almost perfect symmetry throughout, as if he's cinematically attempting to match the formality of Styron's style. And working with the brilliant cinematographer Nestor Almendros, he's worked out a wonderfully evocative color scheme in which the Brooklyn sequences have the lush ripeness of pungent memories, while the Auschwitz sequences (in desaturated color) seem like faded magazine illustrations, as if their content were simply too blistering for conventional photography.

Meryl Streep's performance as the extraordinary Sophie is likewise a masterpiece of ambition; this is her movie in a way few movies have belonged to few stars. Alternately radiant and carnal, merry and exhausted, sweet and duplicitous, beautiful and degraded, she almost makes you believe that a single performance can carry a film.

But in a certain way Pakula hasn't been quite ambitious or accommodating enough. The film is long — 2 1/2 hours — but it seems short; in his mad plunge to get *everything* in, to be as expansive and all-inclusive cinematically as Styron was literally, he leaves significant themes inadequately dramatized, so they don't pay off when they click into play in the story. It's as if there's simply too much book for a single movie; the Duchess of

Windsor notwithstanding, it is possible to be too thin, and that's how the movie feels. This is the low-cal "Sophie's Choice."

(I kept thinking, as I watched, how much more satisfying was the Operation Prime Time adaptation of John le Carre's "Smiley's People." The six-hour format almost afforded the dramatization the novelist's luxury to explore and develop his themes; there simply was no rush.)

The film, though somewhat compressing and streamlining the events of the book, is slavishly fair to its spirit. A young, unpublished Southern writer nicknamed Stingo comes to Brooklyn in 1947 to write a novel, taking up residence in a pink rooming house. He quickly falls under the spell of the mad couple upstairs: Sophie, a concentration camp survivor who is nevertheless voluptuous and full of life, and her crazed, flamboyant lover-Svengali, Nathan, a brilliant Jewish biochemist who has nursed her back from the dead.

These three play out an extraordinary drama over the course of a summer in which Stingo's innocence struggles with his lust (for Sophie, and anything in skirts), Nathan's madness struggles with his brilliance and charm, and Sophie's love of life struggles with her guilty need for death. In time, all the secrets come out: Neither Sophie nor Nathan is what he or she seems and, instead, the reality forms a tapestry of human folly and deceit woven on the warped loom of modern history.

The true climax of the book — and of the movie — arrives when Stingo at last cuts through Sophie's defenses and manages to uncover the source of her guilt and her attraction to death, in the form of the dangerously suicidal Nathan: the truth about her "choice." I doubt you'll ever see a scene more searing. I know I haven't.

And in point of fact, the Auschwitz segments (shot in Czechoslovakia) are the most impressive and unforgettable of the film. This pale, grainy death camp looks and feels authentic from the sucking mud of its grounds to its bleak barracks and its ghostly, doomed prisoners (Pakula was advised in these segments by Kitty Hart, a survivor).

But Pakula has miscalculated: The concentration camp sequences are so searing they tend to blow away the surrounding story into which they are fitted as flashbacks. After Sophie's ordeal and her losses at the hands of the Third Reich, her adventures in Brooklyn seem undernourished.

After she makes her choice, in other words, one feels so shaken that one tends to lose emotional contact with the film, derailing its tragic denouement. In fact, for a movie ending in a domestic tragedy of a particularly wasteful sort, it leaves its audience surprisingly unmoved. I stood in the lobby of a Washington theater and watched the crowd file out: There wasn't a wet eye leaving the house.

There are other troubles. Stingo (Peter MacNicol) was two characters in the book: Stingo the younger and Stingo the older. The younger, burning with an ardent struggle with the great god Literature and the great goddess Sex, frequently amused and delighted and occasionally irritated the older fellow, the published writer and man of the world, remembering his younger incarnation's exuberance. It was the tension between the two that sustained the book much more effectively than the twisted love affair it chronicled. Here he's only one character (though Stingo the Elder is represented in an occasional patch of purple narration by Josef Somer) and he's dim. He is the key character, our access to the story, yet MacNicol never really makes him interesting — or perhaps it's Pakula's script that never finds much for him to do except stand and watch. Curiously muted, this Stingo never seems to be capable of growing into the man who could write "Sophie's Choice."

Kevin Kline, on the other hand, in the potentially disastrous role of Nathan, is rather good. Movie-star handsome, he never lets Nathan's flamboyance degenerate into sheer theatrics; when he seems largely to vanish from the last 40 minutes of the picture, the movie loses much of its vitality.

"Sophie's Choice" isn't quite the fair, excellent thing one hoped it could be, the pure wallow. But the compelling power of Streep's performance — and of the Holocaust — make it unforgettable.

Article:
THE HOLOCAUST ON THE SCREEN
May 4, 1986

Filmmakers have tried many ways of dealing with Nazi atrocities.

In the 1943 Sam Goldwyn film "North Star," a melodrama about the German invasion of Russia as it affects a single village, screenwriter Lillian Hellman tried to come up with a suitable atrocity to jar the civilized American conscience and display the evil of the Third Reich. She thought up the worst thing she could imagine: The German doctors were bleeding Russian children for plasma for their own wounded.

Horrible, indeed. Yet the moment also might be perversely noted as a monument to naivete, a last twitch of innocence in the pre-Holocaust world; it shows just how limited the imagination for evil was before 1945. In late 1944, Soviet troops would finally move through the deserted ruins of Auschwitz; the British would liberate Belsen in spring 1945, and then the Americans would hit Dachau a week or two later, accompanied by the indefatigable photographers from *Life* magazine.

Thus it became clear that a few children had not been harvested for plasma — ironically, there's no record of that particular crime happening — but that a million had been gassed, perishing not because, as part of the war's terrible sloppiness, they were in the wrong place at the wrong time, but because they were in the wrong culture at the wrong time; perishing, indeed, not in spite of the fact that they were children but *because* they were children. Along with them perished 5 million of their parents, all of them Jewish; perhaps another 6 million of various Russo-Slavic heritage were gassed. The estimate is now held to be 12 million victims of what the Germans called Endlossung — final solution.

The civilized world reacted with predictable horror and guilt and fascination; but it wasn't long before the scale of the crime found its way into the film world. Perhaps that process has at least reached a measure of completion with the arrival last year of Claude Lanzmann's epic "Shoah," easily the most devastating and impressive invocation of the tragedy yet.

But the journey has been tortuous. Film culture, like the large culture it is part of and reflects, has struggled clumsily to "Come to Terms" and find the appropriate expression of grief and outrage; these expressions have been frequently vulgar, trashy, sentimental, occasionally quite moving, sometimes completely lascivious.

One thing that becomes immediately apparent is the inability of conventional drama and melodrama to deal with the meaning of the event; I think it could be argued that no great and precious few good films have been (or will be) made from the Holocaust, and that Lanzmann's peculiar approach — radical though it is — is the only method available by which we may comprehend the incomprehensible. In fact, to appreciate the brilliance and the reach of "Shoah," it's necessary to examine what preceded it.

Initially, the Holocaust was viewed by filmmakers as the setup for a crime story. It was, furthermore, not a radically different crime, nor a new crime with a new dimension of meaning, but some indistinct evil that neatly provided a pretext for the manhunt dramas that ensued in the immediate postwar period, and perhaps reached their apotheosis in such 1970s American films as "Marathon Man" and "The Boys from Brazil."

One of the first American films to deal with the Holocaust at all, and one of, if not *the* first, to include actual concentration camp footage, was Orson Welles's "The Stranger," which dates from 1946, and is generally considered the great but uneven director's worst film. Welles plays an escaped German war criminal, Franz Kindler, come to roost in a quiet Connecticut school town. But an indefatigable U.S. war crimes investigator (Edward G. Robinson) tracks him down and begins to zero in on him. Finally, Kindler, exposed, is driven to a clock tower, where he pauses in his flight next to a gothic demon that conveniently symbolizes his evil soul, then plunges to an exotic death, impaled on the sword of a statue below.

"The Stranger" is never much good except in its incidental

details and its stylistic flamboyance, but it establishes one theme derived from the Holocaust that will perhaps never cease to haunt the popular imagination. This is the Nazi as Master Criminal, as Superman of Evil, whose theatrical darkness and mesmerizing hold on the imagination, at the expense of the victims, who generally remain invisible, is undeniable. (This might be seen as the Nazis' one terrible victory of the war.)

The convenience of the "Theatrical Nazi" as a narrative device may be easily seen; he was, in his time, like today's mad psycho. He was the first high-concept movie character: He didn't have to be explained; his terrible iconography — the jackboots, the black tunic, the double flashes of the SS emblem, the twisted cross on his armband — identified him immediately and set up certain expectations.

But beyond the manhunt dramas, there's a whole body of work that might be seen as an attempt to deal with the pathology of the killers while at the same time drawing their primary energy from the theatricality of such figures. These include "The Night Porter," in which Charlotte Rampling plays a concentration camp victim who again puts herself under the domination of an SS man; "The Serpent's Egg," Ingmar Bergman's unilluminating meditation on Germany's adventure in death, and "The Damned," Luchino Visconti's operatic account of a Krupp-like family absorbed into the perversities of National Socialism as located within deeper sexual inadequacies.

Of the American explorations of this theme, perhaps the most notable was Stanley Kramer's orthodox, earnest "Judgment at Nuremberg," which tracked the case of a German jurist (Burt Lancaster) who accepted the legal basis of the Third Reich. In the 1961 film, an American judge (Spencer Tracy) is instructed that, because West Germany is now an ally, he should be merciful in his judgment of the German; but he decides that justice is absolute and may not be tempered by pragmatics, which is exactly how the German judge he is trying faltered.

The first American film to deal directly with the victims — and to pay no attention to the killers at all — may have been

1953's "The Juggler," in which Kirk Douglas plays a camp survivor who, in Palestine, runs away from the probability of imprisonment with a small boy (the director, incidentally, was also Edward Dymtryk).

But the highest expression of the victim drama had to be George Stevens's 1959 version of "The Diary of Anne Frank," with Millie Perkins. Though praised at the time of its release for its high moral vision, the film's reputation has all but collapsed; today, it's seen as a piece of near-kitsch that has the tragic effect of not memorializing the Holocaust, but trivializing it by turning it into a soap opera (a tradition NBC observed with its "miniseries," "Holocaust," of 1978).

The film is ludicrously undone by Hollywood box-office compromises, notably the casting of a 20-year-old starlet as the 13-year-old victim, particularly a starlet whose similarity to the reigning box-office champion, Audrey Hepburn, had to be more than a coincidence. Indeed, the teen-ager's book was updated into a treacly love story, with all-American boy Richard Beymer as her fella. The lush, violin-heavy score by Alfred Newman underscores every dramatic event to the point of absurdity; the ultimate result is to reduce the irreducible in an unsettling, unseemly way (indeed, the only thing that really got reduced was George Stevens's reputation). In the end, "Anne Frank" points up another unsuccessful approach to the materials.

Perhaps the most impressive and successful American film to deal with the Holocaust came in 1965; this was Sidney Lumet's version of the Edgar Lewis Wallant novel, "The Pawnbroker." In a way, it precedes the method of "Shoah" in that it's technically an account of the power of memory.

In the film, Rod Steiger plays Sol Nazerman, a survivor of Auschwitz who has remained sane by sealing himself off from emotion and becoming almost mechanical. Into his small Harlem pawnshop come the wretched of society; but Nazerman, whose wife and children perished in the ovens, is bled dry of grief and cannot respond to their agonies. The chronicle of the movie is the way in which Sol allows himself, by slow degrees, to feel again, primarily by permitting himself to develop affection for his young Puerto Rican assistant. The force of the Holocaust is represented in subliminal flashbacks — quick cuts that last no more than a frame or two — which convey stunningly the process by which the experience has penetrated to the deepest level of Nazerman's being and flashes out of the past to distort his view of reality.

But underlying "The Pawnbroker" was a metaphor that constricted its meanings far too powerfully. That was the idea of the Holocaust as "disease"; Steiger is clearly viewed as "sick" and in need of a cure. The process of the film is almost medical; it watches as, through the healing powers of the medicine of love, he is made well again, whole again, able to feel pain again. In its own way, this is dishonest: Again, like the lower and more meretricious uses of the event, it trivializes the experience, and fails to appreciate the wider meanings.

In the end, it appears to be the documentary alone that can comprehend the Holocaust. The fiction film is irredeemably cheapened by its necessity to draw energy from the theater of the event or to sentimentalize it; the feature film represents a process of emotional miniaturization.

So it's no surprise that the two best films on the Holocaust are documentaries. The first is Alain Resnais's "Night and Fog." This short, shattering 1955 film elicits complex responses because, in contrast to more bombastic expressions of rage and pain, it is so completely understated. Basically, Resnais cuts between lyric shots of the camps as they were in 1955 and documentary materials showing the way they were in 1944. The sites themselves are quite lovely, or at the very least mundane: empty buildings overgrown with lush grass, under sunny skies. Then he'll cut brutally to photodocuments of the event in grainy black and white, the very gracelessness and artlessness part of the horrible power of it. Underlying this is a quiet musical score, and a quiet narration, spoken simply by an actor.

"Night and Fog" does many things with power and economy, but one of the most interesting is the way in which it demythologizes the sense of "place" of the Holocaust. By this I mean it disconnects the events from the places in which they occurred and instead returns them to the realm of human responsibility and memory. It wonders at the phenomenon by which one can go to a camp where millions died and feel only bafflement or one's own inadequacy at feeling nothing. This is all right, Resnais seems to argue: The Holocaust is not a phenomenon of "camps" and "sites" that may be safely fenced off and turned into monuments, then forgotten when they are out of sight. It is, rather, everywhere. As Annette Insdof points out in her "Indelible Shadows: Film and the Holocaust," "The effect is not only opposition (of now and then) but a deeper unity in which past and present blend into each other."

On this trip through the Holocaust, "Shoah" is the final destination. As has been widely noted, it makes several radical choices. The first is that by its very length, it separates itself from every other document on the Holocaust outside the professionally historical (i.e., Raul Hilberg's 1,000-page "The Destruction of the European Jews"). This length makes a statement in and of itself: an event that requires almost 10 hours of screen time is like no other in history.

Another radical decision: Lanzmann uses no documentary material. The familiar iconography of the Holocaust, against which we have become pitifully inured, is absent; no heaps of corpses, no pits, no blazing crematoriums. Instead, Lanzmann, in an artful and consistently amazing way, finds subtle visual suggestions of Holocaust motifs in the authentic world. For example, he finds the stacked cordwood at a camp site standing for the stacked bodies; in the shimmering leaves in the trees that have returned to blossom, he makes us see the souls of the perished; in the cranking Polish railroad cars, he makes us see the machine that brought millions to their deaths. His suggestion is similar to Resnais's: The Holocaust is everywhere.

But he does one other thing, perhaps the core of his method. Unlike the countless documentarians who have approached the topic on their knees, Lanzmann swaggers in, looking for a fight. His quarry is memory and truth, and he's merciless in pursuit of it. He bullies survivors without letting up, forcing them to tell more and more, to penetrate to the heart of their memories; he's interested in honoring the dead, not the living. So instead of giving us that exalted figure, the Survivor, cloaked in special grace and given special space, he shows us people whose humanity is not that far from our own, whose very normality seems their most astonishing psychic aspect. He's equally merciless in his probings of the Nazis he uncovers. He discovers something new: not the legendary, black-booted SS man of yore, but a passel of quivering, wretched self-deluding wimps. He completely obliterates the theatricality of the Third Reich and displays its evil in palpitating banality.

In the end, Lanzmann has done something no one else has and probably ever will. He's given us the Holocaust not as a political or historical event, or as a cultural or a theatrical one. He's removed it from the realm of the historical, the melodramatic, the mythological, the cultural, and returned it to the actual: He's given it a human face, which makes it hurt all the more.

Article:
SECOND THOUGHTS ON SPIELBERG BUT NO SECOND GUESSES
February 5, 1994

In accordance with the universe's most rigid principle — no good deed goes unpunished — it develops that Steven Spielberg's superb "Schindler's List" has attracted the inevitable backlash.

In publications as disparate as *The Washington Post, The New York Times, The Village Voice* and *Commentary*, revisionists of a variety of stripes are striking back at Spielberg's human epic of the Holocaust.

The charges take many forms, but basically they come down to two ideas: The first is the irreducibility of the event itself and its moral unsuitability to artistic representation. The second grants the filmmaker the right to choose his subject, but questions his approach to the story materials.

To take them sequentially, the first indictment runs that the Holocaust was of such magnitude that to reduce it to drama, to story, in some way trivializes it, particularly when the reducer is a popular entertainer best known for such childish confections as "E.T." and "Jaws." The late Terence Des Pres, in his study of victim testaments, "The Survivor," was among the first to articulate the notion that certain events are so beyond the scope of human knowing that no artistic representation can do them justice. This concept seems to have caught on — though anyone with a memory can recall when those in Holocaust-culture felt utterly ignored by an American popular culture that preferred more upbeat topics.

Such critics far prefer non-fictional or at least non-narrative invocations, the most powerful of which is Claude Lanzmann's "Shoah," which never attempts to re-create or represent. It doesn't even use the familiar archival material of the Holocaust, believing, perhaps rightly, that such material is ipso facto banal (if simply through overexposure) and that most people encountering it will respond in equal banality. Instead, the event is created in reflection, almost abstractly. One feels the weight of the event rather than experiencing the particulars of its existence.

To bring such a charge against "Schindler's List" is not entirely without merit. At the movie's most powerful moments, Spielberg's technical glibness is at its most fluent. As much as I admire it, I felt queasy when Spielberg unleashed visual tricks that blasted me into feeling a certain way, and no other. In the harrowing set-piece that is the core of the movie, Spielberg chronicles the razing of the Krakow ghetto. Though in other sequences he's gone to great pains to shelve his vaunted "technique," here he unleashes it to full dramatic effect.

The sequence climaxes on the night after the action, when German SS troopers hunt stragglers hiding in attics and cupboards. Spielberg "aestheticizes" this grotesque reality by building the sequence around the gun flashes in the night, pulling back from a darkened close-up to reveal a bleak cityscape a-flicker with gun flashes, an infinity of gun flashes. There's something almost indecent about the willed beauty of the shot, and its self-consciousness. I think the shot is a mistake.

However, leveling such charges reflects an essentially elitist bias and misses an elemental truth, which is that man has always sought to comprehend reality by re-imagining it to a certain pattern, the pattern of the drama. This is not even a particularly western device, but common to all cultures with minor tonal variations. When Spielberg, after the novel by Thomas Keneally, "reduces" the Holocaust to drama, he does something that not even the majestic "Shoah" could manage — he inserts it into public consciousness, where it absolutely belongs, in a way that only Hollywood could manage.

"Shoah," for all its power, was a recondite document; its radical length and obstreperous lack of dynamism made even the act of watching it a physical ordeal. This in and of itself exiled it from public experience. Moreover, it was so subtle in construction and evocative in deliverance that it was nearly abstract. It was documentary as high art and it demanded a refined intelligence and a good deal of experience in the technique of cinema to enter fully. It simply was not built to be a mass document. But the point is not to invalidate it — no critic could do such a thing — but rather to point out that its existence does not invalidate or preclude the wider appeal of "Schindler's List." Both, in their ways and for their different audiences, are necessary.

The issue of approach fundamentally revolves around the question of appropriateness, and it strikes at Spielberg's most problematic decision. That is, granted that he sought to make a film about the Holocaust, about the murder of 6 million Jews. Why did he select a story in which the Jews themselves are barely seen? They are reduced almost to stereotype, as in the figure of Ben Kingsley's quavery, grave Itzak Stern. It is strange, they argue, that the film chose instead to focus on Germans.

Indeed, the two foreground figures in "Schindler's List" are Schindler, an industrialist who sought to profit from his exploitation of slave labor, and Amon Goeth, the SS officer who was a specialist in the Final Solution, first supervising the razing of the Krakow ghetto and then becoming commandant of the Plezkow labor camp.

One might further complain that under it all, "Schindler's List" conforms to the dramatic arc of the much-reviled "liberal movie" — "Cry Freedom" is a good example. In these, the sufferings of the oppressed have no inherent meaning except that they provide a searing experience by which the white male movie star at the center comes to feel their pain and dedicate himself to . . . writing books and giving speeches in London.

But "Schindler's List" is better than that, except in a teary final speech in which Liam Neeson's Schindler makes explicit that which has been implicit for the previous three hours. Spielberg is nevertheless primarily a storyteller and not a moral lecturer. He knows what makes a story work as well as anybody, and he knows — oh, some other boys, like, say, Melville, Shakespeare and Aristophanes, knew this, too — that a demonic villain is absolutely essential to the story.

Thus the driving force of the film isn't really Neeson's somewhat opaque Schindler, whose motives remain unclear. Rather it is the young British actor Ralph Fiennes, absolutely demonic as Goeth. The movie invites us to share his debauchery, his moral squalor, his utter surrender to the culture of murder where, to amuse himself or to make a droll point to his fellow SS scum, he'll randomly shoot a prisoner, then go back to his schnapps. So intense is Fiennes's Goeth that he does, indeed, blanch the details from the faces of the victims; he's like a huge, incandescent flare bleaching details from the night with its brightness. In his power you shiver and wince. Yet, I would argue, this is not inappropriate but absolutely essential to any inquiry into the nature of the Holocaust. For surely as we struggle to explain it, the one question we owe its victims is: Why? That answer won't be found in boxcars or gas chambers disguised as showers, or in crematoriums. It can only be located in the testimony, the paper trail, the memories of the murderers.

Thus Spielberg, bravely, I think, engages the most cheesy and banal of stereotypes — the Nazi bully — and tries to find his human heart and understand the forces that led him down the path to mass murder. One might profitably compare this German — haunted and vicious, debauched and desperate, somehow both repugnant and queerly tragic in the misapplication of his gifts — to the blond-haired, blue-eyed cliche inhabited by jut-jawed Wolf Kahler in Spielberg's "Raiders of the

Lost Ark." One is a beautiful angel fallen so far beyond redemption that extermination is the only sane response; the
other is a movie gag.

Likewise, it should be pointed out that in these matters
Spielberg is entirely in line with the thrust of the first several
decades' worth of Holocaust scholarship. Work that examines
the culture of the Jews, rather than the culture of the Nazis, is a
relatively new phenomenon. Such books as Raul Hillberg's
nearly all-encompassing "The Destruction of the European
Jews" or even Lucy Davidowicz's "The War Against the Jews"
were obsessed with the bureaucratic mechanics of the killing
operations and paid scant heed to the faces and names of the
victims. Hillberg looked for the killers in their own files;
Spielberg, following on that tradition, shows the killers as men.

RACE IN AMERICA
"Struggling with rage, ambiguity and native ugliness"

A SOLDIER'S STORY
September 28, 1984

Norman Jewison may have been drawn to Charles Fuller's "A Soldier's Story" for the wrong reasons, but he's made the right movie.

Certainly Jewison was attracted to the Pulitzer Prize-winning drama on the basis of its similarity to one of his greatest hits, "In the Heat of the Night." The story, the setting and the hero of both are remarkably of a piece: The setting is the Deep South and the story involves a murder with possible racial implications, and the hero is a sharp, hip, black detective who triumphs where the white power structure has been oafish and derelict.

And the fact that Howard E. Rollins, Jr., the star of "A Soldier's Story," bears an uncanny resemblance (especially with his sunglasses on) to Sidney Poitier certainly doesn't hurt matters.

And there's another similarity: Both are crackerjack entertainment, mystery stories that whistle along to the ultimate solution with sweet bravado.

The differences, however, are equally significant: The setting of "A Soldier's Story" is an Army post, the year is 1944, and the hero isn't a cop but an Army officer. More important, where "In the Heat of the Night" was a sleek commercial entertainment that tooted a reassuringly liberal tune, "A Soldier's Story" is intellectually provocative and like its hero, isn't afraid to look for the answers, no matter how hard they are to find and whom their discovery hurts.

For Fuller pulls off what is so rare: He manages to use the format of the thriller — in this case the murder mystery — as a vehicle by which to probe an intellectual issue. In this case, what is at stake is not merely a crime, but a philosophy of social evolution — that is, how blacks themselves will determine their own destiny in a racist America and a segregated Army.

The victim in the crime, dispatched point-blank by a .45 in the opening seconds of the film, is one Master Sgt. Vernon C. Waters, a middle-aged, scrawny black lifer who runs Company C of the 221st Smoke Generating Unit — that is, who coaches the baseball team. As to who killed him, there can be little doubt. He was, after all, "uppity," and this is, after all, Louisiana. If it wasn't the Klan, it must simply be other, less organized white racists. And the Army isn't about to make a fuss about the death of one obscure black NCO when there's a much larger war to be fought.

But the case will not go away and an investigating officer is sent down from Washington.

When Capt. Richard Davenport climbs off the bus, the salutes fly, but with something less than their usual precision and something less than their usual enthusiasm. Captain Davenport, like Sergeant Waters and the men of Company C — but unlike virtually anybody else on post — is black.

Davenport meets with little cooperation; local authorities are fearful that he'll identify the white culprit and insist upon prosecuting, and an ugly racial incident will occur on the already tense post. And that's initially where the captain's suspicions lead him.

But as he investigates, he begins to think differently.

It turns out that Davenport isn't much of a character — he's a device, really, to get into the complex flashbacks that explain Waters and the company. What little style and brio he musters come entirely from Rollins's own considerable panache and presence. Nevertheless, the investigation becomes a remarkably intriguing journey.

Company C really reflects black American culture. Represented among its men seem to be all the attitudes of the black community: C. J. (Larry Riley), for example, believes you have to go along to get along, and is eager to please and obey; Private Wilkie (Art Evans), busted by the Sarge, is a cringing sycophant; Corporal Ellis (Robert Townsend) is a smooth-talking entrepreneur; Pfc. Peterson (Denzel Washington) is a fighter, but he's too undisciplined to do anybody any good.

And lording over them is Master Sergeant Waters. The role is played in the film, as it was on the stage, by Adolph Caesar, and it's a remarkable, Oscar-scale performance. If you've been in the Army, you'll recognize Waters immediately: the tough, leathery, utterly confident little martinet who really makes the organization run. Waters seems cut from mulehide and held together by Springfield '03 grease. He's the sort of trooper who, blindfolded, could field-strip a water-cooled Browning faster than anyone else could recite the alphabet.

But Waters is also a proud black man and, in his way, more virulently racist than any of the whites on the post. "Not havin' is no excuse for not gettin'," he preaches, sometimes with his fists. He torments the men under him with his vision of perfection, particularly the amiable, slow-stepping C.J. Waters, who is almost a secret Nazi: He wants to cut loose the "Geechees" of his race, so that the survivors will be lean enough and tough enough and smart enough to make it in the white man's world. As Captain Davenport realizes this, he also realizes that no white man murdered Sergeant Waters.

Sometimes the film gets a little confused in its complex flashback structure — there are occasionally flashbacks *inside* of flashbacks — and one of the performances feels way out of key. Jewison cast Dennis Lipscomb as Captain Taylor, the unit's white commanding officer, and the performance is a disaster in just about every way; Lipscomb doesn't have the strength or the charisma to stand up to Rollins and he just about vanishes from the movie.

There's another irritation. Evidently in a concession to mainstream entertainment value, Jewison has cast Patti LaBelle as a waitress-singer in an off-post black bar, which enables him to spring some grotesquely inappropriate Las Vegas-style production numbers on us that smack of phony-Hollywood.

And Jewison also opts to end the movie on a note of triumph when, the mystery having been solved, the black troops march out toward shipment overseas in parade formation. Jewison films this with the soldiers marching thunderously toward his telephoto lens, and the visual suggestion of the inevitability of the civil rights movement and the coming of equality is both phony and trite (in the play, the men were all killed in a World War II battle).

But "A Soldier's Story" is nevertheless crisp and taut and thoroughly gripping.

MALCOLM X
November 18, 1992

Call him the Defiant One. Born Malcolm Little in Omaha, Neb., and orphaned young by racist violence, Malcolm X's journey is inspirational not merely for African-Americans but for the dispossessed as a category: for all the peoples of color or economic desolation who have somehow been subtly informed over the years that America really isn't for them.

But before he was an idea, long before he was a hat or a potato chip, he was a man. And "Malcolm X," Spike Lee's 3-hour, 21-minute biographical account of the hustler who became a separatist agitator on his way to becoming a passionate humanist, has this great strength: It never loses sight of the man.

And in a funny way, Malcolm X's life, as told by Lee, projects the American dream at its purest, a Horatio Alger story to end all Horatio Alger stories — except that the poor boy whose rise in the world it chronicles doesn't find a pot of gold but something infinitely more valuable; he finds his soul. Perhaps the most amazing thing about the film is how restrained it is. All this time we've been thinking Spike Lee wanted to be a bad boy when he grew up, and it turns out he wanted to be the most conservative of good boys — David Lean.

And it turns out he *has* grown up.

Lee's "Malcolm X" is many things, fraught or freighted with multiple meanings as was the life it chronicles, but mostly it's solid, responsible filmmaking that transcends the limits of the bio-pic genre until it becomes something moving and resonant.

No screwball theories underlie it, no screed of racial divisiveness howls out of it; to ape a famous white boy, Ben Franklin, it says merely, let us hang together or we shall surely hang separately.

To begin with, it's the shortest 3-hour, 21-minute movie ever made. Lee divides Malcolm Little's life into five stages, giving each a visual style all its own. But more important, he develops a coherent theory of the life, so that each stage is logically dependent on what came before and seems organic. In other words, the story is rooted in the most basic of Western narrative traditions, the notion that character is fate and that people act rationally in terms of their beliefs and always face the consequences. It also has a weird streak of Greek tragedy. Facing that old blue-eyed devil himself hubris, the beast of pride Denzel Washington is able to give us a Malcolm whose fame and popularity seem to breed a subtle smugness that dooms him. The heir to the throne became bigger than the throne; then he saw through the throne; and then they killed him. He's Thomas Becket to Elijah Muhammad's Henry II.

At first, though, all of this seems so far away. In the early part of his life, in Roxbury, outside Boston, where he was a zoot-suited bad boy, Malcolm is consumed in the quest for his own pleasures. Lee insists on seeing this part of Malcolm's life as a period of innocence. The movie has the almost childish feel of a late-'40s MGM musical, including a great dance sequence, and it's shot in gaudy primary colors. The conk — a lye bath by which African-American hair could be chemically mutilated into a parody of Errol Flynn's lank look — is the key image, not only of Malcolm's foolishness but of his vanity, too.

New York is darker, more sensual, more tempting. He drifts into the orbit of a West Indian gangster, well-played by Delroy Lindo. A quick image rehab has him ritzed up in the shape of an upscale Mafioso, his sleek, well-tailored suits masking the seething tendency toward violence inside.

But Washington's Malcolm really doesn't have it for this kind of heavy hitting; he's not a killer, and when it appears that he's going to be killed, he heads back to Boston for some petty burglary. Here, his self-loathing is represented by his yearning for white women, as if to escape the burden of his own blackness. He has as yet no conceptual framework against which to interpret his increasing rage.

Arrested for burglary, he spends seven years in prison; there, he meets an acolyte of Elijah Muhammad and begins his awakening. Gifts that had been repressed are discovered, painfully. The metaphor for this spiritual rebirth is a voyage through the dictionary, one word at a time.

He emerges from prison a new man, humble in appetites, intellectually alive. And he finds his true gift. Malcolm X really wasn't a political leader, in the sense of organizing and acquiring power and leading a mass movement; he certainly was no guerilla, though he never shirked from the implication of his statements. However much he represented himself as a servant, it appears that he was serving his own ego as much as the larger movement that he embraced.

But he was a spellbinding speaker, and his eloquence was driven forward by an incisive mind that cut like a knife through the polite fog of liberal rhetoric in the early '60s. He emerged first to the public consciousness as a kind of anti-Martin Luther King, a Mick Jagger to King's John Lennon, with more edge, and much more danger. All respect is due Lee for showing just how ugly Malcolm X could be, and for not looking demurely away from the most loathsome few minutes of Malcolm's life, when he issued ugly utterances upon the death of President Kennedy.

Lee is equally open-eyed on the Muslims, particularly Elijah Muhammad, played as a kind of dotty imperial presence by Al Freeman Jr. Possibly he romanticizes the splendor and stability of Elijah's offices (it looks like the Harvard English department!), but his view of Muslim leadership and the factional bitterness that arose against Malcolm X as he became more and more famous feels honest.

If Lee gives the story short shrift, it is perhaps only at the end, at which an exiled Malcolm X's trip to Mecca (first time ever shown in Western cinema and alone worth the price of a ticket) and his epiphany that all men are brothers under the eyes of God are less felt than narrated. His final return to a death he knew awaited him seems the highest act of self-sacrifice. Whatever else Malcolm X had or didn't have, he had guts.

Washington is brilliant. He makes the trajectory from ignorance to hate to comprehension believable, but his angry Malcolm X, seething with pride, his barbed tongue puncturing the illusions that flew before it, his hatred of the blue-eyed devils radiant as the heat off a fire, is truly an impressive creation. He seems a true prince of our disorder.

I wish Lee had dipped away from the temptation to use celebs in ironic cameos — Al Sharpton as a street corner lecturer, William Kunstler as a tough judge — which seems a jokey self-indulgence. Ossie Davis's funeral oration, delivered over a crescendo of images at the end, is another indulgence: We know these images because we've seen them; telling us again is redundant. But in the end, "Malcolm X" can only be described in one word: Magnificent.

DO THE RIGHT THING
June 30, 1989

With Spike Lee's "Do the Right Thing," what you get is what you bring.

For a certain kind of viewer, it will confirm the worst stereotypes of blackness: It's a vivid portrait of a black culture that is crazed with destructive masculinity and a pathological evasion of responsibility — quick to anger on the streets and quick to rest on the job. It captures a language so densely packed with the ugliest 12-letter word in English that it achieves a kind of poetic absurdity. It portrays the fecklessness of certain kinds of black activism. It charts the way in which the most enlightened of goals can stutter-step in a nanosecond into violence and death.

And for a certain kind of viewer, it will confirm the worst stereotypes of whiteness: It's a furious portrait of Caucasian intransigence and brutality, a crazed, self-destructive inability to acknowledge the plurality of human behavior and the different norms within different ethnic groups. It shows whites — particularly a working-class Italian-American family, owner of a small pizzeria in the blighted Bedford-Stuyvesant section of Brooklyn — as almost universally aggressive and predatory, responding to every challenge by reaching for the baseball bat.

Perhaps "Do the Right Thing's" most disturbing quality is that neither of these groups will quite "get it" and will see it as a literal rather than an ironic document. Some will laugh when a pizzeria goes up in flames; some will cheer when a black youth is killed. That is the truth, Ruth. And that is the tragedy.

But for the rest of us, somewhere in the middle, stewing awkwardly about a problem that will not go away and whose solutions seem only to lead to new problems, what of us? Well, for us it's a particularly brilliant movie, moving, funny and deeply unsettling. Far from an anthem to racial violence, as has been claimed in some quarters, it's more of a cautionary tale that shows how fundamentally decent people can be gulled by passion and resentment and clamped in the great vise of an oppressive urban heat wave — Lee really gets the steamy, desolate quality of city heat — into behaving in their own worst interests.

All the way through, you feel Lee the artist in conflict with Lee the ideologue. (It's like Gillo Pontecorvo's "Battle of Algiers" in that respect because, although it frankly takes sides, it refuses steadfastly to assign decency and goodness to the "right" side.) In other words, almost always, the artist wins out over the ideologue, which is what makes the film so beguiling. In fact, Lee gives his sweetest and most human scene to Sal's family, as Sal (Danny Aiello) and his son Pino (John Turturro) sit in the sunlight in the front window of their shop and Sal explains to the angry and hatred-clotted young man how good it makes him feel to have fed this neighborhood for 25 years and watched the young people grow to adulthood on the sweat of his brow and the sauce on his pie. It's a complex, wonderful moment; you feel the older man — basically as racist as they come — nevertheless trying desperately to reach into his own son's hateful heart and free him of the rage that so cripples him. Sal is a pragmatist of the old school: He believes you've got to go along to get along. Poor Pino, the boy, knows that his destiny is to be in a pizzeria he hates in a neighborhood he hates.

But the film is at its best as it demonstrates a particularly persuasive theory of the psychology of racism: that men who feel their power and place in life slipping for reasons that are beyond them tend to channel their own self-loathing onto the nearest available human being of a different shade. We see this happen all through "Do the Right Thing." In fact, the movie is in one way similar to a Rubik's Cube of racial hostility, in which, no matter how you rearrange the parts, you expose some new pattern of hatred. At one point, Lee even stops the film in its tracks and allows the various characters to unburden their toxic ids. One by one they face the camera and let 'er rip: a torrent of racial invective and fury cascading out upon the audience. The effect is brilliant — you see the way in which all men may be brothers in their hatreds alone, but you also see how the hatred deforms them, turning their faces pinched and ugly and pathetic. And, in such tumultuous expression, the language loses its meaning and becomes almost hilarious, a collection of goo-words and baby talk.

In the end, "Do the Right Thing" is like a prism: You beam your own hot glare of racial animosity onto it, and it refracts it into a rainbow spray of understanding. It tells you why you hate, which may be the way to stop hating.

BOYZ N THE HOOD
July 12, 1991

In the Hood, you're quick or you're dead; sometimes you're quick *and* you're dead; sometimes you're just dead. And, sometimes, you get out.

The Hood — the word is a hip-hop reduction of "neighborhood" — is Crenshaw, in South Central Los Angeles. A casual tour might suggest to visitors that they'd traveled back in time to the Saigon of the late '60s. Overhead, the choppers hover, their lights probing the alleys and back streets; at night, automatic weapon fire splits the air; nobody goes out if he doesn't have to; and every morning the bodies are found.

Yet John Singleton, whose powerful "Boyz N the Hood" is the most penetrating examination of the Crenshaws of America to date, isn't quite ready to surrender to despair: He also finds love and loyalty, and particularly the strength of a devoted father who can pull a son back from the craziness.

Singleton's thesis is painfully clear: The boys without the father die; the boy *with* the father lives. Family is destiny. Lack of family is death. So obvious, then, is the thrust of the movie that it somewhat lacks suspense. One knows what will happen, because it's inevitable, given the thesis. And that thing happens. And the movie is over.

Yet to dismiss the film on the basis of its predictability is to absolutely miss the point. Singleton creates a vibrant portrait of a culture at flash point, devouring itself, subject to its own pathologies. And he creates a vivid sense of the power of friendship as well as fatherhood.

The movie is a kind of black urban "Stand By Me," differing from the rural white work in that it has three friends standing by each other rather than four. The three are Tre (Cuba Gooding, Jr.), a sensitive intellectual; Doughboy (the rapper Ice Cube), a hell-raiser with a good heart but a furious temper; and Ricky (Morris Chestnut), an athlete who dreams of attending the University of Southern California.

Ricky and Doughboy are half-brothers, with no father present; Tre's dad, a tough, no-nonsense savings and loan officer, is played brilliantly by Larry Fishburne, and one mark of the 23-year-old Singleton's uncanny artistic maturity is that he doesn't over-sentimentalize Fishburne's character, "Furious" Styles. Furious is a grump and an autodidact and he's not afraid to raise a hand to his child. He's no idealized paragon; he has a mean streak and an attitude problem. But he's one other thing: He's there. And, there's a lot of there there.

Furious guides and bullies and sometimes torments Tre; most important, he gives him an image of male responsibility. And you can sense, behind the brittleness, his love.

Poor Doughboy and Ricky: They're wonderful young men,

loyal, strong, sweet of heart, but, lacking that guidance, they drift. Doughboy seems the most tragic: He's the guy you'd want next to you in the foxhole on a long night in the middle of a war. But in the gun-rich and temptation-dense culture of South Central L.A., his self-destructive tendencies are given vent; you can feel him spinning toward destabilization. Ice Cube is brilliant in the role.

Ricky is probably the least well imagined; he's the only one of the three boyz n the hood who feels like a cliche, and as he struggles to make a passing grade on his SATs so that he can get his scholarship, one feels the approach, on little elephant feet, of tragedy.

But "Boyz N the Hood" has the artistic strength to tell a truth on its own terms; it's a terrific movie.

BETRAYED
August 26, 1988

In the end, "Betrayed" double-crosses everybody, including its cast and its audience.

This troubling but deeply flawed film purports to examine political and racial violence at the furthest extremes of the American right, but what's so ultimately dispiriting about it is that it seems to offer no hope, or at the very least, no middle ground. It's a portrait of a polarized America that seems to stem from a European liberal's most hyperfervid nightmares, in which, by the generalizing power of cinema, all jeans-wearing rural men with rolled-up T-shirts and baseball caps who drive pickups with gun racks are revealed to be murderous racists plotting to overthrow the government. The Greek-born French director Costa-Gavras ("Z," "Missing") can find no others.

At the same time, he has it that our best line of defense, the Federal Bureau of Investigation, is a colony of careerist scum, ruthless and detached from larger meanings; it operates with flagrant unprofessionalism, is completely incapable of protecting its own agents in the field and, in its own way, is just as neurotically drawn to violence as are the men it is trying to protect us from.

In between is Debra Winger, betrayer and betrayee. When first glimpsed, Winger is a "combine-girl" — part of a traveling squad of harvesting machine operators who wend their way up north through the heartland, working the harvests for the smaller farmers unable to afford their own combine machinery. In a small town in an unnamed Midwestern state, she's attracted to a handsome, widowed farmer, a Vietnam War hero who appears to be one of those decent, laconic, country chaps. And he — Tom Berenger — is attracted to her.

Here I must give away the movie's best — and really, only — surprise, but it's one that's already been sprung by the national critics. Winger, 20 minutes into the movie, heads out to visit her "sick mother" and in seconds of screentime is in a nondescript Chicago skyscraper surrounded by men in ill-fitting suits with gimlet eyes and suspicious bulges under their jackets. They're feds; she's a fed, and it's a measure of Winger's extraordinary range as an actress that she's able to convince both as a combine girl and as FBI agent sent into the heartland to investigate a right-wing conspiracy. It's also a shame that she's wasted as the film then simply uses the specter of political violence as a clumsy and unconvincing backdrop for a complex but never convincing psychodrama played out among Winger, Berenger and John Heard, as her FBI supervisor, former lover and extremely ruthless player in the game.

The movie just doesn't quite know what it wants to do. The screenplay, by Joe Eszterhas, is an exercise in conspiracy theory that goes to great extremes to connect dots that no journalist has yet connected; it links a number of violent screwball crimes — the murder of Denver talk-show host Alan Berg being the most famous — into a single tapestry of deceit and, to further sour the plot, it invents several more. Of these, the most repellent is a "coon hunt" — where Berenger and several of his pals laughingly hunt down a kidnapped black man, simply for the sport and to inflate their own sense of racial superiority. This scene is so cold-bloodedly violent it completely shatters the mood: Like the famous Russian roulette sequence in "The

Deer Hunter," it just blows the rest of the movie away, and it's a good 10 minutes before you can concentrate on what's going on.

What is going on is a fictional Cook's tour of the psychopathic right, but one that's queerly misfigured. At one point Berenger reveals that he and his fellow nuts are connected by home computer networks, and the movie seems to be suggesting that home computers are potentially evil. Ban computers, not guns, eh, Monsieur Costa-Gavras?

The single most convincing sequence takes Winger, Berenger and his two kids to a kind of nut-case hootenanny in the deep woods. Costa-Gavras retains his pictorial brilliance, and the image of Winger open-eyed in horror behind a car window on which is reflected the slow cavalcade of burning crosses is indeed terrifying and compelling. But nothing else is, quite. The material cries out for the validation of investigative journalism, rather than the fervor of fiction. You want answers, not story: Do these guys exist? Are they this well-organized? How many have they killed? Are they a real threat or are they just another mob of self-deluded crackpots, blowhards and know-it-alls? It's in the movie's best melodramatic interest to see them as a real threat, but it never comes close to proving the case.

At the same time, the relationship between Winger and Berenger is taking on an exceedingly neurotic cast. Perhaps this is inevitable, given Berenger's clear pathology. What's hard to swallow is Winger's helpless involvement with him. She's certainly the most ambivalent FBI agent in movie history, and certainly the most unprofessional. Next to her, Matthew Modine in "Married to the Mob" seems like Eliot Ness. She completely loses her moral bearings — something nobody has ever accused the FBI of doing, as certitude, for good or ill, is that organization's bedrock. The final drama of the film is trying to anticipate whether she'll be able to do her duty. At the same time, he's beginning to act suspiciously human and weak: He deliberately opens himself to her professional side and to her Smith & Wesson, demanding either her endless love or 147 grains of her .38-caliber lead.

Behind the Berenger-Winger love story, there's an exceptionally feeble assassination subplot, which is meant to give the movie its big jolt at the end. But the subplot does the opposite: It's so sketchy and preposterous — turning on a right-wing plot to zap a right-wing presidential candidate so as to make a martyr of him and propel an even harder rightie into office — that it ultimately trivializes the issues the film raises.

Sure to be controversial, "Betrayed" raises the darkest issues of the republic, then frivolously tosses them away in search of cheap thrills.

THE COLOR PURPLE
December 20, 1985

"The Color Purple" arrives in living black and blue: It's a long chronicle of pain and abuse, in which the blows are much more powerful for not being explicitly displayed. But if it's about pain, it's also about the powerlessness that makes pain inevitable, and the one thing it does brilliantly — and the one thing that will linger for years after the details have fled from memory — is depict with frightening precision the sense of life on the very bottom of the pyramid of oppression. You know what rolls downhill, and it all ends up on Celie.

Celie is ugly, black and poor in the rural Georgia of 1910. As the various systems of society operate — white racism and black male chauvinism, the one an ugly stepchild to an ugly parent — they seem to have no other purpose than to mash her, though of course their primary aim is to sustain themselves.

Steven Spielberg's film, drawn from Alice Walker's Pulitzer-Prize-winning epistolary novel, follows Celie (Whoopi Goldberg) from her rape at age 14 by her stepfather through 20 years of tribulation as the wife of a brutally self-involved, though prosperous, farmer known to her only as Mister (played by Danny Glover), who sees her as chattel while he obsessively pursues another woman. It is a rough transit: "I'm too busy trying to stay alive," says Celie at one point, "to fight back."

At the same time, other characters move through the story:

Mister's son Harpo, who marries the strong-willed Sophia (Oprah Winfrey), whose natural defiance spells her own near doom; Shug Avery (Margaret Avery), a blues singer who is Mister's worshipped lover but a woman strong enough to live on her own terms; and Mister's father (Adolph Caesar), a wizened, leathery little martinet from whose unfeeling heart the legacy of anguish is dispatched into this world.

Yet this is really a story of triumph and escape, almost a jailbreak picture. We watch Celie grow from victimhood to selfhood; we watch her become beautiful and strong, and deliver herself from evil. We watch as love — for her lost sister Nettie (Akosua Busia) and her stolen children — empowers her to, in Faulkner's words, not only endure but prevail. And the film certainly builds to a moment of scalding bliss, even if a few of the strings that Spielberg pulls are jerked too clumsily. The movie ultimately soars on the strength of its compassion and the strength of its love.

Still, it's a struggle. The primary pleasure of "The Color Purple" is provided not by Spielberg, who does almost as many things wrong as he does right (which gives the movie its lurching pace and ragged inconsistency), but by an extraordinary cast which finds the truth that so often eludes Spielberg.

Begin with Whoopi Goldberg. In her first movie, this extraordinary young actress fills Celie with authenticity. Anyone who has seen Goldberg's Broadway show or her HBO special, in which, without benefit of make-up or props, she creates five characters and leads each through funky humor to a chattering epiphany, cannot be surprised at Goldberg's subtlety and artistry. And what a narrow line she must tread. If she's too passive, Celie becomes a punching bag, not a character, and the movie becomes a drag; if she's too perky, the movie's delicate emotional scheme explodes. Goldberg underplays; we watch her grow in the role.

Then, move to Winfrey. Forget that people are talking, forget Chicago, forget Baltimore; here she is fabulous. Her Sophia, a woman mountain of a figure, is an extraordinary creation, although the one that Spielberg handles worst. Sophia is at the center of a ham-handed indictment of white racism that lurches into stridency; she is made to suffer grievous beatings, miracle cures, the slings and arrows of outrageous fortune. Her panties are shown. At one point — Spielberg's cheapest shot — the director zeroes in on her eyes filling with rage just before she smacks someone, and it's almost a Disneyesque touch: She looks like the whale in "Pinocchio" filling with smoke. Yet Winfrey survives and endures. Her Sophia never becomes parody but remains a defiant individual.

The menfolk have the worst rows to hoe. Danny Glover is so likable that he brings a human texture to Mister's misogyny, although perhaps his likability in some sense subverts the film. Willard Pugh's Harpo is another excellent character.

But the real manfolk who's failed is Spielberg. Part of his failure results from the book's essential unfilmability; as an epistolary novel, it had the freedom to range all over the place, and Manno Meyjes's script attempts clumsily to accommodate the novel's expansiveness. It brings in and dispatches story lines inelegantly; it covers necessary events in awkward narration; it relies far too heavily on time-date announcements and Celie's voice-overs; it feels patchy.

When Spielberg and Meyjes invent, the results are mixed. There is a wrenching, horrifying sequence in which Mister attempts to rape Nettie, then expels her from the farm and exiles her from Celie's life for what looks to be forever. It may be the most powerful and best sequence in the Spielberg canon; it's certainly the scariest. But on the other hand, there's a dreadful phony turn when Shug Avery reunites with her daddy that's shot like a swatch of Disney's "Song of the South" in the best zip-a-de-doo-dah fashion.

And I think Spielberg has erred gravely in the visual style of the film. It's lush and dense, whereas Walker's book is harsh and spare. He uses cinematographer Allen Daviau, who also shot "E.T." for him, and the film has a bit much of what might be called the Spielberg Look: a romantic, satiny finish to images that would feel more authentic if they were more harshly and grittily photographed.

The harsh and gritty truth of "The Color Purple" is in the performances.

(Editor's Note: Before Oprah Winfrey's rise to national prominence, she co-hosted a television talk show in Baltimore called "People Are Talking.")

DOMESTIC VIOLENCE

"When love has fled"

WHAT'S LOVE GOT TO DO WITH IT?
June 18, 1993

With a mountain of polyester hair, a voice like melted choco-late cascading over broken glass, and body language that made her seem to throb like a well-lubricated piston, Tina Turner was a sexual and musical icon of the '70s, a Circe whose siren melded the best of black blues and the hottest of white rock. Who could listen and not respond to that call? But who could know that when this proud Mary of a woman left the stage, her old man used to whack the hell out of her?

That twisted story is the substance of "What's Love Got to Do With It?" with Angela Bassett as Tina and Laurence Fishburne as Ike. It's an astonishing movie, first because, de-spite the pathology of the relationship, it's not only about vic-timization; it's a celebration of spirit, both religious and human, about a woman who finally found the guts (and the faith) to say "No more," and went on to invent a new life for herself.

But it's also a clinical examination of a relationship so com-plex it defies easy explanation: Why didn't she just leave? Be-cause in some way she understood that he created her and that all things came from him, the bad with the good. She couldn't begin to imagine a different life. She had to see herself as an independent human being — rather than as an extension of his ego and creativity — before she could leave. For his part, Ike isn't just an arbitrary bully and wife-pounder. Though the movie portrays him in all his brutal splendor, it's honest enough to suggest a theory behind his brutality, and to suggest the pain that drove the anger.

But not at the start. In the St. Louis of the late '50s, Ike Turner was quite the man. With his sleepy eyes and unobtrusive but insistent musical genius, he dominated the black club scene and trained a generation of musicians to cross the bridge between black and white worlds. He himself was thwarted in that ambition until one night a raw young woman just up from the South mounted the smoky stage to hum a few bars — a gimmick of Ike's band.

When Anna Mae Bullock opened her mouth, Ike knew he'd reached the promised land. Something in her tonalities had such richness and resonance it was a river of grief and pain, yet it hit with the impact of a charge of buckshot. He hired her on Monday, changed her name on Tuesday and married her on Wednesday. They cut their first record on Thursday and were stars by Friday. OK, an exaggeration, but only a bit: It took a couple of years, but Ike was a shrewd judge of what America wanted to hear, and in the late '60s a brief window opened in the wake of Elvis's white/black sound, and a number of black groups, including Ike and Tina Turner, broke through to the big time.

In a curious way, the story resonates with echoes of that primal show biz legend, "A Star Is Born." Ike invented Tina and watched as she grew and grew and he himself, in her shadow, shrank and shrank. Where's the rest of me, he must have wondered, and these rogue impulses soon transmuted into anger and then horror and finally violence. That which he created had become its own thing, and others yearned to take it from him. The only way he could keep it was by terrorizing it.

Angela Bassett doesn't look a lot like Tina, but she's evidently been pumping all the iron that Arnold Schwarzenegger no longer pumps, because she's turned herself into a proto-Tina, all muscle and on-stage sass. As she leaves Anna Mae behind and transmutes into Tina, she seems to alter her very body. And she's mastered the Turner stage presence, particularly that high-heeled strut that spoke so eloquently to the inchoate millions.

But that's only half the trick. In its horrifying and intimate moments, "What's Love Got to Do With It?" completely convinces. One feels these figures as true people, not as stuffed imitation celebrities; and the sense of Ike, like some bitter, dethroned lion-king, lurking menacingly in the background, nursing his wounded ego with cocaine and other women but just waiting to explode, gives the movie incredible tension.

Fishburne has always been a wonderful actor, but this Ike is quite a creation. He makes you see the intelligence and the creativity that were unshaped by education but hardened in juke joints and bars. His eyes seethe with intelligence and when he talks, people listen. I think the movie — about as pro-Tina as can be imagined — somewhat underplays his genius, but Fishburne on his own communicates it.

"What's Love Got to Do With It?" is also one of the few American movies of the past several decades to honestly embrace the issue of faith. In Tina's case, it was a commitment to the verities of Buddhism that gave her the strength and self-knowledge to break free from Ike and sever the horrible push-me-pull-you of the relationship. The movie doesn't give any attitude on this: Tina took her strength where she could find it, and unashamedly she embraces the powers of the new system of belief. So the answer to the question posed by the movie's title is "nothing." Faith, though, has *everything* to do with it.

THE WAR OF THE ROSES
December 8, 1989

"The War of the Roses" is a triumph of theory that warrants admiration for its daring consistency of tone, its willingness to hew to its own nightmarish logic, and its refusal to relinquish its dark vision for the sake of market considerations. Give it the Jean Anouilh Drama Prize. Elect Danny DeVito to the National Academy of Arts. Analyze it in *Partisan Review*.

Just don't expect to enjoy it very much.

Though the wonderfully energetic trailers prepare you for a kinetic cartoon romp through the hell that is a disintegrating marriage and a blood-letting divorce, the film itself plays far too leadenly and brutally for much laughter. It's black humor with much of the humor left out, but none of the blackness, a kind of suburban "Lord of the Flies" in which extremely comfortable people devolve into savagery rather than yield on an issue.

But the issue itself is dispiriting. "The War of the Roses" is not fought over love or betrayal or custody or any of the great themes that divide men and women: It's fought over property.

The Roses — Michael Douglas and Kathleen Turner — have a very nice house in the Washington suburbs. It's a kind of theme park of bourgeois aspiration, a white clapboard quasi-mansion, to which they devote 20 years of decorating, heaping the rooms with expensive knick-knacks and inserting a sauna into the basement. It's a monument to conspicuous consumption but, pardon the snit, the fact that their goods include not a single book suggests to me that Oliver and Barbara are pretty shallow people, even for a lawyer and his wife.

DeVito is very good in charting the calculus of physical disgust — the tics, odors and body noises that suddenly cease to be invisible — that signifies the death of affection in an intense relationship. Turner's cruel imitation of Douglas's braying, suck-up laugh is vividly amusing.

And when love has fled, the house remains; it is, after all, what their life has really been about.

DeVito, working from a script by Michael Leeson out of a novel by Warren Adler, is never able to convince us that the house battle is a displacement for larger passions. Instead of building a theory by which the house comes to stand for something, and you can see the way the two combatants pour their fury into achieving what is essentially a meaningless objective, DeVito lets the film languish in the literal: It's really about people who like their house so much they're willing to kill or die for it.

The movie is also peculiarly structured. It is narrated by DeVito, who plays a lawyer with a successful divorce practice, as a cautionary tale for a prospective (and wholly silent) client. This enables the 20-year fable to unfold with considerable telescoping, but not much coherence. It's all high points; and DeVito's comic timing, so adroit in "Throw Momma from the Train," seems badly off as scenes play too long and punch lines fall flat.

Particularly by movie's end, when the story has lost all connection to the comic impulse and is simply about a suburban hunting party, it has become laborious. Give it credit for staying the course; the question is, however, will audiences?

SLEEPING WITH THE ENEMY
February 8, 1991

There's nothing particularly bad about "Sleeping with the Enemy," but there's nothing particularly good about it either; in fact, there's almost nothing particular *about* it.

This is disappointing, not merely because it throws away the luminous Julia Roberts in a strictly routine woman-in-jeopardy number, but because the movie's director, Joseph Ruben, previously has done such excellent work in bringing incisiveness and personality to popular materials.

Ruben broke through with his Father's Day card from hell, "The Stepfather," and he consolidated with the eccentric, compelling "True Believer." But in "Sleeping with the Enemy," his work is the big doze, a skimpy, mechanistic manipulation of gooses and shocks to the system that seems over before it ever starts.

Roberts plays the wife of a sleek Boston investment banker. To the world, she has it all: glorious summer home on Cape Cod, exquisite beauty, an acre or so of lips, wealth. To herself, she has nothing: She is not merely abused but abased. The banker, played in the movie's best performance by Patrick Bergin, is an elegant, silky sadist and control freak, for whom jealousy isn't so much an emotion as a condition.

Bergin, notably charismatic in "Mountains of the Moon," is terrific. What's so scary about his performance is its icy control and sense of rectitude. He has no doubts, no irony; the logic that holds him in thrall is absolute. To this man, it makes no difference whether the towels are lined up incorrectly or his wife has looked at another man: Both are flaws that require correction instantly, and he can make no distinction between them. (In this, the movie repeats a theme from "The Stepfather"; it is a portrait of a tyrant whose most dangerous illusion is that he can completely control the world, and when, as it must, the world disappoints him, he goes ballistic.)

In her hell, Roberts finds society no help at all. Judicial restraint orders or police presence will not stop her husband from killing her, as well she knows. So she improvises a fairly transparent phony death, manages to flee and heads out to bucolic Iowa to start anew. But of course she makes a few mistakes, for no other reason than, if she didn't, there wouldn't be a movie.

That's one reason that "Sleeping with the Enemy" begins to break down: The details haven't been well thought out, and the coincidences begin piling up in such a way that Bergin, with amazing ease, sees through the ruse and begins to stalk her again.

Meanwhile, in an Iowa that's so sentimentalized it could have come intact from a '30s Metro picture, she takes up with the first guy she meets, who happens to be her next door neighbor! He's a young drama professor (played by squirrelly Kevin Anderson), and all too quickly the two become an item.

In fact, not only is Iowa sentimentalized but so is the relationship, which is envisioned in childish terms, with the two dressing up and playing games in the theater department's costume department, eating dinners of pot roast and apple pie, and strolling, thumb-locked, through verdant town squares. The movie has great fun playing cornball Iowa against the sleek and heartlessly modern house that Bergin had built; underneath, there seems to be a fable about the glories of the Midwest and the sleek but soulless harshness of the Northeast.

The endgame is thoroughly predictable, though not as extended as perhaps a lesser director would have played out. It's the old darkened house gig, a night passage through shadow and light, full of red herrings, things that go bump in the night, guns that don't go off when they should, all of it standard and only surprising here in how swiftly and with what disinterest Ruben works his way through it.

"Sleeping with the Enemy" never, however, resonates as did

"The Stepfather." It has no echoes, no implicit meanings. It's about only one thing: movie-makers making money.

Article:
CRASH! GO MOVIE MARRIAGES
December 10, 1989

Suddenly, just in time for the holidays, marriages are crashing and burning on screens everywhere.

This weekend brought us the rotten fruit of two spoiled unions. In "The War of the Roses," director Danny DeVito does a dissection of man and wife who literally despise each other exactly as they love the house that becomes their battleground until death does them part. And from the other side of the spectrum, Roseanne Barr fights for vengeance on the beautiful sophisticate (Meryl Streep) who stole her husband in "She-Devil."

When you think about the pent-up aggression billowing into white-hot violence that runs through the accounts of these two rancid connections, you realize in how short a time Hollywood has almost completely revised its image of the vows that men and women make to each other. We've come a long way, baby, from the original notion of marriage on the screen.

You remember it? It was so wonderful. It existed nowhere but on the screen in the Golden Age of Hollywood, and even if you didn't quite believe it, it sank totally into your brain so that you'll always consider yourself a failure because you didn't get it.

It was the perfect marriage.

Nick and Nora Charles — of "The Thin Man" (1934) — spring instantly to mind, but they're only the most accessible symbols of Hollywood's nearly five-decade-long infatuation with the creation of marital bliss.

Nick and Nora, derived from a Dashiell Hammett novel, were portrayed by William Powell and Myrna Loy in a fabulously successful six-movie run of detective-cum-sophisticated-comedy stories throughout the '30s and '40s; they were the urbane counterparts to Dagwood and Blondie, a kind of Mr. and Mrs. America for the smart set.

Powell and Loy were perfect foils for each other, conversing in an arch, ironic banter, amused by the pratfalls of the common man about them. They were utterly unflappable, with a quip for every situation. Yet what they sold was something more wonderful than the often mechanical mysteries in which they found themselves embroiled: It was that total, limitless submersion of one into the other as expressed not only in complete trust but also in the invention of a private language. They communicated in ways beyond the verbal — in body and hand language, in the lift of a brow, the purse of a lip, the puff of a cheek, the clink of a glass, the multiplicity of nuances carried within the single word "Darling" by which they mutually addressed themselves.

Dagwood and Blondie were the opposite ends of the spectrum, but it was the same spectrum. Low-brow and labored, poor Dagwood went about his life as American domesticated male from 1938 to 1950 in 28 movies (three in some years) with the clumsy earnestness of the good-hearted schmo he really was.

Perpetually in trouble, perpetually destroying the universe he occupied with extravagant explosions of slapstick, he relied on one person to get him through, his wife Blondie. "Blooooonnnnnnnddddddddiiiiiiiieeeee!" was the cry of despair, and of course the sublimely competent better half came running to his rescue.

Again the message was the same: Marriage wasn't between the rock and the hard place. Marriage *was* the rock.

Marriages that broke apart were viewed as pathological. "The Macomber Affair," as derived from "The Short Happy Life of Francis Macomber," a short story by Ernest Hemingway, was a typical "bad wife" film of the '40s. In it, wealthy, weaselly wimp Francis Macomber, as played by Robert Preston, miraculously found his manhood by shooting a buffalo while on safari, thus moving manly white hunter Gregory Peck almost to tears. Alas, it severely ticked off wife Joan Bennett, who applied for a divorce with a Mannlicher 6.55 mm as her attorney. The separation of the couple was instantaneous (well, actually about the time it takes a bullet that size to fly from muzzle to target 100 yards away) and the settlement more than generous, with all property going to the widow.

Hemingway's misogyny wasn't atypical, even though it was cruel: It pretty much represented the norm. The woman who couldn't hold on to her man was sick. Witness Scarlett O'Hara, the golden era's most notorious failed housewife. When, at the end of "Gone With the Wind," the man who once loved her so completely no longer gave a damn, his gesture was viewed as the final comeuppance for an uppity woman.

Only the great Orson Welles was able to see through the veneer of social propriety that shielded marriage: In "Citizen Kane" he had the temerity to suggest that the flaws in marriages frequently originated with the male part of the union as well. His Charles Foster Kane lost his first wife in a terrible scandal when he was discovered in a "love nest" (quite innocent) with a "singer," whom he then attempted to promote into an opera star in order to, in Joseph Cotten's memorable phrase, "take the quote marks away from the word 'singer.'" But Welles's point was well-taken: that in both cases the marriage (and its collapse) were not necessarily the woman's fault, and not necessarily anybody's fault. Love, like any product, simply wears out with usage unless it is lubricated regularly.

Yet for decades, the idea of the perfect marriage persisted. It was the ultimate goal of any woman. "How to Marry a Millionaire," from the '50s, is a perfect example, but more generally the thrust of all manner of male-female relationships was toward marriage. The Doris Day-Cary Grant and, later, Day-Rock Hudson films always played coy games with sexual possibility, as Day's considerable virtue seemed in danger, but she was always saved, in the end, by marriage.

Film culture, of course, reflects the larger culture that spawned it. For reasons too complex to recount here — or anywhere — marriages in the millions began failing sometime in the '60s. Suddenly, divorce wasn't the exclusive property of the debauched rich; it had become a middle-class phenomenon and even a working-class one.

Perhaps the key divorce movie of the late '60s was "Divorce American Style" (from, loosely, "Divorce Italian Style"), which announced the arrival of divorce to the Kmart. The exclusively male movie — Norman Lear and Bud Yorkin wrote, produced and directed before hitting the big time in "All in the Family" on TV — made a sardonic account of the inequities of divorce law, featuring a memorable line that hangs around to haunt all those thinking about bailing out. "She gets the uranium mine," howled Dick Van Dyke about soon-to-be-ex-wife Debbie Reynolds, "and I get the shaft!"

Divorce was not only bad, it was something worse: It was instant poverty, terrifying to newly prosperous heroes of the middle class.

The '70s brought something new to the movies: a threatening feminism assaulting some bastions of male power, which resulted in what might be called the upswing of the bad mommy movie. In a typical bad mommy movie, Mommy, infected by feminism, did what only daddies had done theretofore: She walked out to find herself.

The worst mommy of them all was Meryl Streep in Robert Benton's "Kramer vs. Kramer." Mommy walks out; Daddy must be both mommy and daddy, not hard if Daddy is that champion of sensitivity, Dustin Hoffman, able to locate in the crucible of isolation his centers of nurturing and thus become the mother the boy is missing.

A cruel judge and a crueler legal system then find against him in a custody hearing, holding his lessened earning power against him, vis-a-vis Mommy's new-found success as a freelance fashion designer. Of course, bad Mommy relents in the last reel, giving up the child she feels she hasn't "earned." Another variation on the bad-mommy theme was "Author, Author," with lovable Al Pacino as Mr. Mom.

But the '70s also saw what was probably the best of the divorce movies, the only one to achieve genuine art. This was Paul Mazursky's wise and clever "An Unmarried Woman," with

Jill Clayburgh as a New York housewife abandoned by her husband for a younger woman.

Mazursky, a much underestimated American filmmaker, was extremely generous to both parties; he wasn't one of those with an ideological ax to grind in the battle between the sexes. But he was wonderfully observant. In one brilliant moment, Michael Murphy, dumped by his young woman, came by and actually expected . . . sympathy.

But sensitivity like Mazursky's was rare. By the '80s, a new cliche had replaced the cliche of the perfect marriage: the perfect divorce.

In a perfect divorce, the partners exchange no rancor or bitterness and remain friends and confidants. In fact, they have something of the elan and easeful mutual bliss of Nick and Nora Charles. The kids are all right, too. And she still does his laundry and figures out the checkbook. Uh-huh.

The most ridiculous of these, despite its beguiling surface, was Bud Yorkin's "Twice in a Lifetime," in which Gene Hackman dumped his wife Ellen Burstyn for Ann-Margret. But the temerity of the film was that it insisted on seeing all this as an opportunity for "growth." Even Burstyn was a "better woman" for her ordeal.

By the late '80s, divorce had become useful entirely as a badge of exile for existential heroes. It was but another symptom of disconnection for exiled princes, a mark of moral isolation that was part of their purification for ordeals to come. Heavily influenced by film noir states of dissipation, the new divorced man was made strong by his isolation.

In "Black Rain," for example, Michael Douglas was proudly divorced, and the movie went to great lengths to point this out. It was seen as a mark of honor, somehow. Don Johnson, in the otherwise lame "Dead Bang," was in similar straits: the man alone, having driven his woman off. It's one of the reverse-twists in '80s hip: That which was once scandalous and pathological has now become, though seedy, somehow a mark of cool.

Thus "War of the Roses" and "She-Devil" come as anomalies. They return the prospect of divorce to the realm of pain, no matter how comically inflated. They make the point, collectively, that breaking up is hard to do — that you pay for it in oceans of hurt.

THE HAND THAT ROCKS THE CRADLE
January 10, 1992

One of the now-vanished staples of the old B movies was the "vs." film. "Earth vs. the Flying Saucers" is probably the genre's tacky masterpiece. But who can forget Mamie Van Doren's "The Navy vs. the Night Monsters" or the immortal "Billy the Kid vs. Dracula"?

Now along comes "The Hand That Rocks the Cradle," which is a classic "vs." movie, except that the monster doesn't ride a big Frisbee or arise in slimy, gooey splendor from the depths of the sea or suck necks. She dresses in Villager clothes; she's a yuppie from hell. The movie is really "Good Mom vs. Psycho Mom."

With a high level of craftsmanship and almost no moral qualms at all, it sets up a situation in which an outsider conspires to bump a young mother out of her own family and take over. The movie has some violence, but far more effectively it traffics in subtly escalating psychological stratagems and the cold, clammy sensation of watching a cobra track a mouse, setting it up for the strike.

Director Curtis Hanson specializes in this highly refined arena of creepy pseudo-mayhem; he directed the spooky "Bedroom Window" (set here in Baltimore) and more recently offered low thrills in "Bad Influence," with Rob Lowe and James Spader. Working from a script by Amanda Silver, he keeps this project rolling along smoothly, gradually escalating the fears, never over-inflating the violence, until the end, when it gets out of control.

The cast is excellent. In fact, who better to play a deranged yet cool psychopath than kewpie-doll perfect Rebecca De Mornay? De Mornay, with her icy blue eyes and tiny, exact features, already looks as if she came out of a mold, not a womb. She seems not quite human to begin with, and when she makes nice in the early going, we can see through it even if poor Annabella Sciorra can't.

Sciorra is a perfect foil. Unlike De Mornay's glittery, abstracted Aryan, Sciorra has a warmer, Mediterranean cast to her: She's a beautiful earth mother already, her eyes radiating a kind of nurturing warmth. You would never wonder if she hugged her kid today; *of course* she has.

The event that sets the dueling moms up is insidiously imagined. The pregnant Sciorra is molested by her gynecologist; reluctantly, she brings charges. The doctor, destroyed by the scandal, then commits suicide and his estate is tangled up in litigation. His young widow loses everything — her home, her prosperity, the child she was carrying, and worst of all, the possibility of ever carrying another.

The widow, of course, is De Mornay. Unhinged by the destruction of her life, she sets out to counter-destroy the woman she holds responsible — Sciorra, of course. Sweetly obtaining a position of nanny in Sciorra's household, she sets about to seduce away from her Sciorra's two kids and somewhat dim husband.

The campaign is made more horrifying by the background: perfectly visualized upscale Seattle, where large old houses nestle in homey domesticity under towering elms; and Sciorra's husband (Matt McCoy, barely registering), a research scientist, brings home a decent paycheck every week.

In this unthreatening context, the campaign is greatly abetted by Sciorra's fundamental faith in the human race: As her position is subtly undermined, as her children bond to the other woman, as her goofy husband comes to rely upon De Mornay, Sciorra simply can't conceptualize the immensity of the conspiracy against her. She thinks she's just having bad luck when she "accidentally" loses a funding proposal she promised to take to the post office for her husband, or when her sexiest dress turns up with a stain and she's forced to go out in a frumpy frock.

Sciorra's only defenders are a retarded helping hand, well played by Ernie Hudson, and a shrewish best friend, played by

Julianne Moore. However, both are bumblers unsuited for combat with such a cunning adversary.

The movie's unholiest moment is also its best. That's when, much like "Fatal Attraction," the worm turns, and the audience, nurtured carefully to a high pitch of blood-lust, atavistically unites with the besieged heroine and celebrates with a blast of pleasure her decision to finally kick ass.

And, like "Fatal Attraction," "The Hand That Rocks the Cradle" benefits from a number of resonant subthemes. In one sense, it plays on the fears possessed by the millions of working mothers who must turn their child-rearing responsibilities over to others. But there's a political angle, too.

In some sense, this is a film about a liberal education — in street reality. Sciorra and her husband are sweet and decent people, untinged by bias or paranoia, willing to grant anyone the benefit of the doubt, trusting and decent. In the '90s, that means they're free lunch. Only when they find the will to resist violence with more violence — to become, in effect, vigilantes, and demonstrate how short is the distance from the cradle to the grave — do they manage to triumph and restore their lives.

Sad though it is, that's the bleak message — the movie is really about "Us vs. Them."

THIS BOY'S LIFE
April 23, 1993

All boys' lives are different in details, but all are the same, too, in the larger outline. And the largest outline of all sooner or later belongs to that caricature of horror and terror, that buffoon and bully, that dark, unreachable tyrant, that stupid, uncool moron — the father figure.

"This Boy's Life" is a brilliant account of one boy's struggle with the man who controls his life, who happens not to be his blood father but his stepfather. The movie is derived from Tobias Wolff's brief and harrowing memoir of the same name.

In the mid-1950s, Wolff and his mother were more or less

abandoned by his natural father and her husband, a colorful, worthless rogue with aristocratic pretensions whose life was later to be chronicled in a book by Wolff's brother Geoffrey, called "The Duke of Deception." The mother and son wandered, ending up in Washington state, where at last she took up with, and eventually married, a widowed mechanic named Dwight. She and her son moved into his ramshackle rural house just outside of Concrete, Wash. Then all hell broke loose.

It's hard to watch Robert De Niro's brilliant and terrifying performance as Dwight without thinking of the dreadful Vernon Howell, a.k.a. David Koresh. Though Dwight's kingdom was smaller, it seems ruled by the same nearly atavistic forces. He was one of those sad little men of great delusions who, denied power by the more sensible natural world, became addicted to wielding it within the framework of his squalid little fortress and evolved into a braying, self-aggrandizing, endlessly violent monster.

De Niro gets it brilliantly: Dwight's avuncular, down-homey style, his twerpy, country-boy mannerisms ("You can call me anything you want, just don't call me . . . late for dinner"), his petty vanities and cheap clothes, his intense identification with '50s cultural assumptions of fathers knowing best — and his secret, desperate fears. He loves to tell boring stories about his triumphs as a rifle shot and fist fighter, and to paint a picture of himself as idealized male — a gruff, tough, masculine, John Wayne figure. But it's soon clear that these are all delusional fantasies. He's a lousy shot, a coward and sexually dysfunctional.

But he loves to push people around and exert his authority in pathological ways. He simply cannot control his willingness to dominate, while sanctimoniously explaining to his victims that it's for their own good. He and Toby (Leonardo DiCaprio) are mortal enemies from the start.

Perhaps it's that, before his mother does, Toby sees through Dwight. Perhaps it's that he represents that most hated thing, the outside world. Perhaps it's that the child is bright and adventurous and longs to do the one thing that Dwight never could: get out. Whatever it is, it's war.

It begins harshly and accelerates exponentially, from constant hectoring to full-scale violence. In a scene toward the end, Dwight literally beats the young man bloody because he threw out a mustard jar with too much mustard left in it.

But what's best about "This Boy's Life" is that it isn't a self-important victim's song in which an abused child complains about the tragedy of his life. It fairly demonstrates that Toby's own pathologies were a factor — his sullen rebelliousness, his own sense of superiority that was probably a subtext in his stepfather's anger, and subtle patterns of sexual competition between stepfather and stepson for possession of mother (Ellen Barkin).

The movie manages to depict this horrible phenomenon of "child abuse" in complex artistic terms, rather than with the broad brush of victim movies.

Is it a great movie? Yes — brilliant performances, exquisitely conceived '50s details (none of that phony, those-were-the-days garbage), and quietly insistent but never showy staging by Michael Caton-Jones.

Is it fun? Not for a second.

The threat of violence hangs too heavily in the air. The terrified child is vulnerable to the one figure in whom he has placed all his trust. Wolff was clearly one of the lucky ones. He got out.

LEGENDS OF THE FALL
January 13, 1995

"Legends of the Fall" is soap opera for men.

It's about legends in the minds of dreamy city boys who couldn't find the sky without a map that points up. It's full of junk, fundamentally a romantic yearning for the lost power of well-born white men (which it disguises by cloaking itself in political correctness) and other absurdist romantic conceits: poetic killers, loyal women with cheekbones like the Arch of Triumph, subservient but virtuous and wise Indians, handsome clothes straight out of those pretentious Ralph Lauren spreads in *Vanity Fair*, and that rarest of all birds, the good death.

That's the one I like the best, the good-death bit. At the end of the film, one of the heroes dies a good death at the hands of a teed-off grizzly bear. Of course, to get a good death out of the spasm of violence that is an animal's attack, one must smear a pabulum of sentimentality on the lens. Hazy focus, muted colors, ringing music are a must. Otherwise, the reality that it's the most violent, painful and degrading death available in nature might become evident. Anyone calling it "good" doesn't know what he's talking about, which is generally true of the film.

Set between roughly 1914 and 1930, "Legends of the Fall" follows a tribe of men on a big ranch: a father and his three sons, each of whom has a single defining characteristic. One is called Hoss, the other Adam, and the third Little Joe. Oh, no, all right: One is called Cain, the other Abel, and the third Little Cain. Oh, for the last time, all right: They are Alfred (Aidan Quinn), Tristan (Brad Pitt) and Samuel (Henry Thomas, once "E.T.'s" best buddy).

To make things really irritating, the story is narrated in bogus Native-Americanspeak to give it a dimension of poetic drivel that's quite enough, thank you. One Stab (Gordon Tootoosis) recalls the intertwined gyres of the Ludlow boys, particularly Tristan, who "hears his own inner voice with great clearness and lives by what he hears."

The three are the progeny of old Colonel Ludlow (Anthony Hopkins), an ex-Indian fighter turned peacenik. Just a little bit ahead of his time, he hated the Indian wars he had to fight and the exploitation of the Indians, but that didn't stop him from acquiring a huge spread on former Indian territory and hiring no end of stoop Native-American labor to perform the skunk jobs on the place.

It's a kind of demi-Eden in which each boy is free to pursue his star until . . . the woman shows up. Played by the beautiful Julia Ormond, Susannah arrives as the fiancée of young idealistic Harvard student Samuel, but her presence is so erotically galvanizing that she totally miswires the family circuits. Both wild and outdoorsy Tristan and grimly ambitious Alfred take one look and begin to yearn secretly, but nobly.

The apple cart is truly upset when young Samuel insists on racing off to defend Western Civilization against the Hun by joining the Canadian army and getting into the Big Show. Of course, the other two are too darn noble to make time with Susannah while he's gone, so off they go too, sworn to protect him.

War being war, such pledges don't prove easy to keep: Samuel ends up hung out on the wire for German machine-gun practice (the World War I sequences are the film's most harrowing, as director Edward Zwick learned his battlefield maneuvers on "Glory"). Alfred, a staff officer, blames Tristan, a scout, for letting it happen to advance Tristan's cause with Julia.

This sets guilt-racked Tristan out on a lost odyssey in which he gives himself over to masculinity's darker pleasures, roaming the seas as a trader and professional hunter, honing his killer skills (which first were expressed in his vengeance on the Germans back in the trenches), whoring, drinking, and growing his blonde hair really long, thereby generally exiling himself from the community of the well-born.

The self-hatred that courses through Tristan has an odd commonality with Pitt's work in the equally picturesque and solemn "A River Runs Through It." In both, he's the younger brother with a penchant toward self-destruction and a gift for violence who suffers by turning his best side to the camera. It was as unconvincing there as it is here.

When Tristan returns, he finds that Alfred has married Julia and taken her to the hated "city" where he's become a congressman and fallen in with a mob of Irish gangsters who run the town. (By the way, for a movie that claims to be so politically correct, it has no qualms about ascribing the worst kind of stereotyping to the ethnic Irish, who are universally slandered as rapacious gangsters.)

By this time, Hopkins has exiled Alfred from his affections and so mourns the loss of Tristan that he's had a stroke that turns him into Charles Laughton as "The Hunchback of Notre Dame." Really, watching Hopkins chew the fat, the scenery and most of the crew's doughnuts is the one thoroughly amusing pleasure "Legends of the Fall" yields as it plays out the Susannah-Tristan-Alfred love triangle, building to an inept and unconvincingly staged gun battle, in which the Ludlows finally have it out with the Irish boys of the city.

What "Legends of the Fall" lacks is any spirit of rigor. It buys into — indeed, is selling — the oldest of guff: the idea that the violence of banal men is beautiful and righteous. It honors male anger. I'm tempted to contrast it with the as yet unopened "Cobb," which examines Tyrus Raymond Cobb's burning furies.

"Cobb" is rigorous and honest and understands the price of male anger, and how it isolates and degrades its holder even as it may propel him toward greatness. "Legends of the Fall" worships the red shift of men gone nuts on vengeance. It romanticizes gunplay. It's a big movie that's so small on the inside it's not really there.

Article:
MAJOR-LEAGUE ANGER
February 19, 1995

Can it be more than coincidence that in the aftermath of an election that has gone on to define the national mood as the Revenge of the Angry White Man, along comes a movie biography of the angriest whitest man of them all?

That would be the tidal wave of testosterone and fury known as Tyrus Raymond Cobb, who burned the major leagues for 123 records over 24 fierce and bitter years, ending up as the all-time major-league batting champion, with a career mark of .367. Some have said we shall never see his like again. And someone (me) has added: Who would want to?

Who indeed? Cobb, according to filmmaker Ron Shelton and sportswriter Al Stump, from whose work Shelton derived the just-opened "Cobb," was a spectacular misanthrope. He was racist, violent, shrewd, nasty, mean and extremely tough. He hit lefties, he hit righties, he hit women, he hit blacks, he hit cripples. And that was on a *good* day. You should have seen him when he was ticked off, as on May 5 and May 6, 1925, when he became the first man in modern history to hit five home runs in two games, a record since equaled but never surpassed, even by the mighty Ruth, whom, it need not be added, Cobb despised.

Cobb's pathology was so intense, it is really the subject of "Cobb." In no true sense a full biography of the man's life, the movie is more exactly a map of that dark cloud of energy and loathing known as male anger.

The movie takes off from the fact that in 1960, the nationally known sportswriter Stump signed on to do an authorized biography of the dying ballplayer and discovered not an aging warrior going gracefully into the night, but a full-toot, three-sheets-to-the-wind bastard. Focusing on the old goat's last vicious rampage through snowstorms, Tahoe whorehouses, the Hall of Fame and finally the Georgia hospital in which he died, the movie profits from its classical situation: That is, a normal man (Stump is played by Robert Wuhl), who acknowledges society's limits, encounters a rare one who doesn't and is horrified by what he sees. That's our point of view: "We are *the Wuhl*."

But at the same time — and this is what makes the movie work — Stump cannot quite bite down a little bile of admiration. For while it's evident that Tommy Lee Jones's Cobb has paid a terrible price — he's beaten his body to painful shreds, his anger has unleashed all the demons of the night to devour his digestive and respiratory systems, he's got a crab eating at his lymph glands, he is despised and alone, his family hates and has abandoned him, no other ballplayers will have anything to do with him — he's weirdly happy and, in some foul way, the last free man alive. He did it his way and he's tasted something no normal man ever has or ever will. Like George Bailey, he's had a wonderful life.

Whence came all this black fury? What drove Cobb to slide hard into second base, spikes up, when his legs were so bloody and raw he could barely walk on them off the diamond? Whatever things Cobb feared in the dark of his mind, pain wasn't one of them, and as his many fights both on and off the field attest, fear itself wasn't either.

As it turns out, Shelton buys into Stump's penny-ante shrink job on Cobb, as have most Cobb biographers. Cobb, the theory goes, was created out of a family tragedy, when, on Aug. 7, 1905, as the minor leaguer was about to go up to the majors, his father was accidentally shotgunned to death by his mother. It's a killing with dark currents to it. Possibly, as some rumors have maintained, the homicide wasn't an accident, and the much younger Mother Cobb wasn't alone when the much-older Father Cobb came across her and parties unspecified.

Cobb, the theory specifies, was one of those men who adored and admired his father and yearned to please the man. The death having completely sealed off that possibility, Cobb acquired a fund of flaming anger that drove him furiously; or, perhaps in some dank corner of guy-hell, he actually believed his father was looking down on him.

The theory has a nice ring to it, but it's not one I'd buy. It fails to conform to a social truth that haunts us to this day, which is that those who are abused become abusers in return. Cobb was evidently never abused by his father, but more usually was viewed from afar, through a screen of Victorian reserve. Cobb, however, *was* violently abused by his teammates when he joined his first professional baseball team in 1902 as a 17-year-old boy.

Of course, in those far-off days, no concept of child abuse had yet been developed, but read any account of Cobb's early years and you'll discover that the ritual of hazing that the young man underwent went way beyond cruel and unusual. In the raw and violent rural Southern minor leagues of the early 20th century, new ballplayers were seen as either a threat or a menace. At 17, he was really still a child, dumped into a pure Hobbesian universe of misery and predation, undergoing the worst imaginable physical cruelty at the most vulnerable moments in his life.

He was taught that baseball life was war, pure and total, and that the only way to survive was to be meaner and tougher and more merciless than his teammates. This pattern intensified when he reached Detroit at the end of the 1905 season and for three years was subject to almost unbearable hostility. He actually suffered a nervous breakdown from the pressure in 1906 and spent a month and a half in a sanitarium. One thinks of Hemingway's line: "The world breaks many people, but then they mend, and are strongest in the mended places."

In fact, Cobb went from victim to predator so quickly and so irreversibly that there never was a moment of peace for him; he was never hugged or told it was all right. He was like a punk sent to prison to fester among older, more savage inmates — our century's one sure prescription for manufacturing more violent crime. And a criminal he became. He never had a chance to get in touch with his softer, feminine side because the corn-pone cracker killers he lived and traveled with would have ripped him apart if he did. So he entered the world of manhood made so tough he was hardly human and made so paranoid he was hardly alive. He asked and gave no quarter, not merely for the 24 years he played ball but for all the years thereafter; he even publicly horsewhipped his son when the boy flunked out of Princeton.

A phenomenon of such pure, unvarnished anger is rare to baseball movies, which have usually turned on homey pieties of teamwork and sacrifice, and have reduced the most horrific of ego monsters to Cub Scouts or Ronald Reagan. But such people are not rare to movies. That's why everything about "Cobb" feels familiar, however removed from tradition the materials themselves might seem to be.

As a staple of American movies (and of American literature), male anger is an old-fashioned kind of thing. If you look at American movies over the past 50 years, it's easy to see that they've pretty much been about angry white men. In fact, if there's any connection between "Cobb" and the election, it's that the election simply transformed into political reality a current that's been familiar in the culture for years and years.

Not only is the fury familiar; so is the structure that dramatizes it. Underneath the "male anger movie" — there are enough of them to almost qualify as a genre — is always the same relationship that I have previously mentioned: The point-of-view character is always the sane "civilized" man who comes into the sphere of male demonism. He is shocked, scared, devastated, disapproving, morally superior. Yet a certain subversive part of him connects with and is expressed through the outrageous doings of the angry man; he comes away oddly improved, perhaps even made a man by his experience, whatever that may mean.

The root angry-man story isn't, as have been so many of them, a cop story or even a western. It's very eastern, so eastern it's set in the ocean, where angry Ahab tracks down the white whale that destroyed his ship and hideously maimed him. Alas, no decent film has been made of this great American story, though Gregory Peck had some fun baying at the moon in the mediocre 1956 John Huston version.

But Ahab's anger, even if no movie dramatized it sufficiently, also set the pattern for what came after: It was almost always the anger of vengeance, the dark and foreboding sense that something had been taken from the victim and the victim would get it back. Melville was smart enough to understand what no movie-maker has: that anger is fundamentally irrational and that vengeance against the irrational is meaningless. As Starbuck (the mate) says: "It's just a whale, boys. A huge one, but just a whale." Of course, he dies, too.

In the modern film era, the darkest of angry men was surely the Ethan Edwards that John Wayne played in John Ford's brilliant "The Searchers." This was quite a stretch for Wayne, who had generally become a more benign male authority figure whose humanity was always revealed (as, say, Sergeant Stryker in "Sands of Iwo Jima"). It connected with only one of his previous roles, the dark trail master in Howard Hawks's "Red River," and it reached depths at which he'd never arrive again.

It was his greatest role: Ethan Edwards is a shrewd, vengeful man, obsessed with avenging what would appear to be the slaughter of his brother's family by renegade Comanches. But of course, that's not it at all. Look at it carefully, and you see that Ethan's hatred is sexual. He was in love with his brother's wife (Wayne in early scenes with Dorothy Jordan is unbelievably tender). Thus the Comanche crime isn't murder, which after all is pretty much their business, as Wayne understands; rather, it's the death of his romantic illusions and the further tarnishing of them by the raising of Jordan's child as an Indian.

Like Ahab, Edwards is fundamentally a purist, a zealot and very complex. It's clear that he lived with the Comanches, knows their way and that somehow he even loves them as he hunts them. What liberates him is a terrifying act of violence — scalping his enemy — that somehow allows him to return to civilization, having lost himself to savagery and recovered. Yet, as a door closes him out of civilization in the last frame, it's cruelly clear that he can never come back.

After Wayne, the angriest of the angry white men was Clint Eastwood's Inspector Harry Callahan, a tough law-'n-'order cop who detested, in 1972's "Dirty Harry," what permissive '60s social experimentation had unleashed into society. The movie is a jeremiad against liberal values, a diverse society, "feelings" and "communication," and a complete endorsement of male authority. Harry's tragedy is that the world has lost confidence in, or seen through, the values he still believes in. The anger has the same effect as Ahab's and Cobb's: It isolates him totally.

And, like Cobb's and Ahab's, it also enables him. For that's the oddest thing about the movie's pernicious treatment of anger — even as it seems to despise it, it secretly glorifies it. Ahab, Ethan Edwards, Ty Cobb, Dirty Harry: All were heroes. All were capable of almost unbelievable heroic action — Cobb in life (if baseball is life) and the others in the romantic projection of fiction. No true squalor attends them, no true fear haunts them. Their anger is alchemized into pure adrenaline: Harry can stand calmly in the street as an automobile careens at him, pumping bullets at the driver like a Great White Hunter facing a rogue buffalo. The movie pretends to lament his isolation, but it finds his heroism extremely cool.

That's true finally of the greatest of the Angry White Man movies, one of the greatest of all American movies: Martin Scorsese's "Raging Bull" (1980). Another sports bio, it focused on the toughest of the tough and the craziest of the crazy and the angriest of the angry: boxer Jake La Motta. This film, though it features a lot of dynamic fight action, whereas "Cobb" features almost no game action, actually has a great deal in common with "Cobb." Again, it's not a "biography" so much as a pathology, like the cross-sectioning of a brain tumor in a morgue somewhere: It's never interested in sports culture (no working out, no sparring in rings) and feels entirely disconnected from conventional sports bio. Rather, it treats La Motta's fury in the ring as something beyond technique and stamina, beyond, really, even talent: It's simple psychosis.

In a fight, La Motta is beyond civilization, both horrifying and transfiguring the point-of-view character, his brother, played by Joe Pesci. It charts the same action that "Cobb" charts: The rise to greatness fueled by high-octane anger and the eventual collapse of the personality by the same burden. In the end, Jake betrays everybody, especially those who love him the most. He beats his wife, he beats his brother, he ends up alone. Ironically, Pesci would play the Mafia equivalent of Jake La Motta in "GoodFellas," another anger-crazed essay in machismo whose fury would be both the fuel of his rise and the flame of his fall. Anger is a key Scorsese theme, one reason why "The Age of Innocence," which lacked it, was ultimately so dispiriting.

Two years back, there was another Angry Man movie, Joel Schumacher's "Falling Down." Schumacher is no Scorsese, and he's no Shelton: He took a potentially interesting topic and made it cheap and PC. The true anger it stirred was in the audience and among the critics.

But "Cobb" notwithstanding, that doesn't mean anger is passe. The fact is, the movies love Ahab's rage, for it propels men to their most extreme behavior, and for that reason, it can never be completely disowned. Someone once made a film called "The Last Angry Man." As far as Hollywood is concerned, that day will never come.

NO EXIT

"Lost in hell or some suburb thereof"

LAST EXIT TO BROOKLYN
September 27, 1990

When it was published in the early '60s, Hubert Selby's "Last Exit to Brooklyn" was a scandal in a culture ripe to be scandalized. This was before the Beatles, after all.

With its stark portrayals of working-class degradation along the rotting waterfront of Brooklyn, its explicit description of homosexual acts, and its shattering scene of a young prostitute having sex with hundreds of guys during a long night's journey into day, it brought both realism and squalor to American literature.

And now it's the '90s. And now somebody has made an amazingly literal film version of the book.

And now the response:
ZZZZZZZZZZZZZZZZZZZZZZZZZZZZZ.

It's not that Uli Edel's version is bad, mind you. In fact, it's a fairly ingenious adaptation of a work many thought was unfilmable. And it's not that the performances are bad, though some of them are. And it's not that the ideas of the book are bad, though again, some of them are.

It's that what was calculated as an affront to morality is hardly worth a ripple in a society in which photos of men with bullwhip handles up their rectums can be considered art. And lacking that edge, that thrust of defiance, the piece soon reveals its fraudulent nature. It's crude, sentimental, craftless, lurid and phony all at once. It's so overblown, it doesn't begin to move you.

The novel was essentially six short stories held together on the principle of geographic unity, rather than artistic unity. Edel, working from a screenplay by Desmond Makano, does a good job of streamlining these tales into a semblance of coherent narrative, with the disparate strands reflecting ironically on each other. But he's reduced the six to three: the family travails of a brutish metal worker (played by Burt Young), the adventures of the young prostitute Tralala (Jennifer Jason Leigh) and the coming-out of union shop steward and radical Harry Black (Stephen Lang).

The Young subplot can be dismissed quickly: It's routine guff, the old one about the beast with the heart of gold, surrounded by a family of seething, emotional Italians. Young phones in the same hearty-peasant performance that has bought him lunch since he pioneered it in the first "Rocky."

Story No. 2 is equally problematic. This tells the self-destructive spiral of Tralala, who makes a career out of picking men up and leading them into alleys where her pals from the bar mug them. But whatever fires stir in Tralala, Leigh is unable to define them. In the first place, the movie achieves a kind of ratty movie-phoniness off the front, by failing to disguise the young actress's beauty. Prostitutes on the Brooklyn waterfront of 1952 never looked like movie stars, bleached hair or not.

But Leigh as an actress is also somewhat a shaky presence; it's not a performance, it's an impersonation. We never understand what's going on inside that degraded brain of Tralala, what's driving her. Leigh plays her as dumb, not doomed; she's spectacular but shallow.

It's the third story — Harry Black and the Homosexual — that's the most interesting. Stephen Lang is an excellent actor, as he's proven on "Crime Story" (he was the idealistic young lawyer who ended up working for the mob) and in a few movies. His specialty is passion — he's always gritting his teeth and letting his eyes well with tears of anger or pain. He does a lot of both in "Last Exit."

Harry is a small-beer tyrant swollen with power because, as shop steward, he's suddenly become important during a strike. But one day he spies the sylph-like form of an extremely effeminate homosexual and finds responses inside himself that he didn't realize were there and whose name he dare not speak.

As a portrait of a man in the grip of an obsession, this aspect of "Last Exit" is truly interesting, but it's also dated. Its view of homosexuality is problematic: Gay men are all swishes, it says, and they delight in seducing and destroying the straight. Once Harry falls for "Regina" (an actor calling himself Zette), he's dead meat, lost on the road to degradation. He ends up molesting a child — the movie seems not to understand that homosexuality and child molestation are different conditions — and is finally crucified for his crimes.

It isn't very pretty what a town without pity can do.

SID AND NANCY
December 24, 1986

"Morons From Outer Space," a British comedy of somewhat dubious reputation, never played Baltimore this year. But a version of the film has finally reached us: It's Alex Cox's "Sid and Nancy," and it might have been called "Morons from *Earth*."

Whatever their planet of origin, the title characters seem like aliens. The movie is hypnotically fascinating in its chronicle of a drain-plunge to oblivion, as lived by Sid Vicious, the replacement bassist for the rock group Sex Pistols, and his American girlfriend Nancy Spungeon; a journey much accelerated by epic quantities of drugs and alcohol and lubricated with the grease of intense self-hatred. This sad-sack couple managed to tumble from loud mediocrity to quiet hell without much fun in between; alas, Cox doesn't seem interested in infusing the material with tragedy. It feels cold; watching it has the distinctly uncomfortable feeling of watching animals die in a pen.

The story may be summed up briefly: Sid Vicious, the nom de rock of John Simon Ritchie, enjoyed a brief vogue in the London punk scene of the mid-'70s, chiefly for his insanely raw musical style and willingness to harm himself for the amusement of others. At the height — or depth — of his fame, he met and became chums with an American groupie named Nancy Spungeon, who had clear but unsavory goals: to sleep with as many rockers as possible. The two of them had weird chemistry;

they loved, they laughed, they shot up, they dried out, they shot up. They may have even had a little sex. Then Sid killed Nancy with a knife and, a few weeks later, killed himself with a needle. Wise commentators saw them as "symbols" of alienated youth, though it's doubtful they knew what the word "symbol" meant.

I cannot say I enjoyed the movie a bit; on the other hand, I cannot say I looked away for a second; on still another hand, I cannot say that I learned a damn thing. Cox is meticulously accurate, even re-creating, on the same site, Sid's drug-addled murder of Nancy at New York's Chelsea Hotel in 1978. The film's surface feels immaculate, polished, lapidarily scabrous (with one lapse); the acting, by Gary Oldham as Sid and Chloe Webb as Nancy, is nothing short of astonishing; the only thing missing is Cox's attitude toward all this. He observes with a clinical detachment known but to God or another junkie.

The method of the film is curious. To begin with, Cox completely avoids offering any theory on the curious behavior of these one-way kids. He puts them in no wider context, and never bothers to do the simplest scene setting. He treats them as little dolls of self-destruction: Wind them up and watch them suffer. It's as if he's never heard of psychology; he doesn't interpret their behavior by the typical Freudian model of overcompensation for childhood abuses. He doesn't even offer Sid as a kind of conventional misunderstood talent; he doesn't appear to believe Sid had any real talent at all. At the same time, he doesn't see Sid and Nancy as victims exploited first by Sex Pistols promoter Malcolm McLaren and second by Sex Pistols lead singer Johnny Rotten (played with surprising lack of charisma by Drew Schofield) so much as simple idiots. Cox explains nothing; he just shows everything.

There's a further oddity that gives the movie its extremely creepy feel. In its camera work, the film seems to reflect the perceptions of the drug addict. It co-opts us, makes us co-conspirators, co-users. The focus drifts subtly, unanchored, as if the camera itself had just shot up; its attention wanders, finds odd objects interesting, has trouble following conversations and subjects. Or, at odd moments, it will enjoy the illusion of piercing clarity, when the composition of the frames takes on the precious over-designed precision of an album cover. It's as if Cox, who directed the manic and relentlessly hysterical "Repo Man" (about half a good movie), has decided that the only person who could get close to Sid and Nancy would be another junkie and so he's made the audience one.

The film breaks down occasionally. Sid and Nancy make a pilgrimage to Nancy's suburban Philadelphia house, where the family is oversatirized as vulgar American-Jewish creeps to such a degree that it's actually offensive. And a few fantasy scenes have the look of over-produced videos.

But when Sid and Nancy are alone in their hellish little hotel room, desperate to score, the film makes you feel the terror of the deadest end of all.

RIVER'S EDGE
June 18, 1987

A famous rock anthem suggests that the kids are all right, but if you take to heart the bleak message of "River's Edge," you have to conclude that the kids are not all right. The kids are terrifying.

The movie is based upon an actual event, one of those banal atrocities of everyday life in these here United States that somehow never make it into the *Reader's Digest*. In Milpitas, Calif., a 16-year-old boy rather pointlessly strangled his 14-year-old girlfriend. More fascinated with what he had done than possessed of any moral attitude toward it, he proceeded to bring his friends by to look at the body. It was a phenomenon that somehow needed a theory to interpret it, and no theories came forth for 48 hours, until someone got around to informing the police, who then applied the quaintly old-fashioned theory of guilt and innocence. The unaffectedness of the involved kids turned the seedy killing, with some inevitability, into a big media event. All over America, anchormen displayed concern.

Chilling though that is, screenwriter Neal Jimenez and director Tim Hunter have embellished considerably upon it, not necessarily to good effect. They have inserted the event into a more conventional melodramatic plot, involving several other strands of conflict beyond the kids and their incapacity to comprehend murder. They've invented a whole galaxy of subsidiary characters, to push along the movie's central thesis.

Chief among these is the figure of Feck, played by this year's favorite emissary from the land of the drug-wrecked, Dennis Hopper. Hopper, portrayed in the film as a brain-fried survivor of the '60s, acts as a kind of unofficial spiritual adviser to the group of California kids who are confronting the problem that John has just whacked Jamie. But he is very far from a moral anchor: He's more like a windsock, blowing whichever way they do.

Meanwhile, Layne, played with the self-immolating intensity of a speed-fiend by Crispin Glover, is trying to "save" the situation. He's the leader of the pack, and concludes that morality is conditional: Jamie is dead, and beyond help, and John is alive, and therefore not beyond help. Thus he attempts to "rescue" John by bullying the rest of the gang into pitching in. One girl gives quarters. Another thinks about calling the cops, but cannot quite find the nerve.

Finally, Matt (Keanu Reeves), who has tumbled to the fact that murder is, uh, you know, uh, sort of w-w-w-r-wrong, calls the cops. Unbeknownst to him, his neurotic little brother — Joshua Miller — is now hunting him with a gun, for betraying the pack. This last is a bit much.

These are sensational contents, but the movie plays them like black comedy: It's actually very funny in the deadpan vernacular of modern filmmaking, after the fashion of "Sid and Nancy," in which the innocent depravity of the characters is observed with such horrifying clinicalness that it acquired a nightmare humor.

Hunter gets an awful lot out of his imagery, also: The metaphor of the river's edge is a particularly apt one, for these kids are symbolically perched on the edge of the river of life, which rushes onward, while they are unable to partake, being, like inert Jamie turning blue in the high grass, dead. He plays games with her remains, so that they haunt the movie and never let us stray far from mortal issues. Feck, for example, in a grotesque touch, goes everywhere with an inflated sex doll named Ellie, and her presence reminds us of Jamie, white and glossy, at the river bank.

Yet the film is more than clinical: It goes to great lengths to place these children in a larger context and to find a theory to explain them. They are the children of the '60s, their parents all sloppy or indifferent (no adult figure is depicted with anything less than utter contempt). If the kids are dead, the movie is saying, it was their own self-indulgent parents who killed them.

GLENGARRY GLEN ROSS
October 2, 1992

You have to know the territory and David Mamet knows it well: self-doubt, desperation, flaming greed, hunger, terror and, finally, the will to close in for the kill. That's the mind-set of the hunter-gatherer, be he a caveman stalking a mammoth, a Marine sniper stalking an enemy general, or a salesman stalking a recalcitrant victim.

Thus the real estate office of Mamet's "Glengarry Glen Ross" is less a warren of desks and files than some sort of primal glade. It's eat or be eaten. Of necessary consequence to this extreme circumstance, the men who work there are somewhat on edge. Shelley, poor Shelley, who hasn't had a sale in months, knows he's about to be devoured. At the other end of the spectrum is Ricky Roma, a magnificent lion, serene and untroubled, his belly full, his needs satisfied. But even he knows that he's a few thin weeks away from catastrophe.

Mamet's play, now opened up into a film by James Foley, is a little shaky in the plot department, but as a penetration of the desperate culture of salesmen, a corrosive examination of the hunter-gatherer culture, urban-style, '90s-style, recession-style, it's a knockout.

On a rainy night in Chicago, the office manager of Ape Properties has called a meeting. The sales staff — a sagging, moping pack of used-up hangdogs — gathers to listen to what they expect will be another feckless pep talk. But no. Tonight's guest speaker is Blake (Alec Baldwin), from the anonymous horror known as "downtown" — i.e., the realty firm's owners. He's there to kick butt, light fires and shoot the wounded. The boys haven't been moving enough of the worthless Arizona desert to suit management.

Baldwin is only on screen for about five minutes, but he's mesmerizing. He's like a Cro-Magnon in a Rolex watch and Armani suit; you can't see the hatchet, but it's there. He radiates contempt and danger. His message: Kill or die. This office has been performing so badly that headquarters has decided to cut back. In the next 24 hours, the best producing salesman will win a Cadillac, the second best a set of steak knives, and the rest will be introduced to the first day of the rest of their lives.

The salesmen demand new "leads" — contacts with promising buyers. Baldwin tells them leads are only for winners, that to give them out would be to waste them. The leads — a bundle of blue index cards — will be stored in the office manager's office and will go to the leading salesman.

Some wag once noted that capitalism is man against man, and socialism just the opposite. The story illustrates that principle: The long night that follows is a desperate enterprise. Jack Lemmon's Shelley lurches out into the rain and in one desperate ploy after another, tries to get on the road. Mamet may despise him and what he does, but at the same time he's got grudging admiration for Shelley's whining craft, for the desperate tropes he throws out. His favorite is to represent himself as having flown in from out of town with just an hour or two to spare as he brings "financial security" to his marks.

Others — Ed Harris and Alan Arkin — repair in despair to a nearby Chinese restaurant and talk deep plots. It occurs to Harris to break into the office and steal, then sell, the leads. Arkin wants to know, "Are we talking or are we *talking*?", and no one needs to be told the difference. Meanwhile, Ricky (Al Pacino) is nursing a stranger he met at the bar, and we see his high sleaze in action: He's an oily listener, a nudger, who exchanges worthless sympathy for dollars on the bottom line. He's also queasily magnificent, and to watch him flop poor Jonathan Pryce, as the mark, this way and that is like watching foreplay between a large hungry cat and a small, shivering mouse.

Mamet is widely admired for the intensity of his dialogue, but in earlier filmed versions of his works — his own "Homicide" and "House of Games" come to mind — the rhythms have seemed almost sing-songy, hypnotic. The effect then wasn't reality but a kind of higher stylization. Foley has encouraged his performers to get away from playing the rhythm game, and generally they labor manfully to keep the piece as "naturalistic" as possible. To watch the film is more like eavesdropping than sitting in an audience.

"Glengarry Glen Ross" isn't without flaws; one can feel the claustrophobic press of what had been its stage limits — two sets, the office and the restaurant — squeezing in. A long subplot about the police investigation into the burglary of the stolen leads that dominates the third act doesn't quite pay off as it should — for example, too much of it happens off-screen, while Lemmon and Pacino are struggling vainly to keep control of triumphs the night before in the foreground. Foley never quite gets the balance right between these two issues.

But the signal triumph of "Glengarry Glen Ross" is how much raw and crackling drama it finds in the most banal of places. There may be 8 million stories in the Naked City, but few of them are this good.

THE KING OF COMEDY
April 15, 1983

In certain ways, Martin Scorsese has made the same movie over and over again. This time, he gets it right.

"The King of Comedy," Scorsese's new film, is another vivid study of obsession; it's undeniably brilliant and it's also hysterical.

But one should quickly add that it's quirky, claustrophobic and twitchy, and that its vantage point on the events it chronicles is so peculiar that those who attend in search of a broad screen comedy like "Tootsie" will be as disappointed as they are confused. It's dark and hip and quietly malicious rather than farcically hilarious.

It seems also possible that some poor souls will wander in, kids in tow, under the assumption that they are about to see a Jerry Lewis film, full of comic pratfalls and raucous, grating physical shtick; these people will feel utterly betrayed. That's not to say that Lewis is bad in the film; indeed, he's absolutely superb and it's his bone-deep weariness and isolation and his fiercely held dignity that give the movie a moral center and hold it together. It's certainly the best sheer acting that Lewis has ever done. But "King of Comedy" is as far from "The Nutty Professor" as it is from "High Noon."

To begin with, it only arrives at Lewis after some length. Initially, like "Taxi Driver," it takes the form of a madman's journal: It views reality through the nut's eyes, deadpan, without irony, and sees exactly what he sees, imagines exactly what he imagines. But the nut in the case isn't the violent Travis Bickle of "Taxi Driver," the assassin who writes his own name with a .44 Magnum. Rupert wants to be famous all right, but not because of the gun in his hand so much as the quip in his mouth: He wants to go on Johnny Carson. He wants his own show.

Rupert Pupkin — the name is perhaps too cutely schlumpy, but that's the only flaw in screenwriter Paul Zimmerman's work-up of his crazed personality — has been totally subsumed by the show-biz culture that comes at him over the tube. It has taken over his life — it has *become* his life.

At the most prosaic of moments, Rupert is apt to break into a zany reverie, and see himself lunching at 21 with other celebs, or moving with grace and calm through the higher regions of the entertainment industry. But the reality is somewhat more mundane; he's a middle-aged delivery boy, and the closest he gets to stardom is to ask a star for an autograph. But Rupert gets lucky: A chance encounter with America's No. 1 talk show host, Jerry Langford (Jerry Lewis), impels him to ask for his big break, and the weary, cynical Langford agrees to listen to Rupert's comedy tape.

What's funny about Rupert is his dead-on earnestness, his conviction. He utterly ignores the outside world; his most pleasing cues and signals are from his own head, where he's already a star. Zimmerman has a wonderful gift for capturing what might be called the rhetoric of cliche.

Rupert is as polyester as the suit he wears; he's willed himself into becoming the total celeb, and his life is a tissue of the little Borscht Belt rituals of show biz, as represented on the talk shows — the little insincere kiss, the fleeting smile, the casual body posture that offers a best profile to the camera, most of all that utter ease and calm that the show-biz pro radiates.

What Rupert lacks, however, is talent.

The big break results — as it must, and as everybody except Rupert himself knows far in advance it will — in a routine kiss-off, and Rupert is shattered into a more bizarre course. With the help of the devastatingly off-beat Sandra Bernhard, a rubber-lipped female incarnation of Mick Jagger, he kidnaps poor Jerry Langford and holds him hostage for ransom.

The ransom? Stardom. Rupert wants his shot on the show; he wants to do his routine.

And it comes with a sort of terrible inevitability that Rupert's monologue, when he finally delivers it at the climax of the film, is neither terrible nor wonderful: Like Rupert, it's basically nothing except its own jagged vision of itself. He's made a mediocre stand-up routine out of the pain of his own life.

Scorsese shoots all this as if it were a documentary. The look of the film is spare and clean; it is baroque in conception but never in style, and it's this feeling of reality — Freddie De Cordova, for example, Johnny Carson's actual producer, plays himself — that makes the entire contraption work. Scorsese is shrewd enough to know that Rupert's show-biz argot and grotesque self-deception don't need to be underlined cinematically.

Only one sequence — and it's a hilarious one — borders on the grotesque. When Sandra Bernhard, alone with Jerry while Rupert's off courting stardom on TV, pitches one-way woo at him. Lewis, who is nothing but eyes, controls it as he watches helplessly; Bernhard speaks for all the loony, isolated people who've only been able to make emotional contact with flickering images on the screen.

The movie is dogged by some small flaws that seem so unnecessary. Diane Abbott, who plays Rupert's girlfriend, is clearly in the film because she's De Niro's wife. That she happens to be black should shock no one, but it utterly ruins the pretense of reality. Rupert just isn't the sort of man to bring off a bi-racial relationship — he's not hip enough and, frankly, the movie would make a good deal more sense if she were the white-cheerleader type.

But "King of Comedy" has dark vision and high humor and almost unsettling originality. Scorsese, like Rupert, is an obsessive, but unlike Rupert, he's brought it off.

SHORT CUTS
October 22, 1993

The mark of an artist may be how simple he makes the complex look.

That's the key virtue of Robert Altman's brilliant "Short Cuts," which, on the way to being many things, is certainly the shortest 3-hour movie ever made. But it has a degree of pure simplicity to it — unseen in American films in many a year — in the way it deals with small issues honestly. And under its smooth surface, one senses the movement of large and troubling ideas.

It's also a great piece of storytelling. It glides with such dapper effervescence that it comes to feel truly magical, and its considerable technique is completely yoked to the thrust of the dramatic materials. It never condescends or traffics in cheap irony; you don't feel the filmmaker looking down from on high, amused at the littleness of little lives.

We're in the lesser precincts of the City of Angels, far from the grottos and glades of the rich and famous. Nobody's making deals, nobody's selling anybody out; it's just that dreary stuff called life, with a variety of people attempting no loftier ambition than to get by, day by day.

As derived from the late great American short-story writer Raymond Carver, the ambience is definitely Carveresque — that is, middle-class high and low, largely (but not entirely) non-professional, hard-working, fate-fearing, locked in patterns as rigid as tungsten handcuffs. It's as if the Malathion dropped to combat fruit flies by a fleet of helicopters in the early seconds of the film forms a moral vapor that drifts throughout, confusing everything, turning all the blacks and whites to grays, turning heroes to fools and good men to bad ones. As brightly photographed as it is, the movie seems to be taking place in a kind of living fog bank.

And as Carveresque as it is, it's also an evocation of the real "Hell A" that may be the best in movies since Robert Towne's "Chinatown." Altman, working with a core of nine stories and fragments of several others, has deconstructed the Carver characters from the Pacific Northwest and redeposited them in Los Angeles. He's melded, composted, compacted and Cuisinarted, inventing a kind of mythical substructure so that, in some small way, the characters are all interrelated (in the stories, they stood apart) and their lives interpenetrate in ways they don't know but we do. The movie, in other words, gives us God's eye-view but none of His power. We can't change a thing, and in this untidy and terribly unfair universe, so much needs changing.

A small boy is hit by a car. The woman who hits him is a waitress (Lily Tomlin). She wants to take him home but he refuses, saying he's all right. When he gets home, he decides to take a nap and in no time is in a coma. The drift toward oblivion, nudged by such a fragile whiff of fate, is infuriating. And, with his parents (Andie MacDowell and Bruce Davison), we watch in horror. It's so unfair! Yet nothing can be done.

Nothing can be done. That, in a variety of tones, is the general drift of the pieces. Most of them are haunted by death or its opposite, sex. You know those old favorites, Eros and Thanatos, together again! In another story, three quite decent men

(Fred Ward, Huey Newton and Buck Henry) go fishing; in the far beauty of the mountains, they find a grim relic of the complexities of city life: a dead woman, just under the surface. What to do? They ponder, worry, try to deal with it, and do exactly what they would do in real life but in no movie ever made: They do nothing. (That's the metaphorical meaning of the film, by the way: death, just under the surface of the beautiful.)

A jazz singer in a club through which some of the characters drift yammers on about men, forms a musical chorus, and pays no attention as her daughter (Lori Singer), a cellist, drifts closer and closer toward suicide.

Even in playtime, there's a whisper of grim mortality: Adulterous make-up artist Robert Downey Jr. practices on his wife (Lily Taylor), giving her the bruised face of a murder victim, which leads to an exquisite moment of confusion when she gets Buck Henry's pictures of the dead woman and Buck Henry gets her pictures of herself in the beaten-woman make-up.

Confusion, confusion, everywhere. Did I say fog? Think of the gunsmoke that drifted across the fields at Waterloo and Gettysburg, thrown up by fusillades from the war between men and women, who can never really understand each other. A neat touch: Working people Fred Ward and Anne Archer go to dinner at the exquisite hillside house of upper-class physician Matthew Modine and wife Julianne Moore. In a flash, Altman makes the point that the two men are much more comfortable together than either man has been with his respective spouse.

It goes on, it goes on. The movie in some sense recapitulates on a grander scale the opening shot of Altman's "The Player," when the camera, again replicating God's point of view, wanders around a movie studio, eavesdropping on lives and careers, picking up a dozen different pungent dramas at key moments, then moving onward.

There are some wrong notes. Chris Penn, married to earnest little Jennifer Jason Leigh, who makes extra money talking dirty on the phone (while changing diapers and making casseroles), lives in such a penumbra of frustration that it spills out in a terrible crime toward the end, a stroke I found completely unnecessary and far too melodramatic. The Lily Tomlin and Tom Waits characters seemed somehow to be acting on a broader scale than the other performers; not much comes out of Peter Gallagher's destruction of his wife Frances McDormand's home and property.

But for most of a very long part, "Short Cuts" is like a hot steamy shower in the liquid of the actual.

BAD LIEUTENANT
March 5, 1993

There's no defending "Bad Lieutenant." No argument can be advanced to justify it, no insight can coax meanings out of its bloody innards, no shaman can roll bones and feathers across its textures and decode it. It's strictly a take-it-or-leave-it thing.

It's a study of extreme damnation and marginal redemption, as austere and enigmatic as the life of a saint. It's one of the rare films to sport an authentic NC-17 rating, which it deserves to every fiber of its grubby little body. It aspires to be an outlaw work of art, one of those defiant in-your-face proclamations of truth so painful it defies you to deny it. Well . . . they got the outlaw part right, at any rate.

Harvey Keitel plays a New York police officer who has stepped through the membrane into corruption so enveloping it seems to have saturated his genes. He is walking blasphemy. We capture glimpses of a home life, complete with children, a wife, a sister-in-law and a mother or mother-in-law, but the lieutenant's nervous system is so shot he barely notices them. He seems to be receiving about 10 percent of conventional reality. Having lovelessly dropped his boys at school, he hustles off to his life on the streets, which is largely the indulgence of an appetite so gigantic it defies belief. The Bad Lieutenant is congenitally unable to deny himself a pleasure: His working day consists of using his badge to take whatever pleases him. He has no more acquaintanceship with the concept of public service, of police work, than he does with his family.

At the scene of a horrible murder — two beautiful young women shot through the head — he jokes about betting on baseball with his buddies. His response to a horrible rape is voyeurism. He wanders from drug crib to drug crib, helping himself to chemical stimulants and intoxicants and slipping deeper and deeper into a narcotized daze. No defilement is beyond him, including a sordid interlude in which he accosts two teen-aged girls, determines that they have violated traffic laws, and orders them to assume pornographic poses for an act of self-abuse. Besides his pleasure, the only thing he responds to is the financial catastrophe that stalks him as he slips further and further into debt to the Mafia by betting against the Mets in a playoff series against the Dodgers. A New Yorker who bets against the Mets? This pup is really sick.

What "saves" him — it's the most provisional redemption in film history — is that he is moved by the spirit of forgiveness in a violated nun (the scenes of her rape are the movie's most painful to watch), who seeks only to love her violators. Watching and marveling at her most Catholic love in some strange way heals him; he learns to forgive them and through that himself. The movie's lesson: Heaven is attainable even for a festering carbuncle on the body social like the Bad Lieutenant.

The movie has a catechism-like feeling to it: It simply asks questions numbly and answers them numbly, and in so doing categorizes his defilements and his redemptions without a lot of emotional involvement in such frills as storytelling. Properly speaking, it isn't dramatized at all, merely recorded. It doesn't build. It doesn't even use such timeless devices as "the investigation" to hold it together. Other than Keitel, it has no characters. The raped nun is merely a body, the other policemen simply faces. The movie plants you in a lonely place: his skull.

This makes it inert. Only the power of its atrocities drives it forward. The key narrative question isn't "What happens next?" but "How low will he go?" The answer is: "Lower still." Abel Ferrara, who directed, is shrewd enough to leave behind the fancy pyrotechnics of "King of New York." Thank heaven; the only thing worse than atrocity on film is atrocity made beautiful on film. "Bad Lieutenant" is simply in your face.

LATE DEVELOPMENTS

"Slap another Maverick on my Hornet.

I've got aliens to nuke!"

Article:
FILMS UNDER FIRE
June 18, 1995

There you go again.

The "you" happens to be Bob Dole, the Republican senator from Kansas who is running for president. But it could have been President Clinton, who's sounded similar notes in times past. Or Tipper Gore. Or anyone and everyone on back to the Catholic Legion of Decency in the '50s to the Hays Office in the '20s and '30s to the original blue-nose, Anthony Comstock, and his war on "September Morn," which he managed to turn into the most famous painting of the early 20th century.

The charges are familiar. Dole's variant is only remarkable because he is the Senate majority leader as well as the Republican front-runner, because he has not spoken on this issue before and because his famous speech, though woodenly delivered, was brilliantly written by someone other than Bob Dole:

"Society pays a price when the entertainment industry poisons the minds of our young people. We must hold Hollywood accountable for putting profit ahead of common decency."

The thrust is that in some inchoate, unquantifiable but troubling way, the violence that permeates screen culture has numbed and brutalized those who pay to witness it, making them more prone to expressing themselves with a gun or a knife than might otherwise be the case. Moreover, and perhaps more troublingly, the sexuality that oozes from the screen has led to a breakdown in values, as witness the surge of one-parent families, illegitimate births and attendant social pathologies. Hollywood: guilty, guilty, guilty.

"A line has been crossed — not just of taste but of human dignity and decency," said the senator. He cited two films specifically, Oliver Stone's "Natural Born Killers" and Tony Scott's "True Romance," from a screenplay by Quentin Tarantino. They "revel in mindless violence and loveless sex," he charged.

It is not for me to point out the hypocrisies, real and imagined, behind the senator's assault; that's what pundits are for. Nor is it for me to inveigh hoity-toitily against him on constitutional grounds: The First Amendment, it seems to me, should apply to senators from Kansas like Dole as fully as it does to left-wing filmmakers from Los Angeles like Oliver Stone.

Even less is it for me to take a position on the violence issue, as that would be media hypocrisy of the highest nature. I am also a novelist, and Hollywood currently owns and is "developing" (whatever that means) two of my books. Both books and the movies that may spawn from them are, and necessarily will be, extremely violent; I specialize in natural born killers. Thus, it could be argued, if Hollywood insists on ignoring Dole and persists in business as usual, I stand to make more than a few bucks. It could further be argued that if I argue against Dole, I have a secret agenda: I am advancing my own financial fortunes.

What remains, however, are certain issues of film history, certain charges that play the "good" movies of the past against the "bad" movies of today, which it seem to me are rooted more in political expedience and rhetoric than in reality.

The senator wants moviemakers — artists, in general — to be good citizens first and artists second, exemplars of the now famous "family values." He quotes a movie executive, Mark Canton, in calling for more PG films. He infers that the five "blockbusters" of the last year are "friendly to the family," but it becomes instantaneously clear that he has probably not seen any of them and has certainly not seen "True Lies" in particular, which besides being mega-violent has a gratuitous subplot.

As my favorite film critic noted at the time: ". . . [director James] Cameron (who also wrote) stops the film and turns it into a somewhat bizarrely configured Hepburn-Tracy number. The frustrated [Jamie Lee] Curtis becomes the objet d'amour of a sleazy used car salesman (Bill Paxton) whose method of seduction is to tell his targets he's a secret agent; that, in fact, he's her husband Harry [Arnold Schwarzenegger]! But Harry, who has no appreciation for irony, finds out about it and utilizes the full force of his agency to squash the affair and the little man. Then, ickily, he further twists his power to play an elaborate and extremely sadistic prank on his poor wife, blackmailing her (through a secret guise) into taking on the role and performing some of the degrading acts of a prostitute. Jim, it's not very '90s! What it is, is very kinky stuff.''

But that's not axiomatically bad. Cameron — very much like Stone and Tarantino in the two films that so aroused Dole's ire — was trying to subvert expectations and give his story unique life by twisting it in a new direction. He made a conscious decision to portray the family unit, and particularly the sexual tension between husband and wife, as unusually twisted.

Far from the white-bread fantasy of "Ozzie and Harriet," this was a troubled, dysfunctional and exceedingly disturbing relationship that, liberated by passion, turned into something ugly.

In film terms, it doesn't work, just as "Natural Born Killers" and "True Romance" don't work, either. The point is, however, that not everything works. But what definitely doesn't work is what the senator seems to prefer: that exact kind of "family-friendly" fantasy of storybook lives, of perfect neighborhoods, of happy families.

Dole should remember that the most beloved of all Hollywoods family-friendly films is actually about a dysfunctional family, a family where the nuclear unit has been replaced by extended members (an aunt and uncle), where the menial laborers on the estate are forced to function as siblings, where the child herself is so distraught that she takes refuge in a dreamworld that involves casting all her neuroses in fantasy terms: Where? Why, somewhere over the rainbow, in 1939's "The Wizard of Oz."

Dole says, "In the 1930s, [Warner Bros.] made a series of movies, including 'G-men,' for the purpose of restoring 'dignity and public confidence in the police.' It made movies to help the war effort in the early 1940s. Its company slogan put on a billboard across from the studio was 'Good Citizenship with Good Picture Making.' ''

Hollywood may have said that, but was it ever really so?

Or is the senator remembering the movie past the way the movies remember the South — through a patina of yearning and nostalgia, through a prism of romance and selectivity?

The answer is complex. Indeed, one can look at film history and cite family-friendly films like the Andy Hardy series and the Ma and Pa Kettle films and the Little Rascal films and the Disney films, and see a whole litany of happy-happy. One can look at crime dramas where justice always triumphed, where the cops always got their man. One can look at war films where the industry was part of the home front and made movies that got with the spirit of teamwork and victory.

But at the same time, the American movie has persisted in running through cycles where it was as subversive as it was supportive, where it inverted the "official" values of society or at the very least subjected them to ferocious critique.

Look at the war films, for example. As Dole points out, it was a matter of pride and patriotism in the early part of the Second World War for Hollywood to join the team. But the films that hail from the early years of the war, while possibly the most unified and patriotic and government-friendly ever made, have receded into utter kitsch now.

To see a film like "Bataan," with stalwart Robert Taylor — 100 percent pure American hardwood, mowing down the Japanese on a dry-ice-shrouded back-lot paper jungle, calling them "monkeys" while he fires — is to laugh. Such ludicrous heroics might have briefly lifted the spirits of the home folks, but they said very little about the true nature of war and the true level of heroism and sacrifice demanded of and delivered by American troops off in real jungles — as Dole himself would know. Now they seem almost obscene with their antic bloodthirstiness and their racism and their cartoonlike portrayals of good (us) and evil (them).

Late in the war and immediately after, the war movies turned more realistic and seethed with fatigue, terror, bitterness and confusion. They were hardly inspirational. Look, for example, at William Wellman's superb 1949 "Battleground," an invocation of ground combat as experienced by the 101st Airborne in the Battle of the Bulge. It portrays battle as something far more squalid and terrifying than Taylor's glorious martyrdom. Its heroes are tired men, numbly, in James Jones' great words, doing the necessary. There's an overall sense of waste and loss, of precious youth exiled for an uncertain future — not quite the patriotic we-can-do-it pieties that Dole would seem to prefer.

Then there's the extremely troubling issue of "glorifying violence," which the senator invokes, again tacitly comparing today's seemingly value-free pictures with the strict code of justice and morality that informed the past's films. Again, it seems true on the face of it, but if examined carefully one can see that the reality is more complex.

Under the influence of the Hays Office — officially, the Motion Picture Producers and Distributors, Inc., under the direction of former Postmaster Will H. Hays, which took control of movie morality in 1922 after a spate of suggestive movies and movie scandals — it was mandatory that justice always prevail.

This led to absurd circumlocutions. As late as 1956 (11 years after the office itself closed), when Mervyn LeRoy turned Maxwell Anderson's haunting meditation on the nature of evil, "The Bad Seed," into a film, he was obligated by the still extant Code to give it an ending that pushed the just-desserts line. Thus, when chilling child psycho Patty McCormack is left alive on Broadway to continue her evil ways, protected by a mantle of presumed childish innocence, in the movie version a cosmic blast of lightning from the Man himself flashes earthward to punish her. I would love to have attended the story conference that came up with that stroke of genius!

Still, audiences must have enjoyed the subversive power of the story and particularly the chilling intensity of McCormack's Oscar-winning performance. The new ending was the least persuasive thing in the movie; literally unbelievable. Sophisticated viewers would have seen right through it. In fact, the allure of evil is one of the key components of movies made during the beloved heyday that Dole pretends was so socially positive. It's no surprise that three of America's most dynamic stars of the age — Humphrey Bogart, Jimmy Cagney and Edward G. Robinson — achieved their renown in portraits of deviance. You can say that at the end of "Petrified Forest," "Public Enemy" and "Little Caesar," each man gets what he deserves, but that was only after titillating audiences for two hours with the power and majesty of the criminal's life, his pleasures, his ruthlessness, his utter contempt for the square Johns of the law and the daytime world.

"Mother of God, is this the end of Rico?" asks Edward G., perforated with police bullets. The answer, of course, was no, this is the start of Rico, because Rico — the charismatic gangster whose seductive lifestyle transfigures the young and triumphs over any imposed moral message from grown-ups — was about to begin a run that to this day finds its way into gangsta rap and "Godfather" movies, good and bad.

What we have here, essentially, is a conflict between a politician's concept of artist as servant of society and an artist's conceit of himself as irreverent critic of that society, revealing its secret lusts and values. Why can't you get on the team? Dole is asking, as politicians have asked for generations. Because if I get on the team, the artist answers, I lose my soul.

The deeper truth is that art and society don't obey the same laws. In some sense it feels like a combat between the rational and the instinctive parts of the brain. In society, the rational brain commands, order is everything; we need to cooperate, show tolerance and patience, respect authority, play by the rules. But at the same time, the instinctive part of the brain replies, we cannot deny our attraction to those who won't play by the rules, who assert themselves above the rules and who take their pleasure and their identity from defying the rules.

Can the two ever come together? The track record is dismal. At the time of the Russian revolution, a generation of artists, assurgent with hope for the future, liberated their imaginations to turn out a decade's worth of works that were both: a) masterpieces, and b) works in support of the state. It couldn't last; it didn't. Stalin and his apparatchiks took over, and soon enough, artistic criticism in the Soviet Union consisted not of mildly snippy speeches before fat cats in a hotel ballroom but a bullet behind the ear.

THE USUAL SUSPECTS
September 1, 1995

Round up the usual adjectives.

Try "bold." Go for "terrific." Let a "dazzling" fly. Unleash a "stunning." Send forth a "mesmerizing."

That's "The Usual Suspects," which many are calling this year's "Pulp Fiction" — untrue, by the way — but which is really just one of this year's best movies.

The dense, ironic and thoroughly engrossing caper melodrama opens today. It's not really a film noir or a film noir knockoff, as many are calling it, and it assiduously avoids the kind of arch hipness that somewhat dilutes the impact of the Tarantino work. It's not trying to show you how many movies the director has seen; it's trying to show you a good time.

As a genre item, it could be said to trace its lineage back even further than the noirs of the late '40s to the Black Cat mysteries of the '20s and '30s, with their nefarious master criminals like Fu Manchu. The mysterious bad guy here is one Keyser Soze, legendary Hungarian puppet master, who moves through the American underworld like a phantasm, playing the sides against each other in stratagems so subtle it would take a mainframe to decipher them, and leaving a trail as gossamer and variously interpretable as stardust.

Is there a Keyser Soze? A customs agent played by Chazz Palminteri doesn't think so. But he's got a blazing shipful of corpses (27), missing drug money ($91 million) and one conscious survivor, a glib but obviously weak-minded petty con man named Verbal (spacey Kevin Spacey), who narrates the complex events that led up to the inferno, though from an apparently naive point of view.

Thus the film is a "Canterbury Tales" of pulp fiction, a densely packed, quadruple-caper tapestry of events recalled from memory which in themselves are quite clear but which seem not to be related vertically — along cause-effect lines — but rather horizontally — as layers and layers of enameled complexity.

It all began some weeks previously when purely "by chance" (is the hand of Keyser Soze in here somewhere?) five world-class crooks were arrested on suspicion of a common truck heist in New York, then left to fester in a holding tank off the lineup room. They included a suave ex-cop (Gabriel Byrne), a tough punk (Stephen Baldwin), a tough-talking punk (Kevin Pollak) and a strange Hispanic guy named . . . Fenster (Fenster!) (Benicio del Toro). And Verbal.

Left to their own devices and bitter grievances, they come up with a retaliatory caper and rip off a police protection racket. Let me point out that the director, Bryan Singer, has all kinds of fresh and witty ways of imagining the most banal of situations. The heist, the hostage-taker shooting, the robbery, the hit, the gunfight: All are vividly re-invented.

Meanwhile, the plot is melting down into an alloy so dense no human intelligence can decipher it. Things become insanely complex when Peter Postlethwaite shows up, representing "Mr. Soze," with unbearable sangfroid and savior faire. Back in reality — a crummy lieutenant's office in San Pedro — poor Palminteri is trying to stay up with Verbal's re-creation of these events as it slides and dips back and forth in time.

It may ultimately make sense; no one could tell without at least four or five viewings. What is totally commanding, however, is the level of ensemble acting, the adroitness of the storytelling and the nifty way the mysterious Soze comes to dominate the proceedings even if we never see him. Or do we?

What we do see is great acting. Spacey has been a riveting presence at the edge of many films; here as our principal narrator he's slimy and apparently not quite as stupid as he seems. Baldwin is excellent as a tough little weasel who isn't afraid to shoot first and ask questions later; newcomer del Toro registers strongly. The revelation, however, is Pollak, whose career has always taken him into better neighborhoods than this one. But as a little fast-talking rat of a crook, he's extremely memorable, and his sharp, feral features make him seem totally convincing.

The only weak link, in my view, is the conventionally handsome Gabriel Byrne, who never quite radiates the reptile charisma the movie assigns to him. Was Christopher Walken busy making "The Prophecy"? What about Dennis Hopper, was he still on "Waterworld"? Alan Rickman, of the first "Die Hard"?

No matter. The bottom line is that "The Usual Suspects" is cruelly entertaining. And Keyser Soze didn't make me say that. At least, I don't think he did.

TO DIE FOR
October 6, 1995

"To Die For" will give a certain segment of the audience something to live for and another segment something to die from. It's not for the irony-impaired.

Mordant, dark, bitter, funny, sexy, sardonic, it's one of those special-case movies that ride their outrageousness into your heart and demand your affection even as they're brazenly offending you. It fits in that small category of nasty gigglers that includes "Sunset Boulevard," "The Loved One," "Where's Poppa?" and "Pretty Poison."

What bad boy director Gus Van Sant ("My Own Private Idaho") and bad old man screenwriter Buck Henry have done, through the medium of Joyce Maynard's novel, is re-wire the infamous Pamela Smart case into a wicked parable about the power of celebrity in even the smallest of American nooks and crannies. If you recall, Pamela Smart was a New Hampshire high school teacher accused of seducing a teen-age boy into murdering her husband.

As Van Sant and Henry have it, Smart becomes Suzanne Stone (Nicole Kidman), a blazingly ambitious young woman whose ferocity of temperament and utter single-mindedness have landed her a job as a weatherwoman on a cable-TV news station, possibly the least professional media outlet this side of Rhinelander, Wis.

Kidman is mesmerizing as she closes in on this American pathology. Her Suzanne is utterly without irony, without moderation, without morality, completely capable of using her fabulous beauty and body to get what she wants while maintaining the cutest and most banal of personas to friends, family and, most of all, the somewhat dense hunk she's married to — Matt Dillon, as the last man in Little Hope, N.H., to get it. She's the Bad Seed on a Jane Pauley jag.

The movie is structured as a mock documentary, in the wake of a purposely vague post-scandal media frenzy, as various participants in the famous Suzanne Stone case are interviewed by an off-camera interlocutor, leading them into flashbacks that recapitulate the action chronologically. Suzanne herself seems to be a part of this process as, in one of her pretty pink working-gal suits, she addresses the camera and tells her story in an earnest, peppy voice of complete self-seriousness.

Thus the film is one of those sophisticated documents where tone and mood are completely different, where we the audience are understanding things that the characters are too stupid or too self-deluding (self-delusion is a subtext) to see.

We watch as Suzanne essentially takes over, on the power of pure sexual charisma and technique, a clique of slackers at the local high school and turns them to her purposes, which are to bump off poor hubby Larry, who keeps whining about the babies he wants Suzanne to start producing.

The kids are achingly pathetic and poignant at once. Their leader, Jimmy (Joaquin Phoenix, the late actor River's brother), appears to be a semi-retarded chronic masturbator whose eyes radiate two messages simultaneously: "I hurt, therefore I am" and "I'm stupid, therefore I'm not." Yet as pathetic and hopeless as he is, he comes eventually to represent the movie's extremely small heart.

But in this brazen mixture, nothing is simple: At the same time, Suzanne's seduction of him, slow, teasing, utterly contemptuous, is very sexy. "To Die For" is a much hotter movie than the poor dull "Showgirls," because it understands the ritual of sex and takes its viewers through a narrative curve that traces the acceleration of the sexual impulse to climax and then separation.

The performances are uniformly superb, from Illeana Douglas's sarcastic turn as the dim Dillon's smart sister to Dan Hedaya's baffled spin as Dillon's restaurant-owning father. The three kids — besides the incandescent and Oscar-probable Phoenix, they are Casey Affleck and Alison Folland — are achingly real. But the movie is really Kidman's. She manages to define a mind that is predatory and misaimed at once, so doubt-free it seems not really to acknowledge a larger universe. The film will certainly make her an actress rather than a star's wife. Tom who? you'll ask.

Many people are going to hate this movie. It's the ultimate post-modern document with its chilly morality, its deconstructed narrative, its fascination with pathology, its arrival of justice wrapped in clever irony. It's what the best movies are: unsettling and provocative, profoundly irritating and endlessly fascinating.

GOLDENEYE
November 17, 1995

Memo to Bond, James Bond: You have a license to kill. You do not have a license to bore, you idiot.

"GoldenEye," the newest addition to the Bond oeuvre, introduces Pierce Brosnan to the role of the British agent who made the '60s swing, the '70s snore, the '80s irritate and the '90s nauseate. He certainly is a handsome devil, looks great in a tux, carries a gun with believable authority, has a much lower mousse budget than Roger Moore and is quite an enjoyable presence. One problem: He seems to think he's in a real movie.

Thus, foolishly, Brosnan, his blasted talent getting in the way, actually attempts to give the secret agent man an inner life, a hint of regret, a wisp of melancholy. This naturalism feels somewhat out of place amid the 351 explosions, 56,789 gunshots, the 14 vehicular catastrophes and the final shuddering collapse of some kind of structure that looks most like the WBAL antenna.

They blow things up real good in this movie and that's about the only thing they do real good. The plot is a mess. It seems to have to do with some kind of conspiracy by some rump Russian group (never made clear) to rob electronically the Bank of England before hitting the city with a blast of electromagnetic energy (from a commandeered killer satellite), which will erase every computer memory in the British Isles, as well as making all the stoplights go bananas. But the British don't obey their traffic laws anyway, and Nick Leeson has already wrecked the banking system.

So what we're left with is a kind of monotonous ordeal by muzzle blast that eventually numbs us. You need earplugs, not a movie critic. It doesn't help that the movie lacks a vivid villain, with poor Sean Bean (who did similar duty in "Patriot Games") trying gamely to appear interesting. He has the same problem as Brosnan: too much damn talent. (Sometimes really great actors are completely sandbagged by the Bond thing; both Christopher Walken and Klaus Maria Brandauer registered only dimly in their Bond spins.)

And even in the Bond universe, admittedly not the most rigorous of invented worlds, there are some rules that should not be broken. One involves promiscuous death. It's OK to kill bad guys, kill them in the dozens, the hundreds, even the thousands. But this movie blurs a moral line to its own disadvantage: Much of it takes place in the post-breakdown USSR, but it goes ahead and kills Russians by the bushel basket load — particularly in a long sequence when Bond steals a tank and chases a car through the streets of St. Petersburg, gunning and crushing people endlessly.

Excuse me, folks, the Russians are no longer our enemies, remember? You can't kill them any more than you can kill Swedes or Moluccans or Taiwanese or Clevelanders.

On the other hand, all that death does set up a scene in which a stunt driver does a wheelie in a T-74 Sov main battle tank. You don't see that every day.

The director, Martin Campbell, stages the action well, which appears to be his main talent. He's not good with actors, or at least he doesn't recognize the occasional magic that he bumbles into. One such sequence involves Bond's meeting with his new boss, Ms. M, played in no-nonsense style by the distinguished Dame Judi Dench. Boy, is she good, and boy, does the electricity crackle between her and Brosnan, lighting the film up like a meteor shower. Yet she's only around briefly; how much better it would be if these two congenital antagonists, representing not merely their genders but their world views, stomped and pawed at each other all the way through.

There are two bits of good news in the film: Izabella Scorupco and Famke Janssen. Cast as the good and bad femmes fatales, the two former models (Polish-Swedish and Dutch, respectively) are far more comfortable in their cartoony roles than is Brosnan in his. They seem to get it in a way he doesn't, and both performances are based around the sort of extraordinary physical confidence that beauty seems to endow without complication upon those blessed enough to receive it. Scorupco is, how do you say, ooh-la-la, is that the phrase? Anyhow, her radiance is so compelling that she pretty much outshines even most of the destruction.

But on the whole, the thing could be dismissed as: Shaky, not stirring.

HEAT
December 15, 1995

"Heat," from the Michael Mann who created "Miami Vice" and "Police Story," as well as "Thief," "Manhunter" and "Last of the Mohicans," is exactly what you might expect, only a lot better: a big, fat, full-tilt-boogie, rockin', rollin' heavy-metal concert for outlaws, outlaw wannabes, macho sentimentalists and gun cranks — everyone who's ever felt a dribble of testosterone in his or her endocrine system.

This is glandular, not intellectual, moviemaking but it's at the highest end of technical expressiveness. Mann is a great stylist with cheap but potent ideas. He can make a city — even the scruffy environs of bleak L.A. — look like a $4 million sculpture by Picasso after a weekend of first-class absinthe drinking. His colors blaze out like tracer bullets and he can knit images into percussive action sequences that stomp you to a pulp.

At the same time, the guy's an idiot: He loves (and over-inflates) the sense of camaraderie that he imagines is felt between the best cops and the best robbers, and bases his long and violent heist film on the conceit of mutual respect and even affection between them, sentimentalizing it into a kind of cara-melized apple of macho romance. It's a good idea to build a movie on, but, despite all the shattered glass and ejected car-tridge casings, about as convincing as a cancer cure from Oreo cookies.

The two studboys at the top of twin pyramids of the robbery-homicide detail and the armed robbery crews are Lt. Vincent Hanna (Al Pacino) and pro bad boy Neil McCauley (Robert De Niro). One of Mann's little jokes is that each appears to be in the wrong profession: Pacino's Vincent is flamboyant, incoher-ent, just barely in control, his emotional life is a mess. He dresses like a gangster, too, favoring black silk shirts, a flashy handgun with ivory grips, Italian suits, New Age sunglasses. He shouts, his eyes bulge, he can't keep his hands off people.

De Niro's Neil, on the other hand, is a control freak who lives by the Zen of "The Discipline." He can walk out on any job if something goes wrong, no matter how close he is to the score. He has taken the true criminal's existential vow: to have nothing in his life that he cannot walk away from in 10 seconds. He wears blazers and blue button-downs like any IBM mid-management executive; he never yells.

The two great actors only share a single scene (other than a shootout at the end where they speak with their guns) and that's anti-climactic, but their sense of gravitas and commit-ment gives the movie immense weight and power. We feel as if we're watching mythic figures, not movie stars, stalking each other on the plains outside Thebes.

But Mann doesn't stop there. From these two kingpins of their respective worlds, he reaches out to create two vast but parallel (and occasionally intersecting) universes. For each man is a member of a culture, has a network of relationships, responsibilities and expectations, a place in society. Far from lone gunmen, they are men of community who carry their burdens heavily and live by a code they may detest but must obey.

The film opens with a smashing but bloody takedown of an armored car by McCauley's crew (which includes Val Kilmer as a No. 2 guy with a wife and kid and Tom Sizemore as another family-man criminal). Hanna's team, including the great Cherokee actor Wes Studi and the demented Ted Levine, try to solve it by cutting into networks of informants, knowing somewhere someone will talk.

Soon they've identified the crew, which is planning one more bank job. But so professional is the crew and so big is the last score — $14 mill cash — they decide to go ahead with the job, because even as the cops have ID'd them, they've ID'd the cops, giving them a tactical advantage.

Through this central situation Mann threads a dozen other tales: Kilmer's addiction to gambling and his tough but duplicitous wife (Ashley Judd); a counterplot by a scuzz named Waingro (Kevin Gage) to take down De Niro at the behest of one of De Niro's larceny victims; Pacino's shredded home life with Diane Venora and stepdaughter Natalie Portman; De Niro's love affair with Amy Brenneman, and on and on and on. It's crime story as told by Jane Austen on steroids: a panoramic but intimate view of the social tapestry that ensnares a whole world in a bitter net of cause and effect.

All this leads to the bank heist itself, which is a creation of the universe gone psychopathic. It's a machine-gun-o-rama in downtown L.A. that lasts for about 20 minutes and is, without doubt, the most gripping action sequence in an American movie this year. The world is not merely turned upside down and inside out but shot so full of holes it's turned into a giant cheese grater. This is horrible and naturally I loved it.

One oddity. Nowhere in the press notes and in no other reviews have I seen it mentioned, but "Heat" is a remake of a late '80s made-for-TV movie that Mann did called "L.A. Take-down," with Scott Plank and Alex MacArthur in the Pacino–De Niro roles. If it has the feel of déjà vu to some viewers, that's why. It's not another version of the same idea, but from the same script, complete to names, incidents, camera angles and the whole nine yards. The problem with the TV movie (which I have on tape) is its callowness: All the actors are too young and unformed to be believable.

But with Pacino and De Niro, you know you're getting the real thing. It's as if Mann has been haunted by the failure of "L.A. Takedown" all these years, and this time, he's got it right.

BROKEN ARROW
February 9, 1996

Who put the bam in the rama-dama-slam bam? Who put the boom in the bing-bang-boom-boom? Who put the yow in the wow-pow-yow-yow? Woo, that's who!

I wax anti-poetic, but this is a way to express the following reality: With "Broken Arrow," the great Hong Kong filmmaker John Woo not merely becomes a fully fledged American direc-tor, but finds a way to harness his remarkable dynamism and power to American story traditions and cultural norms, and all but reinvents the action thriller.

A definite guy thing, the movie follows as one slightly nuts-oid American stealth-bomber pilot, passed over for promotion too many times, decides to go into the ransom business, by kidnapping two nuclear devices and threatening to blow up a nice little city if he doesn't get his $250 million.

But the wrinkle here is that the pilot (played by John Travolta) doesn't really expect to be disliked for his enterprise. He's so effervescent, so deeply amusing, so convinced of his own infernal charm, that he fully expects the world to rejoice in his cleverness and seems only a bit ticked that it refuses to.

In fact, so sure is Woo of Travolta's power to seduce that he simply backs off and lets him work. As Vic Deakins, Travolta brings a new dimension to the terrorist impersonation: This is terrorist as game-show host, an endlessly inventive font of charm and narcissism and self-serving grandeur. He is the most amusing nuclear terrorist you ever saw.

Sucking madly on cigarettes, his bright blue eyes beaming like industrial-strength lasers, his icy lips pulsating with wise-cracks, he manages to make nuclear terrorism look as if it would finish very highly in the Nielsens.

One day, on a training mission with live nukes, he suddenly tries to kill his co-pilot, Riley Hale (a game Christian Slater); failing, he punches the button and deposits Hale into midair at the bottom of a chute. Then he dumps the unarmed bombs into the Utah desert, bails out himself and, with a crew of goons, sweeps up the warheads and heads off to pure mischief.

Meanwhile, the perturbed Hale bonds with a feisty female park ranger (Samantha Mathis), and the two scramble to catch up. Hale has an unusual advantage in that having co-piloted all those years next to his pal, he knows how his mind works, its subtleties, it tendency toward feint and maneuver. As the bombs move toward the city, Hale and Mathis close on Travolta and his minions (including Howie Long, imposing but not memorable) time and time again.

The sequences play out around modes of transportation or against varying landscapes. One, for example, takes place in an abandoned mine shaft, where Deakins and his guys have planted a nuke. Hale and his new pal Mathis attempt first to disarm it and, failing that, to get out of the way before the bomb detonates. (Only in Woo could nuclear detonation be a throw-away stunt gag!)

Moreover, the subtext is psychological: the duel of wills between two men, one of whom has always assumed the dominant position vis-à-vis the other, but who discovers that maybe he isn't quite the bull stud he thought he was, and that the littler guy knew some surprising moves, too.

Described that way, "Broken Arrow" sounds almost like a rational document, a story put together out of the tissue of emotion, motive, opportunity and decision.

Well, allow me to disabuse you of that polite notion: It is

rather a poem of action, a tapestry of incredible visceral conflict set to secret rhythms so powerfully primordial that they seduce you without connection to the rational part of your brain.

The idiocies sail blithely by, the hero's incredible fortune in always finding maps, tools and weapons not merely handy but which perfectly match the situation. You notice but you don't care; you've given it up for the power of the rush.

Woo is less a storyteller than a weaver of kinetic images, a man to whom the universe, far from seeming a stable arena in which to stage action, seems plastic, infinitely manipulable to be twisted and molded to his impulses, despite the laws of physics. He is an extraordinary craftsman, and he brings a quality of almost dream-like intensity to "Broken Arrow."

This has always been Woo's gift, and he even deployed it in "Hard Target," but in that film he wasn't quite able to get the proportions right. The writing was idiotic, the star a vain jerk, the plot unsurprising.

Here, the script, by Graham Yost, generates a good deal of bitter wit that sounds feasible and expressive in the mouths of smart punks like Travolta and Slater. And the excruciating sentimentality that informed Woo's Hong Kong work, even in films as violent as "The Killer" and "Hard Boiled," has been scraped from the project, either because of Woo's rigor and quick adaptation skills or at the behest of an intelligent producer.

In any event, with this film, Woo ceases to be a cult filmmaker, and we are the richer for it.

FARGO
March 8, 1996

Some states have a nifty tradition of murder. There's bleak Kansas, with its wheat fields and white-trash roamers; there's New York, with its mobsters; Mississippi with its good-old boys high on corn likker, toting shotguns and ropes; and particularly Florida, with its flashy dope dealers, Tec-9's and sleek Corvettes.

But Minnesota? Like, Paul Bunyan on a bad-hair day? Mary Tyler Moore with PMS chirping Ted Baxter to death?

That all changes today, with the arrival of "Fargo," from Joel and Ethan Coen, set on the snow-blind Minnesota prairies. The Coens, who memorialized the desperate small-beer crimes of Texas a decade ago in "Blood Simple," have returned to film noir with a bitter, savage story of more folks driven blood-simple by greed, rage and stupidity.

The stupidity is a Coen trademark. The brothers — Joel directs, Ethan produces, they both write — aren't attracted to glamorous or heroic people, but to dumb ones. Their typical character doesn't really get it, can't see the big picture, operates off motives so base they'd shame a snail, following plans so moronic they'd embarrass a slug.

So it is with "Fargo," about a small-time loser who sets a plot in motion on the basic assumption that all things will go as planned. Of course, they don't because they can't, and a relatively simple scam explodes into a spasm of violence that leaves seven people dead and the snow spattered with blood.

And, did I tell you, it's a comedy?

Our hero is typical: A smart cop who figures it all out, goes after the bad guys and takes them down, one at a time, just like Dirty Harry. But with the Coens maybe there's no such thing as typical: She's also seven months pregnant.

Marge Gunderson (Frances McDormand) is the chief of police in Brainerd, Minn., a small town 90-odd miles across the tundra from Minneapolis–St. Paul. She's so cheerful and chipper she makes Moore's legendarily upbeat Minnesotan Mary Richardson seem like a depressive personality. Nothing throws her, and when she examines two corpses stiffening in the snow, the blood on them coagulated into black Jell-O, she turns to her deputy and asks him to remind her to pick up some nightcrawlers for her husband, a wildlife artist.

In fact, the Coens get at something rarely achieved in films, where the cops almost never have private lives because they're so absorbed into and consumed by the universe of violence.

Not Marge — no, sir. She's from the Midwest, Minnesota style. She does her job, then puts it on the shelf and goes home for takeout from Arby's and a night of watching Johnny on the tube (it's 1987; Johnny's still on the tube). She may not have a tragic sense of life, but she has the conviction that rules are to be enforced and the commitment to duty to see that they are.

It seems for a bit that the sophisticated Coens are goofing on the poor peasants of the plains. Those cheery accents, driven by a substratum of Scandinavian heritage, bounce loonily into the cold air, unmoored by gravity, tragedy or profanity. We're not in Kansas anymore: We're in Minnesota.

"Darn it," someone will say, or "You're darn tootin'!" or "What the heck is going on?" or with that last twist of Norwegian rhythm so that everything sounds like a question, "Cheese, but it's darn cold today, yah?"

But the secret text of "Fargo" isn't superiority, it's humanity: The Coens, who are from Minnesota, come to make us feel the texture of these chilled, repressed yappers.

There's Jerry Lundegaard (the brilliant William H. Macy), an oddly infantile man who has never quite made it on his own, though he's comfortably married to gruff millionaire Wade Gustafson's daughter, Jean. Jerry, in his desperate quest for success to validate himself in Wade's merciless eyes, has gotten himself deeply in debt.

Thus the original idea is his: to hire two men to kidnap Jean, go to Wade (Harve Presnell) for the huge ransom, give the thugs a small part of it and keep the rest for himself to pay off his debts. But in Minnesota nothing is simple: he hires big-talking small-timer Carl Showalter (Steve Buscemi) and the stoic psychopath Gaear Grimsrud (Peter Stormare), whose response to everything is to start hitting or start blasting.

You can't find good help these days, can you? With Carl and Gaear aboard, the plan is doomed from the start; it teeters crazily toward chaos in the first few seconds, escalates into a shootout on the highway that leaves three frozen bodies in the snow, and then begins to disintegrate as the thugs fall out among themselves, Jerry falls out with Wade and slowly, surely, Marge closes in.

It's a miracle: a tough, honest, bloody film set so far from the bright lights it feels as if it's on a different planet, yet knowable and absolutely compelling from start to finish.

"Fargo" is great American moviemaking.

PRIMAL FEAR
April 3, 1996

The only really primal fear in "Primal Fear" is Richard Gere's for the young man who will ultimately replace him, Edward Norton. It's interesting to watch an old actor try to hold his ground against the inevitable course of hormones, talent and time: Gere uses every trick in the book, every twitch his beautiful face ever learned, every flash, sparkle, glimmer, smolder, eyebrow lift, smile, smirk or grimace. He fights valiantly.

But he is doomed: Norton eats him alive and when the film is over, you're thinking, "Who was that kid?"

The terrain for this battle royale between yesterday and tomorrow is a rather slick, conventional commercial thriller about a callow but ambitious lawyer (Gere) defending a seemingly pitiful but guilty drifter turned altar boy (Norton) on a charge of murder of a revered Catholic cleric. Death came for the archbishop, the cops came for Norton and Gere came for the good career move.

At first, it's totally Gere's movie. Insufferably handsome and vain beyond human measure, Gere's Martin Vail fills the screen like Narcissus on a field trip from ancient Greece. He revels in the attention, he radiates smugness like an old radiator billowing heat through the room, he preens and shucks and gandy-dances for the camera, blowing everyone else out of the movie.

When the boy is apprehended, it seems like one more trip to glory for Gere. Norton's Aaron Sampler is a convention: He's almost inarticulate, a drifting Southerner, unrooted and unfocused and, of course, very stupid. His soft, angelic face seems not even in focus; it's a smear of fuzz on the lens. Gere takes one look at him, thinks, "Plead insanity," and sets about to milk the case for maximum pathos with a hope of keeping the boy, somehow, off death row, a triumph that would have professional meaning for him and is completely unconnected to any notion of justice.

The script, again quite conventional, cycles in thriller tropes, all familiar. Backstory: Vail was once the fair-haired boy of the prosecutor's office, is still bitter about his dismissal and can't wait to use the trial to get at the fat cats (John Mahoney, for one) who still run the place. More backstory: His adversary in the case is Janet Venable (Laura Linney, very good), who was once his assistant and lover.

Wrinkles: The saintly archbishop was perhaps not so saintly after all. A disturbing videotape emerges. A second kid is spotted. A gangster (Steven Bauer), who seemed connected to a land and real-estate scandal that might have involved the archdiocese, is found dead. A psychiatrist (Frances McDormand) keeps picking at the drifter, seemingly making little progress. It all seems so normal.

But the movie is secretly being taken over by Norton, which is really the movie's twist, even as I avoid revealing the more mechanistic coup de grâce in the last seconds. What we're seeing is a contest in acting styles. Gere is an externalist, a "big" performer who immediately draws attention to himself. Stirring, but conventional. Norton, like a few others (John Turturro comes immediately to mind) has that rarest of qualities: He, alone among the extremely professional performers on the screen, seems not to be acting at all. Rather, he has simply become: He is, somehow and magically.

Put another way, we know everything we need to know about everyone in the film in the first second that we see them. We only think that of Norton's Aaron, but the process of the movie isn't so much penetrating a plot as a mind, and Norton takes us deeper and deeper through brilliantly deployed dead ends and subterfuges until he alone is controlling the movie. It's a terrific piece of work.

Alas, it's sad to report that "Homicide's" great Andre Braugher appears as Vail's investigator, with hair no less. The part, while well enough performed, is so far from the demonic splendor and concentrated fury of his Frank Pembleton that it feels a little indecent. Can't somebody out there write a terrific script for Braugher and Norton? Let tomorrow begin now, please! I'm tired of waiting.

TAXI DRIVER
April 28, 1996

He wanted to know: "Are you talking to me?" But he hadn't said it quite right, so he tried it again.

"Are you talking to me?"

Nope. Still not right. Try again.

"Are you talking to me?"

Travis liked that one better. Standing there in front of the mirror, he liked the look of incredulity that came across his face, then transmuted in a firing synapse's time-span toward hostility, but, like, cool hostility — hostility in command. And from there it was a simple matter to get the gun out, the big one, the .44 Magnum with the 8-inch barrel, one of three he carried in "Taxi Driver."

"Are you talking to me?"

But nobody was. Nobody ever did. That was the problem.

The words did not connect Travis to society, no matter how tenuously. No, they were a part of his fantasy mechanism, part of the program by which he could bestir himself from lethargy and indolence to become an avatar of action, which, alas, he could not confine within the bounds of his own mind.

With Travis, it was an obsession with slights — minor, almost accidental tremors of disrespect — that he used to propel himself toward mega-violence to no good end except his own self-expression. With Lee Harvey Oswald, it was a crazed interpretation of Marxism. James Earl Ray was possessed by the demon of racism; Sirhan Sirhan was the avenger of Palestinian wrongs.

Travis merely reflected them, but in the reflection was a purer kind of truth: He was the quintessential troubled loner, haunting our century since at least 1963, and possibly earlier.

He's back. He's back in the form of Theodore Kaczynski, purported Unabomber. And Tim McVeigh, purported Oklahoma City Bomber. But he's back in his purest and most inviolate form in Martin Scorsese's "Taxi Driver," where he's named Travis Bickle — a character inspired by one assassination attempt who in turn inspired another one, certainly as unique a claim as can be made in film history.

The 1976 film, in a restored and remastered version, is now at the Charles, where its enigmas continue to haunt, and where its inner meanings remain as obscure. For it asks the crucial question, which cannot really be answered: Why?

Really, isn't that the big one? What is it that turns one embittered nerd — one among millions of such desperate souls, including, at one time or other, all of us — from his loneliness and litany of grudges into an actual killer?

Scorsese's movie, from a script by Paul Schrader, attempts to answer the question, but it can get no further than a description, vividly accurate, but in the end unpenetrative.

The movie takes the classic text of the madman's journal, inspired as much by Dostoyevski as by Arthur Bremer, as its spine. Bremer was the loner who for obscure reasons roamed through the political year 1972 with a trunkful of guns until chance finally put him in a parking lot in Laurel with Gov. George Wallace. Bremer, politically uninformed, wanted merely to count for something; six shots later he was world-famous, and he still languishes in a Maryland penitentiary.

Just as Bremer recorded his utter banalities and insipid mock-insights in a pitiful handwritten diary, so does Scorsese's Bickle.

But to Bremer's madness Scorsese adds another dimension, one might say another dementia: Instead of transpiring against the backdrop of small-beer suburbs and anonymous expressway exchanges, Travis's odyssey is set against the cauldron of New York City, a city throbbing with brutal sexuality and violence, a city down whose mean streets whip the vapors of madness, anomie, chaos, disconnection.

Through Scorsese's gliding camera and Michael Chapman's rich, dark and troubling cinematography, one can hear the city singing its mad melody to Travis, urging him ever onward, making each step of his journey seem inevitable, even natural.

Seen today, "Taxi Driver" still has the intensity of a fever dream, and its invocation of the swelter and weirdness of Manhattan remains just as mesmerizing.

It retains its power and its strange luminosity, so that it seems in some ways more like a fantasy than a reality. Its technique continues to astonish.

Its climax — a massively brutal explosion of gunfire and mayhem in a sleazy brothel — remains just as shattering, particularly with an emphasis still mind-boggling on the damage that bullets can do to bodies.

And the ironic coda, in which Travis is magically restored to health and sanity, seems just as phony and pointless, a true act of movie desperation.

But now the movie feels different, for some reason. Possibly it's a lack of context, a lack of ready connection between life it portrays and the life so many of us live. Possibly it's that the '70s, with their embittered memories of the '60s, turned into the '90s, with their hazy memories of the '80s.

Perhaps it's that everybody's older, especially De Niro, who in "Taxi Driver" seems so callow, unlined, unformed and pristine, he's almost a fetus.

But this time, "Taxi Driver" seemed stranger, more weird, more incoherent to me, and was not at all the movie I remembered. Like a treasured boyhood vacation spot, revisited it shows it tawdriness and cheapness. It seems even more dissociative and surreal. If anything, there's less of a theory behind it.

For many years, it's been assumed (perhaps by me, most of all) that Travis was a Vietnam vet (he wears a Marine aviation jacket, with a gaudy unit patch on the shoulder and a pair of jump wings on the chest, as well as his name stenciled backward, military fashion, on the back). He has a bad scar, he has military sunglasses.

Nearly everybody tumbled to this theory, and he's routinely described, as by Roger Ebert in "Roger Ebert's Video Companion," as a Vietnam vet. The film was regarded as something similar to Hemingway's "Big Two-Hearted River," about an increasingly dysfunctional combat veteran for whom the war was so gigantic an experience that it could not be named and in going unnamed it became all the more ominous, like the famous iceberg that is nine-tenths under water.

But watching it this time, I began to question the assumption: Is Travis a Vietnam vet, or is he something more troubling, an isolated screwball who took to the military look as a pathetic pretense of joining something, of having, somewhere in his past, a connection?

The case against being a vet is certainly as strong as the case for it.

One thing is that jacket, with its patch. Assuming that these things are planned professionally and are not serendipitous, the patch tells a different story. The Marine Corps is a notoriously Jesuitic institution, not given to show. Bright unit patches, with lions or other predators howling off them, are an army thing, not a Marine thing. For the Corps, the Globe and Anchor is enough.

So what's that patch on Travis's shoulder, and why is it sewn on both his surplus jackets (he has two; both have the patches and the jump wings)?

The jump wings are another oddity: The Marines don't have a big airborne tradition, as does the army. The jump wings (they are jump wings; I looked very carefully at the parachute suspended between two wings) may be non-issue.

Again, when he's interviewed for the taxi job, he's asked if he's been in the service, and he says yes, the Marines. But no mention is made of Vietnam, even when the guy interviewing him claims to be an ex-Marine. Unbelievable.

The guns: He buys four handguns from a contraband dealer, and they seem utterly foreign and completely fascinating to him. If he were a Marine Vietnam vet, guns would have been how he made his living, and they wouldn't seem so charismatic. He would connect these little fellas with the big fellas he carried back in the Land of Bad Things. When he bought them, he might say, "Yeah, much smaller than the '16 I used to carry."

The wound: At one point, we see that Travis has had some

kind of grotesque scar on his back, possibly a bullet wound. That suggests Vietnam again. But again: not conclusive.

And check out your basic psychological texts; you'll find that people who are capable of committing violence have an unusual tendency to attract it as well. Many suffer from maimings or the residues of strange accidents. They've seen blood gush before, their own, and that is why the gush of others' blood isn't particularly shocking to them.

Whatever, I like the non-Vietnam Travis better. It removes the blood libel that all Vietnam vets are psycho misfits prone to violence, a truism of 1976 that one would prefer to think a great director like Scorsese would see through.

And without Vietnam, Travis becomes much more interesting and troubling. He seems beamed down from another planet, an alien, with almost no entry point into the society that swirls about him. And his problems are therefore purely sexual.

The movie is a great black salute to the ugly power of frustration. Poor Travis just wants to have fun, but he has no idea how to go about it. Thus the city, with its venues of trashy professional sex, both attracts and repels him. He yearns to cleanse it (cleanse himself), but at the same time he cannot stop going to porno films; he cannot stop fantasizing.

Thus he's attracted to the blondest of women, not for their beauty but as emblems of purity. This leads Scorsese into obscure situations, such as the frankly absurd one where Travis, a complete social retard, walks in off the street to a campaign headquarters and starts hitting on Cybill Shepherd's Betsy. And she is intrigued enough to go out with this geek.

Yeah, right. Then he takes her, in evident complete innocence, to a porn movie, predictably grossing her out and blowing the relationship for all time.

What planet is this boy from? This cannot be the act of any even remotely socialized American male in the world. It's a fundamental truth of boy culture that the line between taboo and mainstream sex culture is completely known. No one would take a pretty girl to a scuzzy downtown porn theater. Unthinkable! It rings utterly false, unless of course Travis is so messed up he is literally insane as Hannibal Lector or is some kind of wild child, untarnished by adult knowledge.

In fact, all the way through, Travis remains childlike, untouched by the world except for his abiding psychosis. Thus he's moved next by the innocence of Iris, a child prostitute, played by Jody Foster. She becomes his symbol of corrupted beauty in a corrupt world.

The screenwriter Schrader works out the psychological equation quite neatly: Travis feels frustration from his rejection by Betsy. He invests in the well-being of Iris. Feeling powerless in both relationships, he retreats into madness, his changes in hairstyle reflecting his mental state. Acquiring an arsenal of guns, he loses himself in fantasies of power and elects to strike out at the dirty world by murdering the man for whom Betsy worked. Thwarted by the Secret Service, he goes in a rage to Iris's squalid block of Hell's Kitchen, starts blasting and ends up killing her pimp (the demonic Harvey Keitel) and two Mafiosi.

In the film's cheapest irony, his madness is taken for heroism. Suddenly loved by society, he is restored to wholeness and takes up his old life again. But this time, we are given to understand, he is more comfortable within himself. Yeah, right.

This breaks down at nearly every realistic level, chief among them being that he has wantonly killed three men who were doing him no harm, and it does seem that either the state or their employers, the Mafia, might have some investment in his future, no?

But "Taxi Driver" is a triumph of technique over sense. You can point out a hundred reasons why it shouldn't work, yet miss the one reason why it does.

Scorsese so infused it with demonic energy, and he so completely found a visual vocabulary that expressed the one-track mind of its central character, that the movie roars by all literal objections like a freight train.

Is it a fair picture of the mind of an assassin? Probably not; it's too localized for that. Is it almost undeniably powerful and does it have the thrust of nightmare-state logic to it? Yes.

One thing that still must be said about "Taxi Driver": It goes all the way.

INDEPENDENCE DAY
July 3, 1996

"Independence Day" is like a Tom Clancy novel on steroids from outer space.

Big, loud, long, cornball, F-18-crammed, indisputably exciting, patriotic as an anthem, it's something for everybody, and, most of all, unstoppable.

It doesn't really have a plot, only a situation, with which anyone who has watched TV is familiar: World meets invaders, world loses to invaders, world gets invaders. It's 1956's "Earth vs. the Flying Saucers" on an A-budget of millions, bigger and brighter, and with enough computer-generated effects to make Bill Gates's eyeballs go tilt. But the movie is still irredeemably tacky. I mean, what do you expect when you do a cheerful adventure flick with a body count of about 200 million?

Actually, its absolutism is one of its charms. When They finally come, They are not benevolent critters with the fuzzy eyes of Steven Spielberg's warm and Popsicle-flavored dreams, but slimy, geeky space Nazis with no agenda for our frail species save the crematoria. We have it, they want it — the Earth. No peace, no justice, no negotiation: just flat out, kick-butt interspecies warfare to the last man or ectoplasm.

H.G. Wells still did it first and best, but Roland Emmerich, when he isn't staging living Marine Corps recruiting posters, can be stirred to a high level of pictorial splendor. Indeed, "Independence Day" 's best thing is its sense of spectacle. The invasion force appears to have been designed by the inventor of the original Frisbee, but these Frisbees are 15 miles wide and festooned with skyline. Think of New York City wrapped around a pie plate that stretches from Towson to Columbia.

Emmerich gets great mileage out of shadows as the big ships maneuver, separating earth from sun: the ominous slide of darkness as it envelops structures that we humans envision as grand but are instantaneously revealed to be dwarfish vanities when compared to the scale of the saucers. The early game is strategic, not violent: The ships slip into position and hover

over their targets, communicating and mysteriously coordinating.

The movie, in typical disaster-flick fashion, flashes back and forth among the human beings at various levels of society. The President, played by Bill Pullman, blandly handsome enough to be believable in such a role, is dismayed but hopeful. His press secretary (Margaret Colin) is plain scared. A cocky Marine pilot (Will Smith) salivates at the prospect of combat, but his girlfriend (Vivica Fox) is also scared. A drunken ex-'Nam fighter jockey and current crop duster (Randy Quaid) gets drunker. A SETI researcher (Jeff Goldblum) tries to figure it all out. All are good; the only loser in the bunch is Judd Hirsch, as Goldblum's father, overplaying the kvetching Jewish Daddy thing to the point of excess.

Meanwhile, back in the plot, it's Goldblum who deciphers the code and realizes that the bad boys are getting set to pull the trigger. In one of the film's endless litany of brain-dead coincidences that help tie the untidy story together, he just happens to be the press secretary's estranged husband, so he's able to get through to the White House just in time to get the national leadership out of danger before the aliens fry the cities.

A good portion of the subversive fun of "Independence Day" is indeed watching the saucers throw a few more burgs on the barbie, just as it was in both Ray Harryhausen's "Earth vs. the Flying Saucers" and George Pal's excellent 1953 film version of "War of the Worlds." I'm not sure what obscure human need it satisfies, but the audience (of which I was an enthusiastic member) really tripped out as the Empire State Building and the White House were deconstructed into napalm meringue. What is so comforting about the end of civilization as we know it?

In the rubble of the first attack, the President tries to rally the troops while the various other components of the story try to crack the case.

The movie is artfully constructed to play to marginal space-freak fantasies, including the one about the recovered saucer from Roswell, N.M., being stored at the mysterious installation called Area 51, don't you know? All the dysfunctional drifters who've been sustained by this fantasy over the years will find that "Independence Day" is their wish come true.

It's at Area 51 where various mad scientists and cocky Marines and concerned leaders finally crack the case, and figure out the inevitable last gambit that will save the Earth. Hmmm. Somehow I think that the makers of this movie have seen a couple or so other movies set a long time ago in a galaxy far away.

But because the imagery and rhythms of the climax of "Independence Day" are borrowed from the "Star Wars" movies doesn't make it any less effective. Emmerich cares enough to steal from the very best. He's no deep thinker, but he's an incredibly dynamic filmmaker and the movie mounts and mounts in electric tension as it hustles to its explosive and picturesque ending. He even gets the President into the cockpit of an F-18 to lead the last airborne charge.

But, I kept thinking, winning a war didn't get Bush re-elected, so what good's it going to do Bill Pullman?

COURAGE UNDER FIRE
July 12, 1996

Edward Zwick's "Courage Under Fire" has the taste of old wine in new bottles, except that the product in the shiny container is a virtue, not a beverage.

That virtue is courage and the movie can be seen, among its other meanings, as a celebration of the traditionally male thing of battlefield guts as it passes to the other gender — in the form of a tough-as-nails chopper pilot played by Meg Ryan. During the Persian Gulf War, Ryan takes out an Iraqi tank, sets up a perimeter defense, shoots, kills, spits and curses like Sgt. Rock on a good day.

Or does she? Constructed as a post-mortem investigation, the movie follows as Lt. Col. Nat Serling, brilliantly played by Denzel Washington, talks to witnesses and survivors of the firefight to determine if the late Capt. Karen Walden deserves to be the first female recipient of the Medal of Honor. Of course nothing is easy: Bush's White House, represented by an unctuous Bronson Pinchot, wants the medal for its PR value six months after the war. It would make a terrific photo op. So the political pressure is on Serling to rubber-stamp an earlier inquiry and get on with his career.

But as Serling digs, he encounters small discrepancies in the story between witnesses (another downed chopper crew a hill away) and the survivors of her air crew. The issue turns on an M-16 that was heard firing as the Iraqis closed in and the air crew abandoned its defensive position to make it to the MedEvac. Who was the mysterious shooter?

Serling has his own set of problems. An armored officer, he is himself the object of scrutiny from above and investigation from without over a friendly-fire incident (in the confusion of night combat, he incinerated his executive officer's tank); he feels the weight of his own guilt exiling him from the military community. He turns to drink. He wants to do the right thing to redeem himself, for a crime of which he may not even be guilty but for which he feels enormous responsibility.

"Courage Under Fire" is basically an exercise in point of view as the tormented but ennobled Serling recounts the mission through the eyes of all the survivors. We see it replayed over and over again with slightly different emphasis: the crash, the long night on the ground, an Iraqi night probe, a larger daytime assault as ammo and fortitude run low. Each retelling reflects the personality of the teller.

The most compelling witness is a staff sergeant played by Lou Diamond Phillips, a pickled-in-salt NCO, who has no room in his leathery shred of heart for a female officer. As Phillips tells it, she panicked on the ground and only his professionalism got the tiny unit through the night. A medic — Matt Damon — represents the other side, and his account turns the dead officer into a paragon of heroism. But his account rings just as false. Clearly, something happened on the ground that nobody — not even the army brass and certainly not the White House — wants to get out.

Zwick, who directed "Glory" and "Legends of the Fall" to varying degrees of success, does have a natural affinity for physical action and a deep passion for courage. The war sequences, which comprise most of the film, feel very real. For the non-cognoscente, let me point out that much of the drama on the ground revolves around possession of an instrument called a SAW, as in "Gimme the SAW." "I ain't givin' you the blankety-blank SAW." SAW is the acronym for Squad Automatic Weapon, a light machine gun in 5.56 mm that fires from 100-round belts encased in Tupperware. Remember, you read it here, courtesy of the *Sun,* and not in *The New Yorker,* which wouldn't know a hawk from a hand SAW.

Certain small ticks of inaccuracy seem annoying. I cannot for one second believe that Iraqi troops would stand and fight when, as the movie has it, a rescuing force of A-10's and Cobra gunships sweeps in on them. Those flyboys packed mega-heat in rocket pods and incredibly fast-firing Gatling guns and the Iraqi performance in the field was pitiful. Then there's the idiotic issue of the ubiquitous Capitol. Why does everyone in Hollywood believe that the U.S. Capitol can be seen from every single motel window in the greater Maryland-Virginia-D.C. area? Serling sets up shop in a motel in Bethesda, and there's the white dome outside his window!

Despite these irritations, it's Washington who holds the film together and gives it a moral center. He's the good professional: a man profoundly committed to duty, honor, country who perseveres even through his own personal crises and makes us feel not only Serling's professionalism but his humanity as well.

As for Ryan, she's not really in the movie. That is to say, she's dead when it starts and still dead when it ends: What we see of her is her performance on the ground, which is completely at the extremes of bravery and cowardice. She's more of an icon, a symbol of the new woman soldier, than she is a character. At the end, you feel that you owe her a salute, but that you never really got to know her. She's an action figure, not a person.

EPILOGUE

Article:
FATHER OF DARKNESS
June 21, 1981

The cards in all the stores and the ads in all the papers are cheery and warm. The poetry of the day is primitive and heartfelt. But it's a picture of a father I don't know anything about. And there must be millions of Americans on this day who pay lip service to the same myth, make the phone call (if the phone call can still be made), tart themselves up in a fondness they don't feel except out of respect for appearances. They strike the right posture, they say the right things, they smile, they nod. "Yes, dad, how are you?" Or, "poor dad, we miss him so. Dad taught us the lessons, he gave us the strength. Good old dad."

Then they treat themselves to a stiff drink and think, "You old bastard, I beat you."

My father was a handsome man, tall and proud and thin. He was a woefully hard worker. Yet he was shy in an almost pathological way. He hated to meet new people — he hated to do anything. He truly enjoyed nothing. He had no hobbies. He didn't care about sports. He never built anything. For a while, he planted things, but there was no joy in it. He held, he nursed, he *cultured* grudges — against his colleagues, against his wife, against his children.

He was terribly unsure of himself; he was terrified of losing his job, or of being undercut or made to look foolish. For a time, he was quite a success, but he could not live with it. He had everything you were supposed to have in the '50s — a house in the suburbs, four kids, two cars. Yet, he took no pleasure in any of it. He had impossibly high standards for us, but worst of all for himself. I think he'd been damaged severely by his own father, by all accounts a vicious, alcoholic old patriarch who thought his children were worthless. My father took this pain and simply passed it along. In the end that, as much as anything, killed him.

I think we were secretly pleased when he died. He was drinking almost constantly by that time and if he hadn't had tenure they would have let him go long ago. He was in all kinds of trouble, it turned out, with the IRS. He was spending money crazily, and we didn't know what on. His disappearances lasted longer and longer. So we could all say we saw it coming and we could all say that maybe at last he'd found some peace from whatever it was that was chewing him up.

It was, however, a squalid death. There was an element of ambiguity to it. There are certain sections of any city where you don't go late at night if you want to stay alive; he had gone there often. He had a secret life, in other words, and it was a soiled, pathetic secret life, like an ending to an O. Henry short story as it might have been imagined by Edward Albee, which seems at first to solve everything but really solves nothing.

The piece in the Chicago paper was at least circumspect, though you could read the code if you knew it. "University Professor Slain in Robbery," the headline read (and working for a newspaper, I knew just how laconically the item had been handled by editors, how small a deal it was, how it filled a hole in today's Local section, and tomorrow somebody else's death would fill the same hole) and went on to relate that two young men had lured him to an apartment and killed him there; they had been arrested rather quickly, one of them nabbed at the bus station where — he must have been a real piece of sleaze, the stupid sucker — he'd actually been wearing my father's seven-year-old Timex.

My brother had it the worst. Nobody else was home, and they reached him first, so he had to go down to the morgue to make the ID. He said dad didn't look too bad, it wasn't gory, it wasn't anything like the movies. He also saw the two guys they arrested. "Just crackers," he said, "worthless crackers."

My dad's only surviving brother came to the funeral, as did quite a number from that side of the family. They are prosperous farm people from a semi-rural, vaguely southern state where, I'm told, the family is locally famous and huge, with cousins and uncles and sets of aunts spread all over several counties. My dad had hated that, fled it, and brought us to the city. And so seeing my dad's brother that weekend for the first time in 20 years was a real shock: He was stockier through the body and much stronger. And he had a farmer's temperament — his heartiness, his love of weather jokes and folksy sayings — and he was touchingly naive about what had happened to my father in the city and would not — could not, I suppose — really believe it. Yet for all that was different about him, his face was shockingly the same. It scared me a little. I've been invited out there a hundred times since and I always say no and I always will.

The service, conducted by an unctuous university chaplain, was mercifully brief. He asked us to remember dad at his best. I tell you I tried. But I have never understood what little dark thing hid inside that man. When I tried to remember the good things, I thought of all the other things too.

I guess he loathed himself so deeply that he loathed everything else. He hated it when his kids failed and he resented it when they succeeded. He never let my oldest brother forget how second-rate he was, what a disappointment he was, and then, when Phil went out and became a success, dad used to hold him up to the rest of us as an example.

When he drank — and it was often — he turned grotesque. He loved to hurt people when he was drunk, because he didn't have the guts to hurt them when he was sober. When he drank, all sorts of terrible things gushed out. He'd say anything to anybody.

The last several times I returned home, with my pretty wife and my good job and my healthy, pleasant life, he was simply gone.

I think he was cremated. I don't even know where the ashes are.

Yet I saw my dad a few days ago in some pictures. It was all there: the receding hairline, the thinning hair, a peculiar thickness between ear and crown; the funny way he had of cocking his head and squinting when he listened; the awkwardness of the body, held in tightly, the body of a man never truly at ease. The slight paunch, the sloppy clothes. He is holding a child — a son — and it's hard to read much from the relative postures of the figures. There's some awkwardness there, a little tension. The kid has a pugnacious handsomeness, a wildness to him, and the father is clearly a little unsure about the whole business — he doesn't know where to stand, where to yield.

But I like to tell myself there's some love in that picture too, and, I hope, enough to build on. Because it's my dad's face all right, but it's also mine, and that's my son I'm holding.